History and Subjectivity

History and Subjectivity

The Transformation of Marxist Theory

ROGER S. GOTTLIEB

Temple University Press
Philadelphia

Temple University Press, Philadelphia 19122
Copyright © 1987 by Temple University. All rights reserved
Published 1987
Printed in the United States of America

Library of Congress Cataloging-in-Publication Data
Gottlieb, Roger S.
History and subjectivity.
Bibliography: p. 289
Includes index.
1. Political science—Philosophy. 2. Political socialization.
3. Historical materialism.   4. Dialectical materialism.
5. Philosophy, Marxist.   6. Left and right
(Political science)   7. Feminism. I. Title.
JA74.G68 1987 335.4 87-1875
ISBN 0-87722-494-3 (alk. paper)

To My Children

— Aaron, whose spirit blessed my life
— Anna and Esther, whose spirits bless it now

And to Children Everywhere

— That we may make a better world for them

Contents

Preface

IS THERE HOPE FOR MARXIST THEORY AND SOCIALIST PRACTICE? IN THIRD World countries and the Eastern bloc the ideas of Marx, Engels, and Lenin are ideologies for totalitarian bureaucrats or the rallying cry of anti-Western modernization movements. In Europe and America, working-class activism has eroded to parliamentary and welfare-state liberalism. Simultaneously, the capitalist state controls a population saturated by an administered culture of spectacle, dehumanization, and boredom.

Yet we may hope that the quiescence of dissidence in the West is temporary. Currents of political and social activism—socialist and radical feminism, ecological action, pride in race or ethnicity, anti-imperialism—may have achieved permanent (if small) places in the culture and politics of opposition. Also, the twentieth century has shattered illusions about our capacity to know what the future of society will hold. The next oppositional mass movement will probably take new and unexpected forms—just as the radicalism of the 1960s stunned activists of an older generation.

In any event, this book is motivated by the *hope* that the United States will again witness politically radical mass movements and the *belief* that traditional Marxist theory must continue to be transformed if it is to be useful to such movements. More particularly, I have written this book in order to sort out some of the complicated relations between traditional Marxism and the practice and theory of the radical political movements of the last two decades. I have tried to determine—for my own mind at least —how much of traditional Marxism has become obsolete and how much has not; and whether or not the seemingly incompatible accounts of social life offered by traditional Marxism, different forms of neo-Marxism, feminism, and various minority political movements could possibly be synthesized into a more comprehensive and politically useful social theory.

A Brief Overview

How does *History and Subjectivity* contribute to this task?

Part I explains and theoretically defends the book's central thesis: a transformed Marxist theory must reject Marx's claim that the mode of production possesses sole social primacy and recognize that contemporary society possesses three different but equal forms of social primacy. Economic class, processes of socialization, and politics, I argue, are now co-primary in determining social life. Part I also shows how a critical Marxism must see social life as the product of both "History" and "Subjectivity": social regularities or structures *and* fundamental changes in social life initiated by the consciousness and will of social agents. This point is critical because traditional Marxism mistakenly took Marx's theory of competitive capitalism as *the* model for theories of any society. In fact, however, precisely because social regularities are only temporary solidifications of human intentionality, the "laws" of one historical period can be altered by the changed experience and action of collective social agents.

The abstract and philosophical exposition of my theory is followed by much more concrete historical justifications of that theory. Part II shows that attempts to universalize the form of analysis Marx provided for competitive capitalism are mistaken. The social primacy of the economic is not found in either European feudalism (Chapter 3) or contemporary capitalism (Chapter 5). Chapter 4 offers hypotheses as to why traditional Marxism served so successfully as an analysis of competitive capitalism. These chapters document the historical uniqueness of the competitive capitalism that Marx took as the model of social life in general.

With the politicization of the economy (Chapter 5), economic development is shaped by political forces and the outcome of socialization processes. The social primacy of the mode of production is thus limited to the creation of a range of social and political possibilities (Chapter 6). Socialization processes and political life—the second and third forms of social primacy—determine which of these possibilities will be realized.

Part III begins by describing how Communist totalitarianism and the political failures of Western radicalism gave rise to Western Marxism and socialist-feminism (Chapter 7). Western Marxists (Chapter 8) initiated the transformation of Marxism by denying that social life was governed by historical laws based in the mode of production. They stressed the separate social primacy of socialization processes—which mold individual human infants into adults whose beliefs, values, and personalities are compatible with exploitation and domination. Only a working class that has broken through its socialization, argued such writers as Lukács, Gramsci, and Horkheimer, can turn economic crises into socialist revolutions.

Despite their enormous achievements, Western Marxists were sexist in their accounts of the normative foundations of critical theory, their descriptions of socialization processes, and their concepts of class consciousness. These deficiencies have been overcome by contemporary socialist-feminism. Feminism's stress on the political meaning of personal life confirms and deepens the Western Marxist assertion of the primacy of socialization processes. Personal experience—especially that shaped by gender—emerges as a critical force tying the working class to capitalism. Socialist-feminism has also fundamentally transformed traditional Marxism's concept of exploitation and has shown how "class interests" are fragmented by the social differentiation of gender. Finally, socialist-feminists have joined accounts of the critical role of political subjectivity with the demand that radical theory be seen as an expression of the theorist's personal life. These issues, as well as the ways in which class remains socially primary for gender, are treated in Chapter 9. Part III concludes with my own account (Chapter 10) of how socialization processes mold a "dominated self" incapable of radical political action.

Part IV analyzes the third form of social primacy: politics. This form expresses itself at two distinct poles. On the one hand, economic instabilities and political challenges to contemporary capitalism are managed by a state apparatus. Expressing both social structures and self-conscious strategies, the state serves the shared interests of both the economic ruling class and other dominant groups (Chapter 11). On the other hand, when ruled groups break through the submission-inducing socialization processes given so much attention by Western Marxism and feminism, they do not do so as members of a politically unified working class. Rather, they act as socially differentiated groups—defined by race, religion, gender, sexual preference, and so on—which possess distinct political experiences, needs, and agendas. This claim is developed in detail for American blacks and for Jews (Chapters 12–13). Finally, I apply the model of three forms of social primacy to the history of the American left, showing how its successes and failures reflect the interdependence of class, socialization, and politics (Chapters 14–17).

A Note on Class

The fundamental economic and social changes of the last century have refuted Marx's belief that industrial factory workers would become sufficiently homogeneous, numerous, and radical to create a socialist society. We have witnessed increases in workers' standard of living, the rise of the service economy, women's entry into the labor market, racial conflicts, and radical movements of students, people of color, gays and lesbians. Facing the complexity of contemporary society, therefore, many Marxists have tried to determine who the "real" workers are: to draw the line between "the proletariat" and low-level technical workers, supervisors, service workers, government employees, and professionals; and to analyze the "class position" of people on welfare, part-time laborers, housewives, and students.

Why then have I written a long book on contemporary Marxism and pretty much ignored such questions? Some may find it less than satisfying, but my answer is simple. Throughout this book the term "working class" refers to a broad category of: (1) salaried workers who have little or no individual control over their own conditions of labor or over the labor of very many others; (2) their economic dependents; and (3) people dependent on government assistance. The working class thus includes industrial and service workers, housewives and students, technical workers and teachers, welfare mothers and people in the armed forces. This category is designed to include virtually all *groups* whose structural position in capitalist society gives them an interest in creating socialism.

For three reasons, my definition of class is very broad and intentionally ignores questions of working-class leadership or "vanguard." First, history shows that at different times various groups—for example, farmers, industrial workers, students, the unemployed—have been the most radical and politically active. The continually changing character of capitalist society suggests that future "vanguards" will be different from past ones and will possess their vanguard status only for a limited time. Second, I believe (and argue at length in Part IV) that cooperation among different fragments of the working class is essential to any movement that hopes to challenge capitalism. Such cooperation, in turn, requires that different groups within the working class recognize and respect one another's specific experiences and needs, *not* compare credentials of oppression or structural centrality to capitalist accumulation. Third, theoretical claims about which group is "really the working class" or "really the vanguard" are usually a form of self-aggrandizement by political groups representing (or claiming to represent) one sector or another of the working class. This self-aggrandizement is inimical to the socialist project and recapitulates oppression within supposedly liberatory social movements (see Chapters 14–17).

While cooperation among a significant majority of workers is at least a necessary condition for the overthrow of capitalism, workers experience their social situation as members of socially differentiated groups, not as that Marxist theoretical abstraction: the proletariat. Thus the tired questions of the exact boundaries of the working class or the comparative importance of economic exploitation and sexism or racism are false ones. In any case, there are precious few "workers" to oppose to (for instance) blacks, women, Jews, or homosexuals: virtually all "workers" are members of at least one socially differentiated group. In the end, a serious challenge to capitalism is not possible without the political cooperation and mutual respect of all such groups.

A Note on Morality

Throughout this book I use a number of morally charged analytic concepts, especially "exploitation," "oppression," and "domination." Marxism originated with a critical, moral impulse, and contemporary critical Marxism should maintain that tradition (see Part I). Furthermore, I believe that any social theory lacking a moral commitment is theoretically inadequate and morally bankrupt. The social theorist has an obligation to assign institutional guilt and propose alternatives to conditions that have caused so much past pain and threaten to extinguish the future.

I use these three moral terms in *History and Subjectivity* in the following ways. "Exploitation" is intended, in something like its original Marxist sense, to refer to a relation in which a group is in a social position of systematically unequal exchange. Workers who produce material wealth are exploited if a nonlaboring ruling class expropriates a significant percentage of that wealth. The paradigm case of exploitation under capitalism is that suffered by wage laborers. The term also refers to the relation of women to men in the patriarchal nuclear family (see Chapter 9). "Oppression" is a broader category than exploitation; it includes the variety of ways in which one group exercises—on the basis of superior power, for its own benefit, and without justification—control over another group. Such control may include allotting the oppressed an unjust share of material resources, denying it self-respect, destroying its culture, or subjecting it to violence. "Domination" refers to the social power that allows one group to exploit and/or oppress another. To speak of "exploitation and domination," then, is to refer to the way in which a group is subject to unequal exchange and to the social condition of unequal social power that sustains them in that condition.

Acknowledgments

MANY PEOPLE HELPED ME WRITE THIS BOOK.

I owe my greatest debt to my political comrades of the New Left—the antiwar and student movements of the 1960s, the New American Movement, Marxist Activist Philosophers, and the Boston Committee to Challenge Anti-Semitism—whose anger, intelligence, and love inspired my commitment to radical politics and shaped my vision of a better world.

In the realm of theory, I have learned the most from Marx and Kierkegaard. More particularly, my understanding of philosophy, politics, feminism, and economics has benefited greatly from the teaching and writings of Henry Aiken, Alasdair MacIntyre, Ann Ferguson, Sheila Rowbotham, David Gordon, Perry Anderson, Jürgen Habermas, Wilhelm Reich, and Isaac Deutscher.

This book discusses a wide range of material. It was only with the help of very many people—friends, colleagues, and strangers—that I was able to cover this much ground with any confidence. Two people deserve special thanks. Lou Ferleger gave me intellectual help in writing Chapters 3–5 and 12, and did his best to convince me that a philosopher could write about history and economics. Iris Young read several chapters and provided enormously detailed and valuable criticisms of them. Many others were kind enough both to criticize sections of the book and to assure me that the overall effort was worthwhile: Richard Schmitt, Rusty Simons, Paul Breines, Thomas McCarthy, Ruth Smith, John Zeugner, James Hanlon, Mari Jo Buhle, Nicole Rafter, Howard Winant, David Alexander, Rochelle Ruthchild, Thomas Shannon, Esther Kingston-Mann, and Steven Zdatny; Marx Wartofsky and William McBride, reviewers for Temple University Press, were tremendously helpful.

I have been fortunate in receiving wonderful support from the staff at Worcester Polytechnic Institute. For typing sections of the manuscript in the early stages and providing cheerful assistance in other ways, I thank Margaret Brodmerkle, Pat Johnston, Penny Whiting, and Jeanne Leclair. The staff at Gordon Library, especially Diana Johnson, helped me with acquisitions. My work-study student, James Doyle, performed boring tasks with acumen and good humor.

The National Endowment for the Humanities supported the initial stages of research with a Grant for College Teachers.

Jane Cullen, my editor at Temple University Press, was a valued source of encouragement in the last stages of preparation. The production staff at Temple University Press, especially Mary Capouya and Patricia Sterling, did wonders for the text.

Finally, my wife, Miriam Greenspan, made critical contributions to a number of chapters, especially 2, 9, 13, and 17. Of much greater importance, she did her best to convince me (a difficult task at times) that I was a good person no matter what was in the book or what happened to it. For her efforts on behalf of my sanity during the six years that I struggled with *History and Subjectivity*, I will always be grateful.

Earlier versions of parts of this book appeared in the following journals:

The second section of Chapter 2 as "Marxism and the Three Forms of Social Primacy," *Journal of Philosophy* 76, no. 10 (October 1979).

Chapter 3 as "Feudalism and Historical Materialism: A Critique and a Synthesis," *Science and Society* 48, no. 1 (Spring 1984).

Chapter 13 as "The Dialectics of National Identity: Left-Wing Anti-Semitism and the Arab-Israeli Conflict," *Socialist Review* no. 47; (September–October 1979).

PART I

Marxism and the Three Forms
of Social Primacy

1

The Essential Thesis
of Historical Materialism

TRADITIONAL MARXISM WAS UNDERMINED BY ITS OWN THEORETICAL SUCCESS.
Marx's theory of competitive capitalism—so powerful in explaining capitalist development and predicting basic social changes accompanying that development—was taken as the model for theories of all societies. Unfortunately, it is a mistake to generalize from the unique, historically specific characteristics of competitive capitalism. This book focuses on the nature of that mistake and seeks to correct it by describing and furthering the transformation of Marxist theory toward the recognition of three forms of social primacy. Traditional Marxism accorded social primacy only to the mode of production. In contemporary capitalism, however, economic class, socialization, and politics possess different but equally important forms of social primacy. More generally, the transformation of Marxist theory reveals that social life is shaped by both "History" and "Subjectivity": social structures that determine the motivations and effects of human action, and self-conscious attempts to understand and alter those structures.

This chapter offers a brief interpretation of Marx and introduces concepts to categorize challenges to traditional Marxism. Chapter 2 presents my theory of three forms of social primacy; the rest of the book uses that theory to describe and continue the transformation of Marxism.

Marx's Theory

There is now a vast scholarly literature that interprets, defends, and attacks Marx's writings. Since it is not relevant to my purpose to offer a detailed study of his works to "prove" what he "really" believed, this book does not add to that literature; my interpretation is briefly stated and not compared to that of others. Nor do I address at length such issues as the

3

exact distinction between forces and relations of production, whether or not Marx was a technological determinist, the precise ways in which ideologies are determined by the mode of production, and the intricate conceptual relations between "economy," "economic structure," "mode of production," and the like. My goal is not Marx scholarship but a demonstration of how and why Marxism has been transformed. It will be sufficiently clear that I reject interpretations of Marx that see him as removing intentionality from social life or according social primacy to forces of production as distinct from relations of production. To the extent that such interpretations of Marx have some grounds in his writings, they are ways in which he himself failed to appreciate the normative basis of his own theory—and they have necessitated the transformation of Marxism.[1] The finer points of my understanding of traditional Marxism are made clear in a number of ways. The book contains numerous examples of how traditional Marxism's accounts of social life and historical change are limited (in understanding feudalism or contemporary capitalism, for example, or in analyzing the oppression of women, blacks, and Jews). Discussions of leftist history document some unfortunate consequences of traditional Marxism's political strategies. Finally, Part III describes in detail the changes in historical materialism initiated by Western Marxism and socialist-feminism.[2]

From the start, Marx saw theory not as a disinterested description of objective facts but as an aid to the "ruthless criticism of everything existing" (in Tucker 1972, 8). This criticism was directed toward helping humanity realize its potential freedom in a society that promoted the full development and free exercise of human capacities. If his proposed alternatives to existing society were to be realizable, however, Marx's normative critique of social life had to be joined by an understanding of what human beings are and what makes them live the way they do. Marx was therefore driven to produce a theory of the essential forces shaping human behavior.

This theory begins with four central intuitions about what people are. First, we are biological creatures with physical needs; to meet those needs, we must interact with nature. Simultaneously, however, human beings are active, creative, self-changing beings whose reality is made up partly of their own intentions and understanding. Third, people meet their material needs collectively, conceiving of and fulfilling those needs in socially mediated ways. Finally, social reality is not static but historical; there have been significant changes in social organization.

These four universal characteristics of social life require that every society possess a "mode of production" in which productive forces are employed to meet material needs, the labor process is organized, and its products are distributed.[3] Of critical importance are Marx's twin beliefs: that the mode of production explains, more than it is explained by, other social relations and historical change; and that ultimately, the internal dynamic of the mode of production shapes human history toward the progressive development of human freedom. The mode of production is socially primary because it creates economic classes, antagonistic social groups with different relations to the mode of production. These classes act on the basis of interests and beliefs derived from their respective roles in economic life. In doing so, they determine—within the limits set by the level of development of the forces of production—the most important features of social structure and historical change. The crucial motivations for class actions are the antagonistic relations between the laboring class (which performs productive labor) and the ruling class (which controls the forces of production, the labor process, and/or the final product). When class relations are more or less static, the ruling class dominates society in all its important aspects. When control over the forces of production and the surplus is challenged, other social institutions and practices will reflect this struggle. Class struggles centered on economic exploitation periodically culminate in dramatic changes in the mode of production. They will eventually create a society that socializes the control of production and ends class exploitation.

I will call these claims the "essential thesis" of historical materialism. This thesis attributes social primacy to the mode of production and includes within primacy the determination of the most important features of the social future.

Marx's initial conception of human freedom will be revealed as utopian or realistic only if he can show that the resources for freedom and the desire to realize it are developing. The essential thesis of historical materialism can be confirmed only by an analysis of social structure and historical change. These two issues coincide in Marx's analysis of capitalism.[4] Marx describes capitalism as a mode of production in which producers and expropriators meet each other as owners of the means of production and wage laborers. Labor becomes the production of commodities, objects intended for sale to further the accumulation of wealth. In this context competition among owners of capital inevitably leads to accelerating improvements in the forces of production. Yet while capitalism vastly increases our technical powers, it inserts those powers into a social context of recurrent economic crises. After each crisis separate capitals emerge, fewer and larger. Driven to a new round of expansion, capitalism supplants other modes of production both at home and in the steadily diminishing noncapitalist world. The destruction of noncapitalist production brings into existence an ever growing working class. This class, bound together by a common work situation and social experience, has a shared interest in overthrowing the capitalist relations of production and replacing them by socialism. As the source of the expropriated surplus, the working class has the potential social power to overthrow capitalism. As the class that suffers most from the business cycle, it has a clear interest in doing so. As the potential inheritor of resources that can shrink natures's control over humanity to a minimum, it has resources for the realization of human free-dom. As the enemy (in theory if not yet in fact) of the dominant class, it has an interest in eliminating all forms of oppression that politically divide workers.

The class struggle between capital and labor is the political expression of a structural contradiction: capitalism develops and socializes produc-tion, but it constrains the economy by exploitative and irrational private appropriation. By creating a class increasingly able and willing to take power, capitalism necessarily leads to its own overthrow. This overthrow is the decisive step toward a society in which freedom from material want and the fullest development of human capacities will coexist. It is, then, the step that will help realize the normative goals with which Marx began.

Economic Structure and Economic System, Lawlike and Non-Lawlike

To understand the claim that the mode of production is socially pri-mary, we need to know two things. First, how do we distinguish it from other aspects of society? Second, in what ways is it the most important aspect of social life? Given the enormous range of Marx's writings, I do not believe that these two questions can have single definitive answers; however, four concepts can help clarify different ways of understanding Marx and some of the major criticisms that have made a transformation of Marxist theory necessary.

All societies produce. Production requires both tools and techniques, and involves certain characteristic social relations: control of the forces of production, authority over labor power, possession of the product. I will call the forces of production and the social relations surrounding their use an *economic structure*.[5] If the essential thesis of historical materialism is correct—and the economic structure is socially primary—then political life (for instance) must in crucial ways be a product of economics. This assertion, in turn, requires that the economic structure be clearly distin-guishable from politics.

Suppose we define "economics" as the social realm of the production, distribution, and consumption of goods and services; and "politics" as the legitimation and exercise of social authority, legally sanctioned rights, and public obligations. Consider, then, Marx's account of what happens in a society where the expropriated surplus takes the form of "labor rent." Here peasant producers are in immediate control of the forces of production (they control or own land, livestock, and tools) and are compelled by law or tradition to provide unpaid labor on the estate of the lord. In such cases "the surplus-labour . . . can only be extorted by *other than economic pressure*" (Marx 1967, 3:791). To decide whether or not the essential thesis applies to this society, we must ask, Is the relation between the lord and the peasant who provides labor rent economic or political? On the one hand, it is an economic relation: it involves production and distribution. Yet it is also a political relation: the lord takes the surplus by force or "right." The *political* relation between lord and peasant is the relation of authority to expropriate labor rent, to economically exploit the peasant. The *economic* relation between them includes the fact that they possess unequal political rights in regard to goods and services. In this society, class relations exist: there is no difficulty in distinguishing immediate producers and exploiters. In this society, there is an economic structure: we can identify labor and expropriation of a surplus. But if we seek to test the essential thesis in regard to the relation between politics and economics, how are we to separate political organization from relations of expropriation? Any assertion of the primacy of economics over politics presupposes that the two can be distinguished. Yet in the case before us the economic structure involves extra-economic coercion: that is, the lord's military power and the norms legitimizing his expropriation of the peasants' labor. Class domination is not based in the lord's role in production, nor in his control of forces of production. Because the immediate producers live on their own farms and possess their own tools, class domination must be "noneconomic."

We can still apply the essential thesis to a society shaped by labor rent. Religious institutions might be endorsing the power of the lords; or we might find the slow growth of a central political authority superior to and distinguishable from the direct producers and their expropriators. Moreover, there might be a basis for historical change contained within the economic structure; for example, because peasants here (as opposed to slaves, say) have a certain number of days of the week for labor on their own plot, they have an interest in increasing their productivity.[6]

Yet we can also see that in this case the economic structure is not separate from political power. Given this crucial fact, only certain forms of the essential thesis are true. It might still be, as Marx and Engels claimed in *The Communist Manifesto*, that "the history of all hitherto existing society is the history of class struggles" (Marx 1964, 1). But it is clearly false that "the sum total of relations of production constitutes the *economic* structure of society, the real foundation on which rises a *legal and political* super-structure" (Marx 1970, 20; my emphasis). In the social form in which labor rent dominates, the base is not the "economic" as opposed to the "political." Rather, labor and expropriation are shaped by relations of power not clearly distinguishable as either "economic" or "political."

In fact, a clear theoretical distinction between economics and politics (as others have observed) is a product of a society in which there is an institutional and normative separation between control over production and wealth and other forms of social authority and power.[7] Such a separation makes for what I will call an *economic system.* The economic system will comprise the forces of production and control over the process and the product of labor. There will also be a realm of politics, involving the exercise and legitimation of power, most especially state power. The distinction between the political and the economic can be made most clearly (perhaps only) for capitalist society and (as I argue in Chapter 5) only for capitalist society during a certain period in its development. Capitalism is based in unequal relations between laborers who own only their labor power and capitalists who own all other forces of production. Such an economic system can coexist with a political sphere in which both laborers and owners possess equal political rights. Here it makes sense to talk of an "economic base" giving rise to a "political superstructure," for here economic and political roles can be distinguished.

Will an analysis of the economy (whether system or structure) enable us to know the effects of acts taken on the basis of class interests? If it will, let us say that it is *lawlike.* As in the case of an economic system, capitalism is the model for a lawlike mode of production. An analysis of capitalist social relations shows that capitalists must take certain actions rather than others in pursuit of their class interests, and that taking those actions will have certain specific effects on society. For instance, competition compels individual capitalists to produce more cheaply. They do so by extending the working day and increasing labor's productivity. Increased productivity requires industrialization, centralization, and monopoly. More controversially, we might say with Marx that actions forced on the capitalist class inevitably create a revolutionary working class.

Economic systems or structures that are not lawlike are much more indeterminate than lawlike ones. In non-lawlike economies, social agents act in accord with their interests to the best of their knowledge and power. Yet the form taken by that action and its effects on society are not knowable in advance by an analysis of the economy. For instance, we know that the feudal lord has an interest in gaining all the surplus he can from the peasants he dominates. But he can do this in a variety of ways. How he does so is not determined by feudalism's economic structure. Similarly, the politicization of advanced capitalism makes its future development indeterminate.[8]

If a mode of production is lawlike, then we might well describe it as moving "with iron necessity towards inevitable results" and possessing "laws of motion" (Marx 1967, 1:8). If a mode of production is not lawlike, we may still claim that class interests determine social behavior, but we cannot know in advance what forms that behavior will take or what effects it will have. Class *interests* will be determinate, but class *strategies* and the *effects* of class action will not.

Capitalism is the model of a lawlike economic system. Since Marx's analysis of capitalism is the center of his theory, it is not surprising that at times both he and his followers have interpreted historical materialism as claiming that all societies possess lawlike economic systems. This tendency is a mistake, as is the converse attempt simply to reverse Marxism's claims about the primacy of the economic over the political. I can clarify this point by criticizing an example of each error.

Etienne Balibar (1970, 223–24) discusses Marx's passage on labor rent as part of a general attempt to show that while the economy always determines social life "in the last instance," it does so differently in different social formations. If the mode of production—the economic structure— does not directly dominate social life, it will at least determine what aspect of society does. Claiming to base himself on Marx's account of labor rent, Balibar argues that because in a feudal economy peasants possess the means of production, they will be expropriated by noneconomic means. Balibar's discussion of this passage seems to accord with mine when he states that where labor rent prevails, expropriation of the surplus will not be determined by the "economic base alone": "*not directly economic, but directly and indissolubly political and economic. . . .* different modes of production . . . do not allow differential divisions and definitions like the 'economic,' the 'legal' and the 'political.'" This statement is compatible with my claim that economics and politics fuse in an economic structure. Yet just above this passage, Balibar refers to the "mode of production" as the "economic instance." And on the next page he claims to show that "In different structures, the *economy is determinant in that it determines which of the instances of the social structure occupies the determinate place.*" In other words, feudalism's *economic form* determines that peasants will be exploited through *political means.*

But how has Balibar established the distinction between "economics" and the other "instances" of the social structure? He defines the mode of production as the particular combination of laborer, means of production, and nonlaborer in the labor process and the control of property. Yet such a definition specifies an economic instance—economic as opposed to political —only if feudal economic relations can be distinguished from what he calls the "direct relation of lordship and servitude": that is, the (political? economic?) obligation of peasants to labor for the lord. As I have argued already, in feudalism this distinction cannot be sustained.

Perhaps Balibar would argue that the form of property determines the role of politics: because the exploiters do not control the means of production (an economic relation), they must therefore coerce the peasants (a political relation). This argument presupposes the existence of a class of exploiters—of nonowners who "must" be expropriating from direct laborers —but the presupposition is unjustified. If there is to be exploitation between classes when the direct producers control their land, it must take the form of physical or ideological coercion. But why must there be exploitation? We cannot derive the form of exploitation from the form of property. Either the two go together in our definition of feudalism, or they are so separated that there is no necessity for the "political" relation to appear at all. If they are joined together, then the economic and the political are connected in the socially primary social structure. Balibar might want to define the "right" to surplus labor solely as a property relation. In such a case, however, property relations begin to expand far beyond the notion of control over the forces of production. For instance, making captured prisoners work at gunpoint would also be an economic—as opposed to a political—relation. This position would enable Balibar to claim that the economy always "determines in the last instance." It would also render his concept of the economic rather vacuous.[9]

Unlike Balibar, Anthony Giddens responds to differences between capitalism and precapitalism by claiming that the social primacy of the economic exists only in the former. Instead of the universal determination of politics by economics seen by Balibar, Giddens sees sometimes one and sometimes the other as having primacy. Giddens defines economics as the "mobilization of *allocative resources*" (for example, raw materials, forces of production, and products) and politics as the mobilization of *authorization* as a resource (for example, control over "social time-space," biological reproduction, and chances for self-development and expression, 1979:108). He believes that authorization predominates in precapitalist societies. Early civilizations pursued neither technological development nor control of property but the "moblization of 'human machines' [slaves or serfs] in an authoritarian division of labor" (163). "Marx . . . may be read as asserting the universal primacy of allocation over authorisation . . . but . . . in class-divided societies, as contrasted to class society [i.e., capitalism], *authorisation has primacy over allocation. . . . only in capitalism . . . is the* mechanism of economic activity the prime mover" (1979: 162).

Giddens is right that Marxism mistakenly generalized its analysis of capitalism. Yet his distinction between allocation and authorization and his claim that authorization is socially primary in precapitalist societies faces serious conceptual difficulties. In a precapitalist society, authority is directly bound up with allocation. For instance, the "authorization" control over labor found in labor rent would not be possible without the lord's simultaneous "allocative" control over large tracts of land. Alternatively, how are we to categorize the obligation to mill flour at the lord's mill and to give, in return, a certain percentage of the grain? Is this a power over persons, to get them to bring their grain to the mill? or a power over things, to take away grain and monopolize mill ownership? Similarly, control of servile labor is control both over forces of production and over people. Slaves are as much property as slavery is a relation of authority. Only in capitalism can the "allocative" power of the capitalist be sharply distinguished from the (supposed) equality of bourgeois democratic political life. In feudalism (and advanced capitalism) we have an economic structure (and one that is not lawlike) but not an economic system.

Giddens's mistake is to think that if economics—or "class" as he is using it—does not predominate, then politics must: if not allocation, then authorization. But asserting the primacy of authorization over allocation means that the two must be distinct. Such is not the case in precapitalist societies. When a social system centers on an economic structure, a clear distinction between a realm of politics and a realm of economics cannot be made; the social relations of labor and expropriation are simultaneously economic and political. Given the difficulty of sustaining the distinction between authorization and allocation, Giddens is ultimately unable to support his claim for the primacy of politics in precapitalist societies. We can agree with him that "only in capitalism . . . is the mechanism of economic activity the prime mover." To be true, however, this statement must be interpreted as meaning that only capitalism (and only during a certain phase of its development) possesses a lawlike economic system. It is false if it means that under precapitalist societies there are distinct economic and political realms and that the political is socially primary.

Criticisms of Historical Materialism

The concepts just discussed make possible many different versions of the essential thesis of historical materialism. The mode of production may be an economic structure or an economic system; it may be lawlike or non-lawlike; and the essential thesis can be asserted about all societies or about some particular society. These eight possibilities are all compatible with something Marx wrote and with positions held by later Marxists. I do not want to prove here what Marx "really" believed; rather, I want to show how challenges to the essential thesis have led to the transformation of Marxist theory.

These challenges may be described by four claims:

1. The mode of production, whether structure or system, lawlike or not lawlike, is not socially primary.

2. The mode of production is socially primary, but Marx significantly misdescribed it. Other activities and relations than the ones he described are essential to it.

3. The mode of production is socially primary but not in the way Marx thought it was: (a) there exist economic structures, but not systems; (b) the mode of production is not lawlike.

4. In regard to contemporary capitalism in particular, (a) an economic system no longer exists; (b) other relations besides those of wage labor are socially primary.

These denials of the essential thesis signal the following changes in Marxist theory.

First, many theorists argue that the form taken by and the conflicts within the mode of production cannot account for social structure or historical change. Other aspects of society—socialization processes and politics—are autonomous from or interdependent with the mode of production. They possess equally important but different forms of social primacy. All of *History and Subjectivity* centers on this claim.

Second, some writers have claimed that while the mode of production is socially primary, Marxism has misconstrued it. For example, the role of women's work in the reproduction of labor power and the autonomy of the gender relations of exploitation have been ignored. I agree with this position and discuss it at length in Parts III and IV.

Third, it may be argued that only capitalism during a certain phase of its developments is a lawlike economic system. Both feudalism and advanced capitalism are fundamentally different. This point is essential to the thesis of *History and Subjectivity* and is developed in detail in Part II.

Fourth, one may apply versions of the foregoing claims to capitalism in particular. To begin with, Marx's account of the initial phases of capitalist development is valid. Because competitive capitalism is a lawlike economic system, he was able to predict the spread of capitalist social relations, the acceleration of technical change, periodic economic crises, and the forced tendency to centralization and monopoly. Yet the initial phase of capitalism has been replaced by a society in which economic contradictions are managed by the state and ideological contradictions by mass culture. From an economic system, capitalism has become an economic structure. Once lawlike, it no longer is. (Specific treatment of contemporary political economy is the focus of Chapter 5. Relations between economics, politics, and mass culture are discussed in Chapters 7–11.)

Further, political life in capitalism is not simply an expression of conflicts of interest between economic classes; for example, racial domination cannot be reduced to an aspect or effect of the power of capital over labor. Alternatively, it might be suggested that racial domination is essentially economic in form. However, since Marx did not include it as a principle governing the social relations of production, his account of the capitalist mode of production is seriously incomplete. Consequently, his prediction that a politically unified working class would develop fails, as does his more general notion that the liberation of the proletariat signals the end of all forms of oppression. This sort of criticism of Marx is discussed in relation to sexism (Chapter 9), racism (Chapter 12), anti-Semitism (Chapter 13), and the failures of the U.S. left (Chapters 15–17).

Finally, though Marx's analysis of capitalism as an economic system possesses a limited validity, it ignores the way capitalism originated and sustained itself as a world system. In this system the development of Europe was made possible by the underdevelopment of other areas. A worldwide division of labor linked industrial capitalism to stagnation and economic distortion of much of the Third World. The initial development of capitalism precluded its own repetition elsewhere. This theme receives unfortunately brief treatment in Chapters 3–5 and 7.

The core error of Marx and of much of the Marxist tradition has been to take capitalism in one phase of its development as the model of human history as a whole. This mistake contradicts some of Marx's initial intuitions. Insofar as humans are self-changing beings with a capacity for freedom, the existence of a lawlike economic system can be only a temporary condition. Society is mechanical only as long as it does not become the object of the collective intentions and actions of its major social groups. Structures of History are compelling only if they are accepted as given by the social agents who participate in them. History's compulsion may be shattered by Subjectivity: the willed attempt by social agents to transform social life. Therefore, the promise of socialism is contained not in the mechanical tendencies of competitive capitalism but in the awakening subjectivity of the working class.

In the chapters that follow, I argue in some detail for the many general claims I have just made.

2

History, Subjectivity,
and Social Primacy

BEFORE I DESCRIBE THE TRANSFORMATION OF MARXIST THEORY IN DETAIL, IT IS necessary to explain what it means to understand social life as a dialectic of History and Subjectivity—and to offer reasons why it is necessary to understand social life in this way. By "History" I mean social institutions and relations that function as objective social regularities, temporarily mechanical forces that produce personal experiences and group actions in predictable ways. "Subjectivity," by contrast, refers to the collective thought and action of human beings who self-consciously defend, challenge, and change a particular form of social life. Because society is shaped by both History and Subjectivity, I argue first that Marxist theory should possess four features. On the one hand, (a) Marxism must be informed by norms, and (b) it must view society as the product of the beliefs and values of the social agents who make it up. On the other hand, (c) Marxism must be alterable by experience, and (d) it must recognize that human intentionality can become reified or sedimented into historically specific social regularities. The first pair of these features reflects the subjective character of social life. The second pair shows social life as historical (in the somewhat unusual sense I am employing here).

Next I argue for a transformed version of the fundamental thesis of historical materialism. Rather than seeing only one form of social primacy, this transformed version recognizes three. It is therefore necessary to define the concept of social primacy and show how three equal but different forms can coexist in the same society. I then summarize my theory: in contemporary capitalism *class relations* shaped by the economic structure, *processes of socialization* creating persons compatible with an unfree society, and *political forms* in which rulers and ruled succeed or fail at col-

14

lectively pursuing their aims possess equal but different forms of social primacy.

The theoretical connections between the first and second sections of this chapter are these. First, like other theories, and especially as a critical social theory, Marxism is informed by norms and interests. These norms and interests, in turn, shape three different but equally important contexts of theoretical inquiry and political practice. Each context is built around particular intellectual questions and practical concerns. Our responses to these questions and concerns lead us to identify a different form of social primacy for each context. Second, since social life is subjective, it is partly constituted by the beliefs and values of social agents. Therefore, its most basic regularities can be fundamentally altered when those beliefs and values change. The existence of such changes requires Marxism to be empirical as well as normative. In particular, Marxism must transform itself from the original version, which identified only one form of social primacy, to a version adequate to contemporary society, which recognizes three. Third, since social life is a product of History as well as Subjectivity, however, these three forms of social primacy must be understood in seemingly contradictory ways. On the one hand, class, socialization processes, and political organization function as objectively determining social forms, creating and constraining human experience and action. On the other hand, these regularities are patterns of action of human agents; therefore, they are only temporary solidifications of intentionality, not products of unchanging laws or impersonal structures. When collective social agents understand the nature and effects of social regularities, they can create forms of action liberated from at least some past constraints. In fact, many contemporary regularities that seem impersonal and objective are the products of past collective struggles. A transformed Marxist theory thus has the same ultimate purpose as the original version: to stimulate a collective understanding of socially primary regularities—and to remake these forces of History into the free creations of an awakened Subjectivity.

A preliminary note is necessary. In what follows I frequently describe Marxism as shaped by the goals of freedom and reason. A full explanation of these terms would take us too far afield, but it is important to clarify three points. First, these terms refer to the human capacity to know, fulfill, and creatively change human needs and wants. Humans act rationally to increase their knowledge of the natural, social, and personal worlds. Humans act freely to alter those worlds. Second, freedom and reason should not be thought of, as they usually are, as either essentially unemotional or essentially individual. Human feelings are essential to rational reflection.

Healthy personalities are constituted as much by relations with others as by autonomy. Third, I use the term "socialism" to refer to a free and rational society. Such a society has never existed. Should it ever exist, it will have little in common with either contemporary capitalism or the bureaucratic state societies of the Communist bloc.

Social Life as Subjective and Historical

Marxism seeks to realize freedom and reason in social life as well as use them in theory. Seeking to awaken human subjectivity, it denies the claim that human behavior is ultimately the product of nonintentional structures to which concepts of freedom and rationality do not apply. If social life is subjective, then, Marxism must take norms as essential to social inquiry and therefore reject any positivist understanding of social theory. If social life is historical, however, human intentionality may be "sedimented" into temporarily lawlike social regularities. Free intentionality and impersonal regularities coexist.

The philosophical arguments that support this account of History and Subjectivity show that critical Marxist social theory is both normative and empirical; that it understands social life as partly constituted by human intentionality rather than solely as a product of laws or structures; yet it simultaneously recognizes that human intentionality can *temporarily* take a lawlike form, making conscious life and action products of seemingly impersonal forces. These arguments are directed against three mistaken claims: that Marxist theory should conform to the positivist ideal of an objective or "value-free" science; that human behavior is ultimately explainable by objective laws or nonintentional structures; that historical knowledge is limited to the description of particulars, not of causal regularities.

Social Life and Subjectivity

Because social life is partly constituted by human subjectivity, social theory is normative and empirical, and rejects the notion of universal laws of social life as the ultimate determinants of human behavior. I focus on each of these points but argue in greatest detail for the claim that human intentionality renders significant laws of social life impossible. This point is specially important because of its relation to the essential thesis of historical materialism. Traditional historical materialism stated the "law" of the social primacy of the mode of production. That "law," however, described only a temporary solidification of human intentionality. As the following chapters show, this solidification was historically specific. Recognition of this fact is essential to the transformation of Marxist theory. Specifically, it leads toward the recognition of three forms of social primacy rather than the original one form of traditional Marxism.

In the last two decades, philosophers from very different traditions have argued that critical norms are integral to any comprehensive social theory. Their arguments begin by rejecting the essential claims of positivism: that natural science is the sole or preferred form of knowledge, that such knowledge is independent of norms or values, and that values or norms are therefore distinct from science and from rationality itself. "Postempiricist" philosophy of science has described how scientific knowledge is a product of communities guided by normative and historically specific concepts of rationality. These descriptions have emphasized that science is the outcome of human interaction guided by values rather than an objective and impersonal process of accumulating and evaluating objective data (Bernstein 1983). This argument has been extended to the empirical study of social life, concluding that such study is necessarily connected to a "critical evaluation of the quality, direction and fate of public life" (Bernstein 1978, 234).

The critique of positivism is the subject of such a vast literature that there is little purpose in repeating the major arguments here.[1] The critical point is that an adequate theory of society is normatively based, especially in the distinction between free and coerced behavior. Social practices and institutions, after all, may stem not from "human nature" but from the unjust use of force and the inculcation of irrational beliefs or personality structures. A social theory must help us determine which of these two possibilities underlies any social regularity. Therefore, our understanding of social life requires critical norms. Without the concepts of freedom and reason, an adequate social theory is not possible. Jürgen Habermas (1975, 102–17; 1979, 1–68) makes this point powerfully when he claims that rational inquiry requires social freedom. He argues that the rationality of a scientific theory (for example) can be assessed only if people are institutionally and psychologically free to challenge it, propose alternatives, and question the competence and sincerity of other speakers. However, our examination of a scientific claim is simply an example of the manner in which *any* belief—and, by extension, the social practices and institutions that express it—can be examined. As science requires communicative freedom, so we need social freedom to assess the rationality of our economic structure, distribution of political power, or family form.

Marxism uses norms to analyze society and looks to find social forces that will act to replace constraint with freedom and irrationality with reason. The ideals of freedom and reason—which enable the *theory* to distinguish between free and coerced behavior—are the ideals that a liberating Marxist *political movement* seeks to realize practically in social life. The goal of this movement is not to serve "laws of history" but to end a lawlike social life that is evading the conscious control of a potentially free and rational population.

The claim that Marxism is necessarily normatively based is essential to the transformation of Marxist theory for three reasons. First, a positivist Marxism misconstrues the dynamic of social change by searching for invariant laws of social development. This search fails to see that such development is crucially shaped by people's experiences and understanding. Past regularities are not indefinitely repeated; rather, collective awareness of such regularities leads to their transformation. The impersonal "laws" of one phase of capitalist development are, in later phases, pursued or avoided by self-conscious social agents. Capitalist development takes the form of a lawlike historical process *until* collective social agents begin to consciously alter that process. Second, a positivist version of Marxism cannot see that "impersonal" historical events have significant historical meaning only relative to social agents' understanding of and attitude toward them. Especially, the social meaning of economic changes—for example, a depression —is determined by the consciousness and political organization of classes. Third, conceiving of Marxism as a positivist science has been used to justify political domination. For this position, the consciousness of social agents is, at best, a determinate outcome of impersonal social processes governed by lawlike regularities. Consequently, the self-proclaimed "masters" of Marxist theory have too often considered themselves justified in exercising power over workers rather than awakening their political consciousness. The view that Marxism is objective and value-free (as, supposedly, natural science is) has thus accompanied clandestine insurrectionism or totalitarianism.

The same subjective character of social life that compels Marxism to be normative necessarily makes it alterable by experience. Because people can learn from experience, social theory must be changed to accommodate shifts in human understanding and action. Therefore, any opposition between the normative and the empirical in social theory is spurious for at least five reasons.

First, Marxism typically makes claims about what type of society people *would* choose *if* unjustified constraints were eliminated. As long as the notion of constraint is given substantive content, such claims are, theoretically, open to confirmation (Geuss 1981).

Second, political struggles often include a process in which people move from relative constraint to relative freedom. In the self-descriptions of people who claim to have liberated themselves from unjust constraints we find critical evaluations of society transformed by experience.[2]

Third, the norms that guide a critical theory and its account of social causality affect each other. In traditional Marxism, for instance, freedom was largely associated with freedom from capitalist control over the means of production. Feminists, however, have criticized the ideology and political style of traditional leftist organizations for ignoring sexism as an autonomous form of social oppression. These thinkers have argued that seeing capitalism as the sole source of social power makes radicals blind to male domination. Consequently, feminists have demanded that Marxist theory be changed to recognize a multiplicity of forms of domination and that socialists directly oppose patriarchy as well as capitalism.[3]

Fourth, the claims of a critical social theory can have a theoretical function not untypical of other scientific hypotheses. For instance, they can be used to analyze the behavior of oppressed groups that turn anger or resentment inward or toward other oppressed people in a self-destructive displacement. The actions of such groups may have to be explained as expressions of resistance to various forms of constraint, a resistance necessarily sublimated because of the inequalities of power that make constraint possible in the first place.[4] Like other "scientific" theories, then, critical theory can be evaluated by its role in explanations where its key concepts refer to unobservable entities or processes.

Finally, while the norms of freedom and reason are essential to Marxism, these norms themselves are not absolute or transhistorical. Our understanding of rational behavior and human freedom, like that of other forms of knowledge, can improve with experience.[5] More particular norms—such as our concepts of expertise in medicine, or sincerity in sexual relations—have been altered by recent political movements.

Suppose, however, it is argued that the concepts of freedom and rationality are irrelevant to social theory precisely because a science of society should show how people are products of structures, not how they generate their own actions. Such a view would eliminate the normative basis of critical theory by making distinctions between the free and the constrained, the rational and the irrational, inapplicable to human action. Both social theory and society itself would be most fundamentally determined by universal laws of impersonal processes. Strictly speaking, this view would eliminate the concept of human *action* itself—for this concept refers to human behavior that expresses beliefs, intentions, and values. Structuralist views, for instance, claim that human behavior is the product not of intentionality but of a structure to which the concept of agency does not apply. In such a model, generalizations about human actions (for example, about institutions, practices, cultures) must be explained by "scientific" theories identifying deep structures, structures themselves essentially different from human action.[6]

This view of social science has been subject to a series of critiques.[7] Two clear and convincing ones are provided by Alasdair MacIntyre. MacIntyre's first argument (1981, 84–102) concerns the effects of human unpredictability. He argues that human actions cannot be explained by theoretical laws of nonintentional structures, because social life fails to meet the conditions of predictability that make it possible to frame such laws. Providing theoretical laws of any type requires the prior existence of universal generalizations; these show the predictability of some group of objects or processes, whose behavior is in turn explained by the laws of a determining "deep structure." Such generalizations are impossible in social life since—as distinct from the natural world—society is partly constituted by the beliefs and attitudes of the social agents who make it up. These beliefs and attitudes, as well as the actions and institutions to which they give rise, are necessarily unpredictable. Conceptual innovation and the effects of one's own and other people's decisions, for instance, make it impossible to predict future social life accurately. The detailed prediction of the airplane and unemployment insurance would simultaneously be their invention. Yet we cannot invent that which has not yet been invented, and such things as jet travel and unemployment benefits during recessions alter society in unpredictable ways. Also, many social situations—labor negotiations or stock market investment, for example—depend on people acting in certain ways just because they have certain expectations about other people. Such situations are unpredictable for three related reasons. Agents here are trying to make other agents predictable and themselves unpredictable. Simply knowing the players' interests will not tell us how they will act. Next, any agent seeking to misinform others is likely to misinform himself. Finally, interests of agents in social situations are often indeterminate. Devoted union leaders approaching retirement may suddenly discover a yen for a government job. Reliable civil servants like Daniel Ellsberg may join an antiwar movement. In short, unpredictability precludes generalizations. And without generalizations, no laws can be framed.

Second, argues MacIntyre (1973), because human institutions are partly constituted by intentionality, the testing of generalizations about society poses difficulties absent in the natural sciences. As a result, cross-cultural generalizations about social institutions and (by implication) generalizations about the "same" society at different periods are prey to crucial dilemmas of confirmation. Consider that, unlike terms such as "gas" or "metal," the descriptive concepts of social science—such as "religion" or "political party"—apply to objects partly because people have particular concepts of and beliefs about them. Because these concepts and beliefs tend to differ markedly in different societies and over time, testing cross-cultural and historical generalizations about "religion" or "politics" is virtually impossible. This is so because testing whether generalizations about religion or politics describe a causal rather than an accidental correlation requires that we search for counterexamples. To find counterexamples we must test the generalizations in very different contexts. For instance, if we go to Africa to test a generalization about political parties based in evidence from the United States, we find (according to MacIntyre) that Africans treat political parties as if they were (what we think of as) religions. When an African "party" fails to behave like the local Republicans, therefore, we cannot say whether we have disconfirmed a cross-cultural generalization about political parties or confirmed one about religion. Generalizations about political parties are thus possible only to the degree to which people in those parties conceive of them similarly. Yet cultural differences and conceptual innovation necessarily limit such similarity. If we find a radically different environment in which to test our generalization, we will find an environment in which the original phenomenon does not exist at all. Consequently, our generalizations about social life are very limited. Social science is simply incapable of finding the purported "laws" of social life.

Finally, someone might argue that human intentionality is itself the product of structures determining behavior on a lawlike basis. Until a field of predictability for human thought is identified, however, such claims seem vacuous. It is also likely that if such laws became known, they would —like the belief in the Phillips curve or the fear that Trotsky was destined to behave like Napoleon—alter the way people act and thus undermine their own predictive power. Knowledge of social regularities is itself a cause of the ending of those regularities.

Social Life as Historical: The Role of Generalizations

Given the absence of significant universal generalizations about social life, social theories focus on the structures of and changes in particulars: the rise or fall of a mode of production, a cultural form, a personality type. Yet while these particulars embody human intentionality, such intentionality is not always conscious or understood by the agents involved. Social reality is a product of History as well as Subjectivity. The former term, again, refers here to the way human intentionality may be collective, taken for granted, or misunderstood. Intentionality can be introjected as unconscious psychic mechanisms and collectively sedimented as institutions and social relations. The forces of "History" are "objectifications" of human action, for the most part ill understood by the agents whose reified and alienated behavior produces them.[8] As such, they lend themselves to being understood by causal generalizations that are essential to claims about social primacy.

MacIntyre's arguments, then, do not exclude the use of socially and temporally limited lawlike generalizations in social theory. Some writers have misunderstood this point, seeking to confine historical understanding to the pure description of a series of particular events. Maurice Mandelbaum (1977, 103), for instance, rules out the use of generalizations (laws) and believes causal explanations in history can be only simple descriptions of the particular historical process in question. He claims that any appeal to generalizations or laws necessarily focuses on abstractions and fails to capture what is specific to any actual historical occurrence. What is critical is to provide a "concrete description" of the historical event, not subsume it under the general description of a "law."

Mandelbaum is correct in asserting that concrete description is a necessary condition for the explanatory use of generalizations. Yet this is only half the story, for concrete descriptions presuppose generalizations. Our descriptive vocabulary *expresses already* a stock of lawlike generalizations. When we talk, for instance, about "poisons" or "disease bacteria," we are talking about entities that behave in predictable ways and have determinate effects. A descriptive vocabulary that did not presuppose laws or regularities would be too impoverished to provide the "concrete description of the particular occurrence" that Mandelbaum sees as preliminary to the appeal to laws.

This point holds for social theory as well as natural science. Describing a historical occurrence requires that we identify institutions and social practices marked by regularities. To call someone a "Catholic" or a "typical woman" or to describe a society as "capitalist" or "feudal" is to identify these regularities. Yet such terms are surely part of Mandelbaum's "concrete description." Gregor McLennan (1981, 79–80) draws the moral: "The particulars of a narrative can be of many kinds: people, certainly, but also institutions, towns, economies, ideas and so forth. . . . The idea that concern for *types* of phenomena, as opposed to individuals, is inappropriate in history is simply dogma."

Claiming logical priority for description of the "concrete" over explanation via generalizations also forgets the necessity of selection in social theory. For Mandelbaum (1977, 97–98, 104), causal explanation does not appeal to generalizations; rather, we explain by describing, in as full detail as possible, all aspects of the process that culminated in the event we wish to explain. Appealing to generalizations or laws is irrelevant: "To give a causal analysis [in history] is to trace an ongoing process that terminated in the specific effect we wish to explain; this involves describing a particular set of *interconnected* occurrences" (my emphasis). Yet without the prior acceptance of a "law" or lawlike generalization, how are we to know what occurrences are interconnected? How are we to know what to include in our account of the "process" leading up to a "specific effect"? For instance, was the configuration of the planets at his birth part of the process that led to Lenin's taking power in 1917? Such a question shows that description is not logically prior to generalization but dependent on it. Thus Mandelbaum's exclusion of generalizations cannot be sustained.

At least three different types of generalizations are essential in describing the sedimented intentionalities of social life. There are, for example, what Richard Miller (1983) calls "auxiliary hypotheses." These hypotheses are essential to explanations of particular events, even though they may not describe the events in question. For instance, we require generalizations in order to decide what kind of evidence is relevant to our research. Such generalizations, in turn, express our beliefs about the society we are studying. In Miller's example, to use a general's diary writings to explain his surrender after a difficult battle depends on an auxiliary hypothesis as to when diary entries are reliable indications of a person's feelings. For a given society, that is, explanations of particular event rely on certain common regularities of personality and institutional life.

Miller (1983, 93) also argues that we typically choose particular explanations over their rivals against a background of theoretical generalizations concerning socially primary forces. For example, some political historians believe that adequate explanations may simply describe actions of political leaders "sufficient to bring about the event to be explained in the circumstances at hand." Other historians require, in addition, the description of the social conditions that gave individual actions their power to produce large-scale effects.

Perhaps most significantly, the logic of explanation turns on what Alan Garfinkel (1981, 28–100) calls "contrast space"; that is, a set of possible alternatives to what actually happened. Explanations single out causes not from all logically possible alternatives but only from a particular contrast space. Contrast spaces, in turn, may be defined by generalizations about what alternatives are in fact possible within a given society. These generalizations describe a society's contrast space by identifying its social regularities. A critical social theory, then, distinguishes between unavoidable social regularities and those which, as products of constraint, limit the contrast space to considerably less than the logical, natural, or even technological possibilities.

As we have seen, the absence of laws of social life does not imply that historical explanations can dispense with generalizations. Our causal generalizations, however, are valid only so long as they are the contexts rather than the objects of human action. Social regularities (for instance, the business cycle) are only temporary solidifications of intentionality and can be altered by experience. Neither universal laws of social life nor biological structures control human behavior. Subjectivity can erupt into a power that transforms History. Critical theory, in turn, searches for the social regularities (institutions, practices, beliefs, and so on) that are socially primary in frustrating or fulfilling the realization of the norms of freedom and reason. It seeks not just to record these regularities but to transform them—because they are human creations that are sustained and can be changed by the understanding and will of their creators.

This general tension between History and Subjectivity is focused in the transformation of Marxist theory. Misled by the seemingly lawlike development of competitive capitalism, traditional Marxists mistakenly believed that social primacy took a form determined once and for all by the laws of social life. Yet the normative foundations of Marxism make it possible for the theory to liberate itself from this illusion. It is necessary next to clarify more concretely how the transformation of Marxist theory involves the interdependence of critical norms and generalizations concerning social primacy.

Marxism and the Three Forms of Social Primacy

Social Primacy

The essential thesis of historical materialism claims social primacy for the mode of production. This thesis implies that we can distinguish the mode of production from other parts of society, and that the mode of production is significantly more important in shaping those other aspects of society than they are in shaping it. Most important, traditional Marxism holds that the mode of production determines long-term historical change and makes politics and culture express and support class interests. In particular, the internal dynamic of the capitalist mode of production was thought to be sufficient, *in and of itself*, to create political forces that would fulfill the norms by which Marxism evaluated social life.

The transformation of Marxist theory is based in a new understanding of social primacy. The one form of social primacy accorded to the mode of production by traditional Marxism is replaced by three different forms.

This transformation involves the recognition that what Marx described as the "iron laws" of capitalist development have been irrevocably altered. Capitalism is now an object of the theory and practice of social agents. A mode of production that was an impersonal *Historical* force has become, at least partly, a *Subjective* expression of contending self-conscious political actors.

Traditional Marxism believed that the historical development of the mode of production guaranteed the eventual creation of a free and rational society. Because it was shaped by the norms of freedom and reason, therefore, Marxism could accord sole social primacy to the mode of production. It has since been recognized—tacitly or directly—that in the present the social effects of the mode of production are considerably more limited. In contemporary capitalism the economic structure may create the material possibility for a liberated society, but other aspects of social life obstruct the fulfillment of that possibility.

Marxism can therefore no longer be satisfied with a single, unequivocal answer to the question, What aspect of society is socially primary? Previously, when capitalism took the form of a lawlike economic system, social life was dominated by what I have called "History": a mechanical and objective form of social life in which people's experiences and actions were determined in ways they did not understand or control. In this period, Marx believed that the capitalist economy would inevitably create the material resources and political preconditions for socialism. He therefore claimed that the capitalist economy possessed sole social primacy.

If we are now to find the major determining forces in social life, however, we must reformulate our concept of social primacy to deal with the complexities of a social system in which History and Subjectivity uneasily intertwine. The transformation of Marxist theory is necessary because Subjectivity has undermined the mechanical power of competitive capitalism. From an economic system it has become an economic structure, and its lawlike tendencies have eroded. Once a mechanical and objective pattern of action that determined social life, it is now thought about and acted on by contending collective social agents. The primacy of the mode of production now coexists with that of two other different but equal forms of social primacy: processes of socialization and politics are socially primary because they determine whether or not the possibilities created by capitalism will be realized. Our commitment to freedom and reason, therefore, leads us to claim that socialization processes and politics are as important as the mode of production. In particular, the dynamic of capitalist development leading toward a politically radical working class has been obstructed. Pacified by socialization processes, the working class has been shaped to accept capitalism's irrationalities. The instabilities of a capitalist economy are managed by an increasingly active state. Finally, when political unrest does surface, activist groups are split by differences in their social experience and opposed by the comparatively unified and self-conscious power of ruling groups.

To fulfill its original interest in the creation of a rational and free society, then, a transformed Marxism must now raise three distinct questions: What aspect of social life creates the possibility of a rational and free society? What forces prevent this possibility from being realized? How can these forces be overcome? Because a transformed Marxism believes that an answer to the first question is *not* an answer to the second and third, it must identify three forms of social primacy. Each of these questions defines a context from which we can identify a different form of social primacy. Thus we see that aspects of social life are *socially primary* if they determine the answers to these central questions flowing from the theory and practice inspired by our critical norms. In other words, a form of social primacy is an aspect of social life that determines social structure and social change (or the absence of such change) in which we have a critical interest. The failures of Marxist theory and the persistence of capitalism have shown that our general critical interest in freedom and reason must be transformed into three more specific interests, each of which makes possible the identification of a different form of social primacy.

Marxism, then, is driven by its evaluative norms and political goals to raise certain questions. The theoretical problems and practical tasks that flow from these questions determine the three forms of social primacy. In the context of the first form, the capitalist mode of production is most responsible for long-term social change and creating the possibilities for socialism. In the context of the second form, socialization processes are most responsible for keeping people from wanting or fighting for a rational and free society. In the context of the third form, the political unity of the ruling class and the social differentiation that divides workers is most responsible for preventing radical social change—even when political discontent surfaces.

Can a coherent theory accord social primacy to more than one aspect of society? Yes, if assertions of social primacy depend on our interests. Three arguments, by W. V. O. Quine and Alan Garfinkel—constructed for rather different contexts—show how this is the case.

1. Quine (1973) wished to refute phenomenalism: the position that only bits of sensory experience—as opposed to either commonsense objects or the theoretical entities of scientific laws—are "ultimately real." In opposing

phenomenalism, Quine did not wish to offer some other single candidate for ontological primacy. Instead, he denied that assertions about whether sense data, physical objects, or theoretical entities are ultimately real could be proved by appeals to "the evidence." He claimed, rather, that assertions of ontological primacy are justified to the extent that they serve to organize experience in each of three goal-defined contexts: teaching people a language, scientific theorizing, gathering or describing evidence. In each context a different type of entity (physical object, theoretical entity, sense data) is "fundamental." Language learning begins when we learn to refer to objects. Scientific theories of deep physical structure often appeal to unseen "theoretical" entities (such as subatomic particles). Questionable or confusing data may be describable only in the language of sensations. Each of the three types of "entity" possesses equal but different ontological primacy. There is no single answer to the question, What really or most fundamentally exists? Rather, that question is reformulated: What really or most fundamentally exists within a goal-defined context? In short, ontological primacy can only be asserted *relative* to a particular purpose. Since we can identify three such purposes, each deriving from a different but equally fundamental human need, there are three distinct but equally important forms of ontological primacy. Similarly, Marxist theory is now defined by three related but distinct purposes. Each of these purposes generates a different form of social primacy.

2. Garfinkel (1981, 10–15, 134–55) developed a somewhat similar argument concerning the relation between interests and explanations. All causal explanations, he claimed, presuppose interests. It is these interests that enable us to separate all of an event's necessary and sufficient conditions into a huge number of background "conditions" and a small number of foreground "causes." The separation is necessary because we use our explanations to help us control that which we are explaining. The causes of events—as opposed to the taken-for-granted background conditions— are those things we are at least potentially able to control. (For example, all the physical laws of electricity and molecular action are necessary conditions of the kettle's boiling over on the electric stove. However, the *cause* of that event, we will say, is leaving the burner on for too long.) How we explain an event, then, is partly determined by our interests concerning it. Similarly, how we identify the socially primary regularities that shape society will depend partly on our critical attitudes toward social life.

3. Of special importance to Marxism, explanatory relevance in social theory is determined by whether we challenge or accept the structural conditions that determine a society's "contrast space" (defined above). If we

take class structure for granted, for instance, we will explain a political event by immediate causes: a recent election, the personality of a political figure, recent developments in foreign relations. If we think of basic class arrangements as alterable, more immediate causes are less explanatorily relevant than the general form of class structure. Which explanation we use is partly determined by our critical attitude toward fundamental social structures (Garfinkel 1981, 44–99). By extension, which aspects of society we identify as primary will partly depend on our evaluative and theoretical perspective. We will view aspects of society as socially primary, that is, partly depending on what we think our society can become and what we want for it.

Quine claimed that different types of entities were equally ontologically primary. Similarly, we may characterize different aspects of social life as socially primary. Both Garfinkel and Quine argued for the crucial role of purposes and interests in determining (respectively) ontological primacy and causal explanation. Similarly, we may identify three separate but related critical interests *each* of which shapes the basic explanations by which we identify three different types of social primacy. Combining these insights, we may describe the transformation of Marxist theory as the recognition of three distinct but related purpose-defined contexts of social primacy. In the first context we focus on the aspect of society that determines long-term historical change and creates possibilities for a liberating society; in the second and third contexts we focus on those aspects of society that prevent those possibilities from being realized.

Is this new theory still, in any recognizable sense, part of the Marxist tradition? Yes, for two reasons. First, Marxism's original goal has, under current social conditions, necessarily devolved into three more particular interests. The point, again, is that Marxism originally thought that its central question—what will create a rational and free society?—would be answered by one aspect of society: the mode of production. Holding one question and one answer, traditional Marxism could go on to identify one form of social primacy. But historical developments in the twentieth century have eroded this position. There is no longer one question. Rather, the original theoretical and normative goal prompting that question has been transformed into three. The mode of production still creates the possibilities for socialism. However, socialization processes shape a population more at home in domination than in freedom. Political relations split insurgent groups when they break through their socialization, allow ruling groups to solidify, and define the social meaning of economic changes.

Second, as we shall see in succeeding chapters, the recognition of three forms of social primacy has emerged out of the efforts of Marxist theorists to make the original theory adequate to political struggles in a changing social world.

The Three Forms

So far, this account has been necessarily—but perhaps obscurely—abstract. It is time to examine somewhat more concretely the particular forms of social primacy identified by a transformed Marxism.

The first form of social primacy is possessed by those social relations that determine a society's basic and long-term structural changes. Since the dynamic of capitalism is primary in explaining social structure and historical change in contemporary bourgeois societies, this first form of social primacy is possessed by the mode of production. The capitalist mode of production has led to such long-term structural changes as industrialization, urbanization, the destruction of precapitalist economies, imperialism, the entry of women into the labor market, the expansion of state functions, and increases in per capita income. An analysis of the basic tendencies of capitalism also provides us with a nonutopian political perspective on the society in which it is embedded. For this perspective, class relations determine the working class (broadly conceived) as the group most likely to lead the political struggle to create a free and rational society.

Though the mode of production is socially primary, Marx's characterization of it is at times seriously mistaken. For instance, he did not take gender relations seriously; consequently, his theory cannot explain the features of capitalist society determined by patriarchy.[9] However, historical changes in patriarchy are more determined by the mode of production than it is determined by them. By "determined" I mean that the systematic and lawlike character of competitive capitalism—knowable from an analysis of the capitalist economic system in abstraction from its accompanying politics and culture—explains basic changes in patriarchy. The reverse is not the case: we do not appeal to a dynamic of patriarchy to explain changes in capitalism. (This claim, and comparable ones concerning capitalism and racism, are argued at length in Parts III and IV.) Similarly, it is clear that capitalism could not have developed without ideological mechanisms such as religion or popular culture, the political organization of the state, or socialization processes based in a male-dominated family. But the histories of religion, politics, and the family, in their broadest outlines, express interests shaped by the social relations of production. The reverse is much less the case.

A brief example may help clarify this point. Given the long history of women's social inequality, why have feminist movements developed only in the last century and a half? Two fundamental facts, both tied to the development of capitalism, are essential to an explanation. First, there is the development of a characteristically early capitalist ideology of political equality. While originally limited to white, male property holders, this ideology was adopted by other groups, including women. Second, capitalism's systematic tendency to expansion has come to undermine its earlier gender categories of paid and household laborers. As women are forced to work for wages outside the home, a significant part of the structural basis for sexist ideology is undermined.

The primacy of capitalism over patriarchy is shown here by the fact that no analysis of the condition of women in, say, the eighteenth century can make later changes in women's social position or the rise of feminist politics seem likely. Capitalism's systematic character explains changes in patriarchy because men and women have lived out their class identity in a dynamic form, while other aspects of their identity have changed in response to altered class relations. Though men exploit women, relations between men and women have not motivated social change to the same degree as have relations between economic classes. Patriarchy has not been, up to the present, systematic in the same way as has competitive capitalism. Without collective actualization of gender-based conflicts, the oppression of women is an "accepted" social fact. As such it plays a secondary part in social change.[10]

Other examples illustrating this point could be chosen. Consider, for instance, the relation between capitalism and the rationalization of technological innovation, the rise of a consumer society, and the initial motivations for anthropology. These three developments reflect capitalism's need to cheapen labor power, to sell goods under monopoly conditions, and to justify imperialism. Though the functional relation provides an initial explanation, we can also show the direct historical relation of capitalists to their creation.[11] By contrast, we will find no adequate explanation of the most general characteristics of these developments from an analysis of premodern science, precontemporary culture, or early nineteenth-century social science. The separate histories of technology, culture, and social science, that is, make little sense if they are not related to the dynamic of capitalist development.

Modes of production are not always as systematic and lawlike as competitive capitalism. However, they may still possess social primacy if they determine social groups whose contradictory interests motivate actions that are primary in explaining social structure and historical change. A mode of production whose later developments cannot be seen as a necessary consequence of its earlier form may still shape class interests and actions expressing those interests.

Given the nature of capitalism, a critical theory of that society identifies a broadly defined working class as the group both interested in and potentially capable of transforming society in the direction of greater rationality and freedom. But this transformation has not occurred. Only confidence that a lawlike and systematic capitalism make it inevitable would allow us to confer on the capitalist mode of production the *sole* form of social primacy. Such confidence should have been shattered by the history of the twentieth century. The success of Marx's structural analysis of the future of capitalism has not been matched by the success of his predictions concerning the response of the working class to that system. The belief that capitalism would necessarily create socialism is challenged by the repeated failure of socialist politics in advanced capitalist societies. We must then ask, What allows capitalism to continue? Similarly, the totalitarian form taken by "socialist" and "communist" governments raises the question, Would the overthrow of capitalist property relations necessarily lead to a significantly more rational and free society?

With these questions we move to an analysis of the second form of social primacy. This form is defined by the theoretical purpose of discovering how a capitalist society maintains itself despite social inequality, economic crises, and cultural contradictions.[12] The explanatory framework determined by this question is shaped by auxiliary hypotheses and critical norms. These include the beliefs that people are capable of freedom and happiness; that, all things being equal, they would prefer them to their opposites; and that capitalism both creates the material possibilities of freedom and happiness and keeps people from realizing them.

The second form of primacy is possessed by the processes of socialization. These processes shape an individual human infant into an adult whose beliefs, values, and personality are compatible with society more or less in its present form, and incompatible with a social transformation in the direction of greater rationality and freedom. Socialization involves the inculcation of false beliefs, but it includes far more: learning to feel certain emotions and express them in particular ways; developing exploitative or deferential attitudes toward other people and nature; repressing physical and sexual spontaneity and intellectual creativity; identifying particular figures as role models or authority figures.

It might be argued that socialization processes are not as socially primary as the mode of production because socialization processes are expressions of interests defined by the mode of production, and because capitalism sustains itself by creating socialization processes that function to preserve it. Yet it is precisely because the future of capitalism has become indeterminate from the standpoint of a critical interest in a rational and free society that this argument is faulty. The outcome of the conflict of interests defined by the mode of production depends to a great extent on the way socialization processes function. While they are "effective," class conflict will lead only to modifications of the system, not to its overthrow.

Recognition of the second form of social primacy is a historical product of the failure of Marxism's political predictions and political movements. This recognition requires a change in the critical norms by which we evaluate society, as well as in our theory of how predictably economic changes will alter social life. Emphasis on property relations and the organization of production must be joined with a critique of other forms of human interaction. Critical norms must now be directed towards our emotional capacities, gender roles, sources of pleasure, sexuality, and attitudes to authority. All these can contribute to maintaining a social order in which power and privilege are reserved for a small number and in which human capacities are used destructively.

Except for a cognitively oriented theory of ideology,[13] Marx paid little attention to this problem. Though traditional Marxism never claimed that the economic structure was totally self-supporting, only since the transformation of Marxist theory has it been realized that the outcome of class struggle is greatly determined by socialization. As we shall see in Chapter 5, economic theory can now tell us little about the social future of capitalist society.

Histories of socialization processes must rely on an account of the dynamic of the mode of production. Yet both the existence and possibility of overthrowing the economic structure greatly depend on the strength or weakness of the socialization processes. It will be impossible to overthrow capitalist property relations if we do not free ourselves from a socialization that adapts us to class domination. It was perhaps Marx's most profound political error to think that the dynamic of capitalism made this revolutionary development inevitable. Distinct from capitalist economic structure —private ownership, a "free" labor force—socialization may determine social behavior so that working-class political activity is absent or blunted. When this happens, the instabilities and irrationalities of capitalism do not create social contradictions. Conversely, when socialization processes break down, the possibility for self-conscious collective attempts at political transformation become possible.

It might also be argued that since the long-term developments of the mode of production depend on the continued consent of the population, the context of such long-term developments (the mode of production) cannot be distinguished from that of consent (socialization processes). This is an important point. The logically distinct forms of social primacy coexist in a society at any given time. However, these two contexts can be distinguished in the following way. Let us remember that the processes of socialization reflect class interests shaped by the mode of production. Our personality structures, attitudes toward authority, and normative presuppositions support the current economic structure. We are taught to respect a certain kind of authority, to cultivate or reject certain values and needs. And we are so taught in order to preserve a class structure defined by the relations of production and expropriation. Also, accounts of *changes* in socialization processes must appeal, in their broadest terms, to the dynamic of the mode of production. Changes in affective life centering in the family, or educational practices during the last two centuries, say, cannot be explained without reference to the dynamic of capitalism. The reverse is not the case. One would hardly appeal to new family forms to explain the creation of monopoly out of competitive capitalism or the rise of imperialism.

However, the social primacy of socialization processes remains. As capitalism matures and its contradictions become more apparent, socialization processes prevent those contradictions from becoming social crises. To some extent, then, the social primacy of socialization is historical. It emerges as capitalism matures. The longer capitalism continues to exist despite its profound irrationalities, the more socialization processes are socially primary in sustaining it.

Just as the fall of capitalism can no longer be seen as a necessary consequence of capitalist accumulation, so desirable changes in socialization processes cannot be seen as an inevitable product of changes in property relations. The irrationalities of capitalism may lead to a new mode of production, but without a fundamental change in socialization processes, that new mode will shape a society that is little closer than capitalism to the critical norms of freedom and reason. The history of leftist movements indicates that socialism requires more than economic relations and conscious beliefs. The more that supposedly liberatory social movements exhibit totalitarian tendencies, the more it becomes clear that socialization which supports domination must be overcome if freedom and reason are to direct social life. Neither nationalization of the means of production nor the merely cognitive acceptance of socialist ideology are sufficient. Without changes in attitudes toward gender and authority, for instance, new forms of oppressive and irrational social relations will replace the old. Thus the processes of socialization are primary not only because they inhibit the realization of the possibilities created by the capitalist mode of production, but because changing them is a necessary condition for replacing capitalism with a democratic and humane socialism.

The distinction between the first and second forms of social primacy may be made clearer by the example of nuclear power. Appealing to the first form of social primacy would enable us to explain the development of nuclear power by reference to the interests of the capitalist class and the capitalist-dominated state. Such an explanation, however, will not tell us why the mass of Americans are relatively passive in the face of its dangers. To begin to answer this second question, we would examine typical reactions to nuclear power: "I'm not expert enough to decide"; "We need more power"; "We don't want to depend on the Arabs"; "The experts will make it safe"; "I can't have any effect anyway." We would then examine the socialization-induced attitudes and capacities expressed in such reactions: deference to science and technology; passivity before authority in general; inability to act on the basis of one's own convictions; an obsession with consumption; and national or ethnic chauvinism. Thus an explanation of nuclear power in terms of interests based in the economic structure does not tell us about the socialization processes that allow nuclear power to continue. Nor does it tell us what kind of change in those socialization processes would help create a population that would not tolerate such a threat to human life.

I will suggest here (and argue at greater length in Part III) that an analysis of socialization processes in our society should rely most heavily on an account of gender identity. Gender identity is the first form of personal identity communicated to infants. The male-female relation is both the most widespread of social relations and that which shapes the family, still the major institution of socialization. The gendered experience of domination and subservience, power and service, provides the model for such other forms of social interaction as the authoritarian relations that hold in factories and armies. Gender is central to personal identity as that identity is formed in childhood, and it conditions the most intimate of adult experiences. More broadly, it colors virtually all institutions of cultural life and is reinforced by and reflected in the vast majority of political practices. Finally, it is key to that aspect of socialization in which a transformed Marxism has the greatest interest: the way socialization produces political conservatism and passivity in the working class.

Knowledge of the first form of social primacy helps identify the class that can overthrow capitalism. Knowledge of the second indicates how that class—broadly conceived as those dependent on wages and without individual control over their work conditions—is reproduced in such a way that it fails to do so.[14] However, instabilities in capitalism limit the capacity of socialization processes to deflect the interests of the working class permanently or completely. As a result, there is a third form of social primacy. In this context, the sedimented layers of class and socialization wear thin. The oppressed refuse to let things go on as before, and the rulers consciously seek to preserve power and privilege. Here our theoretical goal is to explain the failures of working-class political activity, activity that arises when the effects of socialization are suspended or weakened. This theoretical goal is connected to the practical purpose of organizing a collective agent that can transform society.

This third form of social primacy is possessed by the political self-organization taken by contending classes. In capitalist society it is located in two contrasting poles: the usually more organized and effective ruling class complements the usually more fragmented and ineffective working class.

The capitalist state is the major expression of the unified organization of the ruling class. In late capitalism the function of the state in managing economic life and social reproduction has expanded well beyond anything imagined in the nineteenth century. The state plays a key economic role, physically represses dissent, and reproduces authority relations in all areas of social life (see Chapters 5 and 11). Like that of socialization processes and social differentiation, the socially primary role of the state is a historical product of a transformed capitalism and thus requires basic changes in Marxist theory.

Similarly, Marxism's understanding of working-class political life has been transformed. The working class, it is now recognized, is fragmented by experiences of social differentiation. Traditional Marxism correctly claimed that political consciousness grows out of social experience. By ignoring social differentiation, however, it incorrectly viewed working-class social experience as essentially homogeneous.

Social differentiation can be understood if we imagine a person walking down the street in a contemporary U.S. city. What will that person be thinking about? What will she or he feel? Answers will depend to a great extent on interlocking sets of socially typical experiences. These sets are composed of those experiences typical to persons of a given sex, race, class, sexual preference, and national or ethnic group.[15] These categories shape a person's self-conception and his or her attitudes toward and relations with other socially differentiated groups.

Consider, for instance, the different emotional experiences of a man and woman walking past a group of lunch-hour construction workers; persons of different economic classes entering an elegant restaurant; individuals of different sexual preferences watching television commercials; blacks and whites hearing slaveholder George Washington described as the "father of our country"; Jews and Christians watching a president light the "national"

Christmas tree. In each case the person's response to a social fact is largely determined by a socially differentiated identity. In each case the response contributes to the formation of socially differentiated, and frequently antagonistic, groups. It is the politically divisive character of this antagonism that makes social differentiation—especially when complemented by a relatively unified ruling class—socially primary.

Let me briefly clarify some of the relations between the first and third forms of social primacy. We can understand broad historical changes by reference to a highly abstract account of social relations. For instance, the rise of German fascism or the recessions of the 1980s can be explained, in outline, by reference to the conflicting interests of and struggles between capitalists and workers. Yet the experience of these historical events by German Protestants and German Jews, or American whites and Americans of color, are very different. It is this difference of experience that makes so difficult the formation of a collective social agent effectively antagonistic to capitalism. One's personal experience of social life, and not one's position in the abstract schemas of the first form of social primacy, determine one's political identity. Even when the processes of socialization weaken and significant portions of the population become critical of key aspects of capitalist social relations, effective political action is often made impossible by distrust of other socially differentiated groups.

It is true that economic class is one of the central forms of social differentiation. Yet class identity is much more narrow in the context of politics than in that defined by the first form of social primacy. In analyzing a mode of production—for example, in analyzing the likelihood of a depression—the distinction between union and nonunion labor may be unimportant. Experientially, however, the difference between being a member of an elite craft union (such as a plumber) and being a nonunion hospital worker can be crucial.

It should also be noted that social differentiation is reflected in the history of the left in two crucial ways. First, leftist movements, while claiming to represent a universal interest, often reflect the partial interests of certain socially differentiated groups. Second, leftists have manifested their own peculiar form of social differentiation and made the "universal" goal of political organizing a private social circle.[16]

Although we can distinguish their social effects, the three forms of primacy are interdependent. The long-term possibilities created by the mode of production are inhibited or furthered by the effects of socialization. Without collective social agents capable of struggling against both economic structure and oppressive socialization, social contradictions are resolved by a comparatively unified ruling class, and thus a transformation in accord with the interests of critical theory does not occur. Yet the experiences of social differentiation and the changing nature of the socialization processes will themselves be explained in outline by the organization of production—for it is this organization that has created the most effective collective social agents. Action by these collective agents, however ill understood by the individuals involved, is the most important basis of historical change.

In sum, while Marx's account of competitive capitalism required only one form of social primacy, changes in capitalist society and the subsequent failures of his theory have engendered a transformation of Marxist theory based in the recognition of three such forms. These three forms of social primacy are described by causal generalizations that indicate their role in shaping social life. They are also altered by reflection and political action. They express, in short, both History and Subjectivity.

The rest of this book will justify the theoretical model developed here.

PART II

The Uniqueness of Competitive Capitalism

3

Feudalism and Historical Materialism: A Critique and a Synthesis

MARX'S THEORY OF CAPITALISM DISTINGUISHES AN ECONOMIC SYSTEM FROM other social relations and uses an analysis of that system to explain social organization and historical change. The enormous success of Marx's theory for one phase of capitalist development has unfortunately led many Marxists to use it as the model for theories of all types of society. In this chapter I argue that it is a mistake to try to find an economic system in feudal society, or to base an understanding of that society's internal dynamic and transition to capitalism on an analysis of its economy's "laws of development." Chapter 4 describes some central features of emerging capitalism that made it a lawlike economic system liberated from other social relations. Chapter 5 focuses on some of the critical differences between contemporary and competitive capitalism. These arguments contribute to a central part of my overall thesis: that a lawlike economic system is a historically specific social form that did not predate competitive capitalism and that no longer exists. While we can retain Marx's original commitment to freedom and reason and accept the centrality of class, we will no longer expect class relations to reflect a lawlike economic system. Consequently, we must look to the distinct forms of social primacy now possessed by socialization (Part III) and politics (Part IV).

Marxism and Feudalism

How should Marxist theory understand the dynamic of feudal society and the transition to capitalism? I approach this question by showing the crucial contributions and drawbacks of three competing Marxist answers: that of Rodney Hilton, Maurice Dobb, Robert Brenner, and Guy Bois (the "class struggle" view); that of Perry Anderson; and that of Immanuel Wal-

41

lerstein. While each theory tells us something of critical importance about feudalism, each seeks—mistakenly—to use one aspect of feudal society as the key to an explanation of its dynamic and its replacement. On the contrary, feudalism and the transition to capitalism can be explained only by reference to the interrelation of three factors: local class struggle centering on production and expropriation; the unique political form of European feudalism; and the genesis of an international system of trade. Attempts to single out any *one* of these as socially primary in explaining feudalism fail to account for crucial details. Consequently, theorists making such attempts must rely heavily on factors that their programmatic statements deem secondary. The moral is that while Marx's method of abstracting one factor of society to explain social structure and historical change works adequately for competitive capitalism, it fails for feudalism.

We are concerned with the following historical developments. Froin the eleventh to the fourteenth century, a distinct pattern developed within the feudal mode of production: a movement *away from* production and exchange based on extraeconomic coercion and forced labor within local, self-sufficient and consumption-oriented economic units and traditional communally owned/used lands—and *toward* production geared to exchange, increases in wage labor, the pursuit of trade and profit, alienable private property in land, and an increasingly complex local and regional division of labor. This movement was accompanied by dramatic improvements in agricultural technique and large population increases. In the fourteenth century, however, three centuries of development in western Europe gave way to stagnation and decline. There was a precipitous drop in population, settlement of new lands was halted or reversed, trade slumped, cities declined, industries failed, and commodity production dropped sharply.

Between the middle of the fifteenth and the beginning of the sixteenth century a fundamentally changed western Europe emerged. Hired labor, the renting of land, and the production of produce for sale replaced servile labor on a lord's demesne. Capitalist agriculture was accompanied by a resurgence of town life, with increasingly stratified social relations based on trade and commodity production. The classes of capitalism—owners and wage laborers—were forming. Simultaneously, centralized states emerged. These states appropriated surplus by taxation, supported the nobility in struggles against the peasantry, and took part in economic life as consumers and as rationalizers of the economic infrastructure. They also participated in the recently created world economy that stimulated industry and agriculture by long-distance trade and provided direct plunder and captive markets for colonial powers.[1]

A theory of feudalism must explain why feudal expansion was followed by a crisis, and why feudalism gave rise to capitalism. What would a *Marxist* theory of feudalism be? Some writers suggest that it must resemble Marx's theory of capitalism by identifying a lawlike economic system; for example, finding feudalism's "prime mover" (Hilton et al. 1979, 109) or confirming a "general Marxist *law* of development that economic society is moved by its own contradictions" (Procacci 1979, 129; following Dobb). In this view, feudalism centers on an economic system, a system constituted by forces and relations of production, and distinguishable from and determining politics and culture. The social classes whose actions shape historical change, in turn, are determined by the places they hold in the relations of production; especially, the places of direct producer of material wealth and expropriator of the surplus. Finally, an analysis of the socially primary structure of feudal society (so conceived) would explain both the dynamic of feudal society and its transition to capitalism.

It is interesting and nonaccidental that Marx did not offer a theory of feudalism comparable to his theory of capitalism. Though he did describe some of the necessary conditions for the emergence of capitalism, he did not view those conditions as inevitable products of a law of feudal development. Unfortunately, too many Marxist theoreticians have thought that the kind of theory Marx provided for capitalism—of a lawlike economic system—is the proper model for theories of any society. They have not realized that the success of Marx's account of capitalism lies not just in his "method" but in the unique, historically specific features of competitive capitalism as well. Only when a law-like economic system emerges can social theory focus on one abstractable aspect of society to explain social structure and social change.

There is an alternative form of Marxian theory that rests on three central premises. First, while class relations are essential, those relations are not determined just by the structure of direct appropriation of the economic surplus. They include widespread and historically specific political relations. The form and distribution of political power partly constitutes—rather than results from—the mode of production. Second, class relations involve not just those classes that seem to confront each other directly in production and appropriation (in feudalism, lord and peasant) but also geographically distant groups connected by a world trade network and/or various forms of colonialism. Third, the absence of a single "prime mover" of feudal society means that feudal history is not the working out of a lawlike economic system. Social life and historical change are indeterminate outcomes of political struggles, not imperatives of a mechanical economy.

When this model is applied to the dynamic of feudalism and the transition to capitalism, the following account emerges. First, attempts by feudal lords to increase revenues without developing productivity exhausted agricultural resources and aroused peasant resistance. Second, the particular structure of political power within feudalism allowed for the emergence of protocapitalist urban centers. Third, a worldwide trading and colonial system provided financial resources for capitalist development and markets for early capitalist "industries," while imported agricultural products allowed for diminished local agricultural production. These three factors were interdependent and mutually necessary.

Class Struggle: Dobb, Hilton, Brenner, and Bois

Dobb, Hilton, Brenner, and Bois, despite some differences, all hold a theoretical perspective on feudalism that resembles Marx's theory of capitalism. Their "class struggle" view places primary emphasis on feudalism's possession of an internal dynamic based in the immediate economic relations between serfs and lords. They deny that feudalism, as writers such as Paul Sweezy would have it, was an essentially static system of production for use that was dissolved by trade and towns. The class-struggle theory considers the decisive elements in the transition to capitalism to be internal to feudalism: class struggle in the context of varying amounts of available labor and land; the motivation of peasants to increase their productivity, given that some of their work time was on their own plots; and the need of nobles to compete for power against other nobles and rebellious serfs— factors that led to a development of commodity production *predating* the growth in international trade.

Dobb claims that this analysis follows Marx's general rule that the "hidden basis of the entire social structure," including the "political form of the relations of sovereignty and dependence," stems from "the specific economic form in which surplus labor is pumped out of direct producers" (Marx 1967, 3:791). In feudalism, this economic form is the coercive relationship by which feudal lords forcibly take services or dues from the immediate producers (Dobb 1947, 35). This method of extracting surplus labor is the "crucial characteristic" of feudalism and is of "greater significance" than other factors, including the "relation of production to the market" (Dobb 1979, 58). As ruling-class demands for revenue grew, lords attempted to squeeze greater income from serfs. In response, peasants "illegally" fled the manors, and agricultural resources were exhausted Dobb 1947, 42, 46). Peasant flight, the use of marginal economic lands, the demographic devastation of the Black Plague (partly a product of the peasants' physical exhaustion), and peasant revolts led the nobility to abandon feudalism in favor of profit-oriented production for exchange, or the sale or leasing of lands to rich peasants.

Why did the nobles seek greater revenue? Not for trade, claims Hilton, but to maintain and increase their power vis-à-vis their rivals and their underlings. This pursuit of class power was "the driving force in feudal economy and feudal politics" (Hilton et al. 1979, 114; cf. 116). Simultaneously, since peasants had at least a certain percentage of labor time to work on their own plots, they were driven toward increased productivity when nobles demanded higher revenue (Marx 1967, 3:794).

In this class-struggle view, feudalism's expansion between the tenth and the thirteenth century, its fourteenth-century contraction, and its subsequent transition to capitalism are quite predictable. Expansion was caused by the interests of lord and peasant. Crisis was caused by an exhaustion of peasants' labor power and of animals and soil (Brenner 1978, 46–47). While feudal lords set dues, rents, and fines and controlled the mobility of labor, they were typically unconnected to the process of production. They had a structural basis for desiring more revenue but not for increasing productivity (Hilton 1978, 9). The other major political powers — the state and the merchants—expropriated surplus through taxes and profits on exchange, neither of which were directly involved in raising productivity. The result was a constant tendency to "exhaust the goose that laid the golden eggs for the castle" (Dobb 1947, 46; Garraty and Gay 1972, 400; Wallerstein 1974a, 200). After the crisis, labor-hungry lords had to give better terms to the surviving peasants; and the use of fertile and more contiguous plots of land led to a resurgence in productivity.

Bois argues that this pattern necessarily led towards capitalism. Since each crisis reduced the capacity of the nobility to extract the surplus that could guarantee its power, each expansion-contraction cycle was resolved by increasing the quantity of capitalist social relations. By the sixteenth century, as a result, nobles were turning to hired labor and production for exchange, rather than trying to retain control of the labor force by traditional means. There was a "sudden upsurge of agrarian capitalism" (Bois 1978, 64; cf. 1976, 193, 336).

The class-struggle theory seeks to be a theory of feudalism. It claims that the direct relation of expropriation of an economic surplus is the key to explaining both the dynamic and the eventual replacement of feudalism. One powerful consequence of this view is that it improves on the earlier position (supported by Pirenne and Sweezy) that feudalism was essentially static and had to be dissolved by the action of urban-based trade. As class-struggle theorists argue, both trade and towns were internal rather than external to feudalism. It was feudal figures—the nobility and the church— who promoted the development of trade and the formation of towns (whatever political and economic independence might have been achieved by the towns once they were established). Also, the response of the nobility to the

growth of trade and towns varied dramatically. In England, the commuta-
tion of labor dues to rents took place furthest from the growing towns. In
eastern Europe the introduction of serfdom, which began in the late fifteenth century, was aided and furthered, if not actually caused, by the rise
of the grain trade with the West. Essentially, the market compelled no
particular action by lords; they could seek to "squeeze" peasants rather
than pursue capitalist social relations or to increase productivity (Brenner
1978; Hilton et al. 1979, 109–12; Merrington 1979).[2]

Despite its accomplishments, the class-struggle theory has serious
drawbacks. Most significantly, it needs to be supplemented by accounts
of politics and (local and worldwide) trade. Such supplementation, however, is rejected by the class-struggle theorists' programmatic statements
concerning the social primacy of the internal dynamic of economic class
struggle.

Let us begin by noticing that, contrary to their stated perspective, the
class-struggle theorists must appeal to the autonomous role of politics
to explain feudal development and decline. Bois, for instance, claims that
the development toward capitalism was much faster in England than in
France because an older English feudalism's greater number of expansion-
contraction cycles had altered the balance of power toward the peasantry
and eroded feudal forms of expropriation. But Bois is wrong: feudalism
was older in France than in England. Bois might reply that this led to the
greater power of serfs in France, enabling French peasants to retain control
of their land and obstruct the creation of a landless wage-labor force. If this
is the case, however, then the tendency toward capitalist social relations
contained in the expansion-contraction pattern may conflict with the political requirements of the transition to capitalism. The increased power of the
serfs can either lead the nobility to renounce feudalism and create capitalism or create an entrenched peasantry that makes large-scale capitalist
development impossible (Moore 1966, 40–109). By itself, the economic
structure does not determine the outcome.

Despite his claims for the primacy of economics, Brenner faces a similar problem. He explains differences between feudalism in eastern and
western Europe, or between early capitalist development in France and
England, by appeals not just to differences in the structure of direct production and exploitation, but to political differences. He believes the comparatively weak communal peasant institutions of eastern Europe allowed
the imposition of serfdom in the fifteenth and sixteenth centuries; in France
(but not England) he sees an alliance between the French state and the
French peasantry enabling the latter to resist the expropriation of their
lands. Again, these political relations are not reducible to consequences of
economic relations.

Of course political relations are relations between classes; however, the central theoretical question is, Are they direct expressions of the form taken by the immediate extraction of surplus labor? In feudalism, the answer is no. If political structure is essential to feudal history, the specific form of exploitation does not *by itself* determine feudal society. We can identify the general interests of feudalism's different social classes. But an analysis of extra-economic coercion—the relation seen as "constitutive" of feudalism by the class-struggle theorists—cannot provide the theoretical connection between the crisis of seigneurial revenues and the development of capitalism. In different places, responses to this crisis took very different forms. Some of those responses led toward capitalism and some did not. The class-struggle theorists must, tacitly or directly, acknowledge that politics and the relations of production are interdependent variables that produce a structurally unpredictable outcome. In the context of feudalism we can give a history of that outcome, but we cannot deduce it from our theory. There is no lawlike economic system producing predictable political effects.

Despite the class-struggle theorists' attempt to emulate Marx, his theory of competitive capitalism is quite different. He did not claim that competitive capitalism led to periodic economic crises and that those crises might be resolved in opposite ways—sometimes leading to greater concentrations of wealth and sometimes "back" toward petty commodity production. Nor did he claim that the imperative to realize a profit could ever be met by limiting or abandoning technological development depending on a society's configuration of political power. Rather, he argued that economic relations between capitalist and proletariat would lead to certain structural social changes, including certain predictable political developments.

Another significant criticism of the class-struggle theorists is that they contradict themselves by both denying the importance of the market and making frequent appeals to it as a decisive historical cause. Dobb, for instance, asserts the primacy of productive relations and processes over those of exchange (1947, 25). Yet he also claims that trade led peasants to produce for a market (1947, 60); that trade helped create urban centers, which became the home of the bourgeoisie (1947, 77); that control of trade in the new towns led to decisive political power (1947, 98); and most important, that profit on trade led to increased stratification among peasants and paved the way for full capitalist production (1979, 167).

Like Dobb, Brenner frequently asserts the causal primacy of class struggles and relations of production over exchange (1976, 31). Yet Brenner often appeals to trade to explain the rise in demand for both agricultural and handicraft goods. The world market, he says, provided an "indispensable contribution to the rise of capitalism" by providing demand and promoting concentrations of capital and "cooperative labor" (1978, 76). We might, of course, consider the growth of a world market an inseparable aspect of the structure of class relations. The identities of trader, producer for trade, and so on, would then be essential to the class relations of late feudal–early capitalist society. In such a case, however, no argument can be made for the primacy of class relations over trade. They are part of the same phenomenon. Also, if roles in trade count as class relations, the "prime mover" of feudalism is *not* limited to the struggle between lord and serf over the disposable surplus.

The critical point is that the growth of international and local trade constituted a decisive change in the class structure by introducing new social actors and transforming old ones. Therefore, no rigid distinction can be made between the effects of "trade" and those of "class struggle." Further, the "direct relations of expropriation" on which the class-struggle theorists base their analysis include the macro relations of the world-system as well as the micro ones of capitalist and wage laborer (Bergesen 1980, 123–24).

Urban-based commodity production and exchange in the western European city were also, contrary to the class-struggle theory, essential to the development of capitalism. Rural overexploitation caused the decline of feudalism partly because it coexisted with an urban realm of trade and petty-commodity production. Brenner claims that towns were basically irrelevant to the struggle for peasant freedom, but there is much evidence to contradict him. Towns, much of whose strength derived from trade, stimulated and supported peasant revolts from 1300 to 1700. In western Europe, towns were havens for discontented peasants and lent considerable aid to rural rebellions (Anderson 1978, 205; Kamen 1972, 331–32; LeGoff 1973, 79; Mousnier 1970, 38–54; Thrupp 1973, 268). Also, differences in urban development between eastern and western Europe were crucial in explaining those regions' different responses to the crisis of the fourteenth century. Undeveloped towns in eastern Europe allowed for the imposition of serfdom and the creation of closed economies dominated by the rural nobility (Anderson 1978, 252; Kula 1976; Wallerstein 1974a, 128–32). Finally, town life made decisive technological and cultural contributions, from developing the pedal-operated loom to popularizing the capacity to tell time (LeGoff 1973, 83, 87–90).

This is not to say that there was a rigid distinction between feudal lords and urban merchants; much of the original impetus for the growth of the medieval town had come from nobles or church leaders eager to reap profits from growing trade. The point, rather, is that trade affects economic development because traders have economic interests. These interests will be expressed in class struggles.

In sum, the class-struggle theory requires accounts of politics and trade to achieve a synthesis which will provide an adequate theory of feudalism. Let us examine each of these factors in turn.

Perry Anderson: The Fusion of the Economic and the Political

Anderson focuses on the importance of political structure, stressing that no purely economic analysis of feudalism can explain the dynamics of feudalism or the transition to capitalism. For Anderson (1979, 405), the method of surplus extraction was not constituitive of feudalism; rather, feudalism was, like all "pre-capitalist economic formulations," shaped by a fusion of "economic production," "juridical property," and "politico-ideo-logical power." If the feudal mode of production is defined without reference to law and politics, claims Anderson (1979, 402), we will be unable to explain why it, of all the situations in which "primitive and tribal forma-tion were superseded," produced capitalism. Why, he asks, do large land ownership, small-peasant production, extra-economic coercion, limited commodity production, and restricted labor mobility not lead to capitalism in Ming China, Seljuk Turkey, Ghenghisid Mongolia, Safivid Persia, Mughal India, or Tulanid Egypt? What is unique to western European feudalism?[3]

Anderson's (correct) answer is that Europe's uniqueness is found in the structure of its political institutions. For him, the social effects of rural class struggle (primary for the class-struggle view) depend on the political organization of feudal society. Politically, feudalism was shaped by a "par-cellization of sovereignty" in which there was no single, central authority· (1978, 148). Peasants were subject to the lord's jurisdiction, yet they also were in de facto possession of their own strip tenancies. The lord, in turn, controlled land and possessed political power as a "fief" to a higher lord— in a chain of obligations that led up to the king. But these obligations were complex, overlapping, and sometimes contradictory. Lord A could owe ob-ligations to Lord B, who owed obligations to Lord C, who owed obligations to Lord A, etc. This absence of a political center, claims Anderson, was "constitutive of the whole feudal mode of production" (1978, 148).

Feudalism's political organization had three main consequences.[4] First, it allowed for the continuity of peasant communal lands, supporting peas-ant interest in increased productivity and peasant classs solidarity. Thus, unlike Bois and Brenner, Anderson sees the political organization of the peasantry, crucial to explaining the transition to capitalism, as essential to European feudalism as such. Second, the parcellization of sovereignty cre-ated political space for the unique medieval town. Unlike those of Rome (whose cities were controlled by country landowners) or China (where the provinces were governed by bureaucrats and a central authority), the European feudal town had a relative autonomy which allowed the development of an urban economy of commodity production alongside a rural economy of production for use (1978, 150). Rather than being "parasitic centres of consumption or administration," towns became vital areas for production and exchange and allowed for the emergence of private property (1979, 422).[5] Third, the decentered structure of feudalism dictated much competition among nobles. Feudal politics, far from being a simple consequence of the direct relations of production, helped motivate the increasing drive for revenue which was part of the expansion–contraction cycle.

Since the feudal parcellization of sovereignty is significant only in the context of the immediate relations of production, Anderson's analysis supplements rather than replaces that of the class-struggle theorists. For one thing, his argument presupposes that an autonomous urban economy is inherently dynamic and that the pressures of coexisting with such an economy will drive a rural economy toward capitalism. For another, the medieval town was crucial in the transition to capitalism partly because it stimulated and supported class struggle in the countryside. Also, capitalist development required that production be removed from the towns to the countryside, away from the constraining effects of monopoly-oriented urban guilds. Yet the countryside could be a field for capitalist development only after class struggle had created rural wage labor, agricultural production for a market, and private property in land (LeGoff 1973, 95; DeVries 1976, 94–110). Anderson's account of the political uniqueness of European feudalism (as he must be aware) cannot be abstracted from feudalism considered as a mode of production in the traditional sense; i.e., as structured by immediate relations of production and expropriation in a particular context of productive powers.

Immanuel Wallerstein: The World-System

The class-struggle theorists define feudalism in terms of the immediate relations of production and expropriation. Anderson adds the unique political organization of feudal society. Wallerstein completes the picture by an account of what feudalism transformed itself into. His description of the underlying long-term causes of historical change adds a missing element to our analysis: the transition from feudalism to capitalism required not only rural class struggle centered on production and expropriation plus a particular form of political organization but also the new relations of a world economic system.

Like the class-struggle theorists, Wallerstein (1974a, 37–38) sees in feudalism both a cycle of expansion and contraction and a long-term tendency to crisis leading toward capitalism. However, he defines the new system as a "capitalist world-system": an integrated system of many political units marked by

an expansion of the geographical size of the world in question, the development of variegated methods of labor control for different products and different zones of the world-economy, and the creation of relatively strong state machineries in what would become the core-states of this capitalist world-economy.

In this world-system the "core" states of northwest Europe specialize in the export of manufactured goods and capital-intensive agriculture. They develop wage-labor and exercise various forms of economic (but not political) domination over the "semi-periphery" and the "periphery." The semi-periphery (southern France, Italy, Spain) utilizes sharecropping and produces intermediate goods. The periphery (eastern Europe and the Latin American colonies) provides agricultural raw material and bullion and coerces its labor through serfdom or slavery. The key to the entire system is the creation of worldwide trading patterns that lock different areas into different roles (Wallerstein 1974a, 95–98). These roles determine how labor will be controlled in each of the three areas. Thus Poland's "second serfdom" is a response to the crisis of feudalism in just the same way as is the development of wage labor in England, northern France, or Holland. Finally, a nation's status also depends on whether it can develop a strong state. Strong states create profitable terms of trade for the core nation. The surplus on trade, in turn, provides resources for the expanded reproduction central to capitalist accumulation.

For Wallerstein, there are no capitalist nations or economies. There is only one unique, evolving world-system of capitalism. In sixteenth-century Poland and the Americas, no free wage labor confronted capitalists owning the means of production. Therefore, traditional Marxist theory does not consider those areas capitalist, even though they were affected by and contributed to the development of capitalism in France, Holland, and England. This position finds capitalism only in regions where private ownership and wage labor predominate (e.g., Dobb 1947, 7). Relations between this region and other areas may support the development of capitalism, but they do not constitute it. For Wallerstein (1974b, 398–400), by contrast, economies are defined not by the micro relations that hold between their local classes but by the macro relations tht hold between them and other parts of the world-system. As long as they produce for sale on a market, they are capitalist. As earlier theorists (such as Pirenne and Sweezy) saw an inherently static feudalism being dissolved by trade, so Wallerstein sees world trade—along with strong state machineries—constituting the new system itself.

The world-system framework explains two crucial aspects of the development of capitalism that other theories cannot. First, it accounts for the growth of particular forms of industry and agriculture. Commercial agriculture in Holland was possible only because of the importation of major basic foodstuffs from Poland. An English textile industry clothed the peasants of Europe. Dutch profits on world trade funded investment in massive shipworks and land reclamation. Second, Portugal, Spain, Holland, France, and England derived enormous revenues from their colonies. The influx of treasure provided a significant surplus for the growing European economy. While Spain "squandered" its wealth in consumption, Holland, England, and France sold manufactured goods and the products of capitalist agriculture to captive colonial markets and managed both the intra-European and the Europe–Far East trade. Exchanging manufactured goods for agricultural products raised demand at home and provided a surplus for investment (DeVries 1976, 37–39, 92–93; Hamiltion 1934; Kamen 1972, 57–93; Miskimin 1977, 34–46, 54–56, 89–95; Vilar 1959; Wallerstein 1974a, 165–200).

Despite its contributions, Wallerstein's focus on the emergence of a world-system of trade is not able, *in and of itself*, to explain the transition from feudalism to capitalism.[6] This point can be shown in a number of ways. First, in his account of the dynamics of feudalism, Wallerstein (Wallerstein 1974a, 52–65) relies on the role of local class struggle and the particular political form of European feudalism. Like Anderson, he appeals to the decentralized political authority of European feudalism to explain why it, and no other economically comparable social formation, led to capitalism. Fifteenth-century China, for instance, possessed sufficient internal trade and technological development to initiate a capitalist "take-off"; however, its stability-pursuing centralized bureaucracy forbade the highly charged competition among nobles and between landowners and towns. Motives for developing economic productivity or acquiring colonies were lacking.

More generally, in Wallerstein's second volume on the capitalist world-system (1980, 31), he places a significantly greater emphasis on class struggle in creating the feudal crisis than he did in the first. He claims that the socioeconomic crisis weakened the nobility in both eastern and western Europe so that peasants steadily increased their share of the surplus from 1250 to 1500. This increase drove the ruling class to preserve its privileges by creating a new form of surplus appropriation.[7]

Yet while he sees politics and class struggle in the crisis of feudalism,

Wallerstein's account of the emergence of capitalism either omits them or reduces them to consequences of the world market. His explanation of the form taken by the emerging capitalist system in the sixteenth century turns on the place various countries have in the world market, not on either the specific features of their political history or the outcome of their local class struggle. Countries become core, semi-periphery, or periphery because they can produce and exchange certain kinds of products, and because their ruling classes can (or cannot) create an adequate state apparatus.[8] Exchange possibilities and the wisdom (or stupidity) of the local ruling class determine the details of the development of capitalism.

Like relying solely on class struggle or politics, this position leaves too many crucial historical developments unexplained. For example, Wallerstein explains the rise of serfdom in eastern Europe in the sixteenth century (the "second serfdom") by that region's role as a peripheral supplier of primary agricultural goods to the northwest European "core." There is considerable evidence, however, including some supplied by Wallerstein's own authorities, that the second serfdom occurred well before the region took its exporter role in the world economy (Anderson 1978, 258–59; Brenner 1976, 53; Wallerstein 1974a, 96–97).[9] It could well be argued that Poland became an exporter because lords were able to impose serfdom. Only then was the Polish nobility able to enforce "coerced cash-crop" production.

In fact, forms of labor control are bound by local forces and relations of production as well as by the market. If labor is too demographically scarce, "free" wage laborers will cost too much. If peasants are well organized to resist the lords, serfdom can cost too much. Finally, agricultural productivity must reach a certain level for wage labor to be profitable. If it does not, then the product of a given working day will only match, not exceed, the worker's wages. Under a system of feudal labor dues, by contrast, the fruit of a given day's labor belongs to the lord, who thus reaps a benefit no matter how inefficiently the labor is performed (Dobb 1947, 20–24, 53–56; Domar 1970). It should not surprise us, then, that in certain areas of Europe the development of intra-European agricultural trade led to the development of a wealthy peasantry rather than a resurgence of serfdom. The crucial variable, which determined the effects market forces would have, was the comparative power of the contending local rural classes (Brenner 1976, 54). The particular form of labor control cannot be explained, as Wallerstein implies (1974a, 111), simply by the desire of the local lord to "draw the largest and most immediate profit."

The general point is that the outcome of class struggle determines how a class is able to take advantage of the market. Consequently, when Wallerstein substitutes the notion of a capitalist world-system for the distinction between local capitalist economies and colonies, he is unable to explain the very different dynamics of these different sectors of the "same" capitalist system. For instance, in Poland one sees the familiar pattern of increased feudal exploitation reducing productivity (Anderson 1979, 290; Brenner 1978, 68–71; Kula 1976, 108–11). Poland could not respond to changes in demand, but only to weather-determined vagaries of the grain harvest. Its "capitalist" export agriculture was less productive than the "feudal" production for consumption of the Polish peasants' own plots. By contrast the "core" in England consistently increased its productivity just because its *local* capitalist social relations joined surplus appropriation with the need to develop productive forces (Brenner 1978, 68). Only under capitalism traditionally conceived are exploiters compelled—and able—to raise productivity. Thus the seventeenth-century economic slowdown led Polish nobles to exhaust both land and serfs. Capitalism responds to crisis by long-term increases in productivity, not by declines (Murray 1977).

Wallerstein might reply that his distinction between "core" and "periphery" explains these differences. It would then appear that many of the old features of the distinction between feudalism and capitalism are simply repeated under a new description. Theoretical stress on the primacy of the world-system is then supplemented by stress on local class relations.

Finally, Wallerstein, like others of the "underdevelopment school," claims that the core of the world-system expands because of the surplus it takes from the periphery (cf. Amin 1976; Emmanuel 1972; Frank 1969). But simply being the beneficiary of unequal exchange is no guarantee of economic development. As in Spain, the fruits of unequal exchange can be used for unproductive consumption rather than for development. England "took off" as the first fully capitalist power precisely because it used its trade surplus and the profit from its internal market economy to develop the means of production. If core status is accorded mainly by trade relations, and not also by immediate relations of expropriation, this critical difference between Spain and England cannot be explained.

In short, the market and local class struggle are mutually determining. The growth of capitalism in western Europe required the resources derived from the exploitation of a world-system. It is hard to imagine early capitalist development without American bullion or Polish wheat. Simultaneously, the surplus from world trade fueled capitalist development because centuries of class struggle had introduced a new set of relations of production. In eastern Europe, by contrast, surplus from an export trade led only toward stagnating productivity and eventual loss of markets to modernized

English agriculture (Bairoch 1973, 459–60; DeVries 1976, 72; Hill 1961, 147–50, 201–4, 269–70; Kula 1976).

I have argued that an adequate theory of feudalism and the transition to capitalism relies on three factors: a pattern of expansion-contraction-crisis stemming from local class struggle; a unique organization of political power; the creation of a world-system of trade and exploitation. If successful, my argument should have shown that an attempt to rely on any one of these factors to the exclusion of the others will fail.

This position, synthesized from the work of the theorists I have been discussing, identifies the interests of the social groups whose actions determined historical change. We know, for instance, that the nobility sought to maintain its power and increase its revenue; that the peasantry sought to lessen exploitation; that merchants and protocapitalists attempted to increase the social space in which to pursue trade and, when successful, often sought entry into the nobility. And we know that at various times all these groups sought the support of or opposed the growing centralized state. However, no theory of feudalism will tell us how—on the basis of those identified interests—a feudal society will change. We can abstract the class structures of feudal and developing capitalist societies from, say, the surrounding relations of religion, art, and the family. But we cannot describe a structure of class relations whose tensions guarantee or even define as highly likely the crucial historical developments that culminated in the triumph of industrial capitalism.

We may thus retain the notion of a "mode of production" or economic structure—and view it as shaping class interests. But an analysis of the mode of production will not abstract an economic system from the rest of society. Class struggle will not be defined essentially by economic as opposed to political relations; and it must be viewed as both local and "world" in extent. Nor will an account of class conflicts reveal a structural determinant of the actual historical developments that led to the rise of industrial capitalism. In the context of feudalism, the embryonic classes of capitalism, and the world economy, class struggle makes possible a variety of outcomes.

In feudalism, therefore, the kind of social primacy that Marx accorded to the economic system of competitive capitalism simply does not exist. In Chapter 4 I will offer some reasons why it did exist in competitive capitalism. Chapter 5 argues that it no longer exists in contemporary capitalism.

4

The Emergence of
Competitive Capitalism

WITH THE ADVENT OF COMPETITIVE CAPITALISM WE FIND A UNIQUE LIBERATION of economic institutions from tradition and political power. This liberation makes it possible to center social theory on the social primacy of the economic. As a lawlike economic system, capitalism mechanically determines the expression of class interest in social action, thus making basic social changes predictable. A theory of competitive capitalism can identify not only class interests but the social changes that the actions expressing those interests will produce. Society becomes a product of "History," as politics, personal experience, and social organization are shaped by an impersonal and uncomprehended economic system.

The creation of a lawlike economic system was the major "accomplishment" of western European society between 1400 and 1850.[1] This chapter examines two aspects of this process. First, there is the creation of the proletariat as a mass of laborers, crucial aspects of whose lives could be manipulated by capitalists. Second, there is the emergence of capitalism as a system in which economic activity gradually escapes from the constraints of monopoly, direct coercion, and government control. These two developments form a society in which decentralized economic actors—compelled to particular forms of behavior by the imperatives of commodity production, competition, and class struggle—necessarily alter society in predictable ways.

Free Labor, Captive Workers

To create a labor force subject to the needs of capitalism, it was necessary to alienate workers from the means of production and to dominate them politically and psychologically. This "primitive accumulation" of an alienated labor force is decisive for the origins of capitalism. Only when accumulated wealth encounters "free labor" (labor that can be freely bought and sold like any other commodity) can capital accumulation fully develop.[2]

The proletarianization of the English peasantry took place through enclosures, forcible evictions from traditional lands (Lazonick 1974). The creation of free labor required the laborers' loss of control over their own dwelling places and lands. Free laborers were also subject to the control of the nascent capitalist class in ways in which no other exploited class had been subject to its rulers. As opposed to slaves, the proletariat was responsible for its own food and upkeep. More important, these workers could be taken on and let go at the capitalist's will. Unlike serfs, they could no longer interfere with turning land into a commodity or with changes to more commercially viable agriculture. Finally, they were of necessity highly mobile: needing wages, they had to go where wages were being paid and leave a place where they were not.

"Free labor" meant captive workers. As labor power became a freely exchangable commodity, the new working class was placed at the disposal of capitalists. And when labor power became a commodity, laborers could be treated like things, just because there was no interest in any part of the laborer except that which had been sold. The intermingling of the economic and political that characterized the "extra-economic" coercion and expropriation of feudalism corresponded to the "patriarchal" relations between master and serf. These relations involved both domination and responsibility, subservience and protection. Serfs had a connection to the land even though they did not "own" it. The noble had an obligation to protect his serfs from violence and to aid them in times of economic distress. While these obligations were inconsistently fulfilled, they were not altogether empty. The creation of free labor, however, meant an end to all such relations. Under capitalism the exploiting class has neither an interest in taking responsibility for its work force nor an obligation to do so. Purchasable on the market like any other commodity, labor power could also be disposed of like any other commodity. The working class could now protect itself from exploitation only through organized political struggle.

There are many ways in which the creation of an alienated work force was essential to the development of capitalism. When workers perform one type of wage labor rather than a variety of home-based tasks, their skill can increase. Simultaneously, as workers lose traditional skills and cannot raise their own food, local demand multiplies. As important as these factors are, I wish here to concentrate on another one: how control of the new working class was gradually but definitely extended to the process of production itself. It was necessary to create a body of disciplined, obedient, trained, and stratified workers to serve two demands: the imperatives of, first, mass and then industrial production; and the control of that production by capitalists.

Unfortunately, this aspect of the creation of the proletariat has suffered from one-sided treatments. Bourgeois historians often describe the process as a transformation of production in accord with the demands of efficiency, superior technology, modernity, and so forth. From Adam Smith to Frederick Winslow Taylor, the modern form of factory organization—with its rigid division of labor, increasing separation of conception and execution, precisely defined rules, coordinated efforts of larger and larger numbers of workers, and hierarchical work force—is said to be objectively necessary for the increases in productivity that are synonomous with capitalism.

From the Marxist point of view, Stephan Marglin (1974) has shown the one-sidedness of the above in his well-known essay, "What Do Bosses Do?" He argues convincingly that much of capitalist factory organization serves only capitalists' interests in maintaining control over the labor force and guaranteeing their place in the productive process. The social function served, he claims, is the accumulation of wealth rather than productive efficiency. In another economy, efficiency might be achieved by very different means, including those that do not involve capitalism's overspecialization and hierarchy.[3] Marglin correctly indentifies a capitalist interest in the rigid specialization of labor that goes beyond any concern with efficiency or productivity. Rigid specialization makes workers easier to discipline, preserves a place for the capitalist in the productive process, and restricts potential competition by keeping workers ignorant of the technology underlying production. Marglin (1974, 93) also notes that the factory system coerced its workers by enclosures and laws compelling them to produce at a given rate.

Yet Marglin overstates his case. He gives us little reason to understand why capitalism succeeded, or why it was marked by dramatic increases in productivity. He seems to forget that capitalists must not only control their workers but also compete against other capitalists and win over coexisting forms of production. In fact, the growth of wage labor both presupposes and encourages the growth of productivity. Under capitalism the working day can be divided into a part that accrues to the capitalist and a part that accrues to workers. Since a necessary minimum of that day must go to keep workers alive for the next day's toil, capitalists seek to raise productivity so that the least amount of time possible can be spent on supplying the workers' needs. Increases in productivity enable the workers to produce their own wages in a decreasing proportion of the working day. For a number of reasons, then, capitalism required both control of the work force *and* the raising of productivity. Marglin tends to focus only on the first of these imperatives and to ignore the second.

Let us consider a particular example in which control and productivity coincided: Josiah Wedgwood's transformation of the labor process and the labor force in his late-eighteenth-century pottery factory. There, a self-conscious creation of a division of labor made laborers more subservient to forces of production and "more vulnerable to changing demand and fluctuations in the market"; however, Wedgwood also raised productivity, developing his workers' skills even as he limited them to particular tasks (McKendrick 1966, 67). He increased their skills by creating a drawing school so that workers could be trained from youth and by enforcing a complicated series of rules and methods to limit the carelessness, waste, and inefficiency that had accompanied traditional potmaking. In this process, the imposition of labor control—bells to control work periods, specified punishments for lateness, stoppages, or refusing to obey an overseer—accompanied the creation of a more disciplined, competent, and productive work force.

This process was both inhumane and, for the capitalist class, self-serving. Yet it also entailed a more productive use of the forces of production. Increased work discipline itself leads to greater productivity of labor —and not just a greater quantity produced on the basis of higher input (that is, more effort by workers), as Marglin claims. Not breaking tools and not wasting materials, to take two aspects of increased labor discipline, are connected with greater efficiency as well as with greater control. Domination and efficiency coincided in Wedgwood's case. Conditions were similar, claims McKendrick (1966, 70) for tunnelers, engineers, machinists, and railway builders.

In more general terms, note that the factory system was designed to supplant the older system of rural industries. Capitalists wanted to overcome rural labor's part-time character and workers' tendency to waste and embezzle raw materials. Also, concentrating workers in one place dramatically shortened the turnover time of fixed capital; it also made reasonable the investment in new fixed capital and thus the employment of the many technological developments whose existence predated their use in the industrial revolution (Crouzet 1968, 170–71; DeVries 1976, 105–7; Lilley 1973, 210–13).

Can we neatly divide these developments into those that are products of economic efficiency and productivity and those that stem from capitalists' drive for control and profit? I do not think so. Capitalism is a two-sided process: a "natural" process of interacting with the physical world in order to meet human needs; and a social process of organizing that interaction in

a particular way. The development of this new mode of production is therefore likely to lead to changes of both a "natural" and a "social" kind. Capitalism's unprecedented political and economic success stemmed partly from
the fact that it had to use its workers "efficiently." From the point of view of
cheapening the cost and widening the scope of production, capitalism was
tremendously successful, partly because capitalists had to do these things
in order to survive. The free laborers were captive not only to the desire of
the capitalists to exploit them but to capitalism's need to do so in a way
that increased productivity.

As a result, an enormous area of social life—the productive activity of
the labor force—came under the direct control of capitalists or was subjected to their interests. The process of production was stripped away from
traditional, patriarchal connections and supports and swallowed by a liberated, autonomous capitalism. Until the later failures of capitalist reproduction, the growth of radical working-class political movements, and
challenges by noncapitalist societies occurred, then, this area of life could
be mechanical and predictable. With society dominated by economic power
and interests, knowledge of social life as a whole could increasingly be
derived from an analysis of the economy. Competitive capitalism emerged
as a lawlike economic system, and the scope of capitalist power meant that
this system would possess sole social primacy.

The Unit of Production and the Social Setting

The creation of a complex system of independent and competing units
of mass commodity production was a gradual process. The stages of this
process are a mixture of developing capitalist and declining feudal relations of production. Each stage is marked by some significant difference
from the earlier mode of production, some feature that makes it more like
capitalism and less like feudalism. To observe further how capitalism could
become a lawlike economic system possessing sole social primacy, let us
examine the evolution of the characteristic capitalist unit of production as
a movement away from constraint and toward competitive freedom.

In the beginning, there is the development of commodity production as
a separate function, a permanent feature of the division of labor rather
than something worked on in spare time. Next, that production is detached
from the manor and located in the cities, becoming by and large exempt
from the control of the landed nobility. Simultaneously, a class of traders
emerges whose wealth derives from the exchange of commodities. Commodity production, commodity exchange, the social realm in which they
unfold—these three phenomena constitute the beginnings of European
capitalism.[4]

This was not capitalism as such, however. For one thing, long-distance trade and guild-dominated commodity production have a contradictory relation to the consumption-oriented manorial economy, both undermining its self-enclosed nature and supplying items not easily obtainable or producible otherwise. Also, the considerable rise of commercial capital usually leaves the process of production untouched. The source of the trader's profit is the different levels of labor productivity in different areas or the fundamentally incomplete way in which production has been universalized. Traders have little of the capitalist motivation to transform the forces and relations of production (Dobb 1947: 19–22, 38–42; Hilton et al. 1979, 23, 149–52; Marx 1967, 3: chaps. 20, 26; Pirenne 1937, 46). Capitalism requires a blending of the functions of the trader and the commodity producer. The producer must produce not for specific customers but for a generalized, wholesale market. The merchant must take control of production: first by supplying raw materials as well as buying finished products; then by selecting the artisans and supplying their tools; and finally by paying wages and controlling the activity of production itself.

The rise of the characteristic unit of production of capitalism is the liberation of production and exchange from both monopoly control and political restrictions. The development of capitalism also requires that the profits of commodity production cease to be the products of extra-economic coercion.

These two claims can be supported by noting some of the crucial differences between commodity-producing guilds and capitalist firms. For one thing, the guilds' workers owned their own tools and purchased their own raw materials—or they could aspire to the status of being able to do so (Dobb 1947, 85). More significantly, the guild system was based in the restraint of competition: within the guild, between the guild and other producers, and between the guild and the suppliers of raw materials. As the response of the feudal nobility to a high demand for revenue was to overexploit the peasantry, so the urban guild pursued wealth by eliminating competitors. In neither case was the typical capitalist solution of revolutionizing the means of production the "natural" response (LeGoff 1973, 77, 89, 95; Pirenne 1937, 184). Profits made by traders and guilds were not from the simple sale of commodities on the open market but from their sale under conditions of political power: "The market was a restricted prize and the 'capture' of it entailed the enforcement of a productive and trading monopoly against the countryside and against encroachment of rival towns" (Merrington 1979, 181).

There is no capitalist drive to increase productivity here. Rather, there is physical power or protection by the nobility and (later) the state. Therefore, the emergence of developed capitalist enterprises in England required the transfer of commodity production from the city to the countryside. Entrepreneurs who organized this transition combined the trader and producer roles mentioned above. They did so in the presence of increasing quantities of "free" labor and against attempts by urban guilds to make their activities illegal. Above all, protocapitalists needed to be free of urban restrictions on the use of certain raw materials, on the processes used, on the quantities involved, and so on (Bergier 1973, 410–12; DeVries 1976, 245; Merrington 1979, 189).

A similar pattern emerges if we examine relations between the European "core" states and their colonies. Of course, these relations were always marked by politically enforced unequal exchange. The surplus accumulated from such exchange was essential in providing a base for capitalist development. However, what is important is that the trading companies of Portugal, Spain, Holland, France, and England repeated the progressive liberation of capitalist institutions from the political power we have found in the guilds. These companies evolved in terms of successively less state control, initiative, and restriction (Coornaert 1967).

The trading *casas* of Spain and Portugal were hampered by too many rules and too many incompetent government appointees. The Dutch and English generated private companies of greater efficiency; however, they were still semi-public bodies exercising monopolies and possessing something like political power over their areas of influence and activity. Their efficiency restricted by administrative favoritism, they focused on trade and ignored the possibility of using colonies as centers of production. Like guilds, these companies "were essentially groups of private merchants exercising a royal monopoly privilege of trading with a certain foreign region. . . . In a world that did not expect long-term growth of foreign markets, men pinned their hopes for gain from trade on their ability to control their markets" (DeVries 1976, 124–28). Also, in their earlier, exclusively commercial form, these companies were (as I suggested such capital would be) external to fundamental changes in productive life (Dobb 1947, 192–96; Wallerstein 1980, 45–46).

Between 1690 and 1720 new merchants and more powerful colonies protested against these limitations. The result was a transfer of economic functions to competing private companies and of political control to parliaments. A new colonial system was created, more independent from the state and more oriented toward production than to simple extraction. In short, the development of these trading companies led to the classic capitalist separation of economic and political roles.

Commodity producers and traders had to move away from the coercive control of a limited market and toward competitive success in productivity.

Similarly, we shall now see, state power had to change its relation to the economy dramatically. The state has been essential to the success of capitalism: controlling the work force, creating favorable conditions for local capitalists against foreign ones, and enforcing unequal relations with the noncapitalist world. However, there is a significant difference between a state that controls or dictates the conditions of production or exchange and one that creates an arena favorable to capitalist enterprises. In the first case we get a state-monopolized economy, with its attendant inefficiencies, favoritism, and stagnations. In the second we get a number of discrete, detached, and competing economic units. These units are not constrained by the political interests of governments: neither by the incompetence of inept government appointees nor by the needs of the state to balance contending class forces. Out-of-date methods of production are no longer secured by decree, and survival is not guaranteed by state funds. "Liberated" capitalist enterprises are clearly more risky than those supported and directed by the government, but they need answer only to themselves and not to the balance of class forces within the economy as a whole. This very riskiness and lack of either guarantees or controls, in turn, provide a spur to development and efficiency. These claims can be supported by a brief examination of the way successive domination of the "world-economy" passed, between the sixteenth and the eighteenth century, in the direction of countries that could integrate colonial wealth into increasingly autonomous capitalist development.

Spain was the first major power. Its American treasure resulted from military conquest and was used for war and consumption, not to develop its economy (Koenigsberger 1958, 322–23; Wallerstein 1974a, 191–95). The feudal form of surplus acquisition and consumption thus carried over into the beginnings of the modern era. Conversely, when Ferdinand and Isabella did try to support Spanish industry, they went about it in a counterproductive way. In the Castilian textile industry, for example, their ordinances froze industrial development, made dynamic improvements illegal, and created a short-lived monopoly that never competed successfully on the world market (Miskimin 1977, 108).

In contrast to Spain, Holland became a leading force in the world economy through a combination of agricultural specialization, industrial production, and commercial control of the Baltic and Atlantic trade. Dutch workers became known for their discipline, and skilled laborers emigrated to Holland. Yet the resources of the Dutch republic could not really compare with those of England or France. Demographic limitations and military weakness led Holland to become a dependent partner with England in the latter's long (1670–1760) struggle with the French.[6]

France might seem to have been the natural heir of the Spanish empire. It had three times as many people as England, plentiful raw materials, and a centralized government interested in economic development. Wallerstein (1980, 84–104) claims that France had little motivation to dominate the world market because it had a sort of "world economy" within its own borders. While England had to seek overseas for both markets and crucial raw materials, developed France—the North—could sell its manufactured goods to and get raw materials from underdeveloped France—the South. Wallerstein also claims (1980, 258–89) that a comparatively weaker French state was not able to carve out a dominant place for France, especially its agriculture, on the world market. Unfortunately, this position does not explain why northern France did not use the rest of France as its "world-system" and thus generate enough demand to match England's late-eighteenth-century industrial growth.

More central to my argument, Wallerstein does not explore either the French bourgeoisie's reluctance to join in capitalist production or the French's state's counterproductive involvement in French capitalism. In France, lending to the state consumed much of merchant profits. State-sponsored trading companies in the late seventeenth century failed because members of a bourgeoisie suspicious of government ventures sought "to invest their surplus in government offices" (Maland 1970, 234) and state loans (Kamen 1972, 171). As a result, even in the eighteenth century the French bourgeoisie was in the main "a financial and official class, not a commercial and industrial one" (Cobban 1970, 239). Then, as earlier, profits from trade and industry were used to buy *rentes*, official posts, land, and titles "instead of applying it in new fields" (Lough 1969, 227–28). The French bourgeoisie clung to the old form of surplus appropriation: extra-economic coercion now applied through state taxation rather than feudal relations. The consequences for French economic development should be obvious.[7]

The French state was "strong" enough to appropriate much of the economic surplus. Yet it could not create the unified social, political and economic conditions necessary for industry and capitalist agriculture. David Maland (1970, 230–32) cites the difficulties facing government minister Colbert in the attempt to modernize the legal structure, and describes how both the nobility and the officer class resisted losing their privileges vis-à-vis the state, including their freedom from taxation.

Finally, even when a centralized French government was able to impose its will, the results were often negative. Government control of production, as opposed to government creation of a favorable climate for it, tended to backfire at this stage in history. Despite Colbert's interest in and support for French industry, government relations with the French economy were often unproductive (Miskimin 1977, 111–17; Wilson 1970, 31). There were petty regulations, incompetent inspectors, and inventions suppressed by the joint action of industry and the state. Only in the later eighteenth century was a push to develop countryside production—free from monopolistic guild limitations—provided (Cobban 1970, 238–39). Rather ironically, by the eighteenth century those industries that received the least government "aid" were the most successful (Wilson 1970, 34). By contrast, England's Parliament attempted to legally restrict the setting up of rural industry during the mid-sixteenth century (Dobb 1947, 130), but the English government—unlike that of France—was too weak to make these regulations stick. Also, economic legislation in France was often motivated by the desire for immediate gains in government revenue rather than long-term development of industry or trade (DeVries 1976, 237–40; cf. Carsten 1969a, 4, 14, 17; Clark 1969, 85). Government influence on British economic growth in the century and a half preceding the industrial revolution helped British exports secure a dominant place in world trade and create a captive colonial market.

As we have seen in the case of Poland, however, a demand for agricultural products does not guarantee increases in productivity. It was not state control but government *lack* of control, that was essential to English economic development. Phyllis Deane (1965) tries to show that the industrial revolution led to state involvement in the British economy on an unprecedented scale, an involvement (roughly between 1760 and 1850) that included war, protecting the working class from some of the most flagrant capitalist abuses, providing poor relief, regulating currency, and enabling railroads to buy land at will. However, most of these functions (poor relief, currency control) were not new in kind. Others (such as supporting railroads) were part of government support of a general economic infrastructure. By contrast, Deane also cites a number of ways in which government became *less* involved in the economy: the elimination of a mass of (inconsistently enforced) "governmental rules and restrictions on economic activity," including laws governing the use and mobility of capital and how things should be manufactured or put on sale; and the "spectacular triumph" of laissez-faire in foreign trade (Deane 1965, 220–21, 227–28). It is precisely this kind of state withdrawal from the economic process that is essential to early capitalist development. While the state was instrumental in the growth of industrial capitalism, the *kind* of involvement Deane describes is quite compatible with the development of capitalism as a lawlike system, liberated from tradition, monopoly, and the state. With the exception of guaranteeing the success of the railroads and allowing the working class to reproduce, there was a general tendency to lessen government in-

terference in production and exchange: that is, to allow economic life to be
controlled by independent economic actors.

The success of *early* capitalism required a peculiar balance. Bourgeois
historians tend to stress the autonomy of the emerging economy, presenting
a picture of bold entrepreneurs adventurously manufacturing wealth for
the tradition-dominated masses. Marxists have sometimes overemphasized
state involvement in economic processes. What was necessary, I am suggesting, is a state strong enough to clear away obstacles and create a favorable international position, yet not strong enough to dominate the process
of production itself. All the state power in the world cannot make inefficiently produced goods cheap on the world market. A favorable position in
world trade is possible only when state support is combined with adequate
productivity. As we have seen, such productivity comes—both locally
and in world relations—when both monopoly and state control diminish.
Finally, the state's participation in economic life must not come at the
expense of the utilization of profit in reinvestment, as it did with the
creation of a *rentier* class in France.

More than anywhere else, this balance was struck in England. As a
consequence, its mercantile profits from the triangular trade could be integrated into its growing textile industry to produce the industrial revolution:
a revolution which continued processes dating back to the sixteenth century (Nef 1954). England's domination of the world market was connected
to its balance between government power and freedom for developing industries, as well as with technical innovation. In dramatic contrast, Spain's
failure was rooted in its inability to develop its productive life.

The emergence of capitalism is the emergence of a lawlike economic system. The efficiency and primacy of this economy, I have suggested, lie in
two factors: tying the interests of the ruling class to continual increases in
productivity; isolating economic life from politics, monopoly, and tradition
so that economic life can function autonomously.[8] Simultaneously, an increasingly powerful state aids capitalists in struggles against workers—
but rarely controls production itself or guarantees the existence or success
of any particular enterprise. Finally, in the day-to-day struggle over wages,
working conditions, and investment, capitalists have control of the means
of production; the working class has an immediate need for wages. The
result is that until the working class develops its own forms of power,
capitalists have the social space to pursue their own ends. Consequently,
capitalism as a system follows its own internal logic and shapes the fundamental institutions and relations of the surrounding social world. The de-
tachment of the economy from the political and cultural systems—this

historically specific development of a lawlike economic system—determines the sole social primacy of the mode of production in competitive capitalism. As Marx saw, however, competitive capitalism generates political and social crises that require fundamental social changes. In the present, the autonomy of the productive unit, unfettered competition, and the separation of the economy from the state no longer exist. To show that this is the case, we must examine the complicated structure of advanced monopoly capitalism.

5

Politicized Capitalism
and Marxist Economic Theory

COMPETITIVE CAPITALISM NO LONGER EXISTS. IN ITS PLACE WE FIND A FUN-
damentally different social structure. Like feudalism, contemporary capitalism does not possess an economic system. Class relations continue to
predominate, yet those relations no longer form a lawlike system but a
politicized economic structure. Predictable mechanisms of capitalist economic development have been replaced by an economic life organized by
contending political agents. In this transition two new forms of social primacy, possessed by socialization processes and politics, have emerged to
join that possessed by the mode of production.

This chapter describes the politicization of the economy and discusses
some crucial implications of that politicization for Marxist economic theory.
This discussion completes my argument concerning the historical specificity
of competitive capitalism. It shows that the kind of knowledge Marx had
of competitive capitalism is no longer possible. Social life is again unpredictable. Class continues to motivate social action—but the future effects of
class-motivated actions cannot be known from an analysis of the economy.

Politicized Capitalism:
From Business Cycles
to the Managed Economy

Even the most autonomous forms of competitive capitalism—those of
America and England—were aided by state action to support particular
industries, physically control the working class, militarily conquer foreign
markets, and secure sources of raw materials. In these ways, the state
helped create a social context favorable for capitalist accumulation. Now,
however, the state is a decisive participant in the accumulation process

itself. It has drastically increased its previous economic activity, and attempted to conceptualize and act on the economy as a whole. These two developments constitute the politicization of the economy. They make contemporary capitalism fundamentally different from its forebears and have crucial implications for the transformation of Marxist theory.[1] Let us examine some of those implications for Marxist "crisis theory" and for the social role of credit.

For Marx, capitalist accumulation depended on the capacity of the capitalist to make a profit. It was necessary that society provide capital goods and labor, and consume commodities in such a way as to provide an "adequate" profit; without it, the capitalist class would withdraw capital from the productive process. The succession of favorable and unfavorable conditions for making profits has become known as the business cycle. Marx correctly claimed that competitive capitalism would inevitably produce these cycles. He also saw a predictable relation between the business cycle and other key institutional changes of capitalist society: concentration and monopolization, periods of high unemployment, technological development, the attrition of small businesses and farms. The inevitability of both the business cycle and its institutional effects was essential to the way in which competitive capitalism was a lawlike economic system, in crucial ways autonomous from politics. Most important, Marxism has frequently envisaged a progression of increasingly extreme depressions culminating in an economic crisis that would precipitate a social revolution.

Since the 1930s, however, there has been a partial transition from an economy marked by predictable and unconstrained business cycles to a managed economy. In this economy, a state apparatus works to facilitate capitalist accumulation as a whole, and international organizations and arrangements seek to rationalize the international movement of investment and trade. Society's capacity to meet the necessary conditions of capitalist accumulation no longer depends on the more or less spontaneous movement of the economy. Rather, it has become much more the product of state decisions and self-conscious political struggles.

Of the many aspects of this transition,[2] my immediate concern is with the way classic Marxist descriptions of a capitalist economy no longer hold for the dominant capitalist nations. To make this point, let us consider how the changed role of the state affects the two most common Marxist theories of the business cycle and economic crises: "underconsumption" and "falling rate of profit" theories.

Marx claimed that the "ultimate reason for all real crises always remains the poverty and restricted consumption of the masses as opposed to the drive of capitalist production to develop the productive forces" (1967,

3:484). This "underconsumptionist" explanation of capitalist crises can be developed into the following argument. Capitalists compete with each other and seek to replace expensive labor by continuously developing the means of production. They do so by using a significant percentage of the total social surplus. The end result of the use of that surplus is an increase in the production of consumer goods. But the percentage of social surplus used to develop the means of production leaves an insufficient amount of wealth in the hands of those (especially the working class) who are supposed to consume what is produced. There is an inevitable failure of demand due to lack of income. The working class cannot consume all that it produces, and capitalism cannot consume it in other ways. The inability to consume leads to periodic economic slumps or crises during which much productive capacity stands idle, the standard of living of the working class falls, and reserve stocks of commodities are consumed (Sweezy 1942, 102–86).

In the foregoing model, workers' capacity to consume is limited by their wages. However, with state involvement in the economy, workers receive not only wages from their employer but also a social wage. The social wage includes welfare payments, unemployment benefits, social security, veterans' benefits, medical care, government-sponsored work programs, and a large number of "public" items for consumption such as state education, parks, and public support for the arts. The social wage significantly increases the capacity for working-class consumption. Most important, the impact of the business cycle is diminished as the structural disjunction between consumption and income is lessened. Unemployment has a much smaller effect on demand when unemployed workers receive half (or more) of their wages for six months. The perennially unemployed constitute a source of consumption even though they receive no wages at all (Gough 1975, 72, 82; O'Connor 1973, 124–44, 158–62).

The second major form of the Marxist theory of capitalist crisis focuses on the falling rate of profit (Mandel 1962, 166–70; Marx 1967, 3:211–66; Sweezy 1942, 96–108). In this view, the ultimate cause of crisis is the fact that constant capital (the means of production) absorbs a steadily higher percentage of capital outlays relative to variable capital (wages). Since profit can be made only from variable capital, it is argued, the rate of profit will fall as the ratio between constant and variable capital (the "organic composition of capital") rises. Finally, intracapitalist competition requires continual expansion of constant capital. Therefore, there is no way to avoid increases in organic composition.[3]

As the state has increased the capacity of workers to consume, so it has socialized many of the costs of production. This socialization cheapens both the means of production and labor power, and helps reduce the organic composition of capital to allow for an adequate rate of profit (Gough 1975, 77–80; O'Connor 1973, 97–123). Constant capital is socialized, for instance, via state contribution to and organization of scientific and technical research. Research is often a source of higher productivity; however, its cost is born not by the industries that profit from it but by society as a whole. Consequently, the firms in question can achieve higher productivity without higher organic composition—and thus without a downward pressure on the rate of profit.

Government expenditures also socialize the costs of labor. Engineers and technicians train at state universities. Workers travel to their jobs on state-financed transit systems. Some medical costs are socialized. In all these cases we see government expenditures complementing money wages to help provide workers an "average" standard of living—thus cheapening the cost of the reproduction of the work force and lowering the necessary level of wages.

State involvement has not eliminated the business cycles of capitalism (Murray 1979). What has ended is their general pattern of increasing severity. The notion that each "crash" would be bigger than the one before was essential to Marx's belief that the severity of the final crash would be instrumental in creating a socialist revolution.

The role of the state is, of course, not limited to its "interference" with the crisis-producing mechanisms of either underconsumption or the falling rate of profit. Less neatly categorizable but of great importance, for instance, is the way the state provides the necessary infrastructure for the consumption of certain key commodities. The automobile industry would have been impossible without state-built roads. The U.S. nuclear power industry required that government limit the industry's financial liability in case of accident.

The contemporary role of credit in the U.S. economy is a third example of how politicized capitalism is not bound by the same structural rules as competitive capitalism. Government-guaranteed credit is essential to public consumption and corporate investment. Government support of home mortgages has been essential to the housing industry, for instance. In general, credit cushions or bolsters what otherwise might sometimes be stagnant consumer demand. For corporations, large-scale borrowing aids in technological development and overseas investment. In certain crucial cases—Chrysler and Lockheed are two of the best known—the state guaranteed loans to large corporations that might otherwise have gone bankrupt. Government deficits served to finance both the Vietnam War and much of the urban renewal of the 1960s and 1970s.

The system of both national and international credit poses certain real risks, from the defaulting of local governments to an international debt crisis (Mandel 1980, 60–78). However, it can also lessen the effects of the business cycle and capitalist competition. The investors and workers who were "saved" when the government rescued Chrysler did not join the ranks of either the bankrupt or the unemployed. The Federal Deposit Insurance Corporation (FDIC) has dictated bank mergers to protect the liquidity of the banking system and the Federal Trade Commission (FTC) has instructed major banks to fulfill debt obligations on which they might have defaulted. In general, government support of and intervention in the credit system leads, again, to an increasing dependence of economic developments on administrative decisions. These decisions are shaped by political advantage, theoretical conceptualizations of the economy as a whole by economists, and contending political forces and interest groups.

The critical point in all this is that elements essential to capitalist accumulation are no longer principally the product of spontaneous interactions between isolated capitalist firms or of struggles between capitalists and isolated groups of workers. Nor are they set by limited state action on fragments of the economy (for example, protectionist tariffs, or aid to a few selected industries). Crucial decisions concerning investment, as well as the mechanisms setting the price of labor and constant capital, have become—to a certain extent—political decisions. They are the outcome of planning, political struggle, and compromise. Politically conscious social classes and subgroups interact with a state that not only functions in the interest of the entire system but *whose actions take that system as a whole as their object.*

Not all the foregoing developments are unique to contemporary capitalism. What is unique is the *degree* to which they shape the economic structure and the way that structure is treated as a totality by contending political forces. Capitalist "rationality" now coexists with the rationality of political struggle and political planning. We do not have an economic system in the sense of an organized set of principles that operate autonomously to produce determinate outcomes. Therefore, the social future of a society centered on a capitalist economy cannot be known from an analysis of that economy.

Politicized Capitalism: Imperialism

The politicization of the economy is global as well as national. While traditional Marxism's expectation that capitalism would spread internationally has been partly confirmed, the capitalist world-system now functions on the basis of a political, not merely an economic, dynamic. Though class interests are revealed in state actions, relations between dominant economic powers and developing nations follow no systematic pattern.

Historically, the capitalist world-system has been dominated by a succession of core nations distinguished by higher levels of productivity, advanced social infrastructures, military power, and superiority in trade relations (Bousquet 1980). However, there have been a succession of different relations between the core country, other capitalist nations, and the periphery of colonies and underdeveloped and developing nations. Imperialist nations have exported goods or capital, sought large markets or employed cheap labor. They have both destroyed local production and distorted the local economy around production for export. Contemporary imperialism profits from labor controlled by totalitarian governments yet, in some places, promotes industrialization and the creation of large amounts of local capital (Baran 1957, 163–248; Magdoff 1969; Mandel 1980, 129–40; Sklar 1980, 558–59; Warren 1980, 125–257).

Since 1945, imperialist relations have been mediated by two critical sorts of political development. First, there is the existence of a militarily powerful bloc of "socialist" nations. Much of postwar U.S. policy has been a response to the perceived threat to U.S. interests of this alternative system of military alliances and social forms. It was not simply the direct economic interests in overseas investment that motivated postwar American support of European and Japanese capitalism; it was a more broadly defined geopolitical concern with maintaining spheres of influence and political power. U.S. trade deficits and devaluations of the late 1960s and early 1970s indicate that this concern was not necessarily directly compatible with some powerful U.S. economic interests. Similarly, U.S. military and economic aid to Israel, El Salvador, or South Korea cannot be explained as a direct result of the mechanisms of U.S. capital. While perceived economic interests may motivate these policies, the policies themselves take no predictable form.

Second, the politicization of the Third World—whether in "liberation" movements, fascist juntas, or cartels of raw material producers—is transforming the role of the Third World in the economy of the dominant capitalist powers. Clearly, perception of economic interest by the central actors shapes these relationships, but we cannot have determinate knowledge of the outcome of actions based on those perceptions. Third World liberation movements may lead to the withdrawal of a previously imperialized nation from the world market (Burma, for example) or to a country's becoming a potentially attractive export market (China after Mao). The United States may create one-crop economies or generate competitors. Raw materials may be obtained at low prices—until political pressures drastically raise their prices (OPEC oil). The predictable spread of capitalism envisaged by Marx is clearly not the sole outcome. Nor, since World War II, is it simply a matter of imperialist powers perpetuating Third World underdevelopment through unequal exchange. As in national capitalist economies, the world-system is very much determined by how economic relations are understood and acted on politically by self-conscious social agents.

The Politicized Economy and Marxist Theory

How does the politicization of the economy transform Marxist theory? First, Marxist theory is now unable to identify one primary mechanism determining the capitalist economy and bourgeois society as a whole. It must be realized that social change depends on the self-consciousness and political activities of contending classes (and perhaps other groups as well). Economic life no longer takes the form of a system, independent of and determining the rest of social life. Second, therefore, the belief that future political change is predicated on the development of present economic forces must be abandoned. Third and more generally, for a variety of reasons and in a variety of ways, the mechanical forces of History have been under-mined—if only partially—by an eruption of Subjectivity. The rest of this chapter focuses on the first two of these points, chapter 6 on the third, thus preparing the reader for the detailed examination of the social primacy of socialization and of politics.

Many writers claim that the stabilizing effects of state involvement in the capitalist economy have only changed the form of capitalist crises, not eliminated them.[4] There may be attacks on the social wage rather than wage cuts, or a combination of inflation and unemployment rather than a classic depression. But the continuing private control of the means of production guarantees that crises will arise. Manuel Castells (1980, 130) for instance, argues that "the intervention of the state takes place within the *structural rules* of capitalism" (my emphasis).

Just what are those "structural rules," and precisely what do they determine? Though they offer different (and frequently directly contradictory) candidates, contemporary Marxist economic theories share an inability to tell us how capitalism's structural rules will affect the future development of either the capitalist economy or bourgeois society as a whole.[5] This inability is the essential characteristic of the transformation of Marxist political economy.[6]

Castells, David Gordon, Samuel Bowles and Herbert Gintis, and Paul Sweezy and Harry Magdoff, for instance, stress that the economic crisis they describe has an indeterminate future. Writing about the Reagan administration's prospective attempts to control inflation, Sweezy and Magdoff (1981) list the variety of effects these attempts might have. They might raise—or lower—the inflation rate. They might cause massive unemployment—or lower unemployment as a consequence of further government organization and the stimulus of corporate investment. Bowles and Gintis (1982) pose the alternatives of increased popular control of government in support of the social wage—or less popular control and a fall in the workers' standard of living.

For these writers and many others, economic crises will be resolved by political forces, *and those political forces are not themselves the determinate outcome of an economic system.* The profitability of investments, labor costs, and consumer demand are determined as much by state action as by the aggregate response of atomized individual corporations. State action is itself described as shaped by many forces: political activity of contending classes and groups; interactions among international political alliances; conflicts between multinational and local capital; and the beliefs of politicians, administrators, and intellectuals.

To recapitulate: during capitalism's competitive phase, especially as the autonomous economy unfolded in England and the United States, Marx analyzed capitalism as a lawlike economic system with a single form of social primacy. The social primacy of the economic meant that capitalist accumulation would predictably produce business cycles of increasing severity, the growth and concentration of corporations, worldwide economic interdependence, and a certain amount of homogenization and politicization in the working class. With the end of the autonomous economy, however, the sole social primacy of a lawlike economic system no longer exists. Future developments of the economic structure and of social life as a whole now depend on the often unpredictable actions of somewhat self-conscious, collective social agents. While these agents belong to classes and relate to each other as members of an economic structure, their membership in that structure is no longer a clear determinant of what they do or of the general social outcomes of their actions. *The crucial transformation of Marxist economic theory is thus a movement from claims about how political forces are created by economic systems to claims about how economic changes are dependent on political forces.*

What are the consequences for Marxist theory when this transformation is resisted?

Both Castells and Ernest Mandel mistakenly understand contemporary capitalism as organized by one continuing principle. Castells (1980, 42–43) argues that a theory of the capitalist economy must identify one central contradiction at capitalism's core. This contradiction, he believes, will determine capitalist development in all its phases. He finds this contradiction in the struggle between capital and labor. Capitalist development is a response to labor's struggle to diminish exploitation, as capitalists seek both to replace labor by sophisticated technology and to increase exploitation: "This basic contradiction is the key to explaining our world . . . the cornerstone of any analysis of the process of social change." Yet Castells is unable to substantiate this claim. When he analyzes particular episodes in the history of capitalism he appeals to many causes that are not products of his single, key principle. He fails to show, for instance, that the particular mechanisms of underconsumption, a falling rate of profit, and the fiscal crisis of the state all stem from the capital-labor relation (1980, 5–8, 81–93, 123–32). Alternatively, it seems that this relation has so many different, and sometimes contradictory, effects that we can explain little by appealing to it alone.

When Castells (1980, 58) deals with the current period, he claims that the major contradiction is the state's role in sustaining the sluggish capitalist accumulation of monopoly capital: "By expanding itself through the state, capital denies its own logic and undermines its hegemony over civilian society." If this is the case, however, then Castells should have realized that the "logic" of capitalism is now partly based in politics, not just in an economically defined system. Politicization of economic life in contemporary capitalism makes it impossible to identify autonomous mechanisms whose determinate operation allows us to predict the future outcome of class struggle. In this sense, the "structural rules" of capitalism no longer exist—or, at least, they are conditioned by the "structural rules" of politicized processes. As Bowles and Gintis (1982) have successfully argued, the rights of persons have become determining social principles alongside the rights of property. Production and distribution reflect not only the search for profit, but also attempts to meet what are seen as people's rights to a certain level of consumption. This transition defuses crucial aspects of the traditional business cycle and makes future economic development dependent on the interaction of the principles of capitalism and those of liberal democracy. Political behavior itself may express class interests, but an analysis of those interests will not tell what specific actions or institutional changes will occur.

Like the class-struggle theorists discussed in Chapter 3, Castells seems to make the mistake of thinking that Marx's original economic theory is the model of any adequate theory of historical change and social structure. But an economy that is no longer a lawlike system can no longer be described by a theory centered on structural rules. That is why Castells cannot offer serious predictions about the future of capitalism, the kind one would think his "theory" of capitalism should offer. He cannot tell us whether corporations will grow bigger, the service sector contract, U.S. overseas investment grow, or state aid to accumulation decline. These issues will be resolved by the politicized decisions of contending classes and political functionaries, as well as by capitalists' search for profits and workers' for higher wages. No abstract rules of capitalist accumulation will control this process, for those rules are now subject to the (partial) understanding and control of collective social agents.

Like Castells, Mandel (1978, 10, 528; 1980, 164–80) considers contemporary capitalism to be what I have termed an economic system.[7] He believes that the "post-war history of the capitalist mode of production" can be explained by the "basic laws of motion of capitalism discovered by Marx in *Capital*." Basic to these laws is the "law of value," which enables larger masses of capital to appropriate larger masses of surplus value by increasing productivity. Investment migrates to these more productive sectors until overinvestment occurs; then a downturn of production follows until a new equilibrium, based on a new "average" productivity, occurs and the cycle of competition resumes.

To this fairly familiar account Mandel adds a theory of the "long waves" of capitalist development. These waves, much longer than business cycles, are (about) fifty-year cycles made up of one expansionary and one contractory phase. Expansionary phases begin when technological innovation cheapens production and wages can be held down. The stagnant phase is caused by an exhaustion in investment outlets for the new forces of production and a "worsening" of capital-labor bargaining conditions.[8]

Mandel wants to show how long waves are "expressions" of the law of value. But he does not succeed in doing so, or—to put it another way—as in Castells's appeal to the capital-labor relation, the ubiquitous law of value has such various effects that it becomes less and less responsible for actual historical developments. These developments are more and more described as the outcome of the "particular conditions" of the time, the interests and organization of classes, and the international balance of power. For instance, Mandel (1978, 636–50) criticizes Paul Baran and Sweezy (1967) for suggesting that price controlling monopolies can evade the law of value. Yet Mandel himself recognizes that state subsidies often determine patterns of investment and that such subsidies may themselves be decisively affected by political considerations that "suspend" the law of value (cf. n. 549). In general, decisions to support a lagging auto industry, defend the interests of auto workers for political reasons, let the industry deal with the consequences of its failure, or alter tax structures to encourage investment for higher productivity express political as well as "purely economic" considerations.

Mandel searches for the fundamental economic contradiction of capitalist society because he believes that the economic system possesses sole social primacy. That he is mistaken may be shown if we examine his claim (1980, 182) that the workings of the law of value will overturn capitalist society. In the present contraction phase of the long wave, he claims, there is a coincidence of economic stagnation and increased strike activity that will lead to a "crisis of all bourgeois social relations." This forecast ignores how the beginnings of past long waves were also marked by economic crisis and political tensions. Yet European fascism and the U.S. New Deal managed the economic crisis and radical working-class movements of the 1930s. Similarly, everywhere but in the Soviet Union, the radical and union movements of the low point of the late 1880s and early 1890s were managed without successful revolutions.

Nevertheless, economic stagnation always poses some threat to capitalism. Therefore, the transition to an expansionary phase requires basic political and cultural as well as technical and economic changes. Capitalist recovery from stagnation or contraction is not the simple product of technological innovation and cheaper labor costs. Because he fails to appreciate this point, Mandel (1978, 310–42, 439–72, 523–60; 1980, 114–23) searches for the economic forces that will make the present crisis the final one. He locates those forces in anti–business cycle measures, especially those concerned with credit. Such measures, he believes, lead to an inflation-producing credit explosion, threatening both global capitalist accumulation and the competitive strength of the capitalist nation it hits hardest.

In seeing no way out of this dilemma, Mandel repeats the mistake of those Marxists who saw the Great Depression as the "final cataclysm" of capitalism. The post-Depression structures of capitalist accumulation have resolved capitalism's "insoluble" contradictions for fifty years. There is nothing in Mandel's description of the "laws of motion" of capital to show that a similar accommodation cannot take place today. International control over the credit cycle is no more antithetical to world capitalism (1978, 440) than state management of national economies. In an era of diminished expectations, the working class may remain fragmented. International control over credit and money may be accompanied by a drastic lessening of the social wage. Advanced capitalist nations may focus new investment on computers, data processing, management, aerospace, microelectronics, automation, petrochemicals, energy, and bioengineering. The Third World may be left with agriculture, raw materials, labor-intensive capitalist industries, and "mature technologies" such as steel (Sklar 1980, 558, 560). After World War II, sophisticated monetary and trade agreements supervised by the United States replaced an outmoded system of British hegemony (Block 1977a; Pindar 1976). Similarly, the disorganization of the early 1980s may give way to yet more sophisticated and internationally oriented mechanisms of control (Sklar, 1980).

Because Mandel believes in the sole social primacy of the economic, he cannot take such a reorganization as a serious possibility. He is thus led to a mistaken alternative: either the law of value necessarily determines capitalist development, or all the contradictions of capitalism have been resolved (1978, 524). If capitalism reorganizes itself yet again, however, we will not have seen the end of its "crises"—but this particular crisis will be followed by another capitalist expansion.[9]

The general point is that capitalist development is defined by a series of historically specific transitions in what David Gordon (1978; 1980; Gordon, Edwards, and Reich 1982) terms the "social structure of accumulation." Economic long waves are generated by a periodic incompatibility between capitalist accumulation and a number of social structures, including labor control, religion, and family. When these structures are not stable or do not fit with the organization of production and distribution, there occurs a social crisis requiring massive social reorganization. Transformations of the social structure of accumulation have included the transition from competitive to monopoly capital, increase in state involvement in the economy, the development of the nuclear family, and the spread of an ethic of consumption. The form of these transitions is at least the partial outcome of the self-conscious struggle of political agents. Even technological development, which for Mandel is the real heart of the expansionary takeoff, is for Gordon (as for Braverman 1974; Edwards 1979; and Marglin 1974) partly an *outcome* of political, social, and cultural relationships, not just their cause.

Gordon's analysis suggests that different phases of capitalist development will be marked by fundamentally different types of crises, not the repeated effects of one unchanging systematic tendency (cf. Wright 1979). A developing capitalist society, drawing labor reserves from an uprooted peasantry, will function differently from a late capitalism in which the labor force is politically organized. We will not explain all crises or all resolutions either by Castells's one basic contradiction or Mandel's "law of value." Rather, later phases will be different from earlier ones *just because* the structures of later phases are solutions to problems that could not be solved by earlier ones.

There is nothing in Mandel's "law of value" or Castell's "structural rules" to prevent this process from repeating itself indefinitely. Capitalist "laws," as guiding principles of the economic structure of capitalism, shape social dilemmas faced by contending political agents. But the experience of the past history of capitalism has helped those agents learn to partially constrain the workings of the law of value or to adapt themselves to it in ways that mitigate its effects. To understand how crises will be resolved, then, it is necessary to understand how the mass of the population is socialized to reproduce capitalism despite its crises (Part III); and how as political agents both working class and ruling class attempt to shape society to fit what they perceive as their interests (Part IV).

PART III

The Social Primacy of Socialization
Processes: Western Marxism, Socialist-
Feminism, and the Dominated Self

6

From Historical Laws to History and Subjectivity

THE ECONOMIC IMPERATIVES OF CAPITALISM PRODUCED A HISTORICALLY SPE-
cific social form in which objective laws seemed to determine social processes. Capitalism appeared to be a system that controlled social life behind
the backs of human beings. This mode of production was a lawlike economic system; a theory of economic processes could, therefore, provide
knowledge of future social development. When system gives way to structure, however, and the lawlike behavior of the mode of production is subjected to self-conscious calculations of collective social agents, such knowledge ceases to be possible.[1] In contemporary capitalism social developments
are no longer shaped by a "mechanism" or governed by laws. Rather, social
life is conceptualized and acted upon by human agents whose actions
express their past experiences and their desires for the future. *Thus socialization processes and political organization—the shaping and political
expression of experiences and beliefs—become socially primary.*

Present capitalism is different from earlier capitalism not because one
mechanical process replaced another. Rather, it is different just because
capitalists, workers, politicians, bureaucrats, and intellectuals have sub-
jectively experienced (in however distorted or ideological a form) and
responded to past events. Changes have taken place because human beings
fought, planned, argued, plotted, pleaded, and ordered that they should.
And people did so because competitive capitalism failed to meet their
interests—or was doing so but seemed to be breaking down. The changed
role of the state, for instance, cannot be understood without seeing how the
major classes of the leading capitalist nations felt about and responded to
the Great Depression.[2]

Because of the specific form taken by competitive capitalism in one
phase of its existence, Marxists mistakenly saw capitalist social relations

83

as expressing the properties of an objectified entity called the "economy" or the "mode of production."[3] They failed to see that this was only a historically specific and temporary form taken by the social organization of human action. In this form, we have an economic system that gives rise to certain characteristic motivations and actions. The social structure of accumulation required that, for the most part, these actions be taken by fragmented, more or less unconnected groups—but that they take place according to a logic supportive of capitalist accumulation.

This society has been transformed. The transformation is comprehensible if we see that social life is the outcome of the action-directing beliefs, attitudes, and goals of the human agents who are its members. Like individuals, social groups may have greater or lesser understanding of what they are doing, both of their actual motivations and of the effects of their actions. The origins and full content of people's motivations are usually somewhat opaque to them, and their actions often have unexpected results. But, also like individuals, social groups can learn from their experiences, evaluate them, and transform their social action accordingly.[4] This ability to think of society as a whole is itself a historical product, a product of the tradition-destroying ideologies of capitalism, and of the conceptual and institutional necessities imposed by the expanded scope of capitalist production. Only with the rise of the ideologies of mass democracy and enlightenment is it possible to think of social life as something which should be consciously reordered according to the rights and interests of the entire population.

The early centuries of capitalist development demanded the rationalization of technical change—self-conscious control of the development of the forces of production. Similarly, late capitalism requires the rationalization of social relations—including but not limited to "economic" relations. As a result, the contemporary state, working-class political parties and trade unions, social groups of women and national/racial minorities, capitalist think tanks and Marxist intellectuals have all developed the capacity to "think" social life in general. Workers' acceptance of mass industrial unions and capitalists' acceptance of state regulation of the economy (to name but two) are examples of social groups transforming society on the basis of changes in their own understanding of the structure of social action. Thus the contradictions of competitive capitalism constitute ways in which major social groups come to see that a "mechanical" form of human action cannot meet their needs.

Responding to these contradictions, the ruling class seeks to defend the system. The crisis-laden history of capitalist economic development motivates the ruling class to monitor and intervene in social life. Also, the twentieth century has produced actual and ideological alternatives to capitalism. For these reasons, capitalism cannot sustain itself as an impersonal process shaped by the actions of fragmented capitalists. The increased power of the state, monopoly pricing agreements, transnational corporations, international agencies, and bourgeois economic theory have all been created to preserve the system.

Similarly, since the middle of the nineteenth century there have existed political movements that take as their goal the radical transformation of capitalism. In practice, mass trade unions, leftist political parties, feminist and racial movements have (however inconsistently) contested for political power.

Despite their efforts, neither the working class nor the ruling class has achieved anything even approximating complete and rational control over social processes. The business cycle has been weakened but not eliminated. Social and economic policies that succeeded in containing previous crises possess contradictions that will give rise to new ones. Rational governmental economic planning for the economy remains obstructed by conflicting interests and by ideological and structural limitations. Similarly, working-class-oriented political parties have not acceded to power in Europe. In the United States such parties do not exist, and only a minority of the working class is protected by unions. While significant political movements of women and ethnic minorities have developed in the last decades, no social movement clearly represents the interests of the working class as a whole. In all cases, attempts by any given group to understand and control society are frustrated by comparable attempts by other groups.

History is Subjectivity because social life is shaped by self-conscious groups who can take the structure of social life as the object of their actions. Subjectivity remains Historical because society creates both the individual and social groups to meet the needs of preexisting social structures. Contemporary capitalism is the product of both History and Subjectivity. The structural rules of capitalism described by Castells and Mandel continue to operate. However, groups now seek to rationally and self-consciously preserve or transform social life. Alienation and reification— the fragmentation and making mechanical of human consciousness and action—coexist with the attempt to rethink and reshape all human institutions: the factory and the family, the state and the hospital.

The truth of radical thought is its rebellion against traditions that fail to meet human needs. The truth of Marxism is its recognition of how rebellion against entrenched power can succeed only as a product of contradictions within the existing order. Yet while the contradictions of capitalism have been manifested many times, the hoped-for transformations have not occurred. The capitalist class and the capitalist state have retained their power partly because they have altered the behavior of capitalism to make it both more functional for themselves and more tolerable for the working class. It may be, as Georg Lukács (1971) suggested, that only the proletariat can see society as a totality in such a way as to eliminate its contradictions. Yet the ruling class has transformed the content of those contradictions and kept capitalism "viable."

Our society is now determined by the interplay of embedded forms of action and the free play of creative responses to the limitations imposed by those forms. We are living out the dialectic of History and Subjectivity. To understand how Marxist theory must see that dialectic as shaped by three forms of social primacy, we now turn to an examination of Western Marxism and socialist-feminism. These two traditions have responded to the failures of traditional Marxism's predictions and the inadequacies of traditional Marxist politics. They have stressed the social primacy of the processes that create a population compatible with the economic contradictions of advanced capitalism. And they have shown just how dramatically socialization processes must change if capitalism is to be overthrown in the interests of freedom and reason.

7

The Historical Motivation
of Western Marxism

SINCE THE 1920S WESTERN MARXISTS HAVE FACED THE FAILURE OR ABSENCE
of socialist revolutions. The conditions that Marx thought would lead to
capitalism's overthrow—economic and social crises in advanced capitalism
—existed, yet power and authority remained with the state and capitalists.
Also, Marxist political parties rigidified into oppressive state powers or
dogmatic and self-serving cliques. In response, Western Marxists have
tried to explain the gap between the social structure of advanced capitalism and the consciousness and political organization of the working
class by stressing the social primacy of the processes of socialization. For
feminists, these issues have been compounded by the sexism of socialist
organizations and the failure of Marxism to comprehend women's social
position. Through its examination of personal life and the family, socialist-
feminism has deepened our understanding of the social primacy of socialization. Feminism's focus on gender relations has also decisively altered
the Marxist concept of exploitation.

As a preliminary, let us note that (short of abandoning Marxism altogether) two basic responses to the failures of Marxist-oriented politics
are possible. First, we may transform the analysis of advanced capitalist
nations or societies into an analysis of a capitalist or imperialist world-
system. In this view, social contradictions between capitalists and workers
have been shifted to conflicts between capitalist nations and the Third
World. The absence of revolution in advanced capitalist societies is made
possible by their exploitation of underdeveloped nations: "class struggle" is
to be found not between workers and capitalists but between the victims of
imperialism and imperialists. When that struggle finally undermines the
economies of advanced capitalist nations, the contradictions between capi-

tal and labor in those nations will return. While Marx was mistaken in thinking that capitalism would create a homogeneous world, he was right in seeing economic structure as primary.[1]

This position rightly sees access to investment, cheap raw materials and labor, and favorable conditions of trade as essential to the post–World War II stabilization of world capitalism. Its weakness lies in the way it retains a basic premise of traditional Marxism: that social primacy lies solely in an economic system. Analyzing that system as a world order based in imperialism rather than a local one based in relations between capitalists and workers leaves unchanged the belief that the dynamic of this system is sufficient to bring about revolutionary social change.

The West has seen a number of massive economic crises. These crises led not to successful revolutions but to the reorganization of the social structures of accumulation, the integration of the working class into those structures, and continued capitalist power. It should be clear, then, that the "conditions of revolution" involve more than economic crisis—whether national or global—and that a transformed Marxist theory requires more than a redescription of the economy. Further, given the degeneration of Soviet Communism and the totalitarian tendencies of Western socialist movements, it is clear that state power in the hands of self-proclaimed "socialists," "communists," or "Marxists" may mean very little in the way of human liberation.

A second response to the failures of Marxism is therefore necessary: to recognize that the dynamic of the mode of production has considerably less influence than traditional historical materialism believed. We now see that socialization processes—by creating a population at home with exploitation and domination even during economic crises—are socially primary. The effects of socialization determine in great measure whether or not economic crises will become social crises; and whether social crises will be resolved by the end of oppressive social relations or simply by their transformation.

This chapter focuses on the weaknesses of Marxist theory and practice that motivated Western Marxism. Central to the transformation of Marxist theory has been the rejection of the orthodox Marxism expressed in the German Social Democratic Party and the Second International, and the Leninism of Russian Communism and the Communist International. Chapter 8 examines some features of Western Marxist theory, especially those concerned with the primacy of socialization processes; that discussion leads naturally to socialist-feminist theory (Chapter 9), which both fulfills and transcends Western Marxism.

Social Democracy

In 1875 German socialists created the German Social Democratic Party (SPD), hammering out a united program that combined Marxist theory with some concessions to the followers of the German socialist Ferdinand Lassalle. Against both anarchism and Lassalle, the SPD affirmed the central role of the industrial proletariat; the need to overthrow rather than reform the state; the desirability of a broad, democratic party rather than a small, conspiratorial one; and the necessity for the workers' movement to be independent from the progressive middle classes. By 1890 the SPD controlled thirty-five seats in the legislature and close to one and a half million (almost 20 percent of the total) votes. Its size and influence made it a model for the smaller and less influential social democratic parties of Europe. With the exception of France, continental socialism looked to Germany for leadership (Joll 1966; Novack, Frankel, and Feldman 1974; Lichtheim 1965).

The Second International was founded in 1889; more than four hundred representatives from twenty countries began an organization that would be the center of European socialism for the next twenty-five years. Two major issues dominated. First, most members chose a revolutionary strategy based on mass parties and parliamentary victories rather than one stressing direct action, strikes, and revolutionary violence. Second, it was assumed that a European war would be prevented because the interests of the proletariat transcended national boundaries and workers would not support their governments' militarism. The failure of the SPD-led Second International was shown most clearly in August 1914, when most of its leaders endorsed their countries' entry into World War I. This failure is directly connected to the Second International's political strategy. While its leaders claimed that social democracy sought the overthrow of capitalism, the SPD's politics were essentially reformist. In his preface to an 1895 reprinting of Marx's *Class Struggles in France*, Engels proposed replacing revolutionary violence of the 1848 or 1871 variety with electoral activity by a mass party. Though Engels recommended such activity as a temporary tactic, it became for the Second International a long-term strategy.

Such a strategy was consistent with the Second International's understanding of Marxist theory. According social primacy solely to what they believed was an economic system, social democratic leaders expected the economic contradictions of capitalism to pave the way for an easy socialist victory. Seeing the breakdown of capitalism as an inevitable consequence of its systematic laws of development, the SPD could reasonably trust in democracy, the increasing size of the proletariat, and its own well-protected organization. Cultivating a politically conscious and militant mass movement seemed unnecessary.[2]

Eduard Bernstein, editor of the SPD's main theoretical journal, sought to rectify this contradiction between radical theory and reformist politics by demanding a fundamental "revision" of Marxism. He argued that capitalism's self-regulation disproved Marx's prediction of inevitable economic crisis and proletarian immiserization. Capitalism had stabilized itself and was providing a steadily increasing standard of living. Socialism would follow the slow increment of socialist parliamentary power and the increased strength of trade unions and consumer cooperatives. Given a climate of political democracy, these institutions would erode capitalist profits to the vanishing point. Gradual progress, not economic crisis and revolution, would lead to socialism.

The SPD formally rejected revisionism, but Bernstein's position reflected the actual practice of the party.[3] As an experienced Bavarian socialist wrote to him: "One doesn't formally decide to do what you ask, one doesn't say it, one *does* it. Our whole activity . . . was the activity of a Social Democratic reforming party" (Joll 1966, 94). Bernstein's revisionism reflected crucial changes in European society, not just the reformism of the Second International. The extended economic crisis of 1873–95 fundamentally altered world capitalism. Competitive capitalism was giving way to trusts and monopolies, and there was a resurgence of colonization. The state's role in the economy was increasing, and social welfare legislation was introduced to contain working-class dissent.

These changes from competitive to monopoly and imperialist capitalism led to temporary political stability and economic affluence in Europe and the United States. A comparatively privileged sector of industrial labor won (after bitter struggle in some cases) improvements in wages, working conditions, and political rights. Social democracy functioned in the service of the limited interests of these workers and their leaders. Cultivating their organizations and trusting their rather vulgar version of Marxism, leaders of the Second International were unprepared for the catastrophic social effects of a world war motivated by the pursuit of Third World markets and resources. Neither could they understand that workers, despite Marxist theory, identified with their nationality as much as or more than with their class.[4]

Perhaps most important, the Second International's acceptance of the most mechanical version of Marxist theory ignored the essential role of human subjectivity in political change. On the one hand, their view of capitalism as an economic system governed by lawlike principles kept them from seeing how the ruling class could learn from the past and modify capitalist society. On the other hand, they did not understand how critically important it was that workers were socialized to accept relations of authority and oppression, and could continue in that acceptance even during economic crisis.

The beginnings of Western Marxism are found in the wave of theoretical and political criticism of the Second International that arose after World War I. The theoretical contributions of Karl Korsch, Lukács, and Antonio Gramsci (examined in Chapter 8) were motivated by their rejection of the way the Second International ignored workers' class consciousness and treated Marxist theory like the objective description of a lawlike system.

Leninism, the Bolshevik Revolution, and the Comintern

Russian socialists, facing an economically and politically undeveloped country, could not successfully employ an SPD strategy dependent on bourgeois democracy. Instead, they had to adapt Marxism to Russian conditions: an overwhelmingly rural society that also possessed a few centers of large-scale industry and militant workers' organizations. This combination meant that the "bourgeois-democratic" revolution, in which a rising bourgeois class creates widespread capitalism and democratic political institutions, could not occur in Russia. Russia's anomalous social structure also made the Menshevik application of Marx's historical model (in which capitalism necessarily follows feudalism and precedes socialism) a mistake. For the Mensheviks, capitalist economic and bourgeois social development would repeat themselves (as law-governed processes) in all modernizing countries. This theory dictated that in political crises the Mensheviks were bound to support capitalists against the proletariat and to ignore the peasants, the vast majority of Russia' population. The Menshevik strategy placed undue confidence in a small and weak Russian bourgeoisie, which was heir to enough political experience to know some of the dangers of allying itself to a now potentially revolutionary proletariat (Horowitz 1969). Because of historical developments after the events that Marx generalized from—including proletariat uprisings in 1848 and 1871 and the rise of socialist parties—Marx's generalizations no longer held. Human experience of past social regularities made those regularities temporary.

Lenin's adaptation of Marxism was more sensitive to the historical particularity of Russia. Initially, he defined himself in opposition to "Legal Marxists," with their stress on legal reforms, and to the "Economists," who limited themselves to trade union activity. Lenin wished to combine both tactics with a more militant struggle for the overthrow of both Czarism and capitalism. This process, he argued, required the leadership not of a mass but of a "vanguard" party. The model of such a party was Lenin's most dramatic contribution to Marxism, the one still most closely identified with the term "Marxism-Leninism." In a series of polemics written between 1901 and 1907, Lenin defined the party as a group of disciplined, highly trained, professional revolutionaries. Only such a party, he believed, could coordinate diverse struggle in the face of state repression and inject socialist class consciousness into a working class dominated by bourgeois ideology (Lenin 1943; 1960; 1970).

My concern here is not with Lenin's vast and not always consistent writings.[5] Rather, I wish only to summarize what Leninism came to mean in the context of the Russian revolution: faith in the vanguard party, alliance between peasants and proletariat under the latter's leadership, and a belief that political consciousness and action—not the laws of history— caused revolutions.

Some weaknesses of Leninism are indicated even in this capsule summary. First, both Lenin and the rest of the party believed that a working class–peasant alliance could hold power and begin to build socialism in Russia only with aid from a postrevolutionary Europe. What would happen, however, if an uprising by the tiny but politically advanced Russian proletariat and both the commune-dwelling and the land-hungry peasants did not spark a European upheaval? How long, for instance, would the alliance between the proletariat and the peasantry last—especially since many peasants wished to retain their own communal institutions, which had no place in Lenin's model of proletarian social dictatorship?

Also, what would happen if the small, professionalized party were to become a power elite, a privileged bureaucracy rather than a selfless revolutionary leadership? This last possibility was anticipated by Trotsky's prophetic critique of Lenin's "dictatorial" methods and ideas at the 1903 Russian Social Democratic Congress. Trotsky warned of a situation in which, once the party was substituted for the class, "the party organization is substituted for the party, the Central committee is substituted for the party organization, and finally a single 'dictator' is substituted for the Central Committee" (Daniels 1960, 1:31). Rosa Luxemburg (1971, 191), similarly, criticized Lenin for confusing "the corpselike obedience of a dominated class and the organized rebellion of a class struggling for its liberation."

Although Leninism's rejection of mechanical historical schemas was an improvement over the Second International and the Mensheviks, Lenin's faith in the knowledge and virtue of a vanguard sowed the seeds of future dictatorship. After its seizure of power in 1917, the Russian Communist Party came to dominate Russian political and social life.[6] Other political parties were eliminated; the soviets, trade unions, and peasant cooperatives were destroyed or turned into puppets of party power. Independent political expression was made impossible.

The Party claimed that its repression was justified by the existence of both internal and external problems. First among these was an economy which, with few centers of heavy industry, was predominantly undeveloped. This underdevelopment worsened after a civil war left the economy in ruins. Far from inheriting an economically and socially modernized country, as Marxist theory forecast, Russian Communists had to direct the modernization of agriculture, industrialization, urbanization, and the process in which consumption is sacrificed to the creation of modern productive capacity.

Second, internal political relations developed in the complete absence of democratic traditions. The outlawing of opposition parties is often taken as evidence of Leninist "dictatorship," yet it should be remembered that opposition members attempted to kill Lenin and negotiated with hostile foreign powers.

Third, the international revolution did not occur. After a series of uprisings, the postwar tide of revolution ebbed in 1923. Instead of sparking— and receiving aid from—European revolutions, Russian Communists found themselves surrounded by antagonistic capitalist powers. They had become the lonely vanguard of history instead of the inspiration of a new world order.

Finally, the original social base of the Bolsheviks, the peasant-worker alliance, collapsed. By 1921 the Russian working class, as an organized group capable of exercising some controls over its political representatives, had ceased to exist. Workers had been killed in the civil war, had returned to the countryside as industry broke down, or had risen into the ranks of the new bureaucracy. With the absence of a self-active proletariat, then, the Communist Party represented little more than itself, its memories, and its aspirations (Deutscher 1963, 9). Even Lenin had to admit that by 1921 the Russian proletariat no longer existed.[7] And to the extent that the peasants supported revolutionary aims, they sought to do so on their own terms, developing their historic communes into autonomous rural institutions. While the Party allied with the peasantry during the New Economic Policy of 1921–28, it would not long permit independent political institutions. The majority of Russia's population was to be, for Leninism, subordinate to the (supposed) representatives of the tiny working class. With the stabilization of Communist rule by the late 1920s, the Party-peasant alliance turned into violent struggle, as some (variously estimated) five to fifteen million peasants were killed or allowed to starve, and autonomous peasant leadership was broken. Some efforts were made to win the poorer peasants to socialist ideology, but no serious consideration was given to sharing power with progressive peasant forces (Kingston-Mann 1983).

In 1921, with the end of the civil war, the "Workers' Opposition" demanded increases in power for the soviets. True to its belief in its own role, the Party responded that

only the political party of the working class, i.e., the Communist Party, is in a position to unite, educate and organize such a vanguard of the proletariat and all the laboring masses as will be able to counteract the inevitable petit-bourgeois wavering of the masses, to counteract tradition and unavoidable lapses of trade union narrowness . . . to direct all sides of the proletarian movements. (Daniels 1960, 2:210)

Reacting to an uprising of the usually supportive sailors of Kronstadt against what they called the "new bureaucracy of Communist commissars and officials," the Party passed a resolution demanding strict unity and banning factions. The democratic reforms of 1920 were curtailed and greater power accorded to the organizational structure of the Party. By 1928 the defeat of the "joint opposition" marked the end of serious intra-party struggles. Justifying its dictatorship by appeals to security, the Russian Communist Party modernized agriculture and initiated the fastest industrialization in world history. It also created a new class of privileged bureaucrats and technical experts.

Far from imbuing the working class with socialist consciousness, this ruling class took Russian society as an object to be controlled. Unlike the early years of the revolution, women's and homosexual rights, progressive education, and collective child rearing were attacked. There was a resurgence of narrow nationalism, anti-Semitism, and support for the traditional family structure (even as women were increasingly entering the work force). In the 1930s a Stalinist reign of terror led to the often completely random killing of millions, including much (perhaps most) of the most dedicated Communist cadre. False confessions were extracted by torture, and history was knowingly distorted (cf. Medvedev 1973).

At the same time, Soviet citizens and the world at large were assured that the Communists were creating "socialism in one country." Just as traditional Marxism had been unprepared for revolution in backward Russia, so Marxism-Leninism could equate socialism with central planning and nationalization of the means of production. According sole social primacy to the economic structure, Marxists could not see how the failure to change socialization processes and the absence of political activity among the mass of Russia's population made the Soviet Union a new form of class society rather than a "socialist republic."

The "success" of Leninism led Communist parties to form throughout the world, all of which accepted Soviet leadership. Affiliating in the Third or Communist International (Comintern), these parties agreed to unconditional support of the Soviet Union; obedience to the executive of Comintern, subject to expulsion; the splitting of previously existing parties on lines defined by the executive, and acceptance of the Soviet model of revolutionary strategy and organization.

As European revolutionary movements faded, Soviet—and hence Comintern—policy shifted. Waiting for a breakdown of capitalism once again seen as "inevitable," Communists were instructed to protect the Soviet Union. Not only a shifting theory but self-interested Russian nationalism motivated this strategy. In a sense, Comintern was the SPD on a world scale. A poverty of theory combined with an unfortunate "wealth" of narrowly national and bureaucratic self-interest masquerading as universal revolutionary morality. Consequently, Communist parties accepted and justified opportunistic deals between the Soviet Union and capitalist nations, allowed themselves to be pushed into catastrophic alliances with bourgeois nationalist forces in colonial countries, and rejected cooperation with social democratic forces during the rise of fascism. On the level of theory, independent ideas and creative Marxist scholarship were replaced by dogmatic justifications of Soviet policies.[8]

As it had initially rejected the Second International, Western Marxism later defined itself in opposition to Comintern. In Korsch's later writings, and those of Wilhelm Reich and the Frankfurt School, we find attempts by isolated radicals to create a Marxist theory opposing both bourgeois thought and a worldwide Communist movement. Somehow, these thinkers believed, it was possible to transform Marxist theory so that it would no longer view society as a law-governed mechanism, nor workers as tools of the laws of history to be manipulated by bureaucrats. Conversely, it also had to be possible to build a critique of bourgeois social relations into a theory of capitalist society. We will now consider to what degree Western Marxists were successful in these efforts.

8

The Contributions and Dilemmas
of Western Marxism

FROM THE 1920S TO THE PRESENT, WESTERN MARXISTS HAVE WRESTLED WITH
the intellectual and political dilemmas just described.[1] Given the sizable
and continuously increasing literature on Western Marxism, I will make
no attempt to treat the tradition as a whole. Rather, I want to focus on
three related points. First, Western Marxists have decisively transformed
Marxist theory by challenging the traditional conception of historical materialism and developing accounts of the primacy of socialization processes.
Second, in stressing how socialization produces class consciousness, Western Marxists have necessarily challenged the positivist Marxism of the
Second International and Leninism. Third, the understanding of class consciousness and of theory in key Western Marxists such as Lukács, Gramsci,
and Max Horkheimer has been limited by male bias. Western Marxism—
including the less sexist and considerably more profound Marxist writings
of Wilhelm Reich—thus finds its fulfillment in the women's movement. In
my interpretation, then, these writers—who are perhaps most associated
with the transformation of Marxism in the twentieth century—are pre-
cursors to contemporary socialist-feminism.

I begin with Korsch's reformulation of the relation between economic
structure and consciousness. Next, I show how the Western Marxist critique of positivism both furthered our understanding of the social primacy
of socialization and also retained an unjustified and regressive yearning
for authority. Lukás, Gramsci, Horkheimer, and Reich stress the social
primacy of working class consciousness and begin the integration of psychology and Marxism. While their work is essential to the transformation
of Marxist theory, it is also sexist. Feminist criticisms of these writers
prepares for the direct exposition of socialist-feminism in Chapter 9.

While my concept of socialization emerges fully only in the course of

96

the whole book, a short explanation of what I mean by the term will help orient the reader to what follows.

Whatever individual capacities or temperament infants are born with, it is clear that their interaction with the people around them determines them as social beings: that is, conditions them to one historically specific set of social relations. Socialization processes, then, are modes of human interaction that transform infants from beings potentially compatible with any form of human society to historically shaped members of a particular one.

This shaping has several stages. The infant initially experiences a certain style or texture of emotional and physical interaction with his/her immediate caretakers. Later, the infant learns particular feelings toward and ways of engaging in body functions, physical movement, cognitive development (tactile, visual, intellectual, symbolic), gender, and play. The young child also experiences the distribution of power and privilege within the household, a distribution that will be presented in ever widening contexts as the child develops. Simultaneously, children develop and witness a limited range of emotional interactions and social relations with peers and with adults. Finally, adult forms of ideology and mass culture reinforce and preserve the lessons of childhood, so that socialization processes maintain in adults what was begun in childhood.

In modern class society the net result is an almost closed system of personhood. People are fitted to a family form, a distribution of authority, and a set of sexual, cognitive, political, and cultural conventions that make them feel comfortable only in conditions of unfreedom. Socialization processes are therefore socially primary in two ways: they preserve class domination even during social crises, and the effects of socialization must somehow be overcome if capitalisms's failures are to give rise to a free and rational society.

Karl Korsch: Economic Structure and Social Consciousness

Two related topics are the focus of Korsch's *Marxism and Philosophy* (1971; first published in 1923): a rejection of the essential thesis of historical materialism and a questioning of the cognitive status of Marxist theory.

Contrary to the "orthodoxy" of the Second International and Leninism, Korsch asserted that ideology, consciousness, and "superstructure" were neither completely logically distinct from nor causally dependent on economics, matter, or the "base." In particular, the classic Marxist distinction between the economic system and politics, ideology, and culture was mistaken: "The material relations of production of the capitalist epoch *only are what they are in combination with the forms in which they are reflected in the pre-scientific and bourgeois scientific consciousness of the period*; and they could not subsist in reality without those forms of consciousness" (Korsch 1971, 88–89; my emphasis; cf. 1971, 98).

This position rejects traditional Marxism's conception of the mode of production as an economic system, separate from and determining the rest of social life. If capitalist "relations of production" are partly constituted by a particular combination of "material relations" and "consciousness," material relations cannot determine the structure of consciousness—for these two do not exist independently of each other. There cannot be an economic system distinct from ideology and politics. Nor can there be laws of economic development that necessarily bring about changes in society as a whole. Further, economic crises will be historically significant only insofar as they are connected to basic political and ideological changes. What traditional Marxism claimed for politics, law, religion, philosophy, and art— that they had no independent history—is here being claimed for the economy as well.

Korsch's position has a major difficulty. He describes the economic structure as the "basis" to which the "legal and political superstructure" "corresponds" (1971, 98), thus seeming to confer some kind of primacy on economics. But if all aspects of society form a totality, how can one part be primary? Like subsequent Western Marxists, Korsch does not wish to deny all primacy to economic structure. To do so, after all, would end any sense of priority in social theory. If all aspects of society were equally part of a whole, then a society could be understood as much by its stamps, chamber music, or sports as by its social relations of production. Korsch claims that economic theory can begin an investigation of bourgeois society, but he would not claim that for *all* ideas. Also, his description of society depends on concepts of production and property. His concern is with *bourgeois* society and *its* characteristic politics, religion, law, art, and so forth. He would not characterize a society by the form of its symphonies or the architecture of its churches. Finally, he believes the proletariat to be the revolutionary class, even though workers' consciousness and political organization are vacillating and often conservative. The working class has a *potential* political destiny because, at present, it has an *actual* role *in production*. Political strategy still depends on economic structure. In short, Korsch rejects traditional formulations of the essential thesis but still retains some sense of the primacy of economic structure.

Two other critical points accompany this insight. First, changes in economic relations will not automatically produce changes in politics or ideology. Thus, while the economic structure retains a certain kind of primacy, other types of primacy emerge. Especially, proletarian consciousness and political action have an autonomous role in creating socialism. Korsch saw that the many failures of revolutionary politics during the 1910s and 1920s —despite the presence of highly supportive economic conditions—required Marxism to abandon the formula, "The economy produces social change." In rejecting that claim he initiated the realization that economics and socialization both possess social primacy. The forms of their primacy, however, are different. The capitalist economic structure creates the material resources and the potential agent for revolutionary change. Yet processes of socialization have both obstructed change and will be essential to achieving socialist goals. These processes shape working-class consciousness: that consciousness which determines the political and social meaning of economic development.

Second, as economic structure and class consciousness are mutually constituting in the broader society, Korsch (1971) argued, so Marxist theory and working-class politics require each other. A revolutionary philosophy disconnected from a mass movement inevitably becomes distorted. For instance, we may see Bernstein's theoretical justification of reformism or Kautsky's "pure theory" which "had no practical consequences" (65–66). By demanding that Marxist theory be tied to radical movements, Korsch challenged those who believed that the purported "scientific" status of Marxism protected it from the ideological biases of other traditions. Korsch's criticisms raised two key questions: If the authority of socialist theory does not rest on its "scientific" status, on what does it rest? If Marxist theory is not the objective study of an impersonal lawlike system, what is it? Thus we see the connection between the critique of traditional Marxism's rigid distinction between economics and the rest of social life and the suggestion that Marxist theory somehow requires an essential connection with a revolutionary mass movement. If social life is not a law-governed system determining human experience and action but is rather a dialectic of person-creating History and history-creating Subjectivity, then Marxist theory must differ from natural, positivist science. If capitalist development will produce social changes that depend on the consciousness of the working class, then the primacy of economics necessarily coexists with the primacy of the processes determining that consciousness.

The writers discussed in the following sections all stress the importance of class consciousness and (at least by implication) of the socialization processes that shape it. They also face the dilemma of justifying their own theories in ways that do not appeal to a disinterested "scientific" perspective. As an introduction to my critique of these writers' greatest weakness—their male bias—I begin by examining this latter issue.

Science as Ideology:
Marxist Theory as Authority

How should Marxists conceive of Marxist theory? The transformation of Marxist theory has fundamentally altered our answer to that question. Beginning with Korsch and continuing with the Frankfurt School and, more recently, socialist-feminism, Marxist theory has progressed *away from* viewing Marxism as an objective science of an impersonal history and *toward* seeing it as both the description of historical forces and the expression of an awakening subjectivity. Two aspects of this progression are Korsch's and the Frankfurt School's political critique of the positivist concept of science; and some important failures in the Frankfurt School's version of that critique.

In 1923 Korsch (1971, 69, 81) had already denied that "scientific social-ism" was scientific in the positivist sense and that knowledge involved consciousness mirroring an independent reality. Since social life was partly determined by the beliefs of its members, social theory could not be simply a reflection of a social reality distinct from consciousness. By 1930, Korsch had developed this position into a critique of the conception of science and knowledge in the Soviet Union. Against Lenin's view that knowledge is the "passive mirror and reflection" of "objective Being" (Korsch 1971, 132–33), Korsch utilized German Idealism's critique of empiricism and anticipated later philosophical refutations of positivism. Specifically, he asserted the role of social forces and evaluative concepts in scientific practice and de-nied rigid distinctions between theory and observation.[2]

Lenin had stressed materialism as a philosophically progressive re-sponse to conservative religion. Korsch (1971, 129), by contrast, saw not religion but a "materialist outlook . . . coloured by the natural sciences" as the reigning ideology. More important, he believed that Lenin's view had disastrous political implications. If knowledge were interestless, a passive representation of the independent and objective world, then possessors of that knowledge would be justified in organizing social life. If Marxist theory were an objective representation of impersonal social processes, the Com-munist Party could rightly form a political dictatorship on the basis of that theory. A positivist version of historical materialism becomes an ideologi-cal prop for Stalinism, a dictatorship "over, not of, the proletariat" (Korsch 1971, 143).

This discussion was the beginning of Western Marxism's long study of the relations between science and politics. Western Marxists have argued that a positivist view of science has two crippling consequences: it can lead to political passivity, as in the Second International's confidence that objective laws of history would bring about the revolution; or it can support political domination, as in the Soviet claim that knowledge of the "laws of history" justifies political power. In either case, Marxist theory is disconnected from the political action of the proletariat. Workers are "objects" of knowledge, to be manipulated in the same way that natural science allows us to manipulate physical objects. As Korsch stated and the Frankfurt School argued at length, traditional Marxism shared this view of science with bourgeois ideology.

From the 1930s to the present, the Frankfurt School has developed Korsch's original point through a critique of "enlightenment." From Plato to Hegel (the argument runs) traditional philosophy identified reason with the capacity to choose ends appropriate to human nature. By contrast, the bourgeois concept of reason sought only an ordered system of propositions describing the world "as it is." The objectivity of theory correlates with the human capacity, under conditions of "enlightenment," to separate reason and interest. Interests, norms, and ends are divorced from reason, beyond the bounds of intelligent argument. Only questions concerning efficiency or accuracy can be rationally posed. The "success" of science and technology are paraded as proof of their rationality, while a rational critique of the effects of physically compelling but destructive technologies and institutions is not possible. "To the enlightenment, that which does not reduce to numbers ... becomes illusion; modern positivism writes it off as literature" (Horkheimer and Adorno 1972, 7). As this ideological conception of science, technique, and rationality spreads, technical experts seem to be the bearers of truth (Marcuse 1941, 431). However, science and technology lead to power without reflection, helping administrators create an "efficient" Auschwitz. When Marxists share this perspective on the relations between reason, science, and technology, their politics will follow the same path.

Pushing beyond anything Korsch envisioned, Max Horkheimer, Theodor Adorno, and Herbert Marcuse also suggested that there are distortions not just in the uses of western science and technology but in their content. The source of these distortions is a misconception of the proper relation between human beings and nature. Despite the theoretical and technical success of modern science, its model of nature as something that exists only to be mastered by human beings constitutes a central flaw in its basic structure. Seeing nature as an object of mastery inevitably leads to seeing human beings in the same light. The control and consumption of human beings—in factories and wars, hospitals and concentration camps—becomes integrated into "scientific" practice (Wellmer 1974, 131; Horkheimer and Adorno 1972, 38–39). The more we humans are emancipated from the power of nature, the more we are socially and psychically enslaved by the system that produces the "emancipation." This result "denounces the rationality of the rational society as obsolete" (Horkheimer and Adorno 1974, 38–39). Moreover, a transformed science would result if we sought the liberation of nature instead of its domination. This new scientific perspective would extend the concept of liberation from society to nature, recognizing "forces in nature which have been distorted and suppressed—forces which could support and enhance the liberation of men" (Marcuse 1972, 66).

Since Horkheimer, Adorno, and Marcuse offer no concrete idea of what science might be like if it did not seek to dominate nature, two examples might deepen their position. Traditional Chinese medicine has fundamentally different premises from those of Western medicine. It employs metaphorical, qualitative concepts rather than quantitative ones. It believes that bodily systems are integrated rather than isolated, and that "mental" and "physical" ailments are reciprocal aspects of a generalized condition determined by sensation, emotion, bodily structure, and the organization of organic energy. It treats illness by seeking to alter energy patterns conceived of as mental, emotional, moral, and physical.[3]

More broadly, consider a "science" of ecology. If we were to define the goal of such a science as "knowledge of the necessary and sufficient conditions for maintaining an environment in which humans and nature could flourish," we would see it as far more inclusive than anything currently called by that name. It would include aspects of contemporary biology and geology, say, yet would insert their more limited knowledge into a framework which included an understanding of social forces. And it would include a normative account of what it is to "flourish."[4]

The Frankfurt School's critique of science has aroused much hostility on the left. Some Marxists have accused Horkheimer and others of confusing class domination with the uses of technology. Habermas (cf. 1970, 81–121) asserted that the problem is that human beings are treated like things, not that things are not treated like human beings.[5] However, the Frankfurt School did not neglect their critique of capitalism when they challenged science's authority (Horkheimer 1972, 215; Horkheimer and Adorno 1972, 168; Marcuse 1969, 12). Similarly, Habermas never seriously questions whether the treatment of natural "things" might help determine the treatment of persons. Perhaps—as Stanley Aronowitz (1981) and Isaac Balbus (1982) argue—Marxism simply cannot see the connection between our attitudes toward nature and our treatment of people. For example, it is radical feminism, not Marxism, that has described the systematic connections between science, capitalism, and male domination.[6] More generally, the "defense" of science seems to presuppose a clear distinction between science and ideology, and to suggest that social forces might never determine research programs or some of science's basic concepts be shaped by social experience. Not only have these positions been disputed successfully,[7] but they clearly contradict a basic principle that leftist defenders of science's objectivity should remember: social relations of production will exercise some constraining influence over all significant aspects of society, including the production of knowledge. Unfortunately, however, the ideology of science reappears within Marxism as a residual yearning for the authority of "objective science."

The critique of science shows that when social life is viewed as an objective mechanism and Marxist theory an objective science of that mechanism, a politics of domination will result. If Marxism is to fulfill its original goals, then, it cannot picture society as an impersonal system or itself as a positivist science.

Unfortunately, however, the critique of science presented so far is incomplete. Like their critics, members of the Frankfurt School in particular still retain a residual yearning to support their theory with some kind of authority. This yearning not only indicates the reappearance of a kind of positivism in these critics of positivism but shows their attachment to a male form of reason. Once again, our discussion begins with Korsch.

Korsch claimed that when Marxism was not connected to an activist movement, it became an ideology. But what is it for theory and practice to be connected? Could Korsch have thought that workers would fully understand a highly sophisticated theory? Also, why should the fact that workers believe it make the theory true? Or did Korsch mean that revolutionary theory was simply a commentary on radical movements? If so, it would have nothing to say during periods of political passivity, and Korsch's own later writings are suspect. Furthermore, even if we agree that a theory has to be connected to a revolutionary movement to be true, *what theory are we to use to tell us which movement is revolutionary?* Korsch's own critique of betrayals by communist and socialist leaders shows that we cannot unproblematically identify the "real" revolutionary group. Similarly, blacks, women, and other socially differentiated groups have criticized oppressive tendencies within the most "radical" of working-class groups.

Writing in the 1930s and after, the Frankfurt School theorists could not appeal to connection with a revolutionary movement, as Korsch and Lukács did in the 1920s (Held 1980, 398; Jay 1973, 47–48). Thus the Frankfurt

School—picking up where Korsch left off—faced a dilemma. Without an objective basis for its critique of bourgeois society, and without Korsch's purported connection to a revolutionary movement, what made Western Marxist theory any more justified than that of the apologists for bourgeois society or Stalinism? If their theory lacked the authority of positivist science, what kind of authority did it have? Western Marxism tried to resolve these difficulties and bolster its own authority by a type of foundationalism: that is, by an attempt (one of many in the history of Western thought) to guarantee the validity or rationality of a theory by characteristics external to the content of the theory itself. It was hoped that the supposed "objectivity" or "neutrality" of science as described by positivism could be replaced by the "interested" and "value-conditioned" stance of the committed revolutionary. As opposed to bourgeois science, it was argued, "critical theory" was shaped by certain interests: socialism, a classless society, justice, human liberation, and the like. These interests are supposed to distinguish Marxism from traditional theory and provide its "objective" foundation. If there is no revolutionary movement, as least there is a revolutionary intention.

For instance, Horkheimer (1972, 213) claimed that critical theory was justified because its goals—especially the goal of "a reasonable organization of society that will meet the needs of the whole community"—are "*immanent* in human work." In another version, Marcuse (1969) argued that an instinctual morality and a need for play are fundamental to the human personality and contradict the unnecessary repression and waste of advanced capitalism. In both cases there is an appeal to some force which, despite appearances in the present, can negate the established order. In both cases, critical theory searches for a theoretical authority to compensate for its practical impotence. It seeks to match—by appeal to immanent meanings or instincts—the authority of positivism.

This search for authority was a mistake. By seeking to ground critical theory in the "immanent meaning" of social labor, Horkheimer returned to a Hegelian mythology of intentions that are larger than persons. Yet meanings adhere only to the conscious or unconscious activities of subjects. Only if humanity creates a rational and just society can an "immanent meaning" be ascribed to human labor as such—and then only as a construction on the past. Until that time the meaning of labor is as ambiguous as that of human history. Is it the pursuit of freedom and justice? At times. But any familiarity with history will tell us that it is equally the pursuit of slavery and degradation. To claim that critical theory is justified because it expresses values to which the human race is really committed—even though it is not aware of its commitment at the present—is to search for a guarantee of success. A similar guarantee allegedly belonged to objective science as construed by positivism. In actuality, however, the power of positivist science was greatly dependent on its social connections: the institutional power of its practitioners, and its compatibility with the established order. Seeking a comparable authority in the absence of such connections reveals that despite its critical intent the Frankfurt School shared one fundamental feature with bourgeois and Stalinist conceptions of reason: the belief that reason has to be a form of authority.[8]

Marcuse's appeal to instinct—the neo-Freudianism of *Eros and Civilization* (1962) or the claim in *An Essay on Liberation* (1969) that new instincts were appearing—is an attempt to find a force that can subvert the totalitarian order of the present. Yet the contradictory array of instincts posited by psychology since Freud makes appeals to them weak at best. More important, precisely because human beings are subjective, even the existence of instincts does not justify a given set of norms. People may freely endorse their instinctual needs or choose to repress them. Marcuse may *hope* that human beings will endorse his "new instincts" of play, creativity, and reciprocity; but history hardly allows him to have confidence that they will. Alternatively, if we cannot help shaping society according to instincts, the appeal to instincts to justify norms is gratuitous.

From John Dewey to Richard Rorty, foundationalism has been convincingly criticized by many writers. I will not repeat their arguments but summarize by stating my belief that Western Marxism's version of foundationalism is undermined by three considerations. We can never be sure of what theorists' intentions are. We do not know why their intentions should have any bearing on a theory's truth. We need theories to tell us which interests are in fact revolutionary or liberating and which political practice serves those interests—and thus cannot unproblematically support a theory on the basis of the "interests" it serves.

At the same time, the intentions informing Marxist theory are not irrelevant to it. In Chapter 2 I described some aspects of the interdependence of Marxism's cognitive claims and ethical goals. A critical theory motivated by the goal of a free and rational society refuses to accept existing social forms as given; will reject unverified models of human beings or social life that reinforce and reflect unjustified power; and will seek to evaluate both its cognitive and its practical claims by as free and open a discussion as possible. However, none of this provides a *foundation* for critical theory; that is, none of it can play the role that the supposed status of science played for either Leninists or bourgeois positivists. None of it, in short, confers authority on the wielders of the theory. There is no ultimate grounding for a critical theory of society; there can only be free discussion, in a free society, by psychically liberated people. The search for a ground is, ultimately, the search for a social authority. Its "rational" basis will be operative only insofar as it is enforced: by the professor, the commissar, or the social worker.

Moreover, a "grounded" reason—reason with a "foundation" of more than simply the free expression of free people in a free society, reason that is more than the expression "my" needs, "your" needs, "our" needs—is a form of *male* reason. It seeks authority in something more than the shared experience of communicating subjectivities. It sets itself apart from the inevitable rootedness and partiality of the particular person, group, and time. In our version of patriarchy such reason is identified with men, while particularity is thought to be female. The male voice is considered the voice of detached objectivity; partiality and emotion belong to women (or other oppressed groups).

This mistaken search for a male form of theoretical authority is echoed in a fundamental error in the Frankfurt School's criticism of the presuppositions of Western science. These theorists claimed that, in seeking to dominate nature, the "naturalness" of human beings was denied. Yet, just because human beings are a part of nature, the domination of nature helps produce social domination. The flaw in this system is that "men" had not really expelled nature from society. The nature *men* denied in themselves was projected onto *women*. The view that nature was solely an object to be known and controlled coincided with the view that nature and women were similar to one another—and opposed to the objective, instrumental rationality of men. In a male-dominated culture, women became the symbols of just that naturalness that men sought to master by "Enlightenment." The spontaneity, fertility, intuition, and capacity to feel men rejected as womanly and natural they nevertheless needed in their relationships with women. "Man" had not cut "himself" off from nature. Men had. And women were part of the nature they sought to dominate.[10]

These remarks are sketchy. They will be developed in the next section and in Chapter 9. What is important is the connection between the critique of science, the primacy of socialization, and the role of subjectivity. Western Marxism rejected the positivist interpretation of Marxist theory and argued that society—the "object" of Marxist theory—was fundamentally different from nature. Consequently, we cannot understand society by a "science" that seeks authority in denying the subjectivity and partiality of knowers. Simultaneously, Western Marxists found that society was not a lawlike system but partly the product of the consciousness and conscious activity of its members. They showed that both social life and social theory depend on the way people experience and seek to change their lives. Thus the processes of socialization that shape people's experience and understanding, and the political forms and struggles that express them, may emerge as socially primary. While the possibilities of society's future have been created by capitalism, their realization will be determined by socialization and politics. Again, there are three forms of social primacy.

Having seen some of the contributions and limitations of Western Marxist's views of knowledge,[11] let us examine and criticize some aspects of their account of subjectivity.

Class Consciousness and Masculine Ideology

Western Marxists faced the gap between the social structure of advanced capitalism and the consciousness and political organization of the working class. They responded by attributing increasing importance to class consciousness, seeing it as the determinant of the outcome of economic crises and a critical obstruction to political activism. Consciousness, however, is the product of complex socialization processes rather than simply class position. Therefore, in the progression from Lukács and Gramsci to Horkheimer and Reich, the primacy of socialization was increasingly recognized. This stress on class consciousness and its relation to socialization is Western Marxisms's contribution to the realization that processes of socialization are socially primary. Despite its groundbreaking contributions, however, Western Marxism's conception of the origins and content of and obstructions to radical class consciousness is sexist.

Georg Lukács

Lukács makes a major contribution to the recognition of the social primacy of socialization: a model of how the working class develops class consciousness. Beginning with the traditional view that classes are determined by position within the mode of production, Lukács (1971, 46) identifies two types of class consciousness: "actual" class consciousness comprises the feelings and beliefs of a given class at a given time; "real" class consciousness, which determines the class's "historically significant actions," involves "appropriate and rational reactions imputed to a particular typical position in the process of production" (1971, 51). Lukács believes that the proletariat will be driven to real class consciousness by its role in capitalist accumulation and come to see capitalist society as the essentially irrational and oppressive totality it is. Looking at society "from the center, as a coherent whole," will enable the proletariat "to change reality" and thus embody the unity of theory and practice (1971, 69).

Real class consciousness will come to the proletariat because the fun-

damental ideological mechanisms of bourgeois society—reification, rationalization, and commodification—contradict what workers feel. Reification
makes all aspects of society, especially capitalist domination, seem given,
or objective. Adopting a positivist perspective on Marxist theory, Lukács
adds, furthers reification. If knowledge is the passive reflection of a given
reality, the knower can adopt only a passive attitude toward that reality.
When attempts are made to understand social life, "rationalization" inhibits
our capacity to conceive of society as a connected whole.[12] Rationalization's
effect on knowledge mirrors the way capitalism combines highly sophisticated social "parts" (a factory, a technology) in an irrational system driven
to economic crises, wars, and oppression.

Though reification and rationalization form the boundaries of class
consciousness in capitalist society, they may be shattered by the contradictions of commodification. Lukács's argument is that while members of the
bourgeoisie (mistakenly) experience themselves as controllers of bourgeois
society, workers experience themselves as commodities. The contradiction
between their social status as commodities and their human reality as subjects will lead the proletariat to revolutionary political action.

This process begins when workers experience their own commodification: "Quantitative differences in exploitation which appear to the capitalist
in the form of quantitative determinants of the objects of his calculation,
must appear to the worker as the decisive, qualitative categories of his
whole physical, mental and moral existence." (1971, 166) Where the capitalist sees a quantitative change in exploitation, the worker feels his personal identity altered. For instance, workers are personally affected when
the working day lengthens: "For the worker labour-time is not merely the
objective form of the commodity he has sold, i.e., his labour power . . . in
addition it is the determining form of his existence *as subject*, as human
being" (167, my emphasis). Since a worker finds in "every aspect of his
daily life" that he ceases to be a subject, he is "driven to surpass this im-
mediacy. . . . [Because] of the *split* between *subjectivity and objectivity*
induced in man by the compulsion to objectify himself as a commodity, the
situation becomes one that can be made conscious" (178–79, my emphasis).
If their existence as commodities is revealed, workers will understand how
commodification affects all of society. They will see through the "fetishism"
that masks relations between people as characteristics of objects. Most
important, workers will overcome the reification of a social life that seemed
unchangeable. Class consciousness, the "*indispensable precondition* for a
politicized proletariat," will emerge (1971, 173). This real class consciousness is a form of self-knowledge, the possession of which transforms the
possessor.

Lukács's confidence that the immediate experience of the working class will necessarily lead it to develop real class consciousness may be questionable. Yet we must appreciate the way he deepens traditional Marxism's simplistic social psychology by directing our attention to that experience. The failure of the working class to develop real class consciousness will then lead us to an examination of those factors structuring immediate experience that prevent the development of class consciousness: that is, the processes of socialization. Also, Lukács views Marxist theory not as a positivist science but as an element in the transformation of worker-as-commodity to worker-as-political-agent. Theory becomes a practical agent in helping workers achieve class consciousness, not an objective description of how a lawlike economic system determines that consciousness.

At the same time, Lukács mistakenly assumes that the proletariat is essentially homogeneous and thus fails to understand the different class consciousness of workers who have different roles in production. Most important, he fails to see any distinction between the condition of men and women or to recognize women's specific role in the reproduction of labor power. Because of his distorted view of "production," he necessarily has a distorted view of the "rational consciousness' that would result from a rational understanding of one's place in production. (These themes are treated in detail in later sections.)

While Lukács mentions "everyday life," he focuses almost exclusively on the experience of the proletariat in paid work. He writes, to borrow Sartre's apt phrase, as if workers were born the day they received their first paycheck; he thus ignores the experience of the proletariat as members of family, religions, or distinct national and racial groups. He shows how the immediate experience of work leads to class consciousness but omits other aspects of workers' life-experience. This omission is crucial. It rests on the assumption that political identity is necessarily dominated far more by one's experience in public labor than by anything else, that the commodification of the worker as worker "must appear" to the worker as decisive for "his whole physical, mental, and moral existence" (Lukács 1971, 166; see also 167).

This assumption misses two central points. First, workers perceive themselves and act on the basis of a variety of social relations. That is why fractions of the working class often develop an active political consciousness based not on their identity as workers but on their race, ethnicity, or nationality.[13] Second, the content of class consciousness is for Lukács limited to a set of beliefs about the organization of society and the interests of the proletariat. He views class consciousness—both in its "actual," distorted form and in its imputed, rational form—as fundamentally conscious and cognitive. He does include its moral and personal dimensions—for example, the willingness to sacrifice present consumption in order to industrialize, or to give up the habits of individualism encouraged by bourgeois society [14]—and thus helps expand the traditional Marxist notion of class consciousness. But for Lukács there is no unconscious side to the worker's consciousness. He does not conceptualize sexuality, unconscious identification with or fear of power, and personality structure; therefore, he offers a distorted account of class consciousness. And this distortion is systematic: it is essentially a male view. Lukács's emphasis on public employment to the exclusion of domestic labor, on conscious rationality to the exclusion of the unconscious and the emotions, on adult life to the exclusion of childhood all reveal that he views consciousness from the perspective of culturally defined masculinity. In our cultural system the public world, paid labor, and rationality have been accorded to men. Emotionality, domestic labor, and private experience have been regarded as quintessentially female. Lukács sees a revolutionary socialist consciousness as coming from male experience and taking a male form. That he describes such experience and such consciousness not as male but as knowledge of the social totality reflects a sexist bias rooted in the sexual division of labor. His account, then, does not show the universality of real working-class consciousness. Rather, it reveals the partiality of a male-dominated class, conceptualized in a sexist form.

Antonio Gramsci

My focus is on two aspects of Gramsci's writings: his concept of hegemony, and his stress on workers' councils as agencies of social transformation.[15]

"Hegemony" is Gramsci's term for the dimensions of class power that are rooted in consent rather than force. Through *bourgeois* hegemony the bourgeoisie ideologically and institutionally dominate the proletariat. *Proletarian* hegemony will arise when the various groups oppressed under capitalism not only are unified in their political aims but also possess a "moral and intellectual unity" (Gramsci 1971, 181–82). Before acquiring state power, the proletariat and other subordinated groups have to stop accepting the legitimacy of capitalism and begin unifying around a radically new conception of the world.

Marxists always believed that workers had to overcome bourgeois ideology; however, this development was foreseen as a natural response to capitalist economic crises and the concentration of labor in large factories. For Gramsci (1971, 184, 410–12), by contrast, economic structure only "set the terrain" for politics and culture, only brought a wide range of possibilities into existence. Struggles in the realms of ideology, culture, and politics—including challenges to socialization processes—would determine which possibilities were realized.[16]

Consequently, Gramsci rejected the notion that Marxist theory could be a positivist science. A self-proclaimed "scientific Marxism" would reveal laws of history to the privileged few—who could then sit back and watch or direct the uninformed masses. Without "laws" of history, however, our knowledge of history and economics can only tell us what possibilities exist. In such a case, Marxist theory is useless unless masses of people use it in the struggle for socialism. Without the internalization of a new "common sense" by a working class shaped by progressive socialization processes, economic crises will be resolved by capitalists and mass radical action mismanaged by party leaders.

Gramsci saw "factory councils" as the practical expression of an emerging proletarian hegemony. Councils were a break with trade unions, a break required because unions were designed to improve the workers' lot under capitalism, not to create socialism. Councils gave workers the opportunity to express themselves in what was for Gramsci their essential identity: that is, as producers. Taking charge of production, eliminating the needless role of a capitalist class whose formerly productive members had become parasites, the proletariat would constitute the core of the new social order. Based on collective recognition of the need for mutual support, socialism would be created by a bloc of blue-collar, white-collar, and technical workers.

Gramsci's conception of hegemony further deepens Western Marxism's conception of how socialization processes are primary. The effects of current socialization—and the creation of new forms—determines the outcome of the possibilities set by capitalist development. Radical working-class consciousness is a possible, not inevitable, consequence of capitalist development. Political and social struggle is necessary to develop that consciousness. Finally, theory is one element in that struggle, not a "scientific" or "objective" description of it.

Gramsci, however, faces some of the same difficulties as Lukács. For instance, he fails to take seriously how the division of labor characteristic of modern productive processes politically divides white-collar, blue-collar, and technical workers (cf. Gramsci 1971, 333). He ignores conflicts of interest between the working class and technical workers and among socially differentiated segments of the working class. Though he does note that the proletariat "must rid itself of every corporatist residue" (Merrington 1978, 158), he does not see that political unity of the proletariat is obstructed not only by ownership and distribution but also by the structure of production.

Thus, while Gramsci acknowledges the potential power and destructiveness of the political elite of trade union and party leaders, he shows little awareness of the power and political role of the "technical" class of engineers and managers.[17] He fails to see that the modern division of labor reveals both the capitalist desire to fragment and degrade workers and also a genuinely increased technical complexity. This technical complexity creates a social group whose experiences and interests differ from those of the traditional working class, a class which (contrary to Gramsci) is far from capable of assuming all the roles in modern production. While Gramsci sees that proletarian hegemony required overcoming political splits between the working class, the peasantry, and the petit bourgeoisie, he assumes unity in the realm of production. Much political history has shown that this assumption is unwarranted (Part IV focuses on this issue).

A similar and much more damaging lack of understanding of conflicts of interests within the working class characterizes Gramsci's misperception of male–female relations. In the one extended passage in *Selections from the Prison Notebooks* in which he does discuss sexual politics (1971, 294–305), his concern is with the "sexual question": that is, sexuality. While there is some recognition of sexual abuse, there is no serious attempt to relate such abuse to the general condition of women's oppression. His suggestion is that the female personality must change if women are to attain "independence." How this might happen without a drastic change in male as well as female personality structures, and also in sex-segregated forms of production and reproduction, he does not say.

Gramsci's sex blindness is damaging to his overall theory in at least two significant ways. First, consider his account of workers' councils as agents of socialist transformation, "pre-figuring" socialism and expressing the reality of the proletariat as producers rather than as wage earners. This position ignores the fact that factory councils provide no political outlet for people engaged in that aspect of productive work which is often defined as "reproduction." This work, almost exclusively that of women, includes child care, housework, and providing emotional nurturance.[18] The sexual division of labor within capitalist patriarchy relegates such work to women, while that of earning a living in the public realm is the province of men. Gramsci's proletariat, his "productive core," was nurtured by the devalued, unpaid, sex-segregated labor of women. Moreover, this female labor was performed by a group of people virtually without political representation or established rights, a group whose social position would hardly be improved by a factory council movement staffed by the same men who oppressed them before councils existed.

Is there any reason to expect, for instance, that factory councils would demand equal pay for equal work and equal work itself for women? Would they develop the infrastructure of day care centers, maternity leaves, training, and so on, that could make women's equal participation in paid labor possible? Would mostly male factory councils push for sexual equality in housework, sexuality, and child care? The obvious answers suggest that Gramsci did not see how capitalism's use of sex-segregated labor was repeated in the sexism of working-class consciousness. One result is that the working class contains significant conflicts of interest. Consequently, Gramsci's overly simple model of "proletarian hegemony" falls apart. In that model a fundamental hegemonic principle can be derived from the role of the proletariat in production. But the sexual division of labor divides working-class men and women. There can be no unified proletarian hegemonic principle, because workers are divided by gender.

These facts hold not only under the comparatively undeveloped capitalism of Italy in the 1920s but also for contemporary capitalism. High concentration in sex-segregated state and service sectors puts women in work situations much less amenable to the ideals of self-management than is craft-oriented industrial production. Retaining primary responsibility for housework and child care, even in advanced industrial societies, they have little time or energy for the discussion and study necessary for self-management (Feldberg 1981). These facts offer little hope that simply integrating women into the public work force will overcome the sexist divisions within the society as a whole or the proletariat in particular.[19]

Second, let us note the effect of Gramsci's sex blindness on his account of hegemony. In identifying the physical power of class domination with the state and the more subtle control of consent with the many diffused forms of bourgeois hegemony, Gramsci misses male violence against women — violence that is part of an overall system of patriarchal power.[20] It might be responded that male violence (such as rape and wife beating) is not legitimized like that of the state; that is, it is not legally sanctioned. This is a confused claim for three reasons. First, the legal system has in fact often tacitly or directly sanctioned male violence against women (for example, in not making husbands liable for raping their wives). Second, patriarchal ideologies have "justified" or excused male violence. Third, because male violence has been cloaked under deceptive misdescriptions, rape has not always been seen as violence, wife-beating as a form of social control, or the psychiatric treatment of women as coercion.

Gramsci's sex blindness prevents him from recognizing that the proletariat is not just a victim of hegemony. Parts of the proletariat exercise hegemony even as they are subject to it; that is, male proletarians exercise the hegemony of patriarchy while they are subject to the hegemony of capital. This dual identity of male workers is integral to the maintenance of capitalist power. It is not only an illusion of hegemony or the effect of bourgeois class power over the institutions of education, religion, the state, and so forth, that makes the proletariat accept bourgeois rule. It is also that proletarian men have some interests in common with bourgeois men: continued rule over women.[21] The creation of proletarian hegemony is thus quite different from the process described by Gramsci. It will require, among other things, that proletarian men sever some alliances and give up some power. Until they do, roughly one-half of the working class retains a stake in the system.

Max Horkheimer

Even more than Gramsci or Lukács, the work of the Frankfurt School developed in a context of the failure of radicalism. Not surprisingly, Horkheimer, Adorno, Marcuse, and Erich Fromm turned to an examination of unconscious mental processes to help explain a political life that seemed so haunted by the irrational.

In 1932 Horkheimer (1932) claimed that Marxists would have to use psychology to explain why social forms remained after their objective necessity disappeared; he (and others) developed a theory of authority to show how the working class internalized the social relations of bourgeois society (see also Horkheimer 1972, 98). At this point a natural attraction to psychoanalysis developed. This theory, it seemed, could describe the mediations between class structure and individual experience. Specifically, it could explain the irrational inability of the working class to overthrow capitalism by describing the way in which infants developed personalities compatible with an unfree society. The Frankfurt School wanted to unify Marxism and psychology so that the latter would no longer reify historically specific forms of socialization and the former would stop ignoring the unconscious, sexuality, and the family. They sought a Freud without ideology and a Marx without psychological naiveté. Since the subjects of psychoanalysis—infantile sexuality, repression, unconscious defense mechanisms—had been foreign to Marxism, their integration into radical social theory was a crucial contribution to the transformation of Marxist theory.

The Frankfurt School theorists were critical of Freud's ideologically bound universalization of many of the historically specific features of bourgeois society. They did, however, accept the claim of psychoanalysis that early childhood experience was an unconscious adaptation of instinctual drives to structures of affection and authority in the family, and that much of adult life simultaneously masks and expresses that unconscious adaptation of early childhood. Most important, they saw collective human behavior as centrally determined by the formation of an authority-oriented superego through the introjection of parental authority figures in response to childhood sexual and emotional conflicts.

The family is central to this process, a major cause of working-class political impotence, Horkheimer believed, because it helps maintain an irrational society by creating personalities habituated to obeying authority. It focuses "psychic life" around order and subordination and saps energies that could otherwise be used to bring about social change (1972, 109). The father–son relation is central to the family's reproduction of social authority. The father's authority stems from his physical strength, his income, and his mastery of work skills needed by his children. By obeying and imitating the father, the "individual" develops the self-control, devotion to duty, and capacity to "reason" that are essential to capitalism. Simultaneously, the "seeming naturalness of paternal power" (1972, 107) teaches the child the habit of obedience. As the young child adapts to the father's power, so he will later accept social authority in general. But by the 1920s, thought Horkheimer, this family structure had begun to weaken; economic insecurity, unemployment, and state interference were limiting the father's power. As a result, children sought to identify with an authority outside the family, a replacement for the now weakened family father. The fascist authoritarian state, claimed Horkheimer, satisfied this unconscious need.

While the family reproduces authority, it is also something of a haven from a market society in which human relationships are shaped by competition and cash. Of course, in this haven "the father was becoming the money-earner, the woman a sexual object or a domestic servant, and the children either heir of the family possession or a living form of social security." But still,

Relationships were not mediated through the market and the individual members were not competing with each other . . . the individual always had the possibility there of living not as a mere function but as a human being. . . . common concerns took a positive form in sexual love and especially in maternal care. . . . the family not only educates for authority in bourgeois society; it also cultivates the dream of a better condition for mankind. In the yearning of many adults for the paradise of their childhood, in the way a mother can speak of her son even though he has come into conflict with the world, in the protective love of a wife for her husband there are ideas and forces . . . which in the bourgeois system of life rarely have any place but the family where they can survive at all. (1972, 114–15)

Whatever its positive aspects, this family is still ruled by patriarchal power, a power that dominates both children and women. As a result, women often have to abandon their maternal protective function in order to support the status quo, which produces the husband's income. Under the pressures of bourgeois authoritarianism, in short, women's "natural" support of loving, anticapitalist maternal relations are replaced by a "concern with her own and her children's economic security" (1972, 120).

Horkheimer made an enormous contribution to our understanding of the social primacy of the processes of socialization, especially the critical role of the family in supporting bourgeois authority. Since workers yearn for authority, they are tied to domination when capitalist development stumbles. Unconscious processes prevent social crises from being revolutions. Thus, until new socialization processes challenge the old ones, capitalism, fascism, or Stalinist totalitarianism will command workers' support.

However, while Horkheimer's contributions (and those of his fellows) have received considerable attention, the sexist bias of his theory has not. The points I raise here are, sadly, usually ignored by other commentators. Mark Poster (1980) mentions the topic in passing; David Held (1980), Martin Jay (1973; 1984), and Phil Slater (1977) not at all.

Horkheimer describes the bourgeois family as a place where children learn to work and reason, to delay gratification, and to prepare themselves to submit to the authority structures of the public world. This description, when applied to a female child, is extremely problematic. In the bourgeois family daughters are socialized into very different capacities and dispositions than are sons. Young girls do not prepare to make a career or submit to a lifetime on an assembly line. They learn to provide emotional comfort and nurturance and to please men. The "maternal" love glorified by Horkheimer in his account of the family's "contradictory" role in modern society is not a product of some eternal female nature. It is the outcome of a socialization different from the one through which male children pass.[22]

But Horkheimer is not really interested in women *except as mothers*. They may be "good" mothers, helping to provide a little "maternal" care so that Daddy can feel better after a rough day in the real world and Sonny can grow up knowing that someone always loves him. Or, driven by concern for their own and their children's material well-being, women can turn into agents of bourgeois authority. As a result, the victory of women's suffrage causes a "conservatising" of society. Thus Horkheimer's romanticization of the family—as the place where human values are preserved against a dehumanizing market society—ignores the fact, mentioned in the same paragraph, that the family has been the major location of women's oppression. Horkheimer sees that oppression—the woman's becoming a "sexual object or a domestic servant"—as a result of the development of bourgeois culture and capitalism. Unfortunately, however, historical, class, and ethnic *differences* in women's family situation have been matched by a pretty much *unchanging* condition of social inequality.[23] Moreover, what

Horkheimer celebrates as the "protective" love of a wife for her husband is partly an expression of female subordination. Such affection must be critically examined rather than uncritically celebrated, especially since it so often takes the form of self-sacrifice.

One reason Horkheimer fails to recognize this point is that for him the family has no economic dimension. He sees the father's financial resources as giving him power in the family, but he does not see that power as part of a system in which sex, nurturance, and emotional support are produced and consumed. It is not just that the woman is dependent on the man because he earns money and she does not. It is also that the man exploits the woman by appropriating her sexuality and consuming her physical and emotional services. Contrary to Horkheimer, the home is not only a haven from, a mirror of, and a support for the wider society. Rather, the family itself—as the primary arena of male–female relations—contains exploitation, domination, and struggle (see Chapter 9). Horkheimer's "integration" of psychology and historical materialism confines psychology to the family and production to public life. Not surprisingly, he is theoretically unprepared for the maintenance of structures of male power and ideologies of male supremacy in societies where the majority of women work outside the home. Nor would he understand why women's paid work so often resembles household labor.[24]

In misunderstanding patriarchy, Horkheimer misconstrues the integral relation of the oppression of women to male personality structure. For Horkheimer, men are socialized into authoritarian personalities mainly by their relation to their fathers. They learn to obey and imitate paternal power. Women-as-mothers either provide a brief respite or reinforce paternal authority. Much of paternal authority, however, is neither just an imitation of and obedience to male authority nor (as Horkheimer approvingly quotes Marx) just a "crude revenge for the submissiveness and dependence [men] have had to show . . . in bourgeois society" (1972, 126). Rather, paternal authority is also male authority over women.

Such authority is essential to the seemingly "autonomous individual" glorified throughout Horkheimer's writing. He sees this individual as threatened by fascism in the 1930s and by mass society in the 1950s. In his later writings he speaks nostalgically of the early bourgeois patriarch as a "free man," guided only by his own conscience, who could become for his child "an example of autonomy, resoluteness, self-command and breadth of mind" (1974, 11–12).

This concept of the individual is doubly flawed. First, Horkheimer offers a male model of adult autonomy: a person who is "his own master," free and very much alone. He forgets that mature adults also need to be able to cooperate, share feelings, and provide nurturance. In bourgeois societies these qualities are relegated to women and devalued. Horkheimer tacitly accepts this devaluation. Second, he has also taken a male fantasy as reality. The bourgeois fantasy of adult autonomy is built on the denial of the bourgeois man's dependence on his mother, his wife, his secretary, and his whore. Characteristics that men have shed to become "free" are still needed. They are provided by women. Women's exploitation is the hidden "truth" of male autonomy.

Finally, Horkheimer cannot see women as subjects. This blindness has been a fundamental limitation of most Marxist writings on women.[25] That is why Horkheimer can evaluate the result of women's suffrage as "conservative," not realizing that no matter how women vote, extending democratic rights to them is an enormous step forward in itself. Critical theorists in general have tended to ignore women as a political force, as a repository of "negative" and subversive thinking. The women's battles for suffrage in the United States and England, about which Horkheimer could have made himself quite aware, represented large-scale movements for social change by an oppressed group. They are invisible to him.

Similarly, the Frankfurt School's otherwise valuable pioneering work misdescribes the effects of mass culture on the formation of the personality structure that supports totalitarian governments of the left or right. The mistake is to suppose that there is or can be one personality type in a patriarchal society.[26] The claim that instrumental rationality, obedience to authority, adherence to administrative regulations, and the like, are hallmarks of modern personality structure is refuted if one examines the socialization of the average woman. Women—as mothers, sex objects, and the focus of romantic fantasies—are hardly compatible with technological instrumentality or positivist reason. Women are, in part, the prize of those who have mastered these modern forms of alienated consciousness. Performance according to the prevailing performance principle is rewarded by "things," especially the possession of a beautiful and devoted woman. Thus contemporary mass culture is very different for men and women. A theory that awards social primacy to the processes of socialization must place this difference at its center.

Lukács's, Gramsci's, and Horkheimer's contributions to understanding the social primacy of socialization processes are decisively flawed. Stressing the crucial role of consciousness, they describe only its male form and see it as stemming only from men's life experience. Their claims to a new and critical objectivity are marked by the pretensions of masculine ideology. In the transformation of Marxist theory it is necessary to retain their emphasis on working-class subjectivity and socialization, but also to move beyond their male biases with the help of socialist-feminism. The work of Wilhelm Reich provides an ideal transition.

Wilhelm Reich

Reich's Marxist essays of the 1930s develop the positions of Korsch, Lukács, Gramsci, and Horkheimer. To show how he furthered their analysis and corrected some of their failings, I will discuss two areas of Reich's work: the relation between Marxism and psychoanalysis, and the concept of class consciousness.

Marxism and Psychoanalysis

Reich criticizes Marxism for having only the most elementary theory of how an ideology supportive of class power dominates capitalist society. Neither the institutional power of the ruling class nor its control over sources of information and culture can explain proletarian acquiescence. An understanding of unconscious mental processes—especially those resulting from repressed sexual impulses—is also essential.

Using Freud, Reich sees personality as an essentially unconscious response to the way instinctual drives are shaped by affection and authority in the family; much adult conscious behavior is in fact an irrational repetition of this response. Perhaps most important, he sees adult behavior as structured by a superego formed by the internalization of authority experienced in childhood. Especially, early childhood conflict over sexuality requires the formation of defense mechanisms, which continue in adulthood.

Reich believes that Freud gave too much weight to instincts in determining the organization of society. Freud's claim that instinctual gratification and the social order are incompatible is a pessimistic generalization based on Victorian society, not human nature. For Reich, the social and political setting, rather than the instincts themselves, determine how instinctual energy is expressed. While the conscious ego must adapt instinctual drives to a "reality principle," reality itself is shaped by class interests. Sexual repression is made necessary by patriarchy and private property. Traditional psychoanalysis, he said, mistakenly attempted to reduce political action to expressions of the unconscious, whereas in fact, psychoanalysis applies only to irrational behavior. Seeing radical politics as an expression of "infantile conflict" made psychoanalysis a tool for conservative politics. Political activity as such can no more be explained in psychological terms than falling bodies can be explained by chemistry.

For our purposes, the details of Reich's particular version of psychoanalysis (for example, his precise views on sexuality) are much less important than his integration of psychoanalytic insights into Marxism. His central point is that capitalism is not sustained just by false conscious beliefs but rather by a "character structure": an entire personality, including an unconscious mental life.

In class society, the ruling class secures its position with the aid of education and the institution of the family, by making its ideology the ruling ideology. . . . But it is not merely a matter of imposing ideologies, attitudes and concepts. . . . *Rather it is a matter of a deep-reaching process in each new generation, of the formation of a psychic structure that corresponds to the existing social order.* . . . (Reich 1976, xxvii)

In short, workers in advanced capitalism are not only economically oppressed and politically weak but also psychically crippled. Sexual repression in the patriarchal family creates a passive population cut off from natural instincts for egalitarian human relations, sexual pleasure, and enjoyable work (1946, 30). "The moral inhibition of the child's natural sexuality makes the child afraid, shy, fearful of authority, obedient, 'good', and 'docile'. . . . It has a crippling effect on man's rebellious forces because every vital life-impulse is now burdened with severe fear" (1946, 64–65). The deadening effects of sexual repression also "enable" people to do the boring, mechanical work that dominates capitalist society. Similarly, dulled by sexual inhibitions, people's creativity and learning ability are sapped (Ollman 1972, 204). The task of psychology, then, is to describe the links between class structure and character structure (1972, 44). Especially, psychoanalysis must explain the irrational political quiescence of the working class: not why a hungry man steals but why he does not steal; not why workers strike when striking is in their interests but what unconscious forces keep them from doing so (Reich 1972, 64).

Reich's Marxian use of psychoanalysis helps resolve certain problems posed by Korsch and Gramsci. Korsch was caught between his rejection of traditional Marxism and his continued assertion that capitalism is socially primary. For Reich, the mode of production *is* socially primary in that its structures define the objective interests of social classes and create the material resources to make the satisfaction of those interests possible; it is *not* socially primary because no analysis of it can explain why, for instance, the ravages of the post–World War I German economy produced fascism instead of a workers' government. This development cannot be understood without an account of the socially primary effects of family-based socialization processes. Economic theory is incapable of describing how these processes shape instinctual desires into an unconscious character structure. This character structure ties workers to authority and keeps them from realizing their collective interests through self-conscious political action. Thus, for Reich, the primacy of the capitalist economy resides in one area, that of the socialization processes in another.

Gramsci failed to see how working-class men exercise hegemony as well as suffer from it. Reich, by contrast, saw a direct link between capitalist authority and authority in the family. Socialization includes a male domination that makes women politically passive and submissive to their husbands. And it conditions male workers to authoritarian social relations. "The right of sexual ownership which men enjoy in a class society, is one of the worst obstacles to the development of class consciousness in all members of a family . . . the man . . . is securely tied by it to the bourgeois order" (Reich 1972, 313). In short, men and women have different relations to bourgeois hegemony. Reich developed this point much more in relation to sexual repression and the family than to a general theory of male–female relations, yet his recognition of it provides a theoretical transition between the sexism of Western Marxism and the development of socialist-feminist theory.

Class Consciousness

Reflecting on the failures of the German Socialist and Communist parties, Reich (1972, 283–84) asked why "the people did not listen to us, why we allowed ourselves to be suffocated by our bureaucracy, why the masses indeed acted against their own interest in carrying Hitler to power." His answer was that "while we presented the masses with superb historical analysis and economic treatises on the contradictions of imperialism, Hitler stirred the deepest roots of their emotional being . . . we left the praxis of the subjective factor to the idealists."

Reich assumes that capitalist society cannot satisfy the basic human needs of its members. No social order that requires the frustration of instincts can lead to human happiness. A fundamental dissatisfaction will always be present, at least in latent form.[27] Radical politics must awaken the "subjective factor" into a revolutionary class consciousness by seizing on this dissatisfaction. For the masses, however, class consciousness is not based in correct theory or heroic self-sacrifice. Rather, it centers on the personal and family needs of everyday life: food, clothing, sex, children, housing, and leisure (Reich 1972, 290). To succeed, then, a concentrated and theoretically sophisticated group of revolutionaries must uncover and cultivate those aspects of working-class experience that contain a "germ of rebellion" (1972, 295). If this process is successful, workers will become aware of their own needs in all spheres of life; identify the barriers to fulfilling those needs created by external class structure and internal psychic structure; and sense that the unity of oppressed groups is a necessary condition for the overthrow of oppressive ones. Since class consciousness stems from "everyday life," it will take a different form for each particular group within the working class. Adult men or women, adolescents, and children have distinctive contradictory elements of thought and feeling leading toward and away from such class consciousness.

Reich (1972, 358) presupposes that conflicts of interest within the working class (for instance, those caused by male domination) can be overcome by a class consciousness that supports mass unity. However, if everyday needs and experiences are so central, why should we expect groups with very different everyday experiences and needs to unify politically? Even if workers overcome socialization processes and rebel, can we expect them to cooperate with one another? (See Part IV.)

This reservation aside, for Lukács, as for Korsch and Gramsci, Reich deepens an earlier position within the Western Marxist tradition and anticipates certain developments of feminism. Two points are particularly important.

First, Lukács claimed that the working class is driven to "real class consciousness" by its subjective experience. Yet what is the actual content of that class consciousness? For example, is each member of the working class to possess a theoretical understanding of capitalist society? Reich's account answers this question. For him, class consciousness is knowledge of one's own needs and of the external and internal barriers to their fulfillment. Class consciousness does not include knowledge of how competition for raw materials between imperialist powers is a root cause of war. Yet it is essential to know that militarism and national chauvinism frustrate needs for sexual fulfillment, emotional satisfaction, material security, and creative work. By stressing the critical role of everyday life, Reich's position also partly overcomes Lukács's male emphasis on paid labor. Further, Reich is aware of significant differences in the life experience of an economically defined class. If such differences are not recognized, there will be no way to identify those elements of everyday life that contain a "germ of rebellion" (see 1972, 352). He thus avoids Gramsci's overly simplified model of a single, unified proletarian hegemony.

Second, we find in Reich's account of class consciousness a possible solution to the dilemmas of the relation between the party and the class. Lukács thought of the party as the moral and intellectual exemplar for the class. The party had attained that knowledge of the totality which the proletariat required. By the 1930s, however, the ravages of Stalinism and the failures of the European left raised the question, What is to protect the working class from its "leaders"? Reich suggests that revolutionary politics must be based in awakening rather than manipulating the masses (1972, 352–53). The German Communist and Social Democratic parties, whatever their supposed opposition to capitalism, functioned on the assumption that class consciousness (in Reich's sense) would not arise. They sought followers: passive masses who would accept closed-door negotiations and defer to party leaders. In this way, leftist parties practiced bourgeois politics.

Reich realized that any self-conscious left-wing group within a capitalist society is in some sense a "vanguard." What this term implies, however, is the task of helping the masses to an understanding of their own needs. The core of socialist revolution is an awareness of certain relations between the self and the social order. If such awareness is not developed, the masses will be psychologically tied to an oppressive society—whether that society is dominated by capitalists or by party bureaucrats. People will be more emotionally comfortable with authority than with freedom. Demonstrators will obey "Keep Off the Grass" signs; factory workers will see the means of production as belonging to someone else; and a general deference to authority will be repeated in revolutionary politics. For Reich, then, the task of Marxist theory and practice is to help transform the working class from products of History into Subjective social agents.

Reich had his limitations: overemphasizing sexual instincts, maintaining a heterosexual bias. Similarly, he had no theoretical account of the complexities of the relations between patriarchy and capitalism. His accomplishments, however, well outweigh his limitations. Far in advance of other Western Marxists, in this area, he offered a detailed account of the simultaneous primacy of economic structure and socialization. Finally, his stress on the interdependence of personal and political life anticipated contemporary feminism.

9

Socialist-Feminism

SOCIALIST- (OR MARXIST-) FEMINISM EMERGED DURING THE LATE 1960S AS radical women became increasingly aware of both the societywide oppression of women and the sexism of radical movements (Mitchell 1973; Piercy 1970; Rowbotham 1973). It combined a theoretical analysis of women's social condition with reflections on personal experience by its own theoreticians. This combination was shared by virtually all elements of the amorphous "women's liberation" movement of the 1960s, finding voice in the claim that "the personal is political." This slogan implied that the family, sexual relations, and emotional life are—like property and politics—shaped by systematic relations of power and inequality. Since capitalism relegates the private sphere to women, it is no surprise that they, rather than men, were discovering and struggling against its systematic inequalities. It is also not surprising that feminists would find traditional Marxism—which saw politics only in the public realm and claimed social primacy for the economic—inadequate. The theoretical limitations of Marxist theory and the politically oppressive behavior of male Marxists motivated feminists to demand a reconceptualization of Marxist theory in light of the experiences and interests of women.

This chapter focuses on socialist-feminism's three major contributions to the transformation of Marxist theory—a redefinition of the mode of production to include gender as well as class relations; an increasingly sophisticated account of how socialization processes inhibit radical class consciousness; and a new understanding of the relation between theory and subjectivity. I first summarize the theoretical challenge posed by socialist-feminism to radical feminism and traditional Marxism. Next, the chapter examines the origins and social role of the modern family and the mutually reinforcing relations between male domination and capitalism. I then locate gender relations in my theory of three forms of social primacy and examine feminism's contribution to our understanding of the relation between political change, subjectivity, and critical theory.

Socialist-Feminism and Radical Feminism

The concept of patriarchy was the first major contribution of the radical feminist theory of the 1960s.[1] Radical feminists believed that gender oppression rather than class exploitation had been the dominant fact of history, that male domination was socially primary in virtually all societies. Therefore, a social theory, such as traditional Marxism, that described the condition of women as a consequence of some more primary structure was necessarily inadequate. Politically, radical feminists rejected the notion that organized workers would liberate women. Rather, women's liberation was a necessary condition for human liberation as such (cf. Firestone 1970; Millett 1971).

Despite its critical importance, the radical feminist concept of patriarchy had certain drawbacks. Radical feminists claimed that male domination was socially primary and supported their position by asserting patriarchy's universality. But, responded socialist-feminists, male domination has varied widely throughout history. Since to explain that variety we must describe how patriarchy has been affected by other structures of domination, patriarchy cannot possess sole social primacy (Hartmann 1981b, 18; McDonough and Harrison 1978, 13; Mitchell 1973, 83). Socialist-feminist writers also criticized the radical feminist tendency to explain the supposedly universal condition of patriarchy by reference to ahistorical, universally distributed causes: for example, an unchanging male personality type or female role in biological reproduction (de Beauvoir 1953; Dworkin 1979; Firestone 1970).

Actually, wide variations in male and female personality types have coexisted with male domination. As Linda Nicholson (1977) points out, for instance, the concept of a "rational person" differs greatly in ancient Greek and modern advanced industrial societies. In Greece, the highest forms of rationality were identified with the contemplation of eternal truths, while "practical" forms of technology and accomplishment were devalued. In modern times, "rationality" is identified with a scientific or instrumental mentality. Nicholson's point is that although each society values very different forms of "rationality," those qualities are identified with men. The personality structures considered as rational may vary greatly but in each case they are considered to be male. Similarly, while women's role in biological reproduction may require that men and women do different social tasks, it does not require that men dominate women. Biology may compel a gender *division* of labor, but not gender *inequality* (Young 1981).

Socialist-feminists rejected personality and biology as explanations of a male domination seen as universally constant. Instead, they sought to describe historical and social variations in women's oppression; how that oppression interacted with changes in the division of labor, family form, and culture; and how such changes affect the prospects for women's liberation.

Sexual domination is related to the production and distribution of specific kinds of goods and services. Therefore . . . as historical factors change the rewards from and opportunities to control these goods and services, men's motives and abilities to control women vary, and the character and degree of patriarchal domination is modified. (Ferguson and Folbre 1981, 316)

Finally, socialist-feminists argued that radical feminism's theoretical limitations created strategic difficulties. If patriarchy is everywhere essentially the same, why should it ever change in the future? If male domination is the single fundamental structure of social life, why expect men to give up their power? If historical change is making the liberation of women possible, women's oppression must be partly shaped by factors which themselves are subject to a dialectic—a historical dynamic. Yet it is just such a dynamic that is incompatible with the existence of single, universal force of male domination. Patriarchy, *in and of itself*, is not socially primary.

Problems with Engels

Explaining the varieties and history of women's oppression led feminist theory back to Marxist analysis. Yet socialist-feminists found that analysis seriously flawed.

According to the materialistic conception, the determining factor in history is, in the final instance, the production and reproduction of immediate life. This, again, is of a two-fold character: on the one side, the production of the means of existence, of food, clothing, and shelter and the tools necessary for that production; on the other side, the production of human beings themselves, the propagation of the species. The social organization under which people of a particular historical epoch live is determined by both kinds of production, by the stage of development of labor on the one hand and of the family on the other. (Engels 1977: 71–72)

This familiar quotation seems to recognize the shared social primacy of material production and biological/social reproduction. Actually, however, Marxists believed that the "mode of production" determined family life and the condition of women. The "kind of production" that occurred in the family was dependent on "labor." This belief made for several major flaws in Engels's account of the condition of women, flaws characteristic of traditional Marxism. I summarize here the essential points of a number of detailed feminist criticisms (Barrett 1980, 48–49, 131–32; Mitchell 1972; Sacks 1974).

First, Engels, like Marx, believed that capitalism would obliterate precapitalist social relations and saturate all aspects of society. This process would lead to the expulsion of women from the home—at least the vast majority of working-class women. Engels failed to see the many ways in which capitalism could benefit from a continuing sexual division of labor and sexist ideology. Female laborers could be paid little, and housewives would raise the next generation of workers at a low cost. Women could provide emotional support for alienated workers and help working-class men feel the power and authority denied them in the workplace. The patriarchal family could create emotional and moral bonds that would stifle political militancy and shelter women for participation in the reserve army of labor.

Second, Engels believed that the fundamental basis for women's inequality lay in their lack of property. The oppression of women, he claimed, arose with the creation of private property and would end with the socialization of property under socialism. Engels missed the power of gender relations to determine the condition of women. He did not see that without equality in the "domestic" sphere, women's access to public forms of property would be correspondingly limited. The traditional Marxist answer to women's oppression, resting on Engels's analysis, has been to get women into the public work force. As advanced capitalism and the bureaucratic state have shown, however, women may enter the work force in massive numbers and still lack equality. In all societies where women are active in the public work force, they still perform the vast majority of housework as well. And the public realm of work is itself shaped by gender relations: women find themselves in segregated, low-paying jobs; when new jobs arise and are filled by women, they are thereby devalued. Seen by others and themselves primarily as homemakers, caretakers of children and men, they remain disadvantaged in the public sphere.

Third, Engels's belief in the homogenizing effects of capitalism and the liberating effects of women's entry into the work force blinded him to conflicts of interest between working-class women and working-class men. He failed to see that one reason why women were oppressed, and would continue to be so under advanced capitalism, was that gender relations gave working-class men some powers and privileges over their wives, mothers, and daughters. He could not foresee that male working-class leadership (in trade unions, for example) would cooperate with the state in excluding or limiting women's participation in public labor; that the general oppression of women would be repeated by socialists; and that women therefore needed autonomous political organizations.

The Sex/Gender System

We must now turn to a somewhat more detailed account of how socialist-feminists moved beyond their criticisms of radical feminism and Marxism to positive theoretical contributions of their own. For my purposes, these contributions begin with the concept of a sex/gender system: the method by which a given society systematically transforms sexual differences and needs into gender-defined roles, practices, and institutions (Rubin 1975). There is a striking similarity between this concept and the traditional Marxist notion of "mode of production." "Mode of production" can be applied to all human societies. As biological, social, and rational creatures, humans interact with nature and each other to meet their material needs. The concept of a sex/gender system focuses on a different universal: the creation of gender in response to sexual, reproductive, and affective needs. The identification of universal structures of gender—structures in some ways comparable to the universal structures of class—was the major breakthrough of contemporary feminist theory, whether radical or socialist in character. The concept of a sex/gender system refers both to certain universal features of social life and to the concrete form those features take in different societies.[2] With this concept, feminists could describe both the specificity and the universality of male-female relations.

Much feminist research in the 1970s focused on the social structures that make up the sex/gender system (cf. Rosaldo and Lamphere 1974). Among the most important studies were those that found gender differences to be rooted in the division between public and domestic life, and the oppression of women to be a product of the social structures and ideology of domestic labor (Rosaldo 1974). It remains debatable how broadly to construe such labor, as well as to understand precisely what its relations are with the labor of the "public" sphere. Yet we can see how socialist-feminist theory identifies as crucial an aspect of social life given little attention by traditional Marxism. As there are class divisions and exploitation in the public realm, so the typical family is structured by gender domination and exploitation. By focusing on the social relations surrounding domestic labor and the division of society into public and private spheres, feminist theory created an analytic tool comparable to Marx's notion of the mode of production. In both cases a systematic allocation of roles in a sphere of necessary human activity constitutes a system of power, exploitation, and ideology. Also, as traditional and Western Marxism showed how the social relations of production influence consciousness and are supported by the family, so feminism shows how production and ideology are affected by relations between men and women.

The structural similarity between the mode of production and the sex/gender system has led many socialist-feminists to claim that gender is as socially primary as class. I argue (below) that this important claim can be fully understood only if it is integrated into my theory of three forms of social primacy. Before that argument can be made, however, it is necessary to discuss in detail the mutually reinforcing relations between patriarchy and capitalism.

The Family

Contemporary feminists have shown that to understand the sex/gender system it is necessary to have some account of the formation and reproduction of gender in the family. Socialist-feminists have built on these accounts, and extended the analysis to the mutually reinforcing relations between patriarchy and capitalism. This section focuses on how the family supports and reflects capitalism. Women's role in paid labor and the autonomy of male domination will be discussed in succeeding sections.

Under capitalism the family is shaped by a gender division of labor in the fulfillment of certain tasks. These tasks include the daily care of adults and children, consumption, reproduction, socialization, and emotional intimacy. The division of labor in the family accords moneymaking and authority to men, childcare, housework, and providing emotional closeness to women. Both partners are responsible for sexual satisfaction (not, however, in equal ways: women provide beauty and sexual responsiveness; men provide desire). In recent years this family form has been strained by the rise of single-parent families, increased acceptance of homosexual relationships, later ages of marriage and childbearing, the massive entry of women into the labor force, and feminist criticisms. In its broad outline, however, it remains the dominant family form, both ideologically and in reality, in advanced capitalist societies.[3] Why is this so?

The capitalist family is historically specific. A rigid division between public (paid) and private (household) labor could emerge only after capitalist commodification had dominated social life. During feudalism neither agricultural nor craft labor were rigidly sexually segregated; still, crucial distinctions between male and female labor did exist. The care of children was left to women, and the control of significant amounts of property (as opposed to peasant plots) to men. The political and ideological powers of the crown, the nobility, and the church were almost exclusively male. Since this society had little wage labor, its sex/gender system could not be based on the distinction between those who received wages and those who did not; rather, it was based on physical domination, religion, and the exclusion of women from public roles carrying social authority (Carroll 1976b; Hall 1980, 45–46; Kesler-Harris 1982; Tilly and Scott 1978, 46).

After an initially high concentration of female factory workers, industrial capitalism developed the family unit of the employed husband and the homebound wife. There have been exceptions to this rule: the use of adolescent girls and young women as cheap factory labor; the large (but temporary) entry of women into the industrial labor force during World War II and the dramatic postwar rise of women as service and clerical workers; a state welfare system to support single mothers. Despite these exceptions, women's participation in the world of public labor remains shorter, more inconsistent and much more poorly paid than that of men.[4] And married women find household labor, child care, and personal relations central to personal identity.

This particular form of the sex/gender system is extremely functional for capitalism: it helps form the industrial reserve army, provides for the inexpensive reproduction of labor power, encourages consumption, and supplies ideological and psychological support for capitalist social relations. Let us briefly examine on each of these points, leaving an account of the limitations of these functional arguments for the next section.

Women's social position makes them ideal candidates for the reserve army of labor, especially in the "secondary" labor market where jobs offer horizontal rather than vertical mobility; provide little protection, few benefits, and low pay; and require few skills. Concentrated in this secondary section, women are sharply differentiated from primary-sector workers; they are easy to manipulate, possess comparatively less interest in their fate as workers, and express little worker solidarity. Seen by society and themselves as having less direct connection to paid labor than do men, women can enter or leave rising or failing industries, and they can accept the lower salaries that lessen the costs of production and depress the salaries of skilled labor (Beechey 1978; Edwards 1979, 163–99).

Meeting needs that have never fully been provided for by commodity production, unpaid domestic labor serves three distinct purposes. First, at least some sectors of capitalism find it more profitable than socialized housework. The labor performed by housewives is unpaid, unrecognized as labor, and yet essential to the reproduction of the labor force. It allows labor power to be purchased below its value: that is, for less than if housewives were paid for their work. Second, however, household labor meets some emotional needs. If male workers had to purchase services equivalent to those of a traditional wife, they might not be satisfied even if they received higher wages in order to do so. Wives' services have an "emotional" as well as a physical value (Gardiner 1979, 185).[5] Consider that when fast-food restaurants advertise to replace domestic food preparation, they claim to "do it your way" and, indeed, "do it all for you." To be wife surrogates, they must provide love as well as hamburgers, caring along with the french fries. A housewife's labor is experienced as love and care, not simply "an expectation of service to the material needs of reproduction of labor power" (Malos 1980, 39–40). Third, privatized housework supports capitalist values. Isolated families breed individualism and competitiveness. Male domination in a family hierarchy supports acceptance of authoritarianism in society at large. The sexual division of labor contributes to the creation of a divided and politically weak working class.

Under capitalism the family not only reorganized social labor; it also created new psychological and ideological forms. Poster (1980, 140–96) argues that in the last five hundred years of European social life we can find at least four significantly different types of families. Poster distinguishes these forms primarily by variations in psychic relations among family members and in ties to the surrounding community, variations reflecting differences in the kind and extent of psychological intimacy. Only in the bourgeois family type—and the working-class family modeled after it—can the sustained intimacy and emotional interidentification characteristic of the modern family be found. The peasant family was deeply involved in the life of the surrounding village. The kin-extended aristocratic family was concerned mainly with preserving property, power, and position. By contrast, the "relations of the bourgeois family were regarded as beyond the province of society"; "the family was a private micro-world, a sanctum into whose hallowed chambers no outsider had a right of entry" (Poster: 170). Productive life was removed from the home, making the family a "place of close, warm, emotive relations" distinct from the brutal world of work. Men, dominant in that world, would be tended to in the home (171). This model of family life was adopted by the working classes as capitalism developed, making for "one of the unwritten aspects of the political success of bourgeois democracy" (196). The intense emotional bonds of the isolated family fit perfectly with capitalism's need for a mobile work force lacking class solidarity.

Bourgeois society also liberated individual energy as it smashed traditional forms of labor and culture. It was up to the home to take up the slack in constructing individual identity. Generally, the modern family is part of the rise of "affective individualism": an ideology and family structure designed to encourage intimate ties among family members, especially between husband and wife (Stone 1977). Affective individualism in the family went along with possessive individualism in the realm of property, laissez-faire capitalism in production, Lockean doctrines of the natural rights of the individual in political theory, and epistemological individualism in philosophy (Stone 1977, 161). In short, a capitalist economy created the individual entrepreneur and the "free laborer." Bourgeois ideology justified individualism in all forms of life. The modern family created the appropriate psychic structures.

These psychic structures involved the transfer of psychic interidentification from the community to the nation-state and the family. Religion, racism, and ethnicity partly inhibited this change (see Part IV), yet to a great extent the transformation—so necessary for capitalism—was made. Workers were not only alienated from the means of production but psychically and socially alienated from traditional forms of identity as well. Ties to place and community were severed or weakened. The psychic strains created by the obliteration of such connections were met largely by the affective individualism of the nuclear family.

The power felt by men in such a family is a substitute for the dependence and submission they experience in public life. The emotional security sought in the family replaces an enduring and stable communal existence. The freedom to order one's family life according to one's own desires compensates for the loss of an organic connection to traditional work. The enormous investment of love and trust in the family leads the child to internalize the parents' values. The result is an obedient, authority-oriented personality structure. Cathected around the parents during childhood, children exchange freedom for love. The fear of possible emotional rejection by the parents becomes an unconscious yearning to accept authority.

The politically conservatizing effects of all these factors should be clear. They have already been suggested in my discussion of Horkheimer and Reich. The compensations of power, security, and love offered by the family support capitalist social relations. Ideologies of masculinity and femininity —conditioning men to authoritarianism and self-denial, and women to submissiveness and nurturance—shape working-class consciousness and lock the modern family structure into place.[6] Two other factors are also relevant. First, the physical and emotional demands on the adults of a nuclear family often leave little time or energy for participation in political activity; this is especially true for women. Second, along with everything else, the nuclear family can provide love and satisfaction, feelings that seem to diminish the importance of public oppression.

The emotionally encompassing family to which we owe our primary loyalty runs counter to the collective consciousness necessary for mass political power. It may at times give rise to economistic action; or it may lead to militancy when women and men see a threat to the physical well-being of family members. But the privatized family inhibits our ability to conceive of society as a totality and engage in political action designed to alter that totality. Families that do support political resistance tend to be inserted into older-style communities shaped by race, ethnicity, or common work situation. These are communities in which the modern form of the family has failed to dominate. By contrast, working-class men (see, e.g., Sennett and Cobb 1973) may experience upward mobility for their families as in conflict with community (and, by implication, class) loyalty. Some contemporary feminists do claim that the family-based "feminine virtues" of nurturance, relatedness, compassion, and noncompetitiveness are antithetical to the current social order, but this assertion is embedded in a political framework committed to the dissolution of a sexist family structure that accords these virtues only to one sex.

Finally, the nuclear family is also highly adapted to the consumer-oriented needs of advanced monopoly capitalism. As Batya Weinbaum and Amy Bridges (1979) argue, the home is the "other side of the paycheck." Privatized housework requires the consumption of commodities many of which would not be needed if housework were socialized; it thus provides a barrier to that socialization. Not surprisingly, an ideology of high-consumption, labor-intensive housework was part of the growth of the contemporary family. Modern city dwellings—with running water, electricity, heating systems serving many families at once—made much traditional housework unnecessary (Rothman 1980, 15–18). However, women were not to benefit. To motivate consumption and fill the new "domestic void," there developed the demand for an increase in housework based in the image of the "educated Mother." While the expansion of capitalist commodity production was undermining the socially productive nature of home life, the domestic science movement denied the adequacy of traditional forms of child rearing and homemaking (Ehrenreich and English 1975; 1979). Women, it was now suggested, "had to be trained to the tasks of motherhood" (Rothman 1980, 97). The educated mother was above all dedicated to the proper patterns of consumption and the welfare of her children. However, when the mother so educated threatened to preempt the public power of male experts, women were returned to their "proper place." Issues of health care, child rearing, and interpersonal relations—supposedly the natural province of women's maternal instincts—were now presented as the property of (male or male-directed) experts (Ehrenreich and English 1979, 52–90, 165–242; Rothman 1980, 135–221).

Thus, as capitalism had to dominate and devalue the traditional worker, so modern patriarchal capitalism has dominated and devalued the housewife. As a result, the post–World War II mother was the endless consumer, the sometime sex object, and the sympathetic though clearly unprofessional ear constantly counseled—when serious emotional problem arose—to seek professional advice. Mandatory universal education, the state, and the television set dominated a family consciousness in which a mother's "expertise" was confined to cooking and overcoming "ring around the collar." With the economy dependent on multiplying false needs, a "knowledgeable, 'scientific' consumer" would be highly dangerous (Ehrenreich and English 1975, 36–37). Like the "degradation of labor" described by Harry Braverman (1974) and Richard Edwards (1979), the degradation of the housewife subjects her to a privatized, repetitive, tedious existence; she is made dependent on a world of commodities produced in a realm beyond her reach. The result is domestic labor without knowledge, service without insight, a degraded role reflected as much in the statistics on the depression of married women as it is in the convenient use of the term "housewife" as an American cultural symbol of ignorance and incompetence. A product of capitalism's transformation of the family, the modern housewife provides love and labor at little cost to the capitalist, caring for the next generation of laborers and providing the sexual and emotional "goods" that reproduce the male worker as a psychic being. Her contributions are unrewarded by pay or direct social security benefits. She tries desperately to fill the void of her family's life by an endless consumption that somehow never brings home quite the "right" product—the one that will, finally, make them all happy. Experiencing the emotional emptiness in her family's life as her fault, she often hides from the wife battering, incest, child abuse, or alcoholism that signal the hidden despair of modern American family life (Friedan 1968; Rubin 1976; Sidel 1978). Believing that the trouble is her fault, or at least her responsibility, she cannot overcome the bleak landscape and battered egos of advanced capitalism.[7]

Thus the modern family is functional for capitalism in many ways. As we shall now see, however, the family—like women's oppression within it—is sustained by gender as well as class domination. Also, women's oppression now encompasses public as well as private labor.

Public Patriarchy and Sex-Affective Production

"Capitalist development creates the places for a hierarchy of workers, but traditional [Marxism] . . . cannot tell us who will fill which places. Gender and racial hierarchies determine who fills the empty places" (Hartmann 1981b, 18).

The interests of working- and middle-class men interact with those of capitalists to determine women's place in the family and in paid labor. Not surprisingly, therefore, women's inequality occurs in the workplace as well as the home; patriarchy is public as well as private (Barrett 1980, 183; Hartmann 1979).[8] A description of women's oppression in the work force and unique exploitation in the home will help clarify the socialist-feminist concept of patriarchy.

Both men and women labored in the earliest capitalist enterprises. Since early capitalism depended on the putting-out system in which work was performed in the home there was no need for a rigid separation between public (paid) and private (unpaid) labor. Similarly, the early factory operatives in England included a remarkably high (over 50 percent) number of women. Rural Englishmen were in no hurry to enter the factories, preferring to send their wives and daughters (Marglin 1974, 98).

Thus the formation of modern sex roles included the retention and transformation of traditional male domination in the public world. Hartmann (1981b, 19–21) attributes this outcome to a "partnership of patriarchy and capital" and describes actions taken by labor unions in the nineteenth century to exclude women from occupational categories. Similarly, Rothman (1980, 163) shows that Progressive Era legislation that was supposedly designed to protect women actually compelled them "to remain in those occupations that were already filled with women." As a result, a labor market developed in which women were poorly paid, less skilled, and had less authority than men. Limiting women's participation in paid work necessarily involved the struggle of the working class for a "family wage" that would support a male worker and a dependent, homebound wife (McIntosh 1978). Women's subordinate position in the labor market then reinforced and was reinforced by their oppression in the family (Hartmann 1979, 217). Capitalist men and working-class men mutually determined that women would be confined to a dependent position in both the private and public realms.

What is women's systematic inequality in paid labor? First, women workers have been highly segregated. Jobs are frequently defined as exclusively or mainly female: secretaries, nurses, "salesgirls," "cleaning ladies," domestic servants, elementary school teachers, clerical workers are routinely women. Notice how each category calls to mind a male superior. Female nurses, teachers, and secretaries, for example, "require" male doctors, principals, and executives. These jobs also replicate many of the nurturing and care-giving functions that women traditionally play in the home.

Salaries and union protection for female jobs are, almost always, significantly lower than those for male jobs. Insofar as a form of work is considered "female," it is defined as unskilled and thereby devalued. This devaluation is partly the result of the fact that women tend to be less trained than men. Also, until recently, both men and women have viewed female paid labor as marginal to the economic life of the family and the personal identity of women. Typically, women have not organized to improve their position in the world of work, and this lack of organization reflects their relations to their husbands and fathers and to men organized in unions as well as their relations to capitalists. For instance, the prototypically female job categories of public school teacher, department store clerk, and typist-stenographer were created by recruiting middle-class women for jobs that demanded comparatively high skills (such as literacy) but offered little pay. Skilled men rejected the low pay; lower-class men (and women) lacked the requisite skills (Rothman 1980, 40–49). In this case *capitalism* benefited by paying low wages to skilled workers. But women could be exploited in this way because of their relation to *men*. Time after time, male workers have refused to coexist in the same labor market with women (Mitchell 1973, 249; West 1978, 248).

Of course, there has been a massive influx of women into the work force: at present 40 percent of the work force is female, and a high percentage of women—even those with small children—hold some kind of paid job. Yet women still earn from one-half to four-fifths of what men earn: they receive unequal pay for the same work and tend to be concentrated in the worst-paid jobs. Also, the higher the female participation in the labor force, the higher the percentage of part-time female laborers (Hartmann 1981a, 391–92). As long as women continue to bear the brunt of domestic labor, their participation in public labor will continue to be less than men's. While women are subordinate in the home, they are unlikely to organize successfully for equality with their husbands and fathers. Similarly, without equal access to jobs, income, and social power, women remain largely dependent on individual men or male-controlled social institutions and are thus largely confined to unequal positions within the family.

While capitalism benefits from women's workplace and household inequality, there is no strict economic necessity for capitalism to have evolved with patriarchy in all classes. One can imagine another scenario: gender distinctions between working-class men and women could diminish, child care and "housework" functions be integrated into a commodity system, while the wives of the bourgeoisie become nonworking "status symbols." Indeed, in the nineteenth century, a Victorian ethos of "frail" womanhood, combined with the intense drudgery performed by lower-class women, approximated this possibility.

Such a development is feasible in abstract economic terms, but it would not have been tolerated by working-class men. As those men organized against capital, they also sought to preserve power over "their" women.[9] Full equality for women at work would have undermined male power in the home. Simultaneously, an end to the domestic division of labor and power would have made women much less likely to accept inequality at the workplace or in any other social context. Clearly, then, women's dual inequalities—at home and at work—make full sense only when seen as connected. As capitalism developed, precapitalist male domination was *transformed* to meet the needs of a changed mode of production and *preserved* to maintain male power and privilege.

Capitalism evolved as a patriarchy because the interests of men of all classes had to be at least partially satisfied for capitalism to succeed. What were those male interests? "The material base upon which patriarchy rests most fundamentally is *men's control over women's labor power*. Men maintain this control by excluding women from access to some essential productive resources (for example, jobs that pay living wages) and by restricting women's sexuality [including reproductive functions]" (Hartmann 1981b, 15; my emphasis). The key to patriarchy is thus material relations that benefit men at the expense of women. There is no need to posit a male drive for power as the foundation for patriarchy any more than to assume a psychological lust for profit as the basis for a capitalist's exploitation of his workers. In both cases, exploitation is its own reward. At home and at work, men benefit at women's expense.

While Hartmann's position is of critical importance, it must be qualified in two ways. First, we must deepen our understanding of men's control of women's domestic labor. Conventionally, the exploiters' control over labor can be measured in terms of goods and services appropriated. In feudalism, this appropriation took the form of days of service, percentage of a crop, or enforced "taxes." Under capitalism it takes the form of surplus value. Female domestic labor also produces use values and services. Banks and governments compute the economic value of a housewife in terms of so many dishes washed, trips made to the store, meals cooked, and the like. However, there is also female "sex-affective" labor—especially childbearing, child rearing, and "the provision of nurturance, affection and sexual satisfaction"—which cannot be easily quantified (Ferguson 1979; Ferguson and Folbre 1981, 316–17; Greenspan 1983, 222–31). Besides child care, sex-affective "labor" includes establishing intimacy, dealing with feelings, and taking responsibility when personal relations go sour. To sustain the affective individualism so congenial to capitalism, women must perform sex-affective labor. The vast majority of men are incapable of doing this "labor of relatedness"—and in our heterosexual society most people would not accept this work from men in any case.

As opposed to other forms of oppression, women's exploitation in the family is possible only if exploiter and exploited share the most intimate of personal relations. In performing sex-affective labor, women produce "services" for men in a relation of unequal exchange. Men enjoy the emotionally intimate family at comparatively little physical or emotional cost to themselves. They have children without having to get up at night to diaper babies; family holiday meals without inviting people, shopping, cooking, or cleaning; someone to care for their emotional needs without having to make themselves emotionally vulnerable. This sex-affective exploitation is reproduced through socialization processes that tie the personal identity of both exploiter and exploited to gender. Gender identity—first learned and most fundamental to the adult personality—is conditioned around domination and service. Men control women's labor not like capitalists but in the most personal of ways. Women serve men, take care of them, and derive much of their sense of self from that service and caring.

Second, Hartmann's claim that men control women's labor power is complicated by class relations. A professional or managerial woman may control the labor of many men. No worker can gain power over capitalists, or economic power over other workers, and still remain a worker. While gender is crucial in determining social position, it is not—as class categories are—synonymous with social position.

Still, while sexism does not mean male domination of all women, it almost guarantees male superiority toward women in the same class. Even upper-class women are subject to violence against women, to oppressive norms of physical appearance and social behavior, and to generalized male control of female reproductive capacities—for example, in laws controlling abortion. (Consider a well-dressed, professional woman walking past a group of construction workers. Even if she is an executive of the corporation that owns this property, she is still subject to catcalls, veiled sexual threats, and the like.) Similarly, lower-class and ruling-class men share an ideologically structured power of status—men are taken as the model of "normal" humanity—based in countless cultural representations of male superiority.

The benefits conferred by patriarchy thus lead men of different economic classes to bond together "against" women. Trade unions and banks, churches and governments, leftist parties (see Chapter 15) and monopoly capitalist corporations all reflect and reinforce male power in manifold ways. Marxism's transformation will be incomplete as long as this fact is unrecognized. The left's long focus on class conflict and its blindness to male solidarity has led many socialist-feminists to condemn recent attempts to join Marxist and feminist theory in an "unhappy marriage," as male-dominated as those of the real world. It has, in fact, been one of the contributions of radical feminist literature to describe the ways in which male solidarity functions across class lines (cf. Chesler 1980). Since both groups enjoy power and privileges at women's expense, both working-class and capitalist men share an interest in maintaining male power: to exploit the sex-affective labor of their wives, and to maintain their superior position to female competition within their own classes.

Women's unequal position in paid labor and their exploitation in the sex-affective system indicate that contemporary capitalist society is shaped by more than one set of exploitative relations. Adding gender exploitation to our account of economic structure is essential to the transformation of Marxist theory. Without doing so, we cannot begin to explain women's social inequality, the structure of the family, or the most important impediment to the development of class consciousness: workers' emotional ties to male domination. Moreover, it is critical to see that patriarchy and capitalism do not govern separate spheres of social life. As we have seen, both patriarchy and capitalism shape the workplace and the family (Young 1981). Still, patriarchy and capitalism are distinct. The interests and actions of men as a group are not the same as those of capitalists (even though most capitalists are male). Adding gender to class will not produce one comprehensive social theory, and the theorists who try to describe capitalism and patriarchy as a unified system have failed. Like Wallerstein's description of both colonizing and colonized countries as capitalist, efforts to provide a unified account of capitalism and patriarchy inevitably end up describing a system with two very different causal principles. Wallerstein could not explain why different parts of the "same" capitalist system developed so differently; similarly, attempts to describe capitalism and patriarchy as one system typically appeal to different structural forces to explain different aspects of social life.[10] Most important, there is a tendency—about which I say more below—to appeal to the dynamic of capitalism to explain long-term changes in patriarchy. The difficulty of creating a unified theory stems from the fact that social life is shaped by overlapping, contradictory, and uncoordinated groups. A variety of types of exploitation and oppression—including those shaped by class, gender, ethnicity, and nationality—makes for a variety of social forces. If the fundamental forces shaping social life express the collective actions of groups, and the groups defined by capitalism and by patriarchy are overlapping but distinct, we should not expect to be able to provide a unified account of social life.

Gender, Historical Change, and Social Primacy

Socialist-feminists reject the essential thesis of historical materialism partly because they see that many aspects of women's social position are not explained by the public mode of production, and also because one of the political implications of the traditional analysis is that women's issues are subordinate to class issues. Driven by the dynamic of a lawlike economic system, the working class was (supposedly) to end all oppression, including sexism. Socialist-feminists correctly refuse any subordination of women's struggles to those of workers. Because virtually all men benefit from their domination of women, no male-dominated political movement will end women's oppression. And because sexism psychologically ties men and women to domination, the struggle against class power will be unsuccessful if patriarchy is retained.

Although the struggle against patriarchy is as politically significant as the struggle against capitalism, the social primacy of patriarchy and capitalism are not the same. Clarifying these issues requires a theoretical model that identifies the different forms of social primacy and their respective political implications. In essence, my position is that class relations, traditionally conceived, possess the first form of social primacy. As the cornerstone of the processes of socialization, however, gender relations are also socially primary. While these forms of primacy are distinct, it is crucial to recognize that they—along with the third form of primacy described in Part IV—are of equal importance.

In this section I develop this model in three ways. First, I argue for my account of the socially primary roles of class and gender. Second, I support my characterization of those roles by showing how long-term changes in gender are dependent on changes in the mode of production. Third, I offer a hypothesis as to why class relations and gender possess different forms of primacy.

The capitalist mode of production possesses the first form of social primacy because it determined past social change and creates the possibilities for a liberated future society. Only an analysis of the dynamic of capitalism can explain the most basic historical changes in patriarchy and other crucial social institutions. In its triumph, capitalism employed the structures of patriarchy, modifying those structures to support capitalist accumulation and social control. Since patriarchy reinforced capitalism, capitalism took a patriarchal shape. Thus capitalists rule in part by supporting and participating in the rule of men over women. Men rule women, in turn, by adapting patriarchy to the new form of social life imposed by capitalism. The first form of social primacy expressed in these interactions lies in the dynamic of economic class.

At the same time, the sex/gender system, as the core of the processes of socialization, possesses the second form of social primacy. The structures of socialization are socially primary because they sustain class domination by forming a population that finds it difficult to recognize or respond to its own oppression. Even as we transcend the material constraints that render class domination inevitable, and our economic system becomes increasingly strained, gender-based socialization still ties people to a social order based on domination.

Thus the social primacy of socialization processes derives partly from their relation to the goals of Marxist and feminist theory: overcoming human alienation and creating a classless and liberated society. The patriarchal socialization of human infants into "men" and "women" both reproduces women's specific oppression and supports other forms of domination. However, even though the essentially static structures of patriarchy are altered by the dialectic of an inherently dynamic capitalism, simply ending capitalism will not end patriarchy. A new form of socialization—one which eliminates our oppressive sex/gender system—must be created. If it is not, the rule of men over women will reproduce both itself and new forms of class domination.

It is critical to my argument concerning the respective social primacy of class and gender that changes in patriarchy are explained, most fundamentally, by the dynamic of capitalism. This claim is supported by the way socialist-feminist writers themselves often appeal to capitalism to explain alterations in women's social condition. Ferguson and Folbre (1981, 318), for example, wish to assert that labor involved in the sex-affective system "cannot be placed lower than other forms of labor in conceptual importance." Yet they provide no account of the different ways in which labor might be "important." When they attempt to explain changes in the sex-affective system, they must appeal to the effects of capitalism. Women's progressive liberation from much sex-affective work stems from the decline of fertility, "compressing the period of full-time motherhood into a relatively small portion of the life cycle." This decline, in turn, is a "virtually ubiquitous result of capitalist development" (1981, 323; my emphasis).[11] Using the dynamics of capitalist development to explain the most basic changes in the conditions of women is common in the writings of socialist-feminists. Such explanations support my assertion that while capitalism and patriarchy are of equal "conceptual importance," their social role is different.

When feminists do not appeal to capitalism to explain changes in patriarchy, the result is an ahistorical account of social life. This fate befalls Nancy Chodorow's psychologistic theory of the social primacy of mother-monopolized child care.[12] In outline, she claims that male power and sexist ideology—the gender personalities of authoritarian, competitive, aggressive, and emotionally detached men and submissive, relational, passive, and emotionally responsive women, and a militaristic, sexually repressive and hierarchical culture—are all rooted in a psychology acquired in early childhood. This psychology, in turn, reflects the universal fact that women care for infants and young children. For Chodorow, exclusively female mothering makes the individuation essential to ego development fundamentally different for boys and girls. The daughter's identity is based in her view of herself as like her mother. Sons, by contrast, become persons by becoming *unlike* their mothers; for them individuation and separation go together, thus requiring rigid ego boundaries and a critical sense of "difference" from others. Since women's separation is less complete, they need and are capable of much greater affective closeness than men. These needs and capacities reproduce women as sex-affective laborers, while men control the public realm. Further, the fact that men "mature" by escaping their mother's love and power contributes to male misogyny.

The work of Chodorow and other "mothering theorists" makes a crucial contribution to our understanding of how gender is essential to socialization and how socialization is socially primary. If we seek the roots of the failure of oppressed groups to rebel against an oppressive system, we must focus on the way their personalities are shaped. As I have suggested, these personalities are initially constructed around gender. The gendered subjects of class society learn the rules of domination and submission, the alternatives of rational competence or emotional closeness. Later, the powers of the capitalist, the foreman, the party bureaucrat, the general, the bishop, and the professor reinforce the models of relations learned in the home. Chodorow's work also helps explain why men, who dominate the working class, find the authoritarian and hierarchical capitalist (or bureaucratic state) societies compatible with their own personality structures. Moreover, the different personalities of men and women lead to a sex/gender system and a sexual division of labor that creates conflict of interests within the working class. Finally, women's attachment to mothering restricts their participation in the public sphere.

Despite its contributions, however, mothering theory fails when its authors represent it as socially primary in determining either female oppression or domination in general.[13] While there is an understandable attraction to positing early childhood experiences as crucial in the development of any given individual, this form of explanation fails for society as a whole. In general, early childhood experiences bear the stamp of an already existing social organization. Identifying with or separating from a female mothering figure is significant only in a society where gender distinctions carry great weight. Issues of closeness and distance, individuation and separation, are part of a system of power and valuation. Thus mothering theory presupposes rather than explains a male-dominated society. Women's emotional closeness could theoretically lead to social power based in female bonding, with competitive and isolated men subjected to the organized power of women.[14] This possibility is not realized because women's mothering is not the source or reproducer of patriarchy. Rather, it is one of patriarchy's aspects.

Equally important, mothering theory tends to depict mothering as a historical universal. Yet history reveals important differences in the mothering relation. In feudal Europe, high infant mortality and the practice of sending children to work in other homes from age seven on led to mother–child relations radically different from those that exist today. Similarly, male personality styles have varied throughout time. While male power and female mothering coexist in tribal, feudal, capitalist, Oriental, Western, black, white, Christian, and Jewish cultures, men are not uniformly emotionally detached, competitive, and instrumental in all of them.[15]

Finally, by positing mothering as a socially primary universal, the mothering theorists cannot explain why anything should undermine it. If we wish to explain the ways in which mothering has changed in the past and could change in the future, we cannot simply appeal to the personality structures produced by mothering. Chodorow acknowledges that family structure has changed in the last several centuries, and at times appeals to capitalism as the cause of that change. Yet she also (in Lorber et al. 1981, 503) wishes to use mothering as an explanation of some of the most salient characteristics of capitalism (for example, fetishism of commodities, excessive rationalism of technological thought). Unfortunately, she cannot have it both ways. Since mothers always mothered, how did ancient Greece escape a fetishism of commodities or India generate an antirationalist mysticism? Similarly, mothering theory suggests that women confine themselves to domestic labor because of the emotional effects of female mothering. This claim ignores, for instance, capitalism's shuttling of women in and out of the labor force to serve the interests of capitalists, the state, male-dominated labor unions, and their own husbands and fathers in ways that coexisted with and had little to do with the constancy of female mothering (Beechey 1978; Brown 1981; Hartmann 1979; McIntosh 1978; Rothman 1980, 42–62). As we saw in discussing the limitation of radical feminism, a theory based in the universality of patriarchy—in this case, the universality of female mothering—is necessarily unable to explain historical change. Female-monopolized mothering may well be an essential ingredient in the reproduction of gender, but it is not socially primary in the way the mode of production is.

The complex interaction of capitalism and patriarchy has become an object of investigation only recently. My attempt to build a new model of primacy based in part on the fruits of these investigations is necessarily tentative. Yet further support for my argument can be found if we pursue the question, How is it even possible to think that women are oppressed and should not be? Both the ideological-political and structural-economic answers to this question will be based on the effects of the rise of capitalism. Thus these answers will help confirm my claim that long-term historical change — the realm of the first form of social primacy — is dominated by the mode of production.

Let us take the ideological-political realm first. From the seventeenth century to the present, there have been remarkable similarities in each separate "outbreak" of feminism. In each case feminist consciousness developed after women participated in the political struggle of some other group. Three examples from books by feminist historians provide support for this claim. In the seventeenth and eighteenth centuries feminist preachers and ministers extended to women the developing ideology of natural reason, equal rights, and the importance of the individual's personal relation to God.

While impatient and radical thinkers challenged so many authorities, judged their betters, expected to be able to consent before being governed and even taught that all were equal, *women tentatively started to take some of these ideas to themselves.* . . . If the only criterion was individual conscience why couldn't women challenge their husbands' and fathers' right to instruct them in what to believe and their power to control how they behaved? (Rowbotham 1974, 23; my emphasis)

Elenor Flexner (1974) finds the origins of nineteenth-century American feminism in the participation of women in the abolitionist movement. These women developed a political understanding of slavery and, simultaneously, came to realize that most men in their movement believed that women's oppression was either "natural" or secondary to that of blacks.

Finally, Sara Evans shows how the women's liberation movement of the 1960s found its political inspiration in the civil rights movement and the New Left. Many of the women who were to form the first radical feminist groups spent the late 1950s and early 1960s working against racism or the Vietnam War. Some of the key political ideas and techniques of women's liberation, such as consciousness-raising groups and stress on personal transformation — can be found in embryonic form in these other movements. Early analyses of the women's liberation movement often employed terminology from other struggles. Women were compared to blacks in a feminist critique of the Student Nonviolent Coordinating Committee, and to victims of imperialism by women in Students for a Democratic Society (Evans 1980, 86–88, 190–92).

Of course, feminist movements have not only applied previously existing ideas; as feminism develops, it transforms its inspirations. These histories show, however, how each wave of feminism was stimulated by the oppressive sexism of movements that professed to pursue freedom, equal rights, and human liberation. The ideological forebear of all these movements was the demand for freedom and equality raised by the rising capitalist class in its struggle with the inherited privilege of the aristocracy. A democratic ideology of equality and freedom was a weapon in that struggle. The ideology of democracy originated in the bourgeoisie's attempt to reorder society according to the interests of capitalism. It continues to be essential to the Cold War in the present. This ideology is the stimulating reference point for the development of feminism in the religious enthusiasm of the Reformation, in abolitionism, or in resistance to contemporary sexist and authoritarian radical movements. Feminist ideology and politics have been triggered by the currents of class struggle as the legitimation for capitalist society is taken seriously by people who are supposed to be controlled by it. This trigger is necessary, perhaps, because one of the effects of patriarchy is to keep women from seeing themselves as political subjects —until, at least initially, they are stimulated to action by politically identifying themselves not as women but as members of some other group.

The structural-economic basis for the contemporary rise of feminism is the changing form of social labor. Early capitalism created the home as a private sphere; late capitalism is undermining some key aspects of the sexual division of labor. It has done so by commodifying the skills and products of housework; by cutting into the family wage so that increasing numbers of women have had to work for wages; and by professionalizing many traditionally female skills, from emotional support to midwifery (Currie, Dunn, and Fogarty 1980; Kessler-Harris 1982, 217–320). Patriarchy and capitalism are thus antagonistic as well as complementary. The more women must enter into the work force to directly contribute to the accumulation of surplus value, the less they can give to the sex-affective system. The more the state must contain economic and social contradictions by legally controlling previously "private" areas of life, the less the husband's word is law in his own house. The power of the husband is thus challenged by that of his wife's employer, by the state, and by his now at least semi-independent spouse. Also, the more women are driven into the work force, the less the ideology of women's inequality can be sustained. As more and more women earn money, just as men do, belief in the universality of their difference from men cannot be sustained. Finally, as women are thrust into the "public sphere" of wage labor, a "public" political identity for women and political alliances between women and men become possible (Brown 1981; Ferguson and Folbre 1981).

The two historical roots of feminism—an ideology of equality, and women's entry into the paid labor force—determine the dominant aspects of contemporary feminism: women's struggle for equality in personal life and for social power in the public realm. The ideologies and economic dynamic of capitalism, however, will not end patriarchy by themselves. As we have seen, women can enter the work force in a "feminized" way, and they can continue to be primarily responsible for sex-affective labor. As in the transition from feudalism to capitalism, women's inequality can be retained as it is transformed. The point, however, is that *it is the dynamic of capitalism* that has created the ideological-political and structural-economic preconditions for the overthrow of patriarchy. Because no equivalent claim can be sustained concerning the relation of patriarchy and capitalism, I accord the first form of social primacy to capitalism. *But since patriarchy is essential in reproducing class and gender power, equal and simultaneous political struggles against both capitalism and male domination are politically necessary.* Nor is it the case that we can understand the reproduction of capitalism simply in terms of the accumulation of capital. Rather, as Western Marxism and socialist-feminism have shown, the continuity of advanced capitalism rests on the reproduction of human beings compatible with it. This reproduction has as its core the reproduction of human beings as gendered.

Under what conditions can a form of oppression become a primary source of social change?

I believe that patriarchy has not been a historically determining force in the same way as capitalism, because men and women have not, by and large, struggled against each other as collective social agents until the comparatively recent past. Male power has been embodied in the church, the army, the state, and the labor union. This power maintained female oppression despite basic social changes, yet women's response to this power has generally *not* given rise to collective forms of struggle. The malleability of patriarchy to the demands of the economic structure can be explained by the absence of such struggle. Peasants and lords were the major collective agents of feudalism. Their class interests were expressed in the struggles between them. Along with a growing group of merchants, they determined the dynamism of feudal society and the transition to capitalism. Workers and capitalists have been the major collective agents of capitalism. Arguments designed to explain the dynamism of capitalism usually turn on the way the interests of these two classes have been expressed.

Historical change has not been determined by patriarchy because the groups defined by patriarchy have not, by and large, been organized as groups in conflict. Despite exceptions to this general rule—for instance, male displacement of women from the healing arts and other trades during the rise of capitalism—women have not tended to struggle collectively for sexual equality. Patriarchy has adapted to changes wrought by other social structures, and male rule over women has not given rise to dynamic struggles comparable to those between peasants and lords, or capitalists and workers.[16] Though women in precapitalist societies performed productive labor, their social position provided no basis for political struggle. Widespread resistance to women's oppression required the stimulus of capitalism's ideology of equality. Women's political action—food riots in response to rising grain prices in the seventeenth century, for example, and union struggles throughout capitalist development—rarely expressed, until the nineteenth century, a significant political movement of women *as women*.[17]

If one misunderstands this point, it is easy to confuse *conflicts of interest* between men and women with *political struggles* between them. Hartmann (1981a) suggests that the family is an arena of gender political struggle *because* women are exploited in it.[18] But though women and wage earners are both exploited, it is workers—not women—who have (at times) understood and resisted their oppression collectively. It is only when women build a lasting tradition of such collective experience that an *objective* conflict of interest can become a *subjective* situation of political struggle. Women's home life and sexual relationships do express political relationships. But these issues cannot be *politicized* until women's experiences in the public realm provide a basis for conscious resistance to their private oppression. Meanwhile, women tend to resist in isolated and often unconscious ways (cf. Greenspan 1983).

As we saw in the preceding section, feminists have argued that one cannot appeal solely to the interests of capitalism to explain the current gender division of labor. Men and male-dominated institutions controlled women's access to public labor and reshaped both families and personality structures to ensure continued male power. Yet because competing capitalists and antagonistic capitalists and workers act on their interests, the dynamic of capitalism has to a great extent been a product of class actions. Capitalists understand the exigencies of competition and the need to control workers. Workers (at least) struggle for higher wages, better working conditions, and political rights. The power of the capitalist class is vested in its control over the means of production and participation in and influence over the state and the cultural apparatus. The male-dominated working class embodies itself, however imperfectly, in ongoing labor unions and political parties. Patriarchy will be the source of its own historical dynamic only when women act collectively on the basis of their interests. We may speculate that the built-in biological interdependence of men and women obstructs a full-fledged gender "war" comparable to class, national, or racial struggle. However, the unforeseen scope of feminist struggle during the 1970s suggests that the future fate of the sex/gender system is an open—and potentially explosive—question.

Since the nineteenth century there have existed intermittent movements of women seeking to fulfill the interests of women as women. They have won legal rights for women; they have raised public consciousness concerning violence against women, sexual and emotional exploitation, the needs of women workers, and gay rights. However, feminism has not produced institutions sufficiently powerful and permanent to provide continuity for women's struggles. The situation of women will possess the power to shape historical change to the extent that women develop political and economic power comparable to that of the working class or the capitalist class. Whether or not contemporary feminism can accomplish this goal is unknown.

Political Change and Critical Theory

Traditional Marxism's simplistic social psychology claimed that a leftist political consciousness was a guaranteed outcome of capitalism's economic contradictions. Reflecting on political history and economic changes in the twentieth century, Western Marxism and socialist-feminism have rejected this consequence of the essential thesis of historical materialism. In so doing, they necessarily rejected traditional Marxism's view of the nature of political change and the role of critical theory. Two central points have emerged. First, a truly liberating political movement can only be the outcome of the development of an awakened subjectivity: the "class consciousness" of Lukács or Reich, the hegemony of Gramsci, the consciousness-raising of women's liberation. Second, theory is not the description of mechanical social processes and objective social structures. While it must describe social regularities, it also necessarily reflects the subjectivity of the theorist. What are some of feminism's contributions to these two interdependent points?

Male descriptions of the revolutionary process usually focus on justice and power. Women are socialized to perform sex-affective labor and thus be sensitive to their own and others' needs and feelings. They are therefore better able and more likely to stress the subjective transformations that lead them to political consciousness. For many women, the key to revolutionary change is the way people come to understand their oppression in the most personal of terms. Moreover, feminist writers do not simply stress the subjectivity of politicized agents in the abstract. Rather, they describe their own subjectivity. The autobiographical reflection of the theorists becomes part of revolutionary theory.

Feminist self-reflection is an example of how political resistance grows when an oppressed group comes to know itself in terms of its own experience. "The vast mass of human beings have always been mainly invisible to themselves while a tiny minority have exhausted themselves in the isolations of their own reflections. Every mass political movement of the oppressed necessarily brings its own vision of itself into sight" (Rowbotham 1973, 27).

One reason the masses of people cannot see themselves is that they do not experience themselves as agents. Miriam Greenspan (1983, 161–231) describes what she calls the "male women": that is, the woman who experiences her own life through the prism of male experience and male categories. Rowbotham (1973, 40) states that she had learned to see herself through the eyes of men: "I had yet to understand the extent to which I identified with men, used their eyes. I was really sliced in two. Half of me was like a man surveying the passive half of me as a woman-thing."

If women are to experience agency, they must begin by understanding their lives in terms appropriate to their own needs and interests rather than to those of their oppressors. Only if their understanding of themselves is transformed in this way will their lives cease to be a constant accommodation to terms set elsewhere. The first step in this process, feminist writings show, is to stop using the oppressor's categories and valuations and thus overcome the split that Rowbotham describes. Recent feminism has, for instance, reevaluated the aspects of women's lives and experiences that sexism devalues. It has shown the critical role of women's domestic labor; it has argued that an "ethic of sharing, cooperation, and collective involvement" derived from sex-affective labor contributes to women's "potential strength as bearers of a radical culture" (Ferguson and Folbre 1981, 329);[19] thus, instead of accepting the male devaluation of women's socialized capacities, it has represented these capacities as valuable.

This process has been two-sided. On the one hand, as countless reports indicate, women came to see that what they had experienced as their private pain was in fact something they shared with women as a group. Such vision enables oppressed people, under conditions of political ferment, to see through the categories that have been imposed on them and allows for the beginnings of radical *collective* action. On the other hand, coming to understand oneself as oppressed and as potentially free requires an intense *individual* transformation: an awakening capacity to overcome the personal limitations imposed by sexism and change the social structures that imposed them. Radical political action, in feminist visions, greatly depends on the achievement of self-knowledge. Self-knowledge was essential to transforming women into political subjects who no longer experience their subjectivity as an extension of the demands and fantasies of men. This form of knowledge is surely an aspect of the knowledge of "totality" described by Lukács, yet it required a feminist analysis to show its full relevance to political theory.[20] We may extend women's experience to suggest that a politically liberating resolution of the contradictions of capitalist society requires that those it oppresses become collective political agents. Such a political development, in turn, requires that each group come to know and challenge its oppression both personally and collectively.

As Perry Anderson (1980) has pointed out, only in the last few centuries has collective political resistance by an oppressed group taken the form of self-conscious attempts to transform society as a whole. Feminists have shown that the consciousness guiding such a group has two aspects: objective knowledge of the structures of history; subjective awareness of the source of motivation to change those structures. Recent feminist theory has proved the necessity of integrating these two aspects of revolutionary consciousness.

What does this tell us about how a transformed Marxism must view the role of Marxist theory? In a male-dominated, scientistic culture, revolutionary theory and strategy will be conceived of in male terms. Consequently, traditional Marxism isolated and rejected subjectivity. The personal involvement of the theorists was considered a distorting rather than an essential factor in revolutionary theory. Social change was seen as a product of a necessary and impersonal process. Western Marxists improved on the traditional view by stressing how the transformed beliefs of the working class must derive from the dialectic of the immediate experience of that class. Yet these writers showed little realization that the theorists and leaders of revolutionary movements are themselves people with "immediate experience." Western Marxism's blindness to gender accompanied an unfortunate longing for the "male" authority of positivism.

The weaknesses of traditional and Western Marxism are thus indications of their sexism. They represent as rational, objective, and necessary a number of characteristics that are culturally male. Unfortunately, both traditional and Western Marxist theorists have avoided self-reflection, seeming to believe that their ideas, as opposed to those of the masses, come from "pure thought" (Rowbotham, Segal, and Wainwright 1979, 115). Yet people change politically, feminism has taught us, because they have come to understand their own lives in new ways. Like other people, theorists must connect their individual subjectivity to a collective movement and see how the biographical features of that process shape the content of their theory. The beliefs of intellectuals come not only from research and reflection but also from their personal experience of work, sexuality, family, creativity, and their own bodies.

Clearly, it will do no good to *substitute* personal experience for sophisticated theory. The task is to join them. Our goal is to transcend the sexist ideology that separates feeling and thought, the personal and the objective, female and male. What is required is a consciousness that is both Historical and Subjective, both an accurate understanding of the reality of social life and a personal understanding and self-transformation of one's habits, needs, hopes, and fears. Speaking of the women's movement, but in terms applicable to all aspects of the struggle for socialism, Rowbotham (1979, 129) writes:

We can recognize and comprehend intellectually without wanting something to change. We can be opposed to hierarchy and elitism and yet feel superior. We can oppose men's control politically and then feel deserted when it is not asserted in our own lives. We can resist being treated as an object and yet still want to be desired in this way.

This analysis could be extended. We might oppose the pretensions of a scientistic Marxism and replace them with the pretensions of a Hegelian one. We might oppose the power of capitalists and yet seek another sort of power over people in our political group. We might hate the capitalist class and yet also be unable to mount active resistance because we hate ourselves and view our friends or fellow workers as victims.

The alienations of thought and feeling, historical knowledge and self-awareness, power and sensitivity, the expert and the mass, male and female have been reproduced in Marxist theory. Western Marxists tried to overcome them, but their attempt was incomplete, partly because they failed to comprehend how their own theorizing was distorted by masculine ideology. Responding to the oppression of women, socialist-feminist theorists have overcome this limitation. They have presented a model in which subjective knowledge and the transformation of the self are combined with a structural account of social life.

This focus on the social primacy of the forces that socialize us into willing objects for oppression indicates that we must resocialize ourselves if oppression is to be ended. The need for resocialization starts first with the recognition of the effects of the pattern of socialization we have undergone and continues to a collective transformation of our beliefs, values, and personalities. If that transformation can be achieved, there is some hope that oppression can be fundamentally lessened. However, experiencing and resisting our own oppression are necessary, not sufficient, conditions for liberating social change. It is also necessary to challenge and overthrow the organized power of the ruling groups and to do so in alliance with groups whose socialization, experience, and oppression are different from our own. These tasks will be the subjects of Part IV.

10

Socialization and Political Power: The Dominated Self

THE LAST TWO CHAPTERS SHOWED HOW MARXIST THEORY HAS BEEN TRANS-
formed to recognize the social primacy of socialization. Western Marxists
and feminists have stressed the critical role of class consciousness and of
the gender-based socialization processes which shaped that consciousness.
In this chapter I examine another dimension of the primacy of socialization, one to which other authors have given comparatively little attention.
Accordingly, I am not summarizing others' work here but—I believe—
adding a new dimension to the discussion. My focus is on the way the
socialization processes of mass culture help to make most people incapable
of challenging existing social authorities.

Legitimation and Selfhood

With the elimination of the autonomous economy, social life is increasingly conceptualized as something that can be rationally ordered. As capitalism matures, consequently, the ruled must believe that social authorities
direct that ordering process justly. While coercion is at times instrumental
in defending ruling-class power, capitalist society does not typically depend
on it. Also, as a numerical minority, the ruling class can act coercively
only with the aid of the ruled. Thus continued capitalist power greatly
depends on the way the working class sees capitalist social relations and
the state as legitimate.

Marxist theorists have described the legitimation of advanced capitalism as resting on the modern ideologies of democracy and science and
on the co-opted traditional ones of religion and patriarchy. Capitalism, it is
suggested, is sustained by the essentially cognitive content of these ideologies: for instance, beliefs concerning equal opportunity, the role of democ-

153

racy, or women's obligations to their husbands. Alternatively, Habermas
(1975), among others, emphasizes how the value orientation of "civil privatism" stresses high interest in career achievement, family life, and personal
consumption at the expense of participation in political or social life (see
Wolfe 1977, 300).

Cognitive acceptance and depoliticized consumption are indeed essential in maintaining a population compatible with advanced capitalism.
Given the attention they have received, however, they are not my concern
here. Focusing on the United States, I want to show instead how social
authority is sustained by a particular form of *selfhood*; that is, a characteristic set of feelings and experiences that limit our capacity to act politically. The concept of selfhood I employ here presupposes that human action
must be understood as expressing the beliefs, attitudes, and experiences of
agents. Those beliefs, attitudes, and experiences, in turn, are essentially
shaped by two factors: the fit between how we experience ourselves and
how we are represented in the public or intersubjective world; and the
degree to which our actions are able to influence both our experience and
the way it is represented. Selfhood is constituted by the interplay of inter-
nality and externality: the way we objectify ourselves (including the way
we relate to others) and the way we experience and feel about that ob-
jectification.

In stressing a characteristic form of the self, I am in a sense reversing
the direction of most discussions of legitimation. Such discussions usually
focus on what members of a given society or class *believe* about the *state*
or the *economy*. My concern, rather, is with what members of a given
society or class *feel* about *themselves*. I stress this point because I believe
that the preservation of social authority requires that the ruled both accept
the legitimacy of existing authorities *and* lack the capacity for popular
power. Such an analysis is not necessary for precapitalist societies, since
their political organization is not based in the (supposed) right of every
citizen to participate in the political process. Selfhood in advanced capitalism supports the various cognitive and value orientations of legitimacy. It
also sustains social authority even when people's values and beliefs might
lead them to challenge the powers-that-be.[1]

The Dominated Self

Two concepts from Hegel (1967) will help convey what I wish to say
about how the self is dominated in contemporary society. In Hegel's description of the "Master-Slave" relation, the "Master" gets his sense of self
and social position by coercing the obedience of the "Slave"—who sees *his*

labor appropriated by another and his own identity lost in the relation. For Hegel, however, the Slave comes to realize that his "slavishness" makes possible the Master's sense of self. The Slave's obedience and labor—that is, his action—are, in Hegel's phrase, the "truth" of the Master's seeming (but false) self-sufficiency. It is just such a transformation of the "slaves" that has been arrested under advanced capitalism. We do not find the direct and personal relations of Master and Slave; rather, there are the impersonal, bureaucratized relations of mass society—or atomized individuals facing mass-produced images. More important, the oppressed in contemporary capitalist society seem almost permanently blocked from experiencing their lives as forms of action, and thus from seeing the manner in which their action constitutes the "hidden truth" that supports social authority. This blockage produces a self-consciousness that can be understood with the help of another Hegelian concept: the "unhappy consciousness." An unhappy consciousness alternates between its awareness that a yearned-for goal is unrealizable and a fantasized realization of that goal that is haunted by suppressed knowledge of actual failure. Hegel used the concept to refer to certain forms of spirituality; I believe that it has relevance also to contemporary mass society. Specifically, I believe that obedience to social authority—remaining in the "slave" relation—is supported by a society-wide unhappy consciousness.

In the contemporary encounter between rulers and ruled, says Richard Sennett (1981, 154, 26), "Personal authority is not based simply on abstract principles of right . . . the legitimacy of personal authority arises from a perception of differences in strength. The authority conveys, the subject perceives, that there is therefore something unattainable in the character of authority." Even when authorities are subject to criticism, "these powers also translate into images of human strength: of authorities who are assured, judge as superiors, exert moral discipline and inspire fear." In this era of frequently exposed governmental and corporate corruption and incompetence, Sennett is making a crucial point. Though we feel authority to be illegitimate, we still tie ourselves to it. We act in a rebelliousness originating in the desire to displease authority, rather than out of our own freely generated motivations. Or we complain continually about authority but require its existence as the scapegoat for all that is wrong in our lives. Or we use the authority as a kind of negative model: if only we had authorities who were the opposite of what we in fact have, all problems would vanish.

Sennett explains these tendencies as products of our desire to affix personal responsibility for pains caused by an impersonal capitalist market.[2] While there may be some truth in this reasoning, he ignores the possibility that we might take control of those impersonal forces and use them in our own interests. Capitalism created not only the market but also ideologies of individuality and political freedom. How then is freedom made to coexist with powerlessness? Why do we tolerate delegitimized authorities when we might constitute legitimate ones ourselves?

Part of the answer lies in the creation of the dominated self. The dominated self is an unhappy consciousness which, in its unhappiness, requires the "support" of social authority, even when that authority inspires a strong sense of illegitimacy. The dominated self of advanced capitalism is not defined by particular beliefs or values; indeed, contemporary capitalist hegemony is maintained despite significant shifts in the conscious beliefs of the general population concerning crucial political and economic issues. Rather, the dominated self is constructed around a fundamental lack, a sense of inadequacy and unreality.[3] A self that is felt as unreal, absent, or lacking is incapable of rational and powerful action, and so such a self sustains social authority even when that authority seems undemocratic and inexpert. Thus a critique of the powers-that-be is all too frequently joined with political passivity rather than with militant mass movements. Or, when the bonds of social authority are weakened, the action of the oppressed takes the form of a desperate search for a selfhood felt to be unachievable.

Let us take, for example, the media. In advanced capitalism, we consume a never-ending stream of images of human beings. These images purport to represent us but are unrecognizable. We are everywhere and always confronted by images of ourselves that represent not us but some other selves that are not us. The result is a permanent sense of unreality in our own lives: a permanent discrepancy between what we know ourselves to be and what we are represented to be, a discrepancy in which we persistently fail to be what we "are." What we are, again, *is not*—for we know that we are not those figures on the television or movie screen. What we are not, *is*: the interesting, beautiful, seductive images of mass culture have a reality that preempts our own shabby, boring, tired existence. In this complex sense, the media, like the state and the doctor, serve as authority figures. Their authority derives from the compelling power of the images they produce—just as the authority of the medieval church derived from the size of its cathedrals.

The media tell us who we are and who we should be. Our persistent inability to follow that direction results in an often unconscious sense of our own unreality and failure. As men, for instance, we are not those handsome, athletic, fun-loving, warm-hearted guys playing their hearts out for a Michelob Light. We do not have such good friends, after all, nor are we so athletic or good-looking. By contrast to them we are failures—in our relationships, our bodies, our lives. All we can do, at the next touch-football game, is *pretend* that we are they—and suppress to the level of unconsciousness the nagging sense of unreality that inevitably accompanies the attempt. As women, we know that we are not those beautiful, well-dressed, perfectly put-together persons meeting handsome, successful men at expensive restaurants; or shifting with ease from career woman (by day) to seductress (by night); or possessing, along with two children, the figure of a seventeen-year-old model. All of us sense that our family holidays never move with the satisfaction and perfect love of the ones in Hallmark ads. And each time a Christmas or a Thanksgiving family event occurs, there is, again, that persistent sense that it is not what it should be.

The general effect is a demand, by media-as-authority, that we be something we are not. And this includes that most insidious of demands: that we feel something we do not feel.[4] The images of mass culture do not only represent externalities—looks, money, accomplishments; the attention of beautiful women, handsome men, and doting families. They also represent certain interiorities—happiness, fulfillment, love, good humor, calm, sexual satisfaction. We face representations of ourselves that direct us to emotional states we are incapable of feeling. Betty Friedan (1968) described this situation—in regard to the frustration and depression of middle-class women of the 1950s—as "the problem that has no name." Certain women supposedly possessed everything that was guaranteed to make them fulfilled. Instead of fulfillment, they felt a profound sense of emptiness.

These reflections suggest that culture does not only tell people what to do or what authorities to obey; it also represents us to ourselves. A mass culture that persistently tells us we are something we are not induces a sort of cultural schizophrenia. Our persistent attempt to be what we are not—or to believe we are what we know we are not—can only create a numbing sense of personal unreality. Such an unhappy consciousness is incompatible with coherent, organized, and effective political action because it is incompatible with the taking of authority. Thus support for authority, even when that authority is considered illegitimate, becomes more comprehensible. An unreal self cannot provide direction for itself. Without authority, it is lost.

Another source of the dominated self involves the relations between the media and the state. The ideology of democracy requires that the government seem to combine delegated authority and expertise, and that there be a free press, academic freedom, and the like. These institutions allow much of public life to become a series of crises requiring public attention and redress by authority: a Three Mile Island accident, a public building that falls apart a few years after it is built, a delay in natural gas shipments during the winter, a catastrophic rise in gasoline prices. At such times the media generate an enormous hue and cry. News conferences are held; television "specials" give analysis and opinion; radio talk shows hold discussions through the night; popular movies may be made on the topic. The fear and anger of the general population are represented for that population through images of public concern. Media-as-authority promise action to redress wrongs, solve problems and restore public safety. Experts-as-authority provide analyses and devise programs.

The social function of these processes is to lead the general population to believe that the authorities are willing and able to handle the particular problem. Often, however, no really significant action need ever be taken. By the time the blue-ribbon commissions and governmental inquiries are concluded, the attention of the general population is focused on another "crisis" with *its* press conferences, television specials, and government statements. National attention was glued to the Three Mile Island plant during the incident and immediately afterward, but how many people noticed the issuing of the presidential commission's report a year later? How many people know what was in the report, or whether its recommendations were implemented?

In these cases, the general population is led to feel that the authorities, functioning on the basis of a popular mandate and scientific expertise, are dealing with a crucial social problem. yet the speed and intensity with which public attention is focused on and then shifted away from social problems leads to an inability to keep track of the concrete relation between "public" outcry and public reality. All that is known is that nuclear power plants continue to have accidents; public contracting in Massachusetts continues to produce shoddy buildings at exorbitant costs; and energy continues to be controlled by oligopolies for private profit. The painful discrepancy between promise and fulfillment, the supposed capacity and interest of government and experts, and the actual inability and lack of desire to do anything, creates a widespread and numbing sense of *political* unreality. The manipulation of political issues furthers the increased political passivity of a general population in the face of a social order that seems, legally and ideologically, to support political activity. The belief that authority is subject to public scrutiny and responsive to crises coexists with the sense that nothing is really changing and that we are still getting screwed. Price-gouging corporations are widely criticized, crooked politicians removed from office, demonstrations mounted, a rash of muckraking books published. Yet little changes.

There is a relation between the unreality of our image of the public world of politics and the private world of consumption and feelings. Our exclusion from active participation and collective control of the public realm is "justified" by the (illusory) rewards of the private. Depoliticization is rationalized by material wealth and personal freedom to consume, to choose a "lifestyle," to express heterodox opinions, and to form and dissolve personal relationships. Because a democratic ideology is combined with mass powerlessness in the worlds of work and politics, too much is loaded onto the family, fashion, hobbies, the latest VCR, mobile home, lace underwear, or therapy group. Because consumerism and personal relationships cannot replace a fulfilling involvement in social and productive life, mass culture must offer highly distorted possibilities of what consumption and personal relationships can do for us. Commodities and "lifestyles" must be represented as offering fulfillment in such a compelling and convincing way that their failure to do so will be internalized as our own. And it is not foolishness or stupidity that leads us to take these images so seriously. It is the fact that real needs are manipulated into false hopes.[5] Our needs for sexuality, love, community, an interesting life, family respect, and self-respect are transformed by the ubiquitous images of an unattainable reality into the sense that our sexuality, family, and personal lives are unreal. And it is this mechanism that sustains social authorities no longer believed to be legitimate.

The same mechanism contributes to the disunity of the oppressed, a psychic disunity that correlates to the fragmenting effects of labor segmentation and racial or gender antagonisms. In this psychic disunity we live out our lives isolated by the distorted images of our own inadequacy, or we are joined in a false unity that only reproduces our isolation.

We may utilize here Sartre's notion of a "series." Sartre (1976, 25) takes as an example of a series a group of people waiting for a bus. The unity of this group is their common relation to something outside of themselves: the absent bus and the hope that it will get them to work on time. No internal connections are forged within this group; indeed, each member is a threat to the others—a threat that the line is too long and that there will not be enough seats. The unity of millions of people desiring the same (unattainable) sex symbol on a television program or cheering the same athletic team possesses a similar falsity. The sexuality of the film star and the triumph of the victorious team are "for us," yet will never be ours. Our physical desire is awakened at the same time that we know it cannot be fulfilled—except in fantasy. Likewise, our rejoicing over "our" team's victory celebrates an action that is not taken by us and which will leave our lives exactly as they were before. The isolation of a fantasized desire shared by millions corresponds to the false solidarity of a meaningless triumph. In both cases real action is excluded. Surrogate action is all that remains: sex in which the Other is experienced is a fantasy; emotional responses to triumphs and failures of another.[6]

The size and complexity of modern mass culture means that the fore-going analysis needs to be extended. We require an account, for example, of the mass consumption of simulated tragedy in the world of soap operas; or the use of intergenerational relations as substitutes for political ones. We also need to understand the compatibility and tension between modern mass culture and the traditional cultures of religion and community. Most important, it is necessary to see how the totality of culture, despite its reproduction of social relations through the dominated self, may at times come into conflict with the social order.

Here, however, the major point is the manner in which the dominated self can coexist with a variety of ideologies and cultural norms. It makes little difference what people believe, think to be "right," or value if they are incapable of decisive, collective action. This point is crucial, for—just like pop music and women's fashions—much of the cognitive content of ide-ology is subject to rapid transformation. Whatever the images of success and adequacy, they must be inaccessible. As Greenspan (1983) has argued, for instance, the transition from the feminine mystique of the 1950s to the superwoman (career, motherhood, and sexuality combined) of the late 1970s leaves women feeling inadequate when they cannot live up to this new unrealizable ideal. Similarly, a "Father Knows Best" 1950s suburban family (white, middle-class, comfortable, "funny," and loving) no more matches the reality of most families than does the two-career, high-con-sumption, childless yuppie couple of the 1980s. Finally, the dominated self is compatible with certain fundamental changes in the locus of sexual re-pression and cultural images of fatherhood, family, and work. It was out of a particular configuration of these that Reich and the Frankfurt School developed their explanations of authoritarianism. Yet social authority re-mains, even while the cultural changes of the past fifty years have rendered much of their analysis somewhat obsolete. Puritan-style repression no longer links sexuality and social authority.

The dominated self, whatever particular thoughts or beliefs it possesses, maintains its general sense of unreality. And as an unreal self, it neces-sarily turns to the greater reality of social authorities as sources of strength, control, and direction—even when it possesses independent doubts or cri-ticisms of those authorities. It will not rely on itself—or on others like it. Unity and action become impossible.

Criticisms and Responses

Some criticisms might be made of this analysis. If I am attempting to describe the "psychology of oppression," why have I chosen to describe the effects of structures or situations that seem so nearly universal? An upper-class, suburban white woman, after all, may be as distant from images of seductive, beautiful femininity as a black welfare mother. A corporate executive may enjoy less male comaraderie than the workers he exploits. Persecuted minorities may often have as much or more family warmth than members of the ruling class. Yet in each of these pairs, the former possess privileges and, in some cases, power at the latter's expense.

In fact, it might be argued, the structures of oppression are not based in a widespread, nearly universal "dominated self," an atomized relation to a generalized condition. Rather, they are rooted in specific institutional and personal inequalities. To understand the psychology of oppression, then, would be to understand how taking a subordinate position affects the oppressed. For every "have not" felt by the oppressed, there is a corresponding "have" of the possessor group. Women's fear of male violence corresponds to a sense of power held by men. Working-class poverty corresponds to capitalist wealth. The high unemployment rate of blacks makes possible a lower one among whites.

Finally, someone could suggest, while some of the "Master-Slave" relations of contemporary society are impersonal, many are not. As I have already argued in Chapter 9, a significant part of male–female oppression is defined by personal relations. The psychology of oppression is operative in encounters between workers and managers, secretaries and their bosses, ordinary citizens and politicians, nurses or patients and doctors, students and teachers. The solution is, therefore, that the oppressed come to a personal and political realization of the true nature of their relation to their oppressors.

These criticisms, I believe, deepen rather than contradict my analysis. First, consider the sense of personal unreality conveyed by mass culture's images. Different types of oppression can be defined partly by reference to the degree to which people cannot find their lives represented by the culture in which they live. Just as different groups may have unequal access to material wealth, so they may have unequal access to the "cultural wealth" of seeing a reflection of their lives in the surrounding public space. Despite the underlying unreality of most of the images of popular culture, it is clear that certain groups are closer to those images than others. White, upper-class, gentile, nonhandicapped heterosexuals see themselves in these images in ways that black, Jewish, homosexual, or handicapped people cannot. Media-as-authority direct us to live a certain life, engage in certain activities, look a certain way. The closer one is to those images, the less one feels that devastating sense of unreality described above.

Similarly, media-as-authority enjoin us to have certain kinds of feelings. For instance, motherhood is represented as a blissful state in which perfect children play in clean (or soon to be clean) clothes, well protected by a totally devoted woman. Despite the unreality of this image, certain women can clearly find aspects of it easier in their lives than can others. A professional woman married to a husband somewhat touched by feminist ideals, with adequate income for quality day care and the best medical attention, will—all other things being equal—find motherhood less frustrating than will a welfare mother.

We may generalize this point by saying that an essential aspect of the oppression of various groups in our society is their disenfranchisement from the mass culture that surrounds them. Social authority is protected and reproduced by excluding certain groups from cultural and psychic representation and thus crippling their capacity to feel themselves as real.

If my analysis is correct, we would expect to see struggles against oppression include attempts by the oppressed to represent their own reality. And, in fact, we do. From the Harlem Renaissance and Black Nationalist movements of the 1920s to the "Black is Beautiful" slogan of the 1960s, politicized blacks have struggled for cultural self-representation. Contemporary feminists have transformed cultural representations of women and developed "woman-oriented" scholarship, music, and spiritual practices. Examples from sources as disparate as the pre–World War I German Social Democratic Party and Allende's Chile could also be offered.

Similarly, if my analysis is correct, we should see mass culture responding to upsurges among the oppressed by a process of co-optation. In this process the demands and concerns of the oppressed are "deflected": situation comedies about blacks or charming Hispanic-American junkmen, male homosexuals on soap operas, black women newscasters. In each case, the demand of the oppressed—that, for instance, the reality of living as a black in a racist society be recognized—is both "accepted" and shown to be compatible with the existing order. If those blacks on television can adapt, why can't I? If Laverne and Shirley, two working-class "girls" who live together, have such comaraderie and good humour, why can't the rest of us? If this or that individual black or woman or Hispanic has "made it" as anchorperson or executive, my failure must be due to personal limitations (cf. Sennett and Cobb 1973). In each case, cultural self-representation is thwarted and the reality of the experiences of oppression obscured.

Moving to my second example of a source of the dominated self, we may note that just as all groups are not equally alienated from mass culture, so they are not all equally alienated from political processes. Not all see their fears and hopes manipulated and frustrated. To take an extreme instance, we might compare the political responses to an urban fiscal crisis of a corporate executive and an unemployed auto worker. The unemployed auto worker is by and large a spectator, a consumer of the news bulletins and statements by government officials, bank presidents, and bureaucratic union leaders. Meanwhile, his services will suffer the most. He may lack the education to understand either the deeper roots of the fiscal crisis or the terminology of the various alternative proposals for curing it. At any rate, he knows that the effort needed to understand is not well spent. Since he has no input into these decisions, he will be better off looking for a job, fixing his house, or watching a baseball game at a bar. The corporate executive, by contrast, is financially cushioned against a rise in gas prices or layoffs of public school teachers. By training and temperament, he is capable of at least a superficial understanding of a fiscal crisis, alternative proposals to meet it, and the complicated institutions called on to act. He may know some of the bankers, politicians, or experts involved; in any event, he moves in the same social circles.

It is obvious that unemployed auto workers and corporate executives possess unequal social authority, and that the political process in advanced capitalist society includes one and excludes the other. It is less obvious, however, that these differences are not limited to income or social position. What the corporate executive has and the unemployed worker has not is a general sense of the reality of his own being, a sense that his actions will have significant effects in the world. The familiar self-descriptions—"I want to be somebody" and "I'm just a nobody"—sum up this phenomenon. To be oppressed is not simply to lack material goods, leisure, or opportunity. It is to be robbed of one's self.

Finally, my stress on the generalized cultural forms that create the dominated self do not exclude person-to-person interactions. Meetings between oppressor and oppressed may be between individuals, but these encounters express the collective realities of oppressor and oppressed. One does not leave behind the sense of unreality produced by impersonal forces when one confronts the oppressor in person. Nor does the oppressor leave behind the psychological advantage of having had some sense of power, some reflection in the generalized culture. A reality confronts an unreality. A slave faces a master. In this confrontation the power of the ruler is sustained by the material structure of the ruled's inability to feel him- or herself as a reality.[7] Institutional power and wealth are joined with the psychological "wealth" of self-confidence and public recognition; institutional powerlessness and material poverty are joined to a lack of mastery of the techniques by which one represents oneself as knowledgeable, expert, and worthy of respect (Sennett 1981, 97–104; Ellman 1968).

In conclusion, then, we see that socialization processes begun in infancy and continued throughout adult life create adult personalities tied to present forms of domination or incapable of resisting them. The failures of the economy provide, at best, a spur to cracking through the resistant shell of internalized social control or the crippling effects of the dominated self. At such times, however, the oppressed face two other formidable obstacles. The unity of the ruling class is expressed mainly (but not exclusively) in the state. Simultaneously, social differentiation keeps different segments of the working class from uniting politically. Consequently, our study of the transformation of Marxist theory now leads to an examination of the social primacy of politics.

PART IV

The Social Primacy of Politics:
The State, Social Differentiation,
and the American Left

11

Political Power as Structure and Strategy

POLITICS, IN ITS BROADEST SENSE, IS THAT ACTIVITY IN WHICH SOCIAL GROUPS attempt to maintain or transform the social order according to their interests. While class and socialization are crucial in shaping political life, politics cannot be reduced to effects of them. Although class conflicts generated by economic structures produce social contradictions, political realities determine how these contradictions are resolved. Similarly, the autonomy of politics from socialization rests on the way socialization processes themselves are partly the outcome of political forces. Consequently, the transformation of Marxist theory requires recognition of the social primacy of politics. Like our changed understanding of the critical role of socialization, recent Marxist theories of political life deny that political organization and change are inevitable consequences of the dynamics of the mode of production. As we saw in Chapter 5, it is now understood that the social meaning of economic life depends on the political responses of collective social agents. Therefore, it is necessary to examine the two major expressions of political life in advanced capitalism: the state and the socially differentiated working class. To meet their interests, workers have needed but have not achieved political unity or cooperation. To a much greater degree, capitalists and other privileged groups have possessed such unity and cooperation. This contrast has determined the ultimate fate of radical political movements.

To support these claims, I will now focus on the political mechanisms by which the ruling class maintains its social authority, and the processes that prevent the working class from developing its own power even when the authority-supporting bonds of socialization are weakened; to contrast the unity of the ruling class and other oppressor groups with working-class fragmentation caused by social differentiation, and the rulers' capacity to act with the passivity of the ruled.

167

This chapter analyzes social authority in capitalist society, mostly by a discussion and critique of some recent Marxist writings on the state. Chapters 12 and 13 describe the significance of social differentiation through an account of the experiences of American blacks and Jews. Chapters 14–17 show that the political fate of the American left has been determined by the interaction of the three forms of social primacy.

Throughout this discussion it will help to keep two points in mind. First, there is the difference between "political power" and "political authority." Here "political power" refers to the capacity of an individual or group to mobilize social forces to forcibly attain desired ends. Thus the state exercises power when it uses the national guard to end a general strike or police to quell a demonstration. "Political authority," by contrast, refers to the way certain types of social power rest on the consent of those over whom the power is exercised. Thus, to the degree to which capitalist ownership of the means of production or the state's right to declare war go unchallenged, they have power over those areas of social life by *virtue of their authority*. Second, it is important to remember that all the forms of authority and domination discussed in this book work simultaneously in capitalist society, even though at different times one aspect may be more important than another. Thus capitalist control over the means of production, conservative socialization processes, the dominated self, gender domination, and the rest, all help keep authority in the hands of those that have it.

Political Authority: The State as Structure

Given capitalism's separation of the political and the economic, an analysis of the capitalist economy does not explain the power, behavior, or legitimacy of bourgeois political institutions. As a result, Marxist theories of the state have faced certain questions. How does the state apparatus achieve and exercise power? How much of that power exists independently of the power of capitalists? Why does the state usually have the support of the mass of the population when it so clearly aids capitalist accumulation? In particular situations, what leads the state to act the way it does? The rise of the politicized economy makes traditional Marxism's responses to these questions inadequate. Two recent complementary answers involve "structural," and "strategic" or "class struggle," accounts of the state. I argue that state action in advanced capitalist society is both an unplanned effect of capitalist social relations and a product of self-conscious strategies by ruling groups. I also suggest that it is a mistake to regard the state as the only repository of political power.

Structural analyses of the state are based in the premise that capitalist relations of production guarantee capitalist political power even though capitalists are not politically unified. While capitalists possess economic power, many crucial institutions and functions are not in the hands of capitalists. The armed forces and the police are controlled by government. Laws are made and taxes spent by freely elected public servants. Professionals are (supposedly) guided by impersonal standards of responsibility and expertise. Moreover, with the development of the politicized economy, previously private economic matters are now often controlled by the state.

How then is political authority exercised? In the structural view, organizational unity either among capitalists or between capitalists and state managers is (variously) unnecessary or nonexistent. Rather, social relations of production impose themselves as constraints on action, as motivations and organizational principles of the capitalist state. The ruling class rules not by virtue of self-conscious *strategies* but as a consequence of fundamental institutional *structures*. The state serves the maintenance of ruling-class power, but while the ruling class enjoys the benefits of power, it does not itself rule. The political unity of the capitalist *class* is constituted by the structures of capitalist *society*.

Nicos Poulantzas was the most influential exponent of this view. Despite some interesting differences between his two works on the state, *Political Power and Social Classes* (1975) and *State, Power, Socialism* (1978), both reject the notion that the state is guided by a self-conscious ruling class: "*History* ... is a process without a subject ... [nations are] not the product of a class acting as subject of history. They are the result of a process, since history itself is the process of class struggle" (1978, 114–15). For Poulantzas, to say that classes are more or less unified subjects endowed with a "class consciousness" implies that all spheres of society will reflect the contents of that consciousness. Consequently, this view must ignore the separation and specificity of the different "levels" of society: the economic, the political and the ideological. While all these may be "determined in the last instance" by the economic, they each possess a "relative autonomy." The state plays a particular role not because state managers take orders from or are controlled by a unified, self-conscious capitalist class; rather, just because the capitalist class is incapable of the kind of unity that would enable it to rule, it requires a "relatively autonomous" state to preserve its power.

The dominance of the economic "in the last instance" is shown, for Poulantzas, by the way capitalist relations of production can explain both the general autonomy of the capitalist state and some of its key features. Precisely because the form of appropriation under capitalism is based in "free" exchanges between alienated laborers and capitalist owners, the realm of political power must be institutionally distinct from that of economic power. Only as relatively autonomous can the state organize competitive and anarchic capitalists. Only as popular and representative can it appear to embody the interests of the "people-nation" in a way that obscures the superior power of the capitalist class. The "relative autonomy" of the state thus enables it to support the ruling class while appearing not to do so. This dual function of simultaneously aiding legitimation and accumulation has been noted by many contemporary Marxist writers. It reveals a basic characteristic of capitalist hegemony: that political domination is represented as popular.

For Poulantzas, the state can maintain a fictional unity among classes in capitalist society while actually serving the interests of the dominant class because of the state's "institutional materiality." This concept, introduced in *State, Power, Socialism*, was an advance over the highly functional language of his previous book (written ten years earlier), which failed to show how the state reproduces capitalist social relations. His later focus on institutional materiality provides part of an account of how this process occurs. His argument is that the state's key institutional forms correspond to and support the reproduction of capitalist social relations in four typical areas: knowledge, individuation, law, and "the nation." In the realm of knowledge, for instance, the capitalist state reproduces the division of manual and mental labor, both in its own apparatus and in the "science" that it funds. In the realm of "individuation," the state atomizes the body politic, fragmenting a class into homogeneous and isolated "individuals."

Poulantzas's earlier work was criticized for a functionalism that focused on the state as the factor of social cohesion and ignored the contradictory aspects of state action (Bridges 1974; Skocpol 1980). In *State, Power, Socialism*, Poulantzas partly overcame this defect by claiming that state action expresses a particular "condensation of a relationship of forces." The balance of contending classes is expressed in the state, while the state itself lacks any independent power (1978, 149). Thus the power of the ruling class (or bloc of ruling classes), when challenged by popular struggle, is maintained by the action of the relatively autonomous state in "provisional compromises." In order to make these compromises, the state must be relatively autonomous—because the capitalist class may not be able to see the need for compromise. As long as capitalist relations of production exist, however, the power of the ruling class will be expressed by the state.

But this expression is threatened by contradictions between the need for increased state intervention and the preservation of capitalist social relations. The state is caught between backing off from the economy and taking it over. To back off would be to cease to make necessary contributions to accumulation and legitimation (here Poulantzas makes many of the points I discussed in Chapter 5). Going forward would threaten capitalist class relations. Though increased power is transferred to the executive in what Poulantzas calls the "Authoritarian State," the goal of stability is not achieved. The determination of the economy in the last instance revenges itself through a continued economic and ideological instability.[1]

Poulantzas presents many themes that can be found in other recent Marxist writings on the state: the tension in state action between accumulation and legitimation; the ideological role of the state in representing a false unity among a class-divided people; the parallel between the institutional separation of state and economy and the noncoercive form of surplus extraction under capitalism; the recent transition to an increasingly authoritarian state, a transition that shows its increasing desperation in the face of unresolved social contradictions.[2] All these points indicate the recent dramatic increase in the complexity of Marxist theories of the state, a complexity made necessary by the enormous increase in the state's social role in the last half-century.

Most important, from my point of view, is Poulantzas's attempt to show that the basic form of state structures—its institutional materiality— reproduces capitalist social relations. As we shall see, there are several crucial weaknesses in Poulantzas's continual emphasis on the absence of "class subjects" in history.[3] Yet his claim that fundamental elements of state practice reproduce capitalism has great importance. The point is that individual state managers need not consciously seek the reproduction of capitalism in order for their actions to serve that end. The state need not seek to be, as Marx put it, a "committee for managing the affairs of the whole bourgeoisie." Neither need there exist a self-consciously unified capitalist class. The objective function of the state, it turns out, is partly based in structures that have specific effects irrespective of the intentions of the agents concerned. State functionaries are the "bearers" of these structures, not their designers or controllers. In just this sense, these structures serve as the "unity" of the ruling class, a unity that enables the continued reproduction of capitalist social relations.

Both Fred Block (1977b) and the editors of Monthly Review (1976) have clear arguments supporting this claim. They describe the dependence of the capitalist state on the interests of capitalists in the absence of formal or informal ties between the two, or even the intentions of state managers to serve capitalism. Funding for the state depends on the general condition of the economy—and thus on the willingness of capitalists to invest. When

state actions threaten the confidence of the business community, investment dries up. Economic stagnation, rising unemployment, a paucity of
state revenues, and a potential social crisis follow. The state's political
power and mass support are weakened. To act at all, therefore, state managers must to some extent satisfy the needs of capitalists. The structural
dependence of the state on an economic power generated elsewhere guarantees that state action will take place within parameters defined by the reproduction of capitalism.

Erik Olin Wright (1979) and Claus Offe (1972a; 1972b) add to this
account by stressing that even in the absence of initiatives by a unified
capitalist class, the capitalist state is organized around policies that preserve capitalist social relations. The mechanisms by which particular policies are chosen, for instance, need not include a Machiavellian, self-
conscious pursuit of capitalist interests. As Offe shows, for instance, it is
often the case that unstated rules automatically exclude certain types of
policies, and the actual method of selection from the consequent small
range of options is disguised.

The structural view I have just summarized makes a decisive contribution to our understanding of the social primacy of politics. The "fit" between
the form of the state and the form of capitalist social relations means that
capitalist power can be embedded in political institutions without having
to be self-consciously managed or manifested. Consequently, those institutions can stifle and resist progressive forces, although they do not seem
to do so. The general population and state managers may be completely
ignorant of the effects of the state, while capitalists (and other groups in
power) reap support and protection.

Taking Poulantzas as representative of the structural view, however, I
must now turn to a series of critical comments. First, he contradicts his
own denial of class agency. For instance, in his analysis of bourgeois revolutions, he attempts to show that such revolutions do not follow the "classic" pattern of political following economic power. In Germany, he claims,
the bourgeoisie was unable to ally with the petite bourgeoisie and the
working class against the large landowners:

> By one of those *errors of judgment* which stemmed from the fact that ideology
> was at that time infiltrating unevenly into developing national formations, the
> German bourgeoisie could not *make up its mind* to break with the nobility: this
> was because *it was obsessed* by the French revolution of 1848 and by memories
> of the Jacobinisms of the Great Revolution. *It therefore left to the state* the task
> of establishing its own political domination. (Poulantzas 1978, 181; my emphasis)

This passage is striking because of its attribution to the bourgeoisie of the
very "class consciousness" that Poulantzas denies. It is not "structures

without subjects" to which he appeals to explain the role of the German state in the creation of bourgeois hegemony in Germany. Rather, it is "errors of judgment" of a German bourgeoisie "obsessed" with memories. In short, a class subject acted (or failed to act) in a certain way because of its understanding of social reality.

Other examples of this kind of self-contradiction can be found in Poulantzas.[4] He is driven to these self-contradictions because the objective political structures he focuses on are themselves products of previous struggles for class domination. Structures may appear to be impersonal, but they are in fact historically determined by past collective action (Esping-Anderson, Friedland, and Wright 1976, 189). In other words, any total opposition between "structure" and "subject" is false. Subjects act in terms of structures; in turn, their actions sustain, transform, and create structures.[5] History (structure) and Subjectivity exist in and for each other. In any particular time, conscious transforming agency may overcome embedded structures—or vice versa. The state is neither merely "functional" nor merely an instrument of the rulers (cf. Gold, Lo, and Wright 1975, 45–46). Therefore, any account of the capitalist state as a structure of social cohesion and class domination must be joined with an account of it as the product of class action, class strategies, and class struggles.

My second criticism of Poulantzas concerns his conception of authority under capitalism. Consider his claim that the state atomizes society into competing *individuals*. There is some truth here, but Poulantzas ignores the way the state also fragments the working class into antagonistic *groups*. While an ideology of individualism may be endemic to capitalism, capitalist society has long been fractured along racial, ethnic, and gender lines. This condition is partly fostered by state action. As Bridges (1974) argues, the state gets different groups to compete for state aid and protection. State manipulation of social conflict represents social benefits as available to one group only if taken away from another. The history of affirmative action and busing show the state acting to sustain antagonistic groups rather than atomizing a class into individuals.[6]

Poulantzas's problem is that he limits social authority to the state and sees the state as the repository and support only of capitalist power. He thus ignores the importance of other forms of authority besides that of the state, and the existence of other dominant groups besides the capitalist ruling class. Defining a social formation in terms of traditionally conceived Marxist categories of labor and appropriation leaves women's sex-affective labor completely invisible to him. Gender relations, unacknowledged in the first book, are mentioned only in passing in the second—and then they are described as dependent on class struggles "properly so called," used to "relay class power" (Poulantzas 1978, 148). This position is unable to answer certain critical questions. Does the state use the power of men or whites simply to "relay" that of capitalists? Do men who control the state have no independent interest in using the state to "relay" their own power over their wives? If the state relays other than class power, might it not be a "condensation" not just of class struggle but of other struggles as well? These questions reveal that other groups besides capitalists have both power and authority in contemporary capitalist society. The state reflects a variety of forms of power, not just that of class.

Also, state managers possess some autonomous power and independent interests. The state could "possess no power of its own" only if the economy were a more or less self-sufficient process using the state as its "instrument." My analysis in Chapter 5 shows that this is not the case. State *power* derives from its essential role in the accumulation process,[7] its control over agencies of physical coercion, and its usual command over the loyalty of the general population. State *interests* derive from the simple desire of state managers to keep their jobs.[8]

Thus, contrary to Poulantzas, it is not merely classes (as he uses the term) that possess power in capitalist society. Power—the capacity to fulfill interests at the expense of another group—is also held, for instance, by men in relation to women, by whites in relation to nonwhites, and by the state apparatus itself. It is the inability to see the complexity of power that leads Poulantzas to explain state action solely on the basis of class power. Such a reduction will not be able to explain adequately state action that controls women's reproductive capacity, for instance, or confines them to certain spheres of the work force. Because society is structured not solely by the distinction between capitalists and workers (with a few intermediate classes) but also by sex and race, a theory of social authority will be incomplete if it is restricted to the way the state reproduces capitalism or "condenses" class struggle.[9]

The Scope of Social Authority

To understand social authority, then, we must see that it includes that of capitalists over production, the state over civil society, various professionals over aspects of "private life," religion and the media over popular culture, spiritual life, and morality. Further, society is divided into groups, some of which have power and/or authority over others: for example, whites and blacks, men and women. These different forms of authority both order and divide society. They focus the power of the rulers and fragment the ruled into powerless and antagonistic groups. In each case social authority is sustained by the *unification* of an authority relative to the *disorganization* of its subjects.

Unified social authorities transform society to meet challenges posed by social contradictions, but they seek to do so in ways that will not alter the essential relations of power and privilege. These relations sustain a number of subordinate groups, each subject to different but overlapping forms of authority and power. In their exclusive concern with a narrow sense of politics, many Marxist theorists of the state have failed to integrate the power of men, whites, and professionals (for instance), with that of capitalists and the state. An adequate theory of social authority must include but go beyond the state. Similarly, it should describe the interaction of different forms of authority: for example, the role of the state in the domination of women, or the interdependence of class and racial domination. We need to describe and explain what David Plotke (1980, 89) defines as "politics"—"the relational, organizing and directive dimension of social life." This usage stems from the notion that most social institutions and practices—sex and government, religion and public education, factories and the media—are shaped by internal and external relations of power, "wealth," and prestige. Internally, every practice or institution distributes roles of unequal power. Externally, each is connected with other structures of power.

Consider, for example, the social authority of the modern medical system. In this system health care is controlled by predominantly white, male experts whose authority is sanctioned by the state. As many critics have shown, modern Western medicine, despite its accomplishments, perpetuates relations of power in the interests of both doctors and other authorities (Doyal 1979; Ehrenreich and English 1979; Foucault 1975). The genesis of medical control over prenatal care is an interesting example of this phenomenon. The contemporary medical practice of the routine, in-office examination came as a response to state and federally funded prenatal and child care clinics in the 1920s. Created by the Sheppard-Towner Act of 1921, these clinics were staffed largely by public health nurses, female physicians, and female volunteers. Their success sparked the American Medical Association to a previously nonexistent interest in preventive medicine: "By including preventive health care in the services of the general practitioner, the AMA was able to persuade the federal government in 1927, as they had not been able to in 1921, that private doctors were the appropriate and the exclusive guardians of all matters of health" (Rothman 1980, 143). The AMA's response combined the ideologies of anticommunism, sexism, and professionalism. It smeared the act's female supporters as communist and justified doctors' claims to sole medical authority on the basis of their scientific superiority over untrained mothers, social workers, and public health nurses. A material interest in capturing state funds and support was joined to that of preserving male power. This control has had some terrible effects. In 1972 the United States ranked sixteenth in infant mortality, after Ireland and Hong Kong (Arms 1977, 43). Procedures harmful to mother and child had become routine. Women received little prenatal education. Childbirth was usually unnecessarily painful, humiliating, and frightening.[10]

The male medical elite's control of pregnancy and childbirth is an example of how social authority constitutes itself as a unity over against the groups it rules. In this particular case, various forms of authority and power (the state, the professionals, men) are set against the fragmentation of disempowered groups of women. A movement organizing to make prenatal and child care serve women was atomized into groups of patients waiting to be treated by male doctors, or nurses serving in male-dominated institutions. Female initiative in gynecology, obstetrics, and early child care was replaced by a reliance on an "expertise" that combined scientific knowledge, myth, and male domination.

This analysis needs to be extended to other forms taken by social authority: for instance, the family, religion, and higher education.[11] An adequate theory of social authority would show how these social forms sustain ruling groups at the expense of the ruled, simultaneously focusing the energy and power of the former and fragmenting that of the latter.

Strategy and Class Struggle

In opposition to the structural view, I have suggested that the state is neither simply the mechanical product of capitalist relations of production nor the product of subjectless class struggle. The history of capitalism shows *political* cycles comparable in some ways to the "long waves" of economic life discussed in Chapter 5. More or less conscious struggle between classes is resolved by the creation of temporarily stable structures of accumulation and legitimation. This temporary stability allows for "unconscious" or "subjectless" domination for some time. However, the structures that sustain social authority are subject to a variety of contradictions. When they arise, the cognitive, value, and psychological supports for social authority are weakened. Ruled groups organize to gain power for themselves and to alter social norms of legitimation. Ruling groups organize to defend their privileges and to make social changes that will placate the ruled without altering the fundamental relations of power. Given this cyclical view, focusing solely on periods either of acceptance (structure) or of struggle is mistaken. Both are essential to maintaining social authority.

A number of specific historical situations are examples of social reorganization designed to perpetuate existing power. The AMA's response to

Sheppard-Towner is one clear example. In regard to the state, Gosia Esping-Anderson, Roger Friedland, and Wright (1976) list urban political reforms in the early decades of the twentieth century; the shifting of inter-governmental grants to cities via federal funds rather than local ones in the 1960s; and the Progressive Era corporatism that brought representatives of working-class groups into government. In each case, a specific challenge was met by specific structural changes.

These changes created new contradictions in turn. In the case of urban reform, for instance, ethnic and working-class political organizations were replaced by "professional" and (supposedly) apolitical city managers. As a result, cities dominated by elites lacked political mechanisms for integrating and co-opting the post–World War II urban underclass of blacks. This lack set the stage for racial conflict in the 1960s. The corporate liberalism of the Progressive Era saw business leaders welcoming both limited unionization and government regulation (Weinstein 1968). However, corporate liberalism's building of the state's economic role allowed political principles of equality, social welfare, and respect for persons to enter economic life—causing crises of accumulation to become legitimation crises.

Alan Wolfe's (1977) description of its successive forms provides a historical schema of the Western liberal state, pushing our analysis beyond descriptions of ahistorical structures (as in Poulantzas) or particular reforms. For Wolfe, the history of the capitalist state is a series of compromises between the politically unobstructed economic activity of "liberalism" and the mass political participation of "democracy." In the early years of capitalism, an "Accumulation State" managed compromises and coalitions among rising industrial capitalists, merchant capital, and sections of the declining aristocracy, and directly aided accumulation. With the success of industrial capitalism, the "Harmonious State" supported the industrial bourgeoisie's most complete power. Laissez-faire combined with state aid to particular capitalists and physical repression of the increasingly rebellious working class. As class conflict mounted in the late nineteenth and the early twentieth century, political corruption and the economic contradictions of competitive capitalism threatened the general stability of the social order (71). The result was a welter of "rationalizing reforms" whose goal was the increased efficiency and workability of the state in the interests of the dominant order.[12]

The subsequent transition to the "Expansionist State" was provoked by the economic stagnation of 1873–96 and the simultaneous rise of working-class parties and trade unions. In response, the dominant capitalist powers sought to overcome economic stagnation and class conflict by colonial expansion (94). The end of state laissez-faire—that is, obvious government support for overseas expansion and protection for key industries at home—affected public consciousness. A realization grew that an "active" state that worked to benefit capitalists could benefit the working class as well (102). The ruling class then cold-bloodedly used racism, anti-Semitism, national chauvinism, and mass culture (for example, yellow journalism, public spectator sports, education) to fragment and manipulate the working class.

The dilemmas of the private struggle for public power were temporarily resolved by the "Franchise State." This state granted authority to various private institutions, allowing for representation of different power blocs in government and separating the state from many actual exercises of class-biased power. With the experience of government organization and intervention during World War I, as well as the steadily increasing power of monopolies, a corporatist structure emerged: that is, the self-organization of the various sectors of the economy to produce stability and productivity with minimal state intervention (119). Though leading industrialists wanted to be the only sector of the society to be effectively organized, they continued to face mass pressure for working-class representation. The Depression of the 1930s destroyed this uneasy balance. The Franchise State mediated competing interests by aiding corporations and extending union protection and social welfare legislation to workers. Organizations such as the AMA and the ASPCA (American Society for the Prevention of Cruelty to Animals) were given public power to regulate and rationalize particular aspects of society.

The Franchise State was subverted by the failure of its various special interest groups to maintain social stability. Regulatory agencies became captives of the industries they were intended to regulate. Councils of "experts" managed the affairs of state in private meetings. A supposedly "neutral" but actually quite partial administrative class was created. "Questions of power, welfare, community, and purposes . . . were discussed, resolved, and administered in the atmosphere of a Middle Eastern bazaar . . . the principles of the free market finally triumphed, not in the private sector . . . but in the public" (168–69). Consequent instabilities led to a resurgence of state activity and intervention. State involvement in the economy increased, as did direct intervention in processes of production through systems management and budget control. Affirmative action and antidiscrimination programs were implemented (173). A fiscal crisis of the state resulted. Torn between legitimation and accumulation, state action began to undermine itself.

I have presented Wolfe's account in detail not because it is correct in all its particulars: some writers quarrel with his accounts of the degree of self-conscious and farsighted ruling-class organization of reform; others accord a higher degree of importance to more or less autonomous action by state personnel (Nordlinger 1981; Skocpol 1980). What is crucial in Wolfe is his convincing description of how the state's relation to the economy in particular and social life in general changes over time as a result of the action of groups competing for power and privilege. Given this account, we do not have to choose between interpretations of the state as an "instrument" of ruling-class power or a result of class struggle. It is both. The state is an instrument of the ruling class when working-class militancy and organization are at a low point. State action is a defensive response to popular militancy when the ruling class is weakened or disorganized. Furthermore, these two situations can coexist. In recent decades, affirmative action and the war on poverty however divisive of the working class, have been ruling-class responses to popular insurgency. During the same period, government support for the nuclear power industry has shown the state as a more or less passive instrument in the hands of power companies. While U.S. policy in southeast Asia was being partly altered by a popular movement, activities in the Middle East were being dictated by the oil giants (Stork 1975).

However, periods of ruling-class disorganization are usually followed by periods of greater ruling-class cohesion and control over state action. As the transition from competitive to monopoly capitalism required the emergence of corporate liberalism, so transnational economic connections, industrial unionism, mass society, modern technologies, and the Soviet bloc required new institutions of and strategies by a capitalist ruling class.

These institutions and strategies have been studied in great detail by William Domhoff and his students. In *The Powers That Be*, Domhoff describes various processes by which the U.S. ruling class—defined by position, income, prestige, and social contact—exercises its power. For example, a *special interest process* allows tax breaks, thwarts regulatory agencies, provides direction to state bureaucrats, and influences legislative committees. By a *policy formation process* the ruling class transcends the narrow self-interests of particular fractions of capital to form policies benefiting capitalism as a whole; for example, in the capital-labor accord of the early twentieth century, the Marshall Plan, Social Security, and Carter's foreign policy. Such policies evolve from institutions like the Council on Foreign Relations, the Committee for Economic Development, and the Business Council. Policy groups train and screen future administrators, discuss policy, hear experts, and make compromises between different sections of the ruling class. By analyzing how private policy becomes state action, Domhoff (1979, 94, 121) shows that at times "corporate leaders, in fact, had a comprehensive view of the social system and the political situation. . . . That is, the power elite is organized 'politically' in the deepest meaning of the term."

Wolfe and Domhoff show how state personnel and interested members of the capitalist class attempt to overcome contradictions between legitimation and accumulation. A clear sense of class interests usually animate decisive transformations in the state. However, these interests were at times not matched by adequate knowledge. Consider, for instance, certain successes and failures of the New Deal. Finegold (1982, 21–22) argues that New Deal agricultural policy was managed by state-trained experts who could plan for agriculture as a whole and for relations between agriculture and the rest of the economy. In industry, by contrast, the National Recovery Administration was staffed by businessmen who had "never been trained to plan for entire industries or for industry as a whole." In general, the vacillation and partial character of the New Deal reflects not the absence of a self-conscious attempt by the ruling class to preserve its place in society but its lack of knowledge of how to do so.

This point may seem to support Theda Skocpol's (1980) criticism of instrumental theories of state action in the New Deal. She argues that New Deal reforms were not developed by farsighted capitalist classes but conceded in response to working-class pressure or produced by a relatively autonomous state apparatus opposed by hostile and disorganized capitalists. Yet Skocpol surely outstrips her evidence when she uses this particular situation to illustrate the general importance of state structures and political organizations. She herself concedes that the 1930s signaled a breakdown of the self-conscious organization of corporate liberalism, which had generated co-opting reforms three decades earlier. Similarly, it is clear that by the late 1930s the U.S. ruling class had regained policy initiatives.

The problem is that Skocpol, like the state theorists she criticizes, wants a single model to explain social authority under capitalism. State action, it seems, must be *either* a product of co-optive manipulation by the ruling class; *or* a functional structure reproducing the relations of production; *or* an agent of accumulation that responds defensively to working-class pressure; *or* the product of independent initiatives of politicians and relatively autonomous state structures and party organizations. But if political life moves in cycles of structure and struggle, business-as-usual and conflict, *History and Subjectivity*, a single model of social authority may not be possible. While ruling groups always want to maintain their power, they may at times not know how to do so. The disorganized response of capitalists to the Depression shows how that class lacked a coherent understanding of social life during that period. Therefore, leadership shifted for a time to a relatively autonomous liberal state in the U.S. New Deal.

While certain crucial historical developments of capitalist society are products of a self-conscious ruling class,[13] not all state action is the result of ruling-class policies. As we have seen, there are situations where other mechanisms predominate. Also, the capacity to formulate and pursue policies does not guarantee that those policies will be successful. As Wolfe, Poulantzas, and others have shown, the increased social role of the state and ruling-class self-organization may coexist with actual impotence. Despite a southeast Asian foreign policy devised and directed by private, limited, or clandestine groups, the United States was unable either to destroy the national liberation movements or maintain popular support for U.S. involvement. Such groups as the Council for Economic Development and the Business Roundtable direct state action in support of U.S. corporations. Yet it was precisely state support of increasingly uncompetitive industries that led to a diminution of U.S. economic power in comparison with Japan and western Europe. As Offe (1972a; 1972b) has observed, adequate state planning often requires input from precisely those groups whom the state must ignore in order to protect the special interests of capitalists. There is a contradiction, in short, between the goal of facilitating accumulation and the political need to do so in a way that excludes anticapitalist policies.

Marxist writers have often been hampered by the presupposition that adequate knowledge of society is already available: possessed by the ruling class and used to manipulate society in its interests; or obscured only by bourgeois ideology—and hence available to Marxists now and to everyone else "after the revolution." The limited confirmations of Marx's original theory should have changed this view. Because people can learn from experience, traditional Marxism foundered on the way social life changes. In fact, capitalist development is decisively shaped by the way capitalists and workers understand its previous history.

Just because capitalism is no longer a lawlike system, political strategy is necessarily subject to uncertainty. Attempts by the state to control social life are thwarted by society's unpredictability, dramatically constricted by a lack of understanding. Despite its pretensions, social science generally produces forecasts with extremely limited validity. Government or public policy institute economists have failed, for instance, to predict such developments as "stagflation" or to make accurate forecasts concerning economic growth (MacIntyre 1981, 85). As we saw in Chapter 2, there are four inescapable sources of social unpredictability in social life: radical conceptual innovation; the way agents' future actions are conditioned by their expectations of others' behavior; an individual's inability to predict his/her own future actions; and pure contingency in the form of anything from power shortages to the sudden discovery of mineral wealth. The generalizations of the social sciences used by state managers are limited to a necessarily temporary institutional and conceptual order. Human behavior is systematically unpredictable, and thus social authorities can be taken by surprise. Society is further complicated by the way people pursue their interests:

Each of us seeks to embody his own plans . . . in the . . . social world. A condition of achieving this is to render as much of our . . . social environment as possible predictable. . . . At the same time each of us, individually and as a member of particular social groups, aspires to preserve his independence. . . . We need to remain to some degree opaque and unpredictable, particularly when threatened by the predictive practices of others. (MacIntyre 1981, 99)

This point can be attuned to struggles between social authorities and the oppressed. Authorities seek to make their subjects predictable, to guarantee a consistent behavior supportive of power and privilege. Yet the unpredictability of social life entails that this attempt will sometimes fail. Contradictions surface in the structure of authority. Strategies backfire. Temporary solutions lead to later problems. Despite social structure and the strategies of rulers, the ruled learn from experience and challenge authority—although this last, decisive source of unpredictability is not guaranteed, unfortunately. The very unpredictability of social life means that at some time society could be split, in Habermas's (1973, 282) words, into the "social engineers and the inmates of closed institutions."

This dreadful possibility is still very distant. Social authority *is* at times weakened by economic or social crisis. Old structures do not work. Strategies cannot be formulated. The "slaves" shatter, at least partly, internalized authority. An authentic self-identity is expressed in political movements that seek to reconstitute social authority on a new basis. Yet these movements rarely express that Marxist abstraction, "the working class." Rather, they embody experiences of partial and often antagonistic groups. Even when internalized authority is weakened, people experience their lives in terms of social differentiation. That experience and its crucial effects on the struggle for socialism are our next subjects.

12

Social Differentiation and Blacks in the United States

IF THE FEMINIST CLAIM THAT POLITICAL ACTION STEMS FROM PERSONAL EXPE-
rience is true, socialists face a crucial political problem: the same personal
experiences that give rise to radical political action divide groups who
must cooperate for such action to succeed. This problem arises because the
political actions of wage earners without social power, household laborers,
and those dependent on government are not motivated by the abstractions
of political economy. Rather, radical politics is based in a nexus of fragmented and overlapping identities created by social differentiation. These
identities include those of class, race, religion, national origin, sex, sexual
preference, geography, and age. These identities are central in determining
political action and thus produce the social primacy of social differentiation
—a differentiation that functions as the political complement of ruling-
class political unity.

Socialism is possible only if the working class can become a collective
subject. This development is obstructed by the processes of socialization,
which repress the emergence of genuine rather than authoritarian subjectivity; and by experiences of social differentiation, which fragment even
those groups that seek to resist ruling-class hegemony. When people break
through their socialization and overcome the dominated self, they tend to
do so not as members of a unified working class but as members of socially
differentiated groups: communities of shared experience and perceived
political interest. Such groups have at times improved their position in
capitalist society by acquiring political rights, union representation, social
legislation; by having some members enter the middle class; and by receiving increased representation in popular culture. Yet they have failed to
forge the necessary political alliances with other socially differentiated
groups. Consequently, they have been contained by ruling-class reform

and repression. The essential exploitation and domination characteristic of capitalism have remained.

Sadly, the history of left-wing movements is marked not only by frequent appeals for working class unity but also by persistent failures to achieve it. This failure is partly a product of structural stratification in the labor market, inherited precapitalist antagonisms between different religious and national communities, the capacity of the ruling class to manipulate and increase tensions between groups, and various forms of oppression supported by members of the working class. All these factors are reinforced by leftists' inability to recognize the primacy of social differentiation. Perceiving political insurgency in terms of economic theory, leftists have not seen the distinct interests, fears, and values of socially differentiated groups. Of course, community is deeply shaped by paid labor. Yet within a broadly conceived working class, work—like other aspects of "everyday life"—is significantly different for socially differentiated groups. Until this fact is realized, political insurgency will remain fragmented, its accomplishments limited to reform. Without recognition of and action to overcome the effects of socially differentiating experiences, working-class unity is impossible. Without working-class political unity no serious threat to capitalism can be maintained. Even if socialization processes are broken through, resistance to authority will fall far short of decisive social change —just because its motivation and effects will be fragmented.

I support these assertions by two different discussions. To explore the social primacy of social differentiation, this chapter and the next examine some of the distinct features of the experience of American blacks and of Jews. Chapters 14–17 argue that one reason the American left has never posed a serious threat to capitalism is that it has both ignored and expressed social differentiation.

This chapter begins with an outline of black history in the United States, examines different explanations of that history, and describes some aspects of black culture and politics. The entire discussion focuses on the relation between two ways of understanding black history. Theoretical explanations of its basic dynamics must appeal to the mode of production as the first form of social primacy. However, black experience, culture, and political movements express a unique condition of social differentiation. Black cultural and political subjectivity has typically lacked socialist ideology and organizational ties to progressive white political movements. Given the social primacy of social differentiation, this lack is inevitable. Unfortunately, however, it has meant that political struggle for blacks has always had limited effects on racism—and has never posed a serious threat to capitalism.

Racism has been a dependent social phenomenon because its history has been broadly determined by the dynamics of capitalism. Changes in the roles of blacks in U.S. society can be explained by reference to the social primacy of capitalist development. Conversely, however, the independence of racism can be measured by two facts: the central social agents of U.S. capitalism have organized themselves along racial as well as class lines; and blacks have responded to the intersection of capitalist and racial oppression by creating a racial community. The social primacy of social differentiation is found in the way the specific experience of blacks in a capitalist and racist society leads them to challenge their oppression through political action based in a socially differentiated identity.

Blacks under U.S. Capitalism

Black oppression has been functional for capitalist accumulation and historically shaped by the demands of capitalist development. At the same time, blacks experienced capitalism differently from whites. Unlike that of whites, black labor was directly coerced: first through slavery and then, in the postbellum South's "plantation economy," by law, custom, a paternalistic culture, and violence. Without slavery, blacks would not have come to the United States to take part in southern agriculture. Without the variety of controls used after the Civil War, blacks might have moved west or north, becoming independent farmers and industrial workers, or at least demanding more than a subsistence income (Mandle 1978).

After the Civil War, the exclusion of blacks from industrial, craft, and skilled labor was accepted by southern planters and northern industrialists. Able to dispense with the black vote, and finding it possible to do business with the emerging capitalist class in the South, northern capitalists allowed southern plantation owners to reassert control over their black workers. Simultaneously, massive waves of European immigrants satisfied the northern demand for industrial labor (Baron 1971; Geschwender 1978, 158–62; Omi and Winant 1983a, 51). The racial definition of the working class was also accepted by white workers, who usually resisted the hiring of blacks for "white" jobs. Seeking a superior place in the slowly developing southern industrial labor and agricultural market, white unions and poor farmers' associations supported racism, sometimes more virulently than did upper-class whites. The rare attempts at racially unified and antiracist organizations were short-lived and often fell prey to the racism of the surrounding community (Broderick 1971, 97–98; Geschwender 1978, 165–68; Harris 1982, 25–28, 34–35; Worthman and Green 1971, 50–51). An elaborate system of unequal treatment left the majority of blacks debt-burdened tenants in the post–Civil War plantation economy. Blacks thus experienced the U.S. capitalist "takeoff" (1865–1918) in a socially differentiated way. The racism manifested by all classes of whites condemned blacks to exclusion from industrial labor; legal and social second-class citizenship; disenfranchisement in most southern states; public segregation; inferior or nonexistent education and social services.

Increasing demand for black labor in the North and decreased demand in the South undermined the southern plantation economy, in which the majority of blacks lived until after World War II. World War I reduced the flow of immigrant labor to northern industry and interrupted cotton exports. The demand for black labor by northern industries increased as a significant percentage of the work force was mobilized for war. After the war, immigration was curtailed to limit the arrival of ideologically leftist eastern Europeans. Subsequently, a series of agricultural crises struck cotton growers, motivating the westward transfer of cotton and the mechanization of cotton growing (Baron 1971, 20–30; Harris 1982, 53–70; Mandle 1978, 73–95).

As it had in the southern plantation economy, black integration into the urban, industrial economy both satisfied the needs of capitalist accumulation and expressed a specific condition of social differentiation. From the end of the Civil War to approximately 1890 the North considerably improved its treatment of blacks, yet by 1900 residential and occupational segregation and racist ideology were again the norm. Blacks were driven out of white districts; whites refused to patronize black shopkeepers and professionals; and the urban ghettos were being formed (Osofsky 1963, 17–105; Spear 1971). Though blacks were often hired as strikebreakers by northern employers, they were limited to the lowest-paying and "dirtiest" jobs. Competition over housing, public facilities, and jobs led to race riots in northern cities immediately after World War I. Confronting established political machines, ghettoized blacks could not achieve the political and economic leverage of city officeholding and patronage (Wilson 1978, 62–87). White unions usually barred blacks from membership, maintained segregated locals, or at the very least ensured that no blacks achieved positions of leadership. Also, from the Socialist Party of the last decades of the nineteenth century through the Progressive movement and the American Federation of Labor in the first decades of the twentieth, most representatives of the white working class pursued policies that supported or ignored racism. Blacks were thus not only at the bottom of the capitalist system but socially and politically cut off from other pockets of actual or potential resistance to it.

By the late 1930s these conditions were changing. The growing black population of northern cities developed a political consciousness; there were attempts at a self-contained ghetto economy, organizations defending black workers, ghetto self-help institutions, and an explosion of cultural creativity (Kilson 1971; Levine 1971; Meier and Rudwick 1979, 200–390; Osofsky 1963, 92–126; Redkey 1971; Spear 1971). The greatest success of political organization came in 1941, when a threatened mass black march on Washington resulted in the outlawing of segregation in defense plants. Also by the late 1930s, blacks were seen as potential allies by significant segments of the white working class and the Democratic Party, and an activist U.S. left was ideologically driven to support black rights (Bonacich 1976, 46; Cayton and Mitchell 1939; Rosen 1968). In national politics masses of blacks renounced their traditional allegiance to the Republican Party to join the New Deal coalition. While little in the way of explicit legislation was forthcoming for blacks from Roosevelt's administration, there was more public attention and respect than in any previous presidency. Also, there were a variety of serious attempts to mitigate at least some of the racism in the administration of New Deal social welfare programs (Sitcoff 1978; Weiss 1983, 34–61, 120–56, 209–35). Last, wartime mobilization made the entry of blacks into industrial labor inevitable.

During and after World War II the integration of blacks into the industrial economy accelerated. By 1960, 80 percent of blacks lived in cities and only 8 percent worked in agriculture (Marable 1983, 312). Once again, however, the relation of blacks to the dominant mode of production was socially differentiated. Despite the recent growth of a sizable black middle class, concentrations of poverty, unemployment, and political powerlessness in the black community are still highly disproportionate. For example, in 1979, 31 percent of blacks—three times the national average—were living below the "official" poverty line (Marable 1983, 312). Blacks are concentrated in the most poorly paid jobs or form a semipermanent welfare class. While black political power in cities has dramatically increased, significant national power in corporations or national government remains practically nonexistent.

Capitalism and Racism

What is the relation between capitalism and racism? Traditional Marxism is poorly designed to answer this question. The claim that the mode of production possesses sole social primacy implies that racism is a by-product of and support for class domination and cannot outlast such domination. Though Marxists have studied the relation between imperialist and imperialized nations and dominant and dominated "nations" in multinational empires (see Chapter 13), there have been few analyses of multiclass communities. The rise of black political movements in the 1950s and 1960s has led, however, to much more sophisticated Marxist thinking about black oppression. I will now examine some recent accounts of the relation between racism and capitalism, beginning with theories of how racism benefits capitalism and then turning to descriptions of racism's autonomy.

Like other theorists, Richard Edwards (1979) has described the contemporary U.S. labor market as divided into three segments, each defined by occupational benefits, training, prestige, mobility, job security, and union representation. At the bottom is the "secondary market," characterized by low wages, lack of unions, absence of education and skills.[1] Some writers have estimated that as of 1973 as much as 50 percent of these jobs were held by blacks (Edwards 1979, 197). Whatever the precise figures, there can be no doubt that blacks are highly overrepresented in this segment. Since labor market segmentation is motivated, thinks Edwards, by the need to control workers, racism provides captive laborers who must accept work in the secondary market.

More generally, it has been argued that black workers serve as a superexploited labor force in any segment of the labor market. Isolated from other parts of the working class by racist ideology, subject to legal or traditional constraints, and denied political power, black workers have had to work for less than the currently established wage (Bonacich 1976, 36–39; Cox 1948; Frank 1967; Hill 1980). These conditions also lead blacks, like women, to serve as an industrial reserve army (Baran and Sweezy 1966, 249–80). State support for this reserve army socializes its costs, while its benefits are concentrated in the corporate sector (Baron 1971, 36). Members of an industrial reserve army are forced to take the jobs that better-off members of the working class refuse; they are also more likely to accept speedups and dangerous working conditions (Hill 1980; Oppenheimer 1974). Finally, antagonism between different sectors of the working class politically divides workers. Anger that should be directed at the ruling class is aimed at other workers, making class solidarity in political or economic struggles impossible (Reich 1980; Sartre 1965; Szymanski 1979).

> Ethnicity is created, or at least nurtured, by the bourgeoisie of the dominant ethnic group or nationality. It is used to mark off the super-exploited as inferior, through ideologies like racism. And it is used to bind the more advantaged workers to the ruling class through the ideology of ethnic solidarity. (Bonacich 1980, 140)

Not only is racism functional for capitalism, but we can provide detailed historical accounts of ruling-class support for racist institutions and ideologies: the creation of slavery, the passage of Black Codes after the Civil War, the use of blacks as poorly paid strikebreakers, confinement of blacks to the secondary labor market, political programs like affirmative action and busing (that help divide the working class racially), and the promotion of racist interpretations of the fiscal crisis of the state.

Yet the functionality of racism for capitalism cannot explain why it is blacks who play the subordinate role and not some other group. In fact, the functional relation depends on racism as much as it explains it. Capitalism can use blacks as a superexploited, industrial reserve army only because racism exists. Consider Edwards's (1979, 184) claim: "Workers *have been divided* into separate groups, each with its distinct job experiences, distinct community cultures and distinct consciousnesses. The inability of working class–based political movements to overcome these divisions has doomed all efforts at serious structural reform" (my emphasis). Now it is a central thesis of this book that social differentiation is socially primary because, as Edwards says, it has doomed working class political movements to failure. Yet Edwards seems to suggest that the separate groupings of the working class are products of the evolution of labor control. Notice his use of the passive tense in the first sentence above. What this perspective ignores is that workers have not just been divided; they have divided themselves. Moreover, to speak of workers as *having been divided* suggests (intentionally or not) that the working class was at one time undivided.[2] But the working class has been undivided only in Marxist theory—a unit in the theoretical construct "mode of production" or a potential social agent whose future existence was deduced from the (supposed) lawlike tendencies of the capitalist system. Edwards, like other writers, thus confuses the political reality of actual workers with the analytic role of "working class." Similar mistakes are made by Morgan (1981) and Mandle (1978), who explain racism by way of the unfree status of black workers and thus presuppose the racist reality that makes blacks unfree.

In general, the functional-for-capitalism approach to racism ignores the fact that groups other than the ruling class have been active agents of racism. It also fails to see that the working class lives out its class identity in socially differentiated ways and that this social differentiation is only partly a product of capitalism. In fact, workers endure capitalist society as members of historically created and personally chosen communities, cultures, and groups. The ruling class takes advantage of these divisions, and the dynamic of capitalist society alters their configurations. But neither capitalism nor the capitalist class create them. From the days of slavery to the present, white workers have manifested racism by resisting white and black coexistence in the same labor market. In Philadelphia between 1800 and 1830 blacks were excluded from their previous positions in the skilled trades (Baron 1971, 8). Between 1881 and 1900, more than fifty strikes were organized by white workers to protest black employment.[3] The migration of blacks to the North was greeted by race riots after World War I, by the solidification of urban ghettos following World War II. Blacks have always been widely excluded from AFL craft unions. The AFL-CIO, after its merger, hesitated to take strong action against segregated or discriminating member unions (Baron 1971; Bonacich 1976; Geschwender 1978; Harris 1982; Marable 1983). Even in the most racially progressive unions, such as the United Auto Workers, locals held hate strikes against upgrading black labor, and there was a general complicity in castelike divisions of work and dual seniority lists (Hill 1980, 51–53; Meier and Rudwick 1982).

Bonacich (1976, 46; 1980, 14–15) argues that employers take advantage of racist structures in the labor market; they do not create them. Dominant workers are threatened by cheaper labor, and racial antagonism is their way of limiting capital's access to it. This position does account for the actively racist practices of the white working class, yet it faces a dilemma. Why should white workers restrict black entry into "white" jobs if racism does not *already* exist? How could blacks constitute "cheaper labor" if they were not already marked off by racism? The use of blacks as strikebreakers —Bonacich (1976, 41) lists twenty-five examples between 1916 and 1934 alone—makes sense only if blacks have been systematically excluded from white unions. Any special desirability of blacks as employees requires a previously existing convention of discrimination. Not only do capitalists benefit from this situation; they help create it.

Bonacich (1980) and Wilson (1978) mistakenly offer this theory of racism as an alternative to the traditional Marxist account. The theory suggests that *if* particular employers sought to hire blacks and were opposed by white workers, *then* racism must have been motivated by (perceived) interests of the working class and not the capitalist class. The mistake is to forget that a general capitalist interest in racism may coexist with an interest by particular capitalists in hiring blacks for a particular industry. Also, notice that the attempt to hire blacks against the wishes of white workers usually reinforced racism: such hiring was usually at lower pay and with less union protection than whites enjoyed. The issue, therefore, is not the support of racism by workers as opposed to antiracist actions by employers. Rather, it is a conflict between racist *exploitation* by employers and racist *exclusion* by workers.[4]

We must understand, then, that whites of all classes have agreed that whites will dominate U.S. society (Omi and Winant 1983a, 59). The traditional Marxist account of racism either ignored aggressively racist behavior by the working class or explained it as a product of ideological manipulation: a false sense of racial superiority, a racial identification with the ruling class, a psychological assurance that the bottom of society was reserved for someone else (Baran and Sweezy 1966, 251–52, 263). This explanation is adequate only if it recognizes that in most cases ideologies reflect as well as distort social life.

Racist ideologies and practices are based in the social reality of the separate ways in which whites and blacks live out their relations to capitalist society. In fact, antagonisms based on all forms of social differentiation are grounded in distinct modes of life: separate ways of relating to changing demands for labor, conditions of work, income, state activity, and such ineluctable aspects of human existence as birth, death, family, and sexuality. The resistance of white labor to black "competition" makes sense only to the extent that blacks are seen by whites as a separate, different, and—in conditions of scarcity—threatening group. To appeal to competition over scarce jobs, housing, and city services to explain the post–World War I race riots is inadequate. In a context of scarcity, whites were competing with whites, and blacks with blacks as well. But the lived scarcity was experienced as a scarcity relative not to *all* others but to the visible Other of a socially differentiated group. Spero and Harris (1931, 131) make similar points about the visibility of black strikebreakers. The socially differentiated Other is taken as a threat because the needs of life are met separately and in different ways by differentiated groups. In the face of the strains of class society, differentiation is easily transformed into antagonism. With unequal power, antagonism can become systematic exclusion and discrimination. Also, "Normal" socialization of all groups has typically involved the introjection of shame and guilt. Antagonism between socially differentiated groups thus includes a psychological component of projection onto the Other of what is both forbidden and desired for oneself (Fanon 1968; Kovel 1970).

Theories focusing on the autonomy and significance of race arose out of the liberal and radical black movements of the 1960s—movements which were activist, progressive, and not motivated by traditional Marxist theory. As feminists have used "patriarchy" to designate the various structures of male domination, so "colonialism" has been used to define relations between whites and blacks in this country. Applying the term to relations within, rather than between, countries implies that blacks in the United States were set off as an entire community, not simply as a "superexploited" part of the working class. Two points are central to this analysis. First, colonization involves relations between national/racial/ethnic communities and not simply between classes. Second, racial oppression dominates in ways that class does not (Blauner 1972, 146). Colonization causes a characteristic dehumanization that defines "the person of color within frameworks that are less than, or opposed to . . . full adult manhood" (Blauner 1972, 41; Cruse 1968, 76). I will describe some of the consequences of colonialism for black consciousness later on. What is significant here is that under colonialism the oppressed correctly experience their dehumanizing oppression as members of a community rather than as members of a class.[5] The recent integration of blacks into the northern industrial economy makes them less analogous to victims of colonialism, yet they are still distinguished from white ethnic groups by the extreme violence of their history of oppression. Moreover, unlike white ethnics, blacks were displaced from skilled or petit bourgeois positions by immigrants who arrived later (Baron 1971, 7–9; Harris 1982, 39–40). Finally, in the history of American labor, only nonwhite groups have been the target of sustained, self-conscious discriminatory policies by organized labor (Newman 1965).

The emergence of a sizable black middle class in the last twenty years suggests that black oppression has taken a new form. This form is misunderstood, however, by William J. Wilson's well-known The Declining Significance of Race. Wilson (1978, x) argues that with the recent stratification of the black community there is no "uniform black experience"; the existence of a growing and significant black middle class implies, rather, that race has declined in importance in affecting the "life-chances" of blacks. For the large mass of black poor, he maintains, their class—not their race—is the central issue.

A number of writers have criticized Wilson for mistakes in his concept of class, confused distinctions between economic and political struggle, and distortions of black history (Marable 1980, 207–18; Shulman 1981). I have already noted that he unnecessarily sees traditional Marxist and split-labor-theory accounts of racism as mutually exclusive. Despite his limitations, however, Wilson has identified a crucial change in the condition of blacks in the United States: the creation of an "Afro-American petite bourgeoisie" (Wenger 1980, 71). Responding to the political struggle of blacks in the 1960s, and accepting the natural consequence of black population increase in the inner cities, white America allowed and channeled the growth of a black elite (Hill 1980). In fact, the rise of the black middle class provided corporate America with an ally: "This new elite told the power structure: 'Give us a piece of the action and we will run the black communities and keep them quiet for you'" (Allen 1970, 17–19).

Besides serving as administrators, political representatives, and processors of the black underclass, the black elite are role models of individual success. Without such role models, "the individual achievement model of national struggle could not be substituted for . . . class struggle" (Wenger 1980, 70). The consequences of this development do not, as Wilson suggests, signal a major decline in the role of race but only a change in the form of racism. Black income, employment, dependence on welfare, and reward for education remain well below those of the white majority (Geschwender 1978, 207–10; Harris 1982, 181, 189; Hill 1980, 50; Shulman 1981, 28–29). There may be less self-conscious racism against blacks now than in the past, but this change will not console the black person who, for reasons of his/her racial history, possesses "life-chances" significantly different from those of whites.

It should also be remembered that assertions of the social primacy of social differentiation are based in the pragmatic goal of political organizing. A small percentage of blacks may find race less important than class and even politically insignificant. But there is still a poor black majority for whom race is central. From the point of view of socialist political organizing, the effect of social differentiation on this group is crucial. Always present to some degree, the recently deepened alliance between the upper stratum of blacks and the still essentially white corporate and state power structure makes most blacks members of a "nation-class": that is, a group defined by the intersection of class and national/racial experiences and interests (Geschwender 1978, 264). For proletarian blacks, still the vast majority, both class membership and racial identity serve as a basis for political identity.[6]

Race and Social Primacy

As is true of women's issues, certain writers wish to stress the centrality of race by claiming that race possesses the same kind of primacy as the mode of production:

Thus today racial dynamics can be particularized as the working out of the *laws* of the maintenance of mature state capitalism and the *laws of black liberation*. (Baron 1971, 1; my emphasis)

The consolidation of racial slavery structured the class system as much as the class system determined the racial order. (Omi and Winant 1983a, 60).

Awareness of the codetermining importance of race and class, just like that sex and class, is a hallmark of the transformation of Marxist theory. Yet, as I have already argued, it is often couched in mistaken assertions of the co-primacy of factors that actually possess *equal* but *different* kinds of social primacy.

Consider Harold Baron's statement (1971, 6, 9, 20–36). On the one hand, he claims codetermination of black experience by the "laws" of capitalism and of black liberation. Yet his article, titled "The Demand for Black Labor," accounts for all significant changes in the condition of U.S. blacks—the rise of slavery, the creation of racist ideology, the integration of blacks into the industrial economy—by reference to changing capitalist demands for black labor. While Baron sees white working-class racism affecting these developments, it is to the dynamic of the mode of production that he appeals to explain fundamental changes in the black situation. We may infer that racism, like sexism, has little historical dynamic of its own. What Baron terms the "laws of black liberation" are part of what I would call the dynamics of social differentiation—that essentially political process by which social groups achieve differing degrees of unity. The key structural factor in the creation of the contemporary black urban underclass is the fundamentally changed nature of the American economy: the declining need for unskilled labor, the decrease in manufacturing in the central city, and the increase of low-paying, dead-end, nonunionized service jobs (Bonacich 1976, 48–49; Harris 1982, 179–81; Mandle 1978, 99–104). An outcome of the dynamic of American and world capitalism, this change made the path of upward mobility taken by white ethnics inaccessible to blacks. That a sizable middle-class black elite has been created has been the result mainly of a political process: the response by the state and other dominant institutions to black political pressure. Again, we see how structural conditions are determined by the first form of social primacy, while the political response to those conditions is shaped by the third: the tension between the unity of the ruling class and the social differentiation of the working class.

The last point seems to agree with the main thrust of Michael Omi's and Howard Winant's position. They correctly stress the central role race has played in the political life of American workers and, consequently, the way in which "political and ideological factors . . . constitute classes in combination with economic ones. . . . Class relationships are never given, objective, or obvious; rather, they are ongoing processes of historical conflict. . . . classes may be understood as political projects" (1983a: 43–44).

This claim is accurate insofar as the thesis is limited to the realm of primacy of social differentiation; that is, to the problematic of political organizing and political expressions of unity/disunity on the part of capitalism's contending classes. Because groups live out their lives in socially differentiated ways, their political activity is manifested in shifting, uneasy alliances. Therefore, a simple economic definition of class cannot serve as the unproblematic basis for a political strategy. Yet the first form of social primacy, that possessed by the relations of production and expropriation, remains. Omi and Winant retain it (like Baron) perhaps against their will. In the same paragraph as the last quotation above, they write: "The working class Eugene Debs sought to create in 1912 was not the working class Samuel Gompers sought to create." And they go on to say that their perspective

on class-formation does not require use to reject economic determination *tout court*. It does not suggest that economic relationships are nonexistent or that locations in the production process cannot be identified. It insists, however, that such locations are occupied by human subjects who are historically produced, live in ideology, and engage in political practice. (45)

It would be hard to find a clearer agreement with my claims concerning the different roles of the three forms of social primacy. The point is that Omi and Winant, on the basis of a more or less traditional Marxist analysis, put their major focus on an economically defined working class. It is precisely the "human subjects" of *this* class who will, it is hoped, achieve political unity and mutual respect. If the authors do not base this goal on a preexistent economic definition of class, why are they concerned with differences between the working class of Gompers and that of Debs? Why would they focus on workers, blacks, women, Chicanos, and so on, and not supporters of a particular sports team, voters for Jimmy Carter, or people over six feet tall? Why, in fact, employ the term "class" at all?

The answer is that the structural determinants of long-term historical change, as well as the political possibilities for a "coherent opposition to the entrenched social order," (39), still derive from the first form of social primacy. In the United States, "*capitalist development created races as well as classes*" (60, my emphasis). At the same time "the self-conscious organization of the working class in the nineteenth century was to a large degree a racial as much as a class project." (60). In other words, structural determination by the first form of social primacy coexists with political fragmentation defined by the third.

Because they fail to distinguish the different forms of social primacy, Omi and Winant must describe a social terrain of political struggle for which there is no underlying logic in political economy. For instance, they note (1983a: 55) that minorities were able to affect mainstream politics during and after World War II. Yet they do not link this fact to increased demand for black labor during this period, the economically based northward migration of blacks (with its consequent concentration of blacks in the cities), or the general role of the interventionist state, a state necessitated by the demands of the Depression. More significantly, when Omi and

Winant (1983b) describe the rise and fall of black political movements in the 1950s and 1960s, they pay no attention to the fact that white America's initially positive response to some of this movement was based in the (inflationary) abundance of the period, and that cutbacks in government programs and the resurgence of racism in the 1970s reflect the downward trend of the latest "long wave." They similarly ignore the fact that the entire working class suffered a worsened standard of living in the 1970s and that this worsening was in part accomplished by decreases in the "social wage" —a form of income on which blacks are disproportionately dependent. The lowering of the social wage, in turn, is part of capital's recurrent need to discipline the working class, lower wages (direct or social), and alter the social structures of accumulation.

Let us briefly note also the weaknesses of an argument that tries to salvage a traditional sense of social primacy for the mode of production. This is the argument that racial oppression, like other sources of social differentiation, has its "ultimate roots" in class relations. After all, blacks had a particular place in the system of labor control during slavery and in the postbellum South. Women provide sex-affective labor. Forms of oppression that are not obviously part of economic exploitation—such as lynching and rape—are actually forms of labor control.

The fundamental problem with these claims is that such an expansion of the concepts of the "economic" or "labor" vitiates the original power of Marxist theory. Marx used these concepts because of their role in his theories of capitalism in particular and history in general. But while racial and gender oppression do involve controlling the labor of racial minorities and women, such control does not form a system—a mode of production— in the sense in which the concept can be applied to the capitalism described by Marx. One may salvage the primacy of production by expanded definitions, but such a salvage operation will not rescue the traditional Marxist aspiration to describe an economic system with lawlike tendencies. Rather, we will find ourselves describing an overlapping and often contradictory set of economic systems: those involving workers and capitalists, men and women, whites and blacks, craft labor and nonunionized labor, and so on.

Another understanding of the autonomous political movements of women, blacks, gay men, and lesbians is possible. Different forms of social differentiation are not homogenized as forms of labor control in a capitalist system. Rather, working-class cooperation is seen as the political task posed by the primacy of social differentiation. The primacy of class in explaining certain aspects of the history of racial oppression should not, as I have already argued in the case of women, confer a subsidiary political status on groups not included in the traditional Marxist concept of class.

For socialists, classes are "political projects" whose end point is the co-operation of all groups who may be thought of as part of a very broadly defined "working class."

Social Differentiation and Black Politics

In Part III, I argued that political action finds a base in the needs and contradictions of everyday life and personal experience. The everyday life and personal experience of blacks and whites have been significantly different. While whites have achieved certain limited racial privileges, blacks have created themselves as political subjects in terms of the lived reality of racial oppression. How do black culture and politics express a particular form of social differentiation rather than a generalized class position?

Black resistance to racism and capitalism have been manifested in a racially defined politics. Such politics are based in the intersubjective reciprocity of communal existence. This perhaps obvious point must be stressed because of traditional Marxism's view of political subjects as either atomized individuals or members of classes. Also, traditional Marxism mistakenly asserted that the homogenization of labor would erase socially differentiated communities. In fact, the contemporary working class is divided by a labor segmentation that reinforces, rather than limits, the importance of community. The point, then, is not to make some rigid distinction between the effects on political consciousness of paid labor and community life. As we have seen for blacks and women, socially differentiated groups experience labor—like other aspects of life—in their own particular ways. Communities also express the sharing of human, symbolic, and institutional resources. These resources are mobilized to fulfill socially shaped needs and meet the ineluctable demands of human existence. In communities we face birth and death, aging and sickness. We form family units, grow up, and have children. We develop spiritual resources to face questions concerning the purpose of life and the foundation of moral judgments; we create role models and spiritual ideals.

Two aspects of black communal subjectivity are essential in understanding black politics. First, a specifically "black" cultural identity is a product of slavery and the plantation system, which weakened previous social connections and cohesion (Frazier 1974, 11). Cultural resources were partly shattered, partly re-formed, as blacks created a black race "from an array of distinct tribes and ethnic peoples" (Blauner 1972, 12–13).[7] Second, black American culture was not solely an amalgam of African religion, newly adopted Christianity, and responses to specific conditions of labor. Rather, a distinctive culture was generated partly as a defense against the white world. Struggle against racism is the core of a "distinctive ethnic culture" (Blauner 1972, 141). Black nationalism is in essence a defensive reaction to racial oppression: it is group solidarity in the face of a hostile environment (Allen 1976, 123).

Black culture and black political life, then, express the unique condition of black social differentiation. While other "immigrant" groups faced discrimination and prejudice, they retained much more of their traditional culture to help them face the alien social setting (Long 1969). Black culture and political identity, by contrast, have been problematic to blacks themselves. In both culture and politics there arises a complex and troubling perspective. Feelings of group solidarity combine with the belief that black culture and the black community remain subservient to the dominant white society. Blacks describe their culture and communities as lacking, and call for the creation or rediscovery of authentic black culture and politics. Consequently, there are frequent demands that black culture and political position be transformed. Yet it is to the black community that they speak; it is with existing black culture that black intellectuals and activists must begin. Also, success in overcoming black poverty and political powerlessness requires an alliance with some segment of the traditionally hostile white community and some influence on the usually oppressive white-dominated state (Baron 1978; Blauner 1972).

This difficult dialectic of personhood, culture, and politics is frequently found in writings by blacks. The need to justify oneself to a world that continually exploits and excludes poses a central dilemma for the culture of any oppressed group.[8] Most significantly, it leads to an internalization of inferiority:

The facing of so vast a prejudice could not but bring the inevitable self-questioning, self-disparagement, and lowering of ideals that ever accompany repression and breed in an atmosphere of contempt and hate. . . . we are diseased and dying, cried the dark hosts; we cannot write, our voting is vain; what need of education, since we must always cook and serve? (Du Bois 1970, 90–91).

These feelings of inferiority are internalized in direct relations to whites, especially white employers or overseers. Richard Wright recalls his first day of work:

I was tense each moment, trying to anticipate their wishes and avoid a curse, and I did not suspect that the tension I had begun to feel that morning would lift itself into the passion of my life. . . . *I was always to be conscious of it, brood over it, carry it in my head.* (In Butterfield 1974, 159; my emphasis)

This kind of oppression produces the feeling that being black and being a person are incompatible. However, it is also felt that one can be a person only by developing one's unique blackness: "This history of the American Negro is the history of this strife,—this longing to attain self-conscious manhood, to merge his double self into a better and truer self" (Du Bois in Butterfield 1974, 95). The black must be black—yet to be black is to be lacking in certain fundamental ways. Thus the goal is both to maintain and to transform the meaning of blackness, not just to live it out. Personality is shaped by the struggle for freedom, a struggle based in the recognition of oppression and its effects. It is especially necessary to free oneself, as James Baldwin (1964, 72) says, from control by "white Americans' images" of what blacks are. Thus there is a common theme for black autobiographers from 1901 to 1961:

> Their politics range all the way from acceptance of segregation to communist revolution, but every writer in this group is driven to assert the fact of his blackness as the starting point of creating a free self. . . . The assertion of black identity means that the author takes pride in being black; but it also means that he . . . must somehow discover roots in a country which does not accept him as a human being. (Butterfield, 94; my emphasis)

It is striking that black authors write books with titles like *Invisible Man*, *Nobody Knows My Name*, *Let Me Live*, and *Darkwater: Voices from within the Veil*. Nor is it surprising to find a certain characteristic tone— alternately angry, desperate, and beseeching—with which black writers and speakers address a white audience. Human speech presupposes a reciprocal recognition of mutual humanity by those communicating. Yet blacks addressing whites have typically faced an audience which denied their humanity. In 1901 George White, last black member of the U.S. House of Representatives for twenty-eight years, felt compelled to list the post– Civil War accomplishments of blacks (so many newspapers, teachers, college graduates, and so on) to "prove" that blacks deserved political rights (in Foner 1972, 23).

Black social differentiation thus produces a distinctive culture. Blacks face challenges and have needs very different from those of the oppressive racial majority. The result is that black political movements have a distinct racial identity.

It is not surprising that politically unrealistic and apocalyptic visions animate much of radical black politics. Marcus Garvey's "back to Africa" movement in the 1920s was the largest black political organization in U.S. history. Its goal was political independence in Africa. Not only was this goal impossible; it may have been for most members more a symbol of black unity than a realistically held program (Redkey 1971, 123). The key point is that such a symbol—escape to a country without whites—should be so attractive to blacks (Garvey 1972, 138). Forty years later, with most

of Africa independent and territorial nationalism excluded, black nationalist rhetoric turned to the destruction of white America—often through
concepts borrowed from antiimperialist movements:

The victim must become the executioner. . . . To those who point to numbers and
say that black people are only ten percent, it must be said . . . "It only takes a
spark to light the fuse. We are that spark." Black Power . . . is only another manifestation of what is transpiring in Latin America, Asia, and Africa. (Lester 1970,
195–97)

The nationalist radicalism of Garvey and Julius Lester does not exhaust
the wide spectrum of black political thought that has existed in this country. However, for each shade within this spectrum, the specific and unique
condition of black social differentiation has had an effect. Booker T. Washington, for instance, has been described as an ideologist of black submissiveness and inequality who offered cheap and obedient labor to the slowly
industrializing South (Broderick 1971, 98–100); and as a representative of
the black middle class, a class essentially alienated from a black community whose labor it could not control (Cruse 1968, 156–62). Whatever the
class character of Washington's politics, he faced a situation in which
blacks, living as a minority in a racist country, could become militant only
at the risk of provoking overwhelming white retaliation. Condemnations of
Washington ignore the fact that during his leadership of the black community (1895–1915), whites had relegated blacks to the bottom of society, and
black self-assertion was met by southerners with beatings and lynchings.
Washington's "bourgeois" or Uncle Tom politics thus had a logic that a
similar politics preached to a white working class would not.

Similarly, consider the specific problems faced by blacks during the
Depression. On the one hand, although unemployment and poverty struck
blacks disproportionately, social and state racism meant that black political organizations had to be critical of the welfare and pump-priming initiatives of the New Deal. Programs that might help whites would help blacks
less or not at all.[9] Black reform organizations like the National Association
for the Advancement of Colored People and the Urban League struggled
against these inequalities. On the other hand, they also endorsed the New
Deal and became increasingly attached to the Democratic Party. This behavior reflects not "liberal" politics but the specific condition of the black
community: "It may be tragic that it took so little to win black support for
the New Deal, but the hard facts are that it was much more than blacks
were accustomed to getting" (Weiss 1983, 298). We can emphasize this
point by noting that during this period black reform organizations put
enormous energy into urging the passage of a law to make lynching a

federal crime (Weiss 1983, 96–119). That the law was not passed, and that so much energy had to be expended in its support, indicates that the black political agenda—unlike the white—included the simple demand not to be murdered. Since they could not take even so little for granted, black working-class movements had political premises fundamentally different from white ones.[10]

This difference made the specifically black political movements of the 1950s and 1960s a rational response to black oppression. Whatever the ultimate effect of the civil rights movement, the ghetto riots, and radical black nationalism, these movements spoke to the socially differentiated conditions of the black community. The absence of strong ties to white workers may have been regrettable, but little else was possible when the white working class had become "conservative, pro-capitalist and anti-Negro" (Cruse 1965, 3).

The strength of these movements was their capacity to activate sections of the black community by defining black identity in positive terms, whether as the "moral exemplars" of the nonviolent movement or as macho revolutionaries (Omi and Winant 1983b, 36–40). Unfortunately, the restricted base of the black community meant that the black movement— like all such partial movements, including (perhaps especially) those of the white, male, "traditional" working class—would be prey to certain illusions. The civil rights movement was tied to the belief that civil inequality was the core of black oppression. Left-wing black movements, inspired by overidentification with Third World revolutions, ignored crucial dissimilarities between Americans in New York or Alabama and (for instance) the French in Algeria. Urban rioters, if their actions were motivated by self-conscious political impulses, overestimated the lasting effects of spontaneous violence. All three movements failed to see that a fundamental improvement in the lives of the majority of black Americans required a sustained alliance with the white working class. The reality of social differentiation hides this fact from both blacks and whites.

Racially based political movements, isolated from the dominant majority (and often from other minorities) are both inevitable and unfortunate. Because sustained political action grows out of everyday experience, black politics expresses the particular tensions of black culture. On the other hand, despite the successes of recent black militancy (including reduced excesses of violence against blacks, bringing blacks into the electoral process, and creating a black middle class), the reality of black poverty and oppression continues (Piven and Cloward 1979, 181–263).[11] In the end, the political unity of the ruling class reasserted itself as the state acted to contain and defuse black activism, and new political alignments disrupted the tenuous alliance between white labor and blacks (Omi and Winant 1983b, 41–45). The 1970s saw a resurgent public racism take new forms: attacks on earlier civil rights gains; racist reception of immigrants from southeast Asia and Latin America; racist and/or national chauvinist conceptualizations of the energy crisis, the recession, the Iran hostage crisis, and so on. Finally, the dwindling of black radicalism renewed the importance of class differences among blacks: "Moderate groups maintained their positions while radical ones were marginalized or suppressed" (Omi and Winant 1983b, 42–43).

Multiple Social Differentiation

Whatever the effects of black political movements of the mid-twentieth century, their implications for the transformation of Marxist theory are crucial. Most important is the general point that workers face the ruling class of advanced capitalism as members of socially differentiated groups.

The "politics of difference" growing out of such groups is further complicated by what might be called "multiple social differentiations": that is, the simultaneous existence of overlapping and often contradictory forms of social differentiation. In my discussion of blacks, for instance, I have ignored differences between black men and black women, yet these two groups face different social conditions. Just as working-class and ruling-class men bond together, so do black and white men. Consider the conflict between the leaders of the women's suffrage movement and the supporters of the Fourteenth Amendment (giving black men the vote). Support for this amendment by progressive whites and militant blacks shows the possibility for and the willingness of certain blacks (men) to ally with certain members (other men) of the white majority at the expense of both black and white women (Flexner 1974, 142–47). Decades later, the Niagara Movement, organized by W. E. B. Du Bois in 1905 to challenge Booker T. Washington's hegemony over black politics, called in its *Declaration of Principles* for full "manhood" suffrage (Broderick 1971 100–101). This "principle" was formulated at a time when a women's suffrage movement had been active for nearly half a century. Another half-century later we find male domination accepted in the civil rights and black power movements. This acceptance led women in SNCC, for instance, to compare their position to that of token blacks in white corporations (Evans 1980, 86).

Just as black workers live a relation to capitalism different from that of white workers, so black women live a relation to racism different from that of black men.[12] Black women endure the burden of both racism and sexism ("Black Sisters" 1970; Cade 1970; Lerner 1972; Marable 1983; 63–104;

Murray 1970). Other examples of multiple social differentiation in the context of race include Eldridge Cleaver's attack on James Baldwin, not just over political differences but because of the latter's homosexuality (Cleaver 1968, 97–110). There is also the tendency of mainstream black political organizations to concentrate on issues of civil equality and social welfare while ignoring those of class power.

Not only are the resources with which people face the demands of advanced capitalist society fragmented by social differentiation, but social differentiation is itself fragmented into often contradictory forms. Thus it is not surprising that the various mobilizations of the U.S. working class have been limited by the effects of social differentiation. Chapters 14–17 will examine this point in the history of the Socialist Party, the Communist Party and the CIO, and the New Left.

13

Jewish National Identity,
the Left, and Zionism

THE SOCIAL POSITION OF JEWS HAS BEEN EVEN LESS AMENABLE THAN THAT OF blacks to a theoretical framework that derives political position from economic role. Consequently, the left has consistently misunderstood both Jewish oppression and the Jewish political response to that oppression.

This chapter continues my examination of the relations between the social primacy of class and the social primacy of politics. In particular, I want to show that when Marxism fails to understand the importance of social differentiation, leftist movements will not only fail politically, but also manifest racial, ethnic, or gender oppression. I support these claims by describing left-wing anti-Semitism, Jewish national identity, and—connecting those two themes—Zionism, and the left's response to it.

Left-Wing Anti-Semitism

By "left-wing anti-Semitism" I mean the way the left has ignored Jewish oppression, denied its existence, or condemned as "unprogressive" Jewish responses to it. There are many examples of this practice: Russian Populists, Socialist Revolutionaries, and Bolsheviks at times justified pogroms as legitimate expressions of peasant political resistance (Levin 1977, 53–55). The U.S. Communist Party, by its own account, endorsed explicitly anti-Semitic attitudes between 1927 and 1935 (Liebman 1979, 492–510). Offered an unambiguous resolution condemning anti-Semitism at its founding congress in 1891, the Second International rejected it (Levin 1977, 97–112). In more contemporary writings by American leftists, the anti-Semitism of the Ku Klux Klan and the U.S. Nazi Party are frequently ignored (cf. Gordon and Hunt 1977–78). Left-wing writers have blamed Israel for the "persistence of the Jewish problem" (Kodsy and Lobel 1970, 135, 123)—without explaining how Israel caused the anti-Semitism in fascist Argentina and Chile, "socialist" Poland, or bourgeois France. Samir Amin (1978, 47–49, 103), a sophisticated Marxist theorist, can discuss the "Palestine Question" without mentioning the Holocaust or Moslem anti-Semitism (cf. *Arab-Israel Debate* 1970, 54). In theory and practice, many leftists have treated Jews with double standards, condescension, and outright denial of experienced oppression.

Left-wing anti-Semitism reflects an anti-Semitic Western culture. It also results when Marxist theory confers sole social primacy on economic structure. Marx believed that national identity was being eroded by the spread of capitalism.[1] Since significant national differences were doomed to disappear, national conflicts were to be evaluated in terms of how they aided economic development. In national conflicts among great powers, or between those powers and subject nations or undeveloped peoples, socialist support was to be given to "progressive" social forces; that is, to those groups that supported the spread and development of capitalism.

Since then, two central categories have been added to Marxist accounts of nationalism. In the context of a multinational Austrian empire, social democrat Otto Bauer defined nations as peoples sharing a common language, character, and culture (Bottomore and Goode 1978, 102–35). Such nations deserved the right of "national-cultural autonomy": for example, control over education and language use. Stalin's (1935) more stringent definition required common territory, national character, language, and economic life; a nation's "right to self-determination" could include complete separation or regional autonomy. For "national minorities"—groups so interspersed with others as to lack a territory in which they were a majority—Stalin proposed "national equality in all forms." With the development of imperialism as a world system, a second new category developed. The essence of imperialism, claimed Lenin (1963, 409), was the "division of nations into oppressor and oppressed." In this view, Western workers shared a common interest with oppressed nations. The defeat of imperialism abroad was essential to the defeat of the ruling class at home, especially since such defeat would curtail the use of imperialist super-profits to buy off the "labor aristocracy."[2]

All these positions are inadequate to an understanding of Jewish oppression.[3] Defining a group's political future in terms of its role in class struggle or its dominance of a geographical area, Marxism had little to say about the unique configuration of Jewish identity. If nations or minorities are defined solely by shared characteristics "internal" to a group (such as shared language or land), a key aspect of Jewish identity—common historical experience of the non-Jewish world—is not seen. As black identity cannot be understood apart from black oppression, so Jewish identity includes relational as well as internal characteristics.[4]

Jewish social differentiation is constituted by the intersection of Jewish cultural-religious identity and the treatment Jews have received from non-Jews. As a cultural-religious tradition, Jewishness reflects both religious beliefs and an experienced or longed-for group solidarity. Religious symbols and practices define the manner in which Jews experience the ineluctable realities of human life, such as birth and death, and undergo these experiences with a sense of doing so as part of a historically defined group. Jewish "national character"—a common psychology of collective experience and shared values—is shaped by the intersection of culture and social experience, especially by the need to respond to anti-Semitism. Historical changes in the Jewish condition—the modification of Judaism, the development of modern capitalism and the bureaucratic state, the destruction of eastern European Jewry, and the birth of Israel—have altered but not ended Jewish social differentiation. A collective history of expulsion, inquisition, pogrom, and Holocaust have made Jews a homeless people in an often hostile world. In this context, to be Jewish is to be treated as alien or evil—or, at least, never to fully belong to the nation in which one lives. Jewish homelessness provides a bond among Jews who may be very different in their religious beliefs. It also provides a basis for Jewish attempts to evade—through Zionism, assimilation or revolutionary politics—the fate of a Jew.[5]

With the Holocaust, Jewish homelessness took on a new dimension. The threat was no longer to a person or a local community but to the future of an entire people. Jews can be hypnotized or crushed by the Holocaust, try to forget it or prevent its repetition. But it cannot be absent from their consciousness.

The many forms of anti-Semitism—religious persecution, Stalinist slander, pseudoscientific Nazism—are rooted in a material base shared by the very different types of societies in which anti-Semitism has occurred. In feudalism, capitalism, and the bureaucratic state there are ruling classes that appropriate an economic surplus, ideologies that justify such appropriation and the scapegoating of isolated groups to direct the anger of the ruled away from the rulers. Also, ideologies of domination typically construct a presumed standard for personhood that provides the basis for denying the humanity of a socially differentiated Other.[6] This standard is constituted by the rejection of difference: masculinity by the devaluation of the feminine, whiteness by the hatred of blacks, national identity by the rejection of "alien" Jewishness. Therefore, political movements of the oppressed begin as fragmented and often antagonistic groups. That is why overcoming such antagonisms is the primary task of socialist organizing. Finally (as I suggested in Chapter 12), socially differentiated groups live out their relations to social structures and the human condition in different ways. Under the pressures of scarcity and oppression, such differences become suspicion and antagonism.

Besides sharing or ignoring the anti-Semitism of the wider culture, the left has also been blind to the fact that Jewish oppression has continued despite a variety of class positions and social roles. In the Middle Ages, Jews often served landowners and aristocrats, performing money-related services before money and exchange were common to economic life. As capitalism developed, however, the "true natives" took over those services, and Jews were persecuted and expelled.[7] The comparative economic success of Jews in contemporary western Europe and North America prevents Jews from resembling more obviously oppressed groups, yet a Jewish vulnerability still exists. Concentrated in the professional and managerial class, Jewish teachers, social workers, psychologists, and lawyers often function as ideological crowd-controllers for capitalist society. In this role Jews can still serve as targets for the misdirected anger of the victims of an alienating society. During the last hundred years, anti-Semitism has been used to disrupt progressive movements many times.[8]

The coexistence of Jewish oppression and vulnerability with a varied class position means that conferring sole social primacy on economic structure has blinded the left to the reality of Jewish social differentiation. The cyclical pattern of Jewish acceptance, use, and persecution in different nations is obscured by simplified schemas of working class vs. ruling class, or oppressed vs. oppressor nation. If socialism means the liberation of the oppressed, and oppression is seen only in immediate economic terms, the necessity for overcoming anti-Semitism will be invisible.[9] Economic success, after all, does not necessarily put Jews beyond the reach of oppression. Nazis murdered rich, middle-class, and poor Jews with the same gusto. More recently there have been public attacks and legal discrimination in countries as different as Chile, Poland, Argentina, Egypt, and France. While fringe right-wing groups in the United States attack Jews publicly, anti-Semitism in this country is usually structural or cultural: for example, quotas in hiring or taking Christianity as the cultural norm.

Finally, the Holocaust, a decisive event for Jewish history in general and a crucial motivating force for Zionism, threatens traditional Marxism's theory of history. Marx claimed that capitalism would necessarily move society toward technological development and political freedom, culminating in a postrevolutionary classless society. Such confidence was contradicted by the triumph of Nazism. In the face of social and economic crisis, the majority of an advanced capitalist country turned to fascism. Two highly developed Marxist-oriented parties could neither win over the majority nor effectively resist. Marxist theory can of course explain Nazism by reference to German imperialism and monopoly capitalism, and fascist ideology as a product of capitalists' need to justify the growth of the state sector and unify an alienated German population in support of a militaristic foreign policy. Yet such arguments do not defend Marx's theory of history against the challenge of a historical regression.[10] Unfortunately, one response to this challenge is simply to ignore the Holocaust, repressing the memory of that which is so threatening to faith in the future. As a corollary, the "success" of Zionism—creating a state where Jews are not oppressed as Jews—is denied. Israel is distorted into simply a colonial-settler state, an agent of imperialism, or a cause of "genocide" against Palestinians comparable to the Nazi genocide against Jews.[11]

It should be noted that left-wing anti-Semitism has at times been manifested by leftist Jews themselves. Internalized oppression often causes blacks to imitate whites, women to imitate men, and Jews to reject their Jewishness: in part by denying the relevance or autonomy of anti-Semitism. The socialist dream of universal emancipation possesses a hypnotic attraction to many Jews precisely because it promises to eradicate anti-Semitism without actually confronting it. Unfortunately, however, the reality of social differentiation is not eliminated by a Jew's attempt to identify with "the people." As contemporary feminism grew out of the realization by leftist women that they were being oppressed by "comrades," so cycles of specifically Jewish radicalism have been generated by left-wing Jews who came to see both the specific social needs of the Jewish people and the presence or toleration of anti-Semitism by the left.[12]

Zionism

While the abstractions of political economy may explain the rise of German fascism or Russian pogroms, Jews experienced not abstractions but death camps and pillage. It was out of those specific experiences, distinct from the experiences of other oppressed groups or a generalized "working class," that Zionism was born. Like the black political movements discussed in Chapter 12, Zionism is both justified and inadequate.

Zionism was sparked by a two developments of the late nineteenth century: a wave of anti-Semitism that swept Europe, and the impoverishment of the 90 percent of Europe's Jews who lived in eastern Europe and Russia (Cohen 1970; Laqueur 1972; Rodinson 1973). Zionists believed that economic and social pressures would continue to lead to anti-Semitism until a specifically Jewish homeland was created. With the rise of racial anti-Semitism, Jews in France and Germany found that while being Jewish meant little to them, it meant everything to their enemies. "Being Jewish" could not be "cured" by assimilation or conversion; hence, a drive for a politically separate state defined the "political" Zionism that came to dominate the movement.[13] Simultaneously, economic development undermined the social position of Jews in eastern Europe, and the Russian empire turned to increasingly virulent forms of anti-Semitism.

All forms of Zionism contained the seed of the future Arab-Israeli conflict, for all forms envisaged an eventual Jewish majority in a land already populated by people who had no wish to become a minority in their own country. Varieties of binationalism—extending equal political rights to both the Arab and Jewish communities regardless of size—were espoused (sometimes sincerely and sometimes strategically) by many leading Zionists.[14] Yet by the early 1940s the main thrust of Zionism was committed to the immediate establishment of a Jewish state. Binationalism had never been supported by Palestinian Arabs, who saw little justice in equal political power for a community whose immigration was made possible by imperialism and for whom their own independence was being indefinitely postponed.[15] Also, because the socialist-Zionist commitment to end the historical Jewish alienation from the land directed Jews to the exclusive employment of Jewish labor and the acquisition of land for purely Jewish use, Arabs saw the development of a self-contained and more economically developed society alongside their own. With increases in Arab resistance, binationalism and the goal of class struggle were replaced by attempts to build a self-contained Jewish society. As was the case in the alliance with British imperialism that made post–World War I Jewish immigration possible, Zionists—if they were not to abandon the entire enterprise—could do little else.[16] Such an abandonment is preferable to people who usually ignore the other factor that made Zionists abandon binationalism and gained Zionism the support of world Jewry: the Holocaust. The rise of Nazism seemed an absolute verification of the Zionist premise. Right-wing Zionist Vladimir Jabotinsky described this threat in 1936:

We are facing an elemental calamity, a kind of social earthquake. . . . I do not deny [that] . . . the Arabs of Palestine will become a minority in the country of Palestine. . . . I fully understand that any minority would prefer to be a majority . . . that the Arabs of Palestine would also prefer Palestine to be Arab state No. 4, No. 5, No. 6 . . . but when the Arab claim is confronted with our Jewish demand to be saved, it is like the claims of appetite versus the claims of starvation. (In Laqueur 1970, 57–61)

The Politics of Social Differentiation

The categories of the first form of social primacy are essential in identifying the social conditions that made Zionism possible. In eastern Europe the major force leading to Jewish impoverishment was the development of an industrial economy. This transformation undermined the Jews' role as petit bourgeois artisans and small traders. Anti-Jewish actions between 1880 and 1907 were part of the Russian government's attempts to fracture the working class, a working class brought into existence by the same forces that had undermined the traditional Jewish role. In western Europe the success of capitalism was accompanied by an ideology of nationhood, civil privatism, and scientism. These forces reduced anti-Semitism and supported Jewish assimilation. As in Russia, however, the development of class struggles in the late nineteenth century led the ruling class to use anti-Semitism to undermine radical movements. Finally, the Zionist project would have failed if it had not been compatible with the interests of the dominant forces of an imperialist world system. First British and later American interests—including maintaining privileged access to oil, using the area for investment and export, and engaging in *realpolitik* against contending powers—dictated those countries' policies (Collins and Lapierre 1973, 108–16, Chomsky 1969, 22–29; Davis 1977; Friedman 1973; Stork 1975).

The impersonal forces of capitalist development and imperialist domination may explain certain features of Jewish history, but such explanations do not provide an unproblematic basis for socialist political programs. In response to their fate, Jews have frequently mobilized politically as Jews, not merely as "workers." The most noticeable form of this response is Zionism. There is also the development of the Russian and Polish Bund, specifically Jewish social democratic parties. Founded by experienced socialist organizers who had begun as assimilationists, the Bund came to recognize both the specific needs of the Jewish workers and the values of traditional Jewish culture. It reached its greatest influence in the 1905 Russian revolution (Levin 1977; Liebman 1979; Tobias 1972).

Early debates between the Bund and Leninists highlight the failure of traditional Marxism to contend with the social primacy of social differentiation. The Bund claimed the right of a national or ethnic minority to be politically represented by its own organization. It also stressed the significance of cultural autonomy as part of the socialist program. Lenin's faction, purporting to represent the Russian proletariat as a whole, rejected Jewish political autonomy and argued that fragmentation into national groups would be a "reactionary restoration of medieval legal relations" (Tobias

1972, 277). While Bolshevism consistently opposed such "medivalism" for a Jewish political movement, it reintroduced anti-Semitism as part of the Stalinist terror of the late 1920s and executed the refugee leaders of the Polish Bund during World War II. Given their socially differentiated perspective, it is not surprising that Bundists were among the first to criticize Lenin for "blind bureaucratic centralism" and for overly stressing distinctions between leaders and followers, intellectuals and workers (Tobias 1972, 266, 268). Similarly, the Polish Bund quickly diagnosed the collapse of democracy in the Soviet Union (Deutscher 1959 and 1963; Gitelman 1984; Johnpoll 1967; Weinryb 1970).

The history of the Bund (like that of radical black politics) indicates that the primacy of social differentiation does more than set the political task of overcoming divisions within the working class. It must also alter conceptions of political strategy. Since Marx, purported or actual representatives of the working class have claimed a universal interest in "socialism" (human emancipation, liberation, and the like), but the claim has often obscured the importance of the separate ways in which socially differentiated groups experience the dynamics of class society. It has also masked the fact (see Chapters 15–17) *that purported universalistic groups have usually expressed the interests of only some fraction of a broadly conceived working class.* As a result, left-wing parties usually represent partial interests as universal ones. Social differentiation, therefore, makes the organizational autonomy of socially differentiated groups politically necessary. The transformation of Marxist theory will be incomplete until this truth is accepted.

Social differentiation also embeds itself in the institutions and culture of particular groups. In doing so, it tends to create conflict situations in which there is a surplus of justified action, an overdetermination of incompatible "rights." The institutions and cultures of the oppressed can be essential to survival and self-defense. At times, however, they may also conflict with the legitimate interests of other socially differentiated groups. Without a recognition of the inevitability of such situations, leftist theory cannot understand the conflicts involved in, say, affirmative action or the Middle East. Such inevitable moral–political conflicts contradict traditional Marxism, which sees a unity of political interests deriving from the abstractly homogeneous class position of the proletariat.

In the case of Zionism, we find that a history of European anti-Semitism, culminating in the Holocaust, precipitated the creation of a national home for Jews at the expense of the rights of native Palestinians. Left-wing rejections of Zionism have ignored the fact that the history of Jewish oppression in the first half of the twentieth century made Zionism a justified political response. They have also ignored the fact that more than half of Israel's population is the product of migrations from Third World countries: Arab Jews fleeing Moslem anti-Semitism. Finally, they fail to recognize that if Israel had existed in the 1930s, it could have been a haven for a significant percentage of Hitler's Jewish victims—as it recently has been for Jews fleeing from Iran, Argentina, and the Soviet Union. Again, one indication of the political necessity of Zionism is the fantastic character of alternatives to it offered by some leftist critics: Jews should stay and "struggle" with dominant anti-Semitic majorities in countries where they reside, or they should accept promises of equal treatment in a "democratic, secular Palestine."[17]

It was not those who caused Zionism's response to the "Jewish problem," however, who paid the price. The Palestinian community, whose nationalism was partly a response to unwanted Jewish immigration, had been committed to national independence from the turn of the century. Zionism displaced the native Palestinian community and, with the Arab nations, created the Palestinians as an oppressed minority in Israel and the Arab world (Antonious 1939; Ismael 1976; Porath 1977; Quandt 1973; Rodinson 1968).

Given the tradition of left-wing anti-Semitism, as well as the role of imperialism in supporting Israel, it is not surprising that many of the world's leftists have been hostile not just to this or that Israeli policy or leader but to the Zionist enterprise itself.[18] Facing an irreconcilable conflict of rights, the conceptual apparatus of universalism cannot comprehend a situation in which injustice coexists with rights on both sides. Neither can universalism comprehend the necessity for a socially differentiated oppressed group—especially one with the anomalous social position possessed by Jews—to direct its own political destiny. Similarly, leftist analysis of the Middle East conflict has frequently ignored the independent part played by Arab states in creating antagonism with Israel and maintaining the homelessness of the Palestinians. Projecting a two-role model —working class (good) and ruling class (bad)—onto complex international relations is one of the pernicious legacies of Leninism's division of the world into oppressor and oppressed nations (J. Ehrenreich 1983). Such a model cannot comprehend that Syria, Iraq, and Egypt might be both victims of imperialism and oppressors in their own right (of the Palestinians, for example); that Israel might be both an ally of imperialist power and a form of justified self-defense for Jews; or that a two-state solution, despite its limitations, remains the only viable alternative to continued warfare and displacement.

In the last two hundred years, three different perspectives have emerged as attempted solutions to Jewish oppression. The first was assimilation into a modern national state. The second, which in its own way was another form of assimilation, trusted to international proletarian revolution to end an anti-Semitism viewed as the product of class and, more particularly, of capitalist society. The twentieth century indicates the limitations of both these responses: the fate of European Jews shows how fragile bourgeois enlightenment can be; Jewish treatment by the Soviets and leftist groups in other countries provide comparable warnings. The third response was Zionism. Its success is questionable as long as the future of Israel is doubtful.

The first two responses were not without merit. Emigration to the United States did solve the Jewish problem of Europe for the majority of European Jews who escaped. Similarly, the socialist solution remains valid to the extent that class domination will always turn social differentiation into oppression. Only a society moving from class domination toward democratic socialism can provide some measure of real security for socially differentiated groups.

As a partial solution, unaccompanied by the liberation of society as a whole, Zionism's success is problematic. Its dependence on the United States, support of right-wing dictatorships, and oppression of the Palestinians make Israel "just another country." Like the United States, Cuba, France, and the Soviet Union, it oppresses minorities and supports dictatorships.[19] While Israeli Jews are free from immediate anti-Semitism, they still face racism, sexism, and class domination. Arabs in Israel and the occupied territories suffer legal and extralegal oppression.

Social differentiation, as I argued at the end of Chapter 12, takes multiple forms. Ending or lessening one form of oppression does not guarantee liberation from others. Given the limited options available in class society, achievements by one socially differentiated group will usually come partly at the expense of another group and be compatible with continued oppression within the group itself (such as black sexism or Israeli racism against Sephardic Jews). If a ruling class can set the terms by which a socially differentiated group is pacified, the price of such pacification will be paid by others. To be overcome, the entrenched power of ruling groups must be met by a political unity that counteracts social differentiation.

14

The Dilemmas of
Leftist Social Differentiation

SOCIAL DIFFERENTIATION NOT ONLY FRAGMENTS THE WORKING CLASS; IT ALSO isolates leftists. An exploration of this dilemma prepares the ground for a detailed discussion of the way the three forms of social primacy have interacted to determine the fate of the American left. My treatment here is largely theoretical, leaving detailed examples of the role of leftist social differentiation to the following chapters.

It is some sixty-five years since Robert Michels (1962) argued in *Political Parties* that all organizations tend to oligarchy: that is, tend to become controlled by and in the interests of a small number of leaders. Michels's thesis was that the leaders of organizations develop interests different from those of other members and acquire the power to enforce policies that fulfill those interests. As a response to the breakdown of the Second International, Michels's thesis provided a plausible explanation for socialist leaders' support of European war. While Michels took 1914 as the principal experience to be explained, my concern in arguing a somewhat similar thesis is with the failures of the Socialist Party, the Communist Party, and the New Left. Many factors—including the U.S. role in the world economy, the overwhelmingly conservative effects of socialization processes, the organized power of the ruling class, and the effects of social differentiation —contribute to those failures. The social differentiation of leftists is also a factor, however, and one that has received little attention.

The history of the American left is marked by a practical dilemma stemming from the social differentiation of leftists. This dilemma derives from the way socialist political organizations necessarily develop needs and values that distinguish, isolate, and alienate them from the groups they seek to organize.

The dilemma does not consist in the fact that leftists have a theory of society different from that of nonsocialists; the issue is not differences in belief but differences in the manner in which persons meet their needs as persons. Nor am I suggesting that leftists have different personality structures from those of other people; I believe (but will not argue for the claim) that leftists are often quite similar to nonleftists in personality structure. Further, I am not basing my analysis on the claim that the petit bourgeois or professional/managerial backgrounds or occupations of leftists make them politically antagonistic to the working class (Ehrenreich and Ehrenreich 1979); my concern is with the social identity of leftists as a group of people, regardless of class background or occupation. And I am not suggesting, as Aileen Kraditor (1981) does, that "uprooted" leftists are necessarily foreign to a community-based working class; the point is that leftists are distinguished by their participation in *isolated* communities of leftists, not by their *lack* of community. Finally, I do not believe that socialist organizing is impossible. Leftist social differentiation is a permanent but not always insurmountable barrier to socialist politics.

Shaped by our culture, leftists have particular psychological needs. Persons need to be, and to be recognized as, individuals with specific characteristics. Individual identity, in turn, must be connected to some larger, group identity: family, community, religious tradition, "lifestyle," or nation. As members of some group, persons seek communally endorsed values that make possible the evaluation of activities and goals, and provide a model for goodness and contentment. Finally, people require concrete images of ideal persons and of happiness.

The personal identity of leftists separates them from the rest of society. Socialist politics faces a dilemma because socialists meet their personal needs in ways alien to the majority, nonsocialist, culture. Through political groups and activities, leftists develop a socially differentiated identity. Supposedly political behavior often turns out to be the way a particular socially differentiated group meets its members' personal needs. In other words, as Michels analyzed socialist leaders simply as leaders, so we must understand leftists simply as persons.

A community of leftists develops its own exclusionary form of life. Behavior is defined as acceptable or unacceptable; models of authority and subservience are developed. Thus the community marks itself off from the rest of society. In doing so it is neither better nor worse but just like other communities. However, two significant features of the socialist world complicate its communities. First, the socialist world is self-critical: its principles and practices are subject to review and improvement. Second, the basis of socialist self-criticism can be found in the overriding goal of organizing for a socialist society: success and failure are measured mainly by the capacity to turn increasing numbers of people into socialists.

It is this goal of expansion that is defeated by leftist social differentiation. In meeting socialists' personal needs and sustaining their community, socialist organizations cut themselves off from the majority mass of non-socialists. Socialist politics becomes contradictory because socialists are driven, consciously and unconsciously, by two incompatible imperatives: meet your needs as persons, *and* create more and more socialists.

I offer specific examples of this contradiction later on, but first I ask readers who have been activists to examine their political experience. Think, for instance, of the ways in which our groups develop norms and practices which can make sense only to people who accept not only socialism in general but also the importance of this particular group. Think of how quickly we create self-identities opposing other members of the organization—an easy factionalism that shows how the organization (rather than the larger society) has become our psychic reference point. Think of how we develop a lifestyle in which personal value is proved by doing things (participating in meetings, conventions, demonstrations; reading certain books) for which the vast majority of nonsocialists could not possibly have the time—but we do, because they are the basis of our sense of self-worth. Think of how a political group becomes some form of family, some type of religion, a little nation—something to love, hate, fear, cherish —and how often we leave because it cannot do what we want it to do for us as persons and also "make a revolution." Think of how at a rally, a demonstration, a meeting, we sometimes stand back and think: what would somebody outside of all this make of us?

I sat Friday in and Friday out in a puce-coloured Labour Party room in Hackney while innumerable species of "Trots" hurled incomprehensible initials at each other in exclusive intercommunication which completely whizzed past my ears. Although they all knew each other incestuously well they addressed everyone very ceremoniously as "the comrades in the tendency at the back . . ." They prefaced every statement with "The correct Marxist position. . . . " Gradually I started to decode the initials and the terms. The main key was the Russian revolution. I was soon able to classify someone's tendency in, at most, their three opening sentences. . . . The speakers all had things called "analyses" which they maintained were absolutely correct. . . . I remained bound to the group by the peculiar blend of guilt and masochism which builds up in such circumstances. (Rowbotham 1973, 18–20)

This description of sect politics in the London of the mid-1960s has a peculiarly European ring to it, but the same sense of inbreeding, self-importance, and private discourse must be familiar to anyone who has participated in the U.S. left. The point, however, is that such groups *necessarily* develop a private discourse. Any group engaged in a significant and complicated activity does so, whether it is made up of Marxists, engineers, feminists, or football coaches.

Contemporary feminism has shown to many of us that the elitist, male-dominated politics described by Rowbotham is a very oppressive politics. Yet such judgments can be made only from the vantage point of some *other* community—a community perhaps less oppressive, but another community nevertheless. As another community, it will develop and manifest its own exclusiveness. For instance, its members may be motivated by a desire to avoid creating a community like the one to which Rowbotham belonged; this desire, in turn, will have a decisive (or at least significant) effect on the structure of the community. In a transition from Marxist-Leninism to feminism, say, rigid political posturing may be replaced by obsessive concern for the feelings of group members. The search for doctrinal purity may give way to the pursuit of emotional safety. Vacillation based on self-examination can replace rigid adherence to the Party Line. But how incomprehensible and alienating this will be to someone who has no familiarity with the first community! The later group, though it will seem to be more expressive of the personal needs of its members than the one Rowbotham described, will in fact, simply be expressing different needs. And both communities will be alien to people with different experiences and interests.

Against what appears to be relativism, someone might now argue: "My leftist group is *not* just another group but one which is fair, democratic, liberating, responsive. . . . " And of course every socialist must believe something like this, or else why set ourselves the task of transforming the world? But to work for socialism is to have very different needs and values than to live under it. Socialist communities express the needs of people who are organizing their present lives to achieve a transformation of society, yet such needs are different from those of people who—even if they accept socialism as a goal—are not committed to achieving it.

Consider "ultraleftism": that is, politics in which the strategy, practices, and norms of a political group are modeled on the (supposed) condition of social life under socialism and/or on the decisive acts of transformation—and this at times when neither the postrevolutionary society nor the revolution are in sight. Ultraleftists act as if the revolution has occurred or is occurring; or as if it will have occurred or will occur if only we act as if it has occurred or is occurring. Examples of ultraleftism include expecting a transcendence of the division of manual and mental labor in political organizations; holding the mass strike as the only decisive political weapon when people are not organized in trade unions; and refusing political alliances with other leftist groups whose politics are not sufficiently "pure."

These distortions tremendously strain the personalities of ultraleftists and therefore affect the dynamics of ultraleftist groups. They generate a host of unfortunate needs: the need to blame someone for the failure of the revolution; the inability to sustain membership for very long, since membership requires distorting reality into the skewed perceptions of the ultraleftist; the need to find out why all those other terrible leftist groups don't join us.

In the history of the American left, ultraleftism has led to some disastrous policies. In the New Left, for instance, many white radicals so identified with Third World groups that they could not begin to communicate with the white working class. In the Communist Party there was an expectation that personal and family ties would be unhesitatingly sacrificed on the altar of "correct politics." In the Socialist Party and the Industrial Workers of the World there was at times a public rejection of religion so virulent that it necessarily alienated potentially sympathetic immigrant workers. More generally, leftists have invested enormous effort in intraleft struggles. Leftists have also divided the working class into the "vanguard" and the "hopelessly counterrevolutionary," with the former typically being the one fraction of the class to which this particular left group has some ties. Finally, there are enormous pressures on members of the group to be pure in belief and lifestyle.

These phenomena contradict the goal of building a mass movement for socialism—and they also inevitably lead to the personal exhaustion of the socialist cadre. Unfortunately, socialists *must* believe that we are contributing to the creation of a transformed society and that our group possesses some of the features of the society we hope to create. Socialists *must* be ultraleftists to the extent that we believe that we are models in at least some of the ways we think, act, and live. If we are not models, why bother? However, when the transformation does not occur, when the revolution seems not only overdue but perhaps permanently derailed, we find ourselves under a peculiar form of emotional and cognitive strain. We ask ourselves (consciously or unconsciously), What is the good of all this if we do not seem to be having any, or enough, effect? How can we understand our struggle and pain if we cannot see them as leading in the direction of victory?

This strain expresses itself in our work, in our beliefs, and in what we want from each other as persons. Once again, it distinguishes us from the nonsocialists we hope to organize. We build a leftist culture—partly—to deal with this strain. Nonsocialists do not. Other people's strain and pain are thus different from ours; they do not see their lives as shaped by the commitment to transform society. They do not find their lives challenged or their personal worth called into question if a political movement fails. We do. And such a difference creates a barrier between our lives and theirs.

Finally, it must be noted that we cannot eradicate leftist social differentiation even by recognizing it. To do so would be to eliminate our identity as socialists, or to eliminate the fact that we find (at least partly) our personal identity in our socialism. We can of course seek to limit the negative effects of leftist social differentiation. This task is, again, not shared by the nonsocialist mass. It is socialists who seek to reach nonsocialists, not the reverse. And thus the tasks created by leftist social differentiation, like that differentiation itself, are part of the peculiarity of our personal existence as socialists.

15

The Socialist Party: Fragments of a Class

THE RISE AND FALL OF THE SOCIALIST PARTY (SP) IN THE UNITED STATES during the first two decades of this century was made possible by fundamental changes in the mode of production. These changes weakened authority-supporting socialization processes and gave rise to a political movement whose stated aim was the overthrow of capitalism. The successes and failures of this movement depended on the third form of social primacy: political unity of the ruling class expressed in co-optive reforms and state repression; social differentiation that prevented the SP from representing the working class as a whole. The changes in the economy underlying these developments were easily predicted by traditional Marxist theory. Yet reliance on a model involving only one form of social primacy kept theorists from understanding the crucial role of socialization and politics in both making possible and defeating radical working-class responses to economic changes. After a brief discussion of the American economy and culture of the period, this chapter focuses on the social primacy of politics in the history of the Socialist Party in the United States.

The Mode of Production and Socialization Processes

U.S. capitalism changed dramatically between the Civil War and World War I. The size and scope of manufacturing grew enormously, as did the centralization and monopolization of the dominant industries. Production and the labor process were increasingly studied and controlled by capitalists and managers. The replacement of traditional skills by machine processes and the expansion of manufacturing capacity degraded much skilled work. While ordinary plant labor became more homogeneous, the working class developed a new hierarchy based in masses of unskilled workers and complex categories of foremen, supervisors, and engineers.

220

(Braverman 1974; Brody 1980, 8; Edwards 1979, 37–71; Gordon, Edwards, and Reich 1982, 100–163). In agriculture, farm size and machine use increased; production was integrated into a world market and subjected to international economic cycles. The skills, national origin, and gender composition of the U.S. working class were changing rapidly. Though workers' jobs became more uniform, their national, racial, and ethnic identities became more varied. The urban work force was swollen by newcomers from the countryside and southeast Europe and by women (Brody 1980, 15; Tax 1980, 28–29). Workers also faced an explosion of industrial technique, an unprecedented increase in the economic and social power of corporations, and the self-conscious attempts by capitalists to combine Taylorist control of work with industrial psychology's strategies for managing workers' attitudes and feelings (Asher 1982; Brody 1980; Laslett 1970; Montgomery 1979).

These changes in the mode of production weakened traditional forms of socialization.[1] Images of male authority tied to the social possibility of independent farming, respected craft labor, stable small towns, culturally and racially homogeneous workplaces, and a clear gender division of labor were destabilized. The integration of white working-class men (and small farmers) into reigning structures of authority was undermined when these men found it increasingly difficult to participate in that authority in the way they had come to expect: by owning their farms, mastering a craft, having wives who labored just for them. Traditional authority was also threatened by an ideology of scientific and technical expertise and by leftist ideologies imported from Europe. The familiar institutions of socialization —family, church, popular culture, government—were still adapted to small towns or detached urban settings. Their inappropriateness to urban, industrial capitalism made "America in the late nineteenth century a . . . society without a core . . . [lacking] national centers of authority and information which might have given order to such swift changes" (Wiebe 1967, 12). Under these conditions, processes of socialization and the legitimacy of authority became objects of concern and struggle. When socialization processes are unable to integrate the oppressed into a society unbalanced by economic changes, the social space for radical political movements opens up. The fate of those movements depends on how well the working class can overcome the barriers of social differentiation to function as a unity against the typically well-organized ruling class. It is thus only by understanding the different but equally important effects of the three forms of social primacy that we can understand the rise and fall of leftist movements in American history.

My major concern in this chapter is the effect of the complementary forces of ruling-class unity and working-class social differentiation on the SP. Yet it is important to note at the outset that this history occurred in a context of socialization processes undermined by basic changes in the mode of production. Detailed support of this claim is beyond the scope of this discussion, but two examples may help clarify it.

First, Bowles and Gintis (1976) describe how American education, previously geared to the production of "independent workers," had to be changed to produce workers fit for modern "capitalist relations of production" (185). Corporate elites selfconsciously worked to create the modern system of mass education, including "tracking, educational testing, home economics, the junior high school, the student council, the daily flag pledge, high-school athletics, the school assembly, vocational education and guidance, clubs . . . and the monopolization of executive authority by . . . professionals" (181). This system was produced, Bowles and Gintis argue, by elites frightened of labor militancy. School would Americanize immigrant groups with a dangerous penchant for European radicalism, discipline a new proletariat, and fragment and eventually stratify workers along racial, ethnic, and sexual lines (186).

Second, consider the role of religion in the struggle against socialist ideas in the working class. Montgomery (1979, 76–79) summarizes the antisocialist role of both Catholic and Protestant groups, focusing on the influence of the Catholic Church in promoting conservative union leaders and offering an "ideological antidote to socialism." American Catholic thinkers also supported a "living wage"; that is, a wage large enough to ensure that the wage earner's wife would be restricted to household work. This support for the sexual division of labor "ruled out such Socialist proposals as kindergartens." It is an example of the familiar connection between support for class power and support for male authority—and hence for socialization processes tied to that authority. When the growing entry of women into the paid labor force threatens the power relations of the traditional family, support for the homebound wife is connected to an antisocialist ideology (White and Hopkins 1977, 218–23).[2]

We could add to these examples the rise of the domestic science movement to redefine women's role in household labor (Ehrenreich and English 1979, 127–64); the appeal to science to justify the emergence of institutionalized medicine as a form of social authority (Starr 1982, 79–144); a redescription of female "nature" to justify female entry into the clerical labor force (Alexander 1984; Davies 1979); and employers' growing concern with the public perception of businessmen (Gitelman 1984).

These examples show that fundamental changes in the mode of production destabilize the processes of socialization by undermining the social power of old authorities and making new ones necessary—or at least making it necessary to actively support and defend authorities that have hitherto been taken for granted. At such times, in short, social authority is up for grabs. From the destabilization of socialization and authority, in turn, come political movements to change society. Whatever the details of their politics, these movements are always at least tacitly rejecting some existent forms of authority. To pacify such movements, then, it is necessary to reformulate the principles legitimating authority. And since one's attitudes toward authority are part of one's personhood, the defense of social power requires a transformation of personal identity. Changes in the social structures of accumulation thus alter personal identity, both to adapt to a new society and to continue accepting capitalism. From this perspective, the vastly increased role of the state begun during the years of the SP did more than help rationalize the economy and respond piecemeal to particular grievances; it generated a new image of the state as an impartial arbiter of social conflicts, a resource to defend the working class against employers. Similarly, the growing social role of professionals and managers was part of an ideology of expertise that provided forms of authority to contain dissent in a changed capitalism.

Social Differentiation and the Socialist Party

Formed in 1901 by ex-populists, former members of the Socialist Labor Party, and left-wing trade unionists, the SP's initial platform joined reformist immediate demands with a call for socialist revolution. Despite internal conflicts, the party spent the next two decades focusing its energies on propaganda, electoral politics, and attempts to promote socialist ideas within trade unions. The twofold primacy of political life—ruling-class unity and working-class social differentiation—determined the limited success of the SP. Its stated goal of a "cooperative commonwealth" was pursued by a fragmented party representing groups of American workers with significantly different interests. Simultaneously, structural changes in U.S. capitalism and cracks in the facade of socialization were managed by governmental reform and repression.

Eleven years after its founding the SP won what remains the biggest socialist electoral victory in U.S. history: it won nearly a million votes for its presidential candidate in 1912, as well as seventy-nine mayoralties and twelve hundred local offices (Green 1980, 80). The SP's vision of a socialist America was joined with the "sewer politics" of urban political reform, often indistinguishable from that of Progressives. Hundreds of thousands read the party's publications; it led multiethnic parades in New York City, summer encampments in the Midwest, well-oiled urban electoral machines; it was at times a powerful presence in the AFL and in particular unions (Laslett 1970; Leinenweber 1977; Shannon 1967; Stave 1975). The SP reflected the diverse political interests generated by changes in the mode of production: skilled workers resisting the degradation of labor, attacks on craft unions, and the entry of immigrants, blacks, and women into the labor force; women facing the commodification of household labor and the demands of factory work; immigrants coping with a new society; farmers undermined by the corporatization of agriculture; city dwellers living under corrupt city administrations in chaotic urban environments; the middle class and the poor experiencing more severe business cycles and the drawnout slump of 1873–96; small towns dwarfed by the economic power of the railroads. With varied success the SP tried to contain conflicts of interests among these different groups, usually siding with men at the expense of women, whites at the expense of blacks, and skilled native workers at the expense of unskilled immigrants. These limitations of the SP's politics, we shall see, stemmed from both the structure of U.S. society and its own falsely universalistic ideology.[3]

The social differentiation of the U.S. working class affected the SP in two central ways. First, there were socialist electoral or union enclaves in which a relatively homogeneous segment of the working class used socialist ideology and the resources of a third political party to express their particular interests. In Milwaukee, for instance, a coalition of local trade unions and the SP was based in skilled German immigrant workers and their descendants. As in other segments of the native-born or "old" (that is, northern European) working class, socialist politics was motivated by threats to the position of skilled labor, the defense of collective bargaining, and the need for urban reform (Laslett 1970; Miller 1973). More unique to the case of Milwaukee were a heritage of socialist ideology from Germany, and the specific need of Milwaukee's large brewers' union for industrial organizing (Laslett 1970, 12–14).

Despite their stated socialist goals, the Milwaukee socialists led a city administration differing little from that of Progressives. Its major thrust was to expand and reform local government so that workers and corporations could coexist within it, never to challenge capitalism seriously (Miller 1975, 65; 1973, 69–91). Citywide support for the SP stemmed from its honest reputation and cooperation with Progressive Republicans on issues such as worker's compensation and the regulation of child and female labor (Miller 1973, 49). Its two-year administration (1910–12) initiated government supervision of utilities, union wages and an eight-hour day for city employees, and a fiscal restraint that got the city an improved credit rating (Miller 1975, 51–52).

The Milwaukee socialists had inherited from German Social Democracy the belief that capitalism would inevitably be replaced by socialism. At the same time, they represented one socially differentiated group within the working class: skilled workers of largely one ethnic background. They sought to defend themselves against both changing technological conditions, which undermined their status and employment, and the importation of unskilled labor, which, they believed, threatened their wage scale (Asher 1982; Buhle 1968, 48–49; Laslett 1970, 295–97; Leinenweber 1968, 1–6).[4] It was to meet these needs, not those of the working class as a whole, that the Milwaukee SP functioned. On such a basis one can pursue progressive politics and defend the interests of a segment of the working class; however, in the absence of a united, classwide movement, gains will be subject to reversal: strong unions may bring higher wages and then witness the decline of the industry, plant closings, and the runaway shop (Montgomery 1979, 155–59). More important, working-class particularism in the guise of socialist universalism will lead to conflicts of interest with other sectors of the working class. An organization like the Milwaukee SP could not be expected to change society to meet the needs of the unskilled, blacks, housewives, female wage laborers, oriental immigrants, or farmers.

Thus it is not surprising that the undisputed leader of Milwaukee's SP, Victor Berger, was an outspoken racist (Foner 1977; Miller 1973, 28, 51–52, 81–82, 118). Nor is it surprising that the AFL, which the Milwaukee socialists took as their reference point in pursuit of trade union support, could call simultaneously for the exclusion of Chinese immigrants and the nationalization of the means of production (Buhle 1973, 254). As leaders of a political machine pursuing jobs and prestige, the Milwaukee SP necessarily oriented itself toward state policy rather than making direct demands that would benefit those with a lesser electoral base (Shannon 1967, 22–25; Weinstein 1968, 25). For Berger, as for Milwaukee socialists generally, the universal promise of socialist ideology was to be realized by a certain segment of the American working class. The contradiction contained in this position made it necessary to represent the white, skilled worker as the "real" American worker (Buhle 1973, 259).

Other forms of social differentiation can be found in most municipal socialisms: from New York to smaller cities like Reading or Schenectady to towns like Haverhill, Massachusetts, and St. Marys, Ohio (Bedford 1976; Salvatore 1982, 238–40; Stave 1975). In all these cases Socialist administrations faced the dilemmas posed by Walter Lippmann (1975, 185–92) in 1913, after having been executive secretary to the Socialist mayor of Schenectady. Bound by their non-Socialist electoral support, the Schenectady Socialists refused to "attack privilege," followed the "policies of the reformer," and used their more efficient administration to reduce taxes rather than to "spend the profits socially" or cut into the returns of property. The Socialists lost their distinctive political identity, used popular candidates who had little understanding of or commitment to socialism, and failed to distinguish themselves from reformers (Brody 1980, 32–36).[5]

Other "enclaves" of socially differentiated groups can be found among impoverished farmers in the Southwest, western miners, and New York's Jewish immigrants.[6] In each case the specific needs of the particular group determined both their participation in the SP and their interpretation of socialism. It was essential to the strength of the SP to provide a political setting for these different groups. Unfortunately, the effects of social differentiation made conflicts among them (as in the party splits of 1912 and 1919) inevitable. It also manifested itself in the second major effect of social differentiation on the SP: the sexism, racism, and nativism of the party's policies and practices.

Between 1901 and 1907, female socialists—motivated by previous political experience and women's massive entry into paid labor—organized a number of independently functioning socialist women's clubs. These clubs were created by women who wanted to organize women, found such work unsupported by the SP, and believed that women's lack of political experience made sexually segregated organizing necessary (Buhle 1983; Dancis 1976, 104–6; Tax 1980, 186). While the SP formally supported female equality and women's suffrage, it was incapable of recognizing significant differences in the experiences and needs of male and female workers. While women were entering industry, their lower wages and gender-connected jobs made them victims of "superexploitation," and they received little union support (Green 1980, 97). At home they remained largely subservient to their husbands or fathers. In society they lacked the vote and legal equality. Women workers were thus socially differentiated from male workers. However, the same theoretical model of false universality that allowed Berger to identify the skilled workers of Milwaukee as the paradigm of the working class led most of the SP to view women in male terms. This problem was reflected in practice as well as theory; for example, meetings were scheduled in places (like saloons) where women could not go (Tax 1980, 187; S. Miller 1983, 85–87). Further, there was throughout the SP a repetition of society's sexism (Buhle 1983, 132–49).

Despite lack of party support, the socialist women's clubs become a sizable national presence by 1907. Responding to the threat that these clubs might become an autonomous national organization, and to directives from the Second International, the SP formed the Women's National Committee (WNC), a group of five leaders directed to reach out to women with the help of a paid organizer (Buhle 1983, 125, 147; Tax 1980, 185–86). The WNC raised issues specific to women workers, supported women's suffrage, stressed the need to organize women into unions, and adapted the place and style of meetings to women's needs. Their efforts helped increase women's membership in the SP from 5 percent to 17 percent between 1905 and 1915. Nevertheless, women never really penetrated the centers of power of the SP. Ad hoc committees appointed by the national leadership were exclusively male (S. Miller 1983, 86). Recognition of women's specific oppression, including that by working-class men, was never integrated into SP ideology. In 1915, claiming that "all party work is for women," the party abolished the WNC (Tax 1980, 195). The female leadership of the SP complained that the WNC never really had party support, and that bringing the autonomous women's clubs into the SP led to their dissolution (Buhle 1983, 166–70; Tax 1980, 196–98).

The SP was hurt by its inability to recognize or represent women's interests.[7] As the party constrained its own female members, it found it harder to recruit and organize new ones; as a result it suffered a decline of female membership (S. Miller 1983, 102). It also lost the beneficial effects of women's participation on its general policies. Women leaders of the SP were outspoken in opposing immigration restrictions, and in encouraging the more doctrinaire socialists to see potential allies in such groups as farmers and teachers. Women's unique position—in and out of wage labor, in and out of unions—made them more willing to tolerate differences among socialists and less likely to assume a single, universal political strategy (Buhle 1983, 68–69; S. Miller 1983).

The SP also had serious weaknesses in dealing with racism. Its platform at the founding convention (1901) was unique in American politics in calling for equal participation of blacks in the party and in providing a fairly detailed discussion of racism, a discussion to which black delegates contributed. Yet the platform was a compromise in which direct mention of lynching and segregation was omitted for fear of damaging the party's position in the South. Moreover, the resolution was never repeated at future conventions, rarely reprinted in the party press, and unknown to much of the membership (Foner 1977, 94–103). Most crucially, the party's position —that "black oppression was but a part of the larger class question and deserved no special attention" (Salvatore 1982, 225)—reflected an inability to understand the effect of racism on relations between blacks and both the ruling class and white workers. Until the 1920s the SP did nothing as a national organization to oppose lynching and disenfranchisement (Allen

1983, 212). Locals in the deep South were segregated, and some national leaders were publicly racist. The dominant element in the party, seeking a foothold in the AFL, left that organization's racist policies unchallenged (Foner 1977, 102–3; Miller 1971, 222). Those few leaders opposed to racism faced a fundamental difficulty: "How could Afro-Americans simply be part of the larger labor question when most white workers refused to work or organize with them?" (Salvatore 1982, 227).

There were a few exceptions to the general rule in the Oklahoma SP, among some socialist workers in Louisiana and Philadelphia and scattered coal miners; the national organization did refuse to accept the Louisiana SP's explicitly segregationist platform (Foner 1977, 128–37; Green 1978, 94–115; Salvatore 1982, 226; Worthman and Green 1971). In 1911 the New York City local hired black socialist Hubert Harrison "to do special propaganda work among the colored people"; by 1912, however, the local had reverted to comparative indifference and suspended Harrison for publicly criticizing racism in the AFL. Harrison quit the party in disgust, "convinced that the party was not basically concerned with promoting the interests of the Negro"(Foner 1977, 206, 217).

A change did appear in party attitudes after 1913: more sensitivity to racist stereotypes in the party press, a New York State SP resolution declaring blacks the "most oppressed" people in the United States; increased criticism of AFL racism (Foner 1977, 261–62). In the war years a small number of radical blacks endorsed the SP and put forward the message of black socialism to the more than forty thousand readers of their newspaper The Messenger. Yet the composition of the party remained essentially white. Greater racial unity might have developed with the northern migration of blacks during the war—Morris Hillquit, Socialist candidate for mayor of New York City in 1917, received 25 percent of the black vote— but by then the party was on the eve of its collapse, and the racism in most unions was too strong to be overcome (Weinstein 1968, 63–74; Foner 1977, 263–64).

The related issue of immigration demonstrated similar dynamics. Despite significant exceptions, the party in its heyday (1901–13) accepted the notion that the American working class (variously conceived as native-born, or native-born plus immigrants from northern Europe) had to defend itself against immigrants of inferior class consciousness. The SP's focus on electoral politics excluded concern with nonenfranchised recent immigrants. Acceptance of mass immigration from Oriental countries threatened the power base of the moderates who largely determined the SP's national positions (Buhle 1973: 257–66; Leinenweber 1968). The party's distance from the new immigrants was all the more significant since immigrants were a majority of the industrial working class by 1909 but only 18 percent of the SP (Leinenweber 1968, 1). This balance changed after 1916, when foreign-language federations made up more than half the membership; by then, however, the politics of the party expressed the political aspirations of immigrants rather than of the native-born. In both periods, the party was shaped by social differentiation, not a universal class interest.

The SP faced the fundamental dilemma that a universal class interest, in any political sense, simply did not exist. That is why the party's sexism, racism, and nativism cannot be dismissed simply as errors or oppressive politics (see, e.g., Buhle 1983; Buhle 1973; Foner 1977; Leinenweber 1968). Sadly, there would have been serious negative consequences for the SP if it had not been sexist and racist. The frequent complaint by southern socialists that only segregated locals stood a chance of winning even a small percentage of the working class must be taken seriously. The depth of racist feeling among poor whites was a political reality that formed the basis for the success of the Democratic Party and the turning of populism in Texas and Georgia to explicit racism (Foner 1977, 97–98, 128–43, 238–54). Supporting female union membership or accepting women as equals in the party would have alienated that vast majority of socialist men who enjoyed their masculine privilege. As one female SP member put it:

Our menfolks, like ourselves, still have the capitalist mind, and they may theorize, read Marx and Bebel, yet when it comes right down to practice, they feel that the only place for women is in the home. . . . women . . . also . . . feel like criminals if they dare venture outside their traditional sphere. (Buhle 1983, 132, 137)

Thus even after changes in the mode of production destabilize socialization processes, social differentiation makes it difficult—perhaps impossible—to create a radical political organization committed to all segments of the working class.[8] Because the lived experience of the working class is the basis of its participation in insurgent political action, that political action takes socially differentiated and often antagonistic forms. Socialists are inevitably affected by this fact, but for the most part they have not recognized it.

Moments of Unity

Social differentiation crippled the Socialist Party's efforts to create a mass movement. Conversely, its greatest victories resulted when it overcame social differentiation. A temporarily unifying spirit expressed itself in support for the presidential campaigns of Eugene Debs, the party seeing in him a representative of its best aspirations. Despite his small-town,

Protestant, native American origins Debs seemed—at least before the split of 1912—to represent the working class as a whole. Regional leaders like Berger, Haywood, and Hillquit were clearly tied to particular groups. Debs expressed the commonality of skilled and unskilled, native-born and immigrant, Christian and Jewish, northern and southern workers. This phenomenon was made possible partly by Debs's own personality: dedicated, self-sacrificing, charismatic, uninterested in sectarian party disputes or bureaucratic power. He had the capacity to make an audience believe that its rhetoric of socialist universalism was embodied at least in the person of its leader (Salvatore 1982, 231–33; Shannon 1967, 12–13, 27; Weinstein 1967, 11–13, 25–26).

There were also some occasions when the SP overcame its political partiality in practice. During the "women's strikes" in the garment industry in New York, Chicago, and Philadelphia (1909–11), for instance, female socialists worked with the more middle-class and less class-conscious Women's Trade Union League to support massive strikes of predominantly female workers. The still male-dominated SP contributed $11,000; Socialist newspapers created valuable publicity; SP volunteers provided legal and clerical assistance. These strikes were won, moreover, without the financial resources and central administration that conservative socialists thought essential (Buhle 1983, 190–97; Laslett 1970, 110; Tax 1980, 205–41). Similarly, the strike by unorganized immigrants at the Lawrence, Massachusetts, textile mills in 1912 was actively supported by the still native-dominated SP. Even archenemies Bill Haywood (of the industrial union supporting the IWW) and Victor Berger cooperated in different but important roles. Political and personal differences stemming from different constituencies were put aside. Until the power of social differentiation resurfaced in the eventual breaking of the Lawrence unions,[9] the temporary unity among the various segments of the working class was an irresistible force.[10]

In Debs's symbolic role and the strategic unity in New York and Lawrence, the SP was a party dedicated to the fundamental transformation of capitalist society, rather than a reformist interest group representing particular sectors of the working class. Yet social differentiation proved more powerful than these moments of unity. Thus, while the SP offered valuable support during the "women's strikes," it offered little continuing support for its own women organizers. Also, though the women's presence in garment unions was becoming accepted, "the missing dimension of outreach toward nonwage-earning women remained maddeningly elusive" (Buhle 1983, 207). The initial victory at Lawrence was broken by employers' manipulation of ethnic antagonisms. The cooperation between the SP's left and right wings, essential to victory in the strike, dissolved as Haywood was recalled from the party's national executive board for having publicly advocated sabotage. Finally, employers cut down production in Lawrence, creating high levels of unemployment there, and helped organize vigilante groups to terrorize the IWW and the more militant workers (Tax 1980, 268–75).

As a general rule, the white-, male-, and (until 1915) native-dominated SP tended to reach out to women, blacks, and immigrants only when social change made such a reaching-out politically advantageous. The acceptance of blacks coincided with the increased presence of blacks in the industrial north and their potential role as voters or strikebreakers (Foner 1977, 263–64; Miller 1971, 226–27; Weinstein 1967, 112). Union leaders tended to accept immigrants mainly after immigrants had formed "cohesive economic units" (Asher 1982, 331). The WNC was partly a response to the prospect of an autonomous, socialist women's organization.

The SP's successes, when they were not tied to an obviously homogeneous group such as the Milwaukee socialists, were still not those of a generalized working class committed to a universally liberating future. Rather, they were temporary coalitions of groups whose self-identification was still very much based in social differentiation. The greatest strength of the SP was found where it became an essential part of community life, a life defined by the experiences and needs of particular groups: socialist parades in New York City expressed community-wide support for strikes and overcame divisions between the workplace and the home; week-long summer "encampments" in the Midwest combined religious enthusiasm and socialist propaganda; a Milwaukee SP baseball game once featured Berger as a player (Leinenweber 1977; Salvatore 1982, 236–38; Shannon 1967, 220).

The SP's strength depended on its connections to the everyday life of different communities. Therefore, divisions among those communities—or changes within them—weakened it. Despite the rhetoric of universal working-class interest, actual or potential supporters of the SP experienced their social situation in socially differentiated ways.[11] A political movement based in these different groups required the recognition of some collective, overriding, shared interest; it necessitated cooperation among groups whose immediate interests and experiences differed.

By 1919, despite internal divisions and government reform and repression, the party had practically regained its 1912 high of more than 110,000 members. Yet as a number of writers emphasize (Laibman 1979, 45–55; Laslett 1970, 302–3), this was not really the "same" SP. Its strength had moved from the rural West to the urban Midwest and East, from native-born craft workers to unskilled immigrants, from Christian to increasingly Jewish membership. Politically, there was decreasing identification with the AFL and increasing support for the Bolshevik revolution. Moreover, the SP's anti-war stand made it an electoral repository for pacifist sentiments which, like its earlier efforts at municipal reform, had no necessary connection to socialism (Friedberg 1974; Strong 1971, 396). This changed party did not recognize the social primacy of social differentiation. Rather, another model of universality was assumed: "a universal proletarian, the worker stripped of all his loyalties save those to his class" (Buhle 1973, 276).

Ruling Class Reform and Repression

The SP lost not only because the working class was fragmented but because the ruling class was not—or at least it was less so. Structural changes in the U.S. economy made possible the dissident political movements of which the SP was a part. They also led to self-conscious attempts by the ruling class to manage political conflict and protect the essential forms of its rule. During the period when the SP flourished, American corporate leaders welcomed government regulation and a certain amount of limited, co-optive unionization (Kolko 1967; Weinstein 1968). The precise success of the National Civic Federation's coalition of corporate leaders and conservative unionists has been questioned (Montgomery 1979, 83, 84). Yet most writers agree that a principal explanation of the failure of the SP was the way government reforms regulated corporate behavior and provided some protection for segments of the working class. "Union leaders," claims Montgomery, found the government's "promise of mediation services" and "legislated standards for working conditions" to be "irresistible." Liebman (1979, 47) argues that many native-born Americans left the SP partly because of "increased economic security and relative prosperity flowing from government reform regulation and higher commodity prices." Green (1980, 87) notes that Wilsonian reforms brought both socialists and progressives into the Democratic Party in 1912 and 1916 (see also Laslett 1970, 302; Salvatore 1982, 224; Shannon 1967, 79).

Government reform not only co-opted dissent but was intended to do so. From 1880 to 1920 the United States witnessed violent mass strikes, the growth of the SP and the IWW, immigrants carrying political inspiration from Russia, increased radicalization of blacks, and the beginnings of industrial unionism. The U.S. ruling class was well aware of these threats. It mobilized to defeat both an unregulated capitalism and political opposition (Forcey 1961, xx; Kolko 1967, 66, 130, 285; Weinstein 1968).

Ruling-class unity also expressed itself as direct repression. In response to the SP's opposition to World War I, hundreds of its leaders were jailed or prosecuted, its publications banned from the mails, and its members subjected to vigilante attacks. The Socialists of the Southwest, for a decade the most concentrated, best organized, and perhaps most truly socialist of the party, were "destroyed by vigilante and government repression during World War I" (Green 1978, xii). Federal, New York State, and National Civic Federation commissions, responding to Bolshevik propaganda and black self-defense in the race riots of 1919, recommended measures to contain what they perceived as a growing black radicalism (Foner 1977, 290–302).

The Role of Leftist Social Differentiation

Two splits mark the history of the SP. In 1912 a minority departed, rejecting the party's condemnation of sabotage and preference for electoral politics. In 1919 the party leadership expelled more than half the membership, rejecting the majority's commitment to violence, revolution, and "proletarian dictatorship" (Shannon 1967, 133). A number of writers have stressed the importance of one or the other of these splits in explaining the failure of the SP (e.g., Liebman 1979; Weinstein 1967). I wish to suggest that they are another expression of the social differentiation of the left.

In both splits "real" political issues were involved. Disagreements reflected the interests and needs of different segments of the party and, therefore, of the working class. Yet the breaks were also caused by the self-important posturing that inevitably results from the dilemmas of socialist identity discussed in Chapter 14. The 1912 split was precipitated by a speech in which Haywood advocated sabotage and other forms of violence as essential to class struggle. Haywood had apprenticed in the brutal atmosphere of western mining struggles and was no stranger to violence. Yet he also had a history of counseling nonviolence during crucial strikes, in Lawrence and Akron, for example. It seems that his personal antagonism to the conservative wing of the party in general and to its New York leader, Morris Hillquit, in particular helped motivate Haywood's speech. He also had a habit of macho self-presentation (Shannon 1967, 37–39; Weinstein 1975, 11–16). While this attitude was appropriate to struggles in the West, its lack of attention to long-term strategy and its contempt for organization were inappropriate to dealing with older and more organized sections of the working class. Comparable tensions—this time centered in images of Bolshevism rather than the IWW—sparked the 1919 split.[12]

In neither case did socialists on either side recognize the absolute necessity of achieving cooperation among different segments of the working class. To put it another way: in both cases a mythical unity based on a false universalization—seeing the AFL or the IWW, the Bolsheviks or the municipal socialists, as the "real" working class—obscured the necessity for a cooperation based in the recognition and acceptance of difference. What was needed was not the pursuit of the "real" working class and its "real" representatives but an acceptance of the commonality of interests of skilled and unskilled, unionized and nonunionized, black and white, those using electoral politics and those faced with direct repression, male and female.

Perhaps the social conditions facing such different groups will keep them from achieving effective political unity. Perhaps oppressive relations between some groups (between men and women, for example) make comradeship impossible. If so, anything even approaching a socialist victory is impossible. Furthermore, if the radicalized members of each of these groups begin with a presupposition of strategic uniformity based in social homogeneity, the social primacy of social differentiation will make political cooperation impossible. The movement will exclude large segments of the working class and inevitably fragment itself. Finally, political unity in the ruling class will subject fragmented radical groups to co-optive reforms and repression.

In the context of political organizing, the disunity of the working class and the unity of the ruling class are crucially important: once changes in political economy and weakened socialization processes make insurgency possible, they become the socially primary factors. Because the ruling class has greater organizational capacity, the working class—if it is to transform society toward socialism—must be unified. Because segments of the working class are motivated toward radical or insurgent political activity by experiences specific to their socially differentiated condition, overcoming social differentiation is crucial to any attempt to organize the working class.

The SP embodied a crucial error of traditional Marxism: the belief that the structures of capitalist accumulation unproblematically determine the political boundaries of a homogeneous working class. While an undifferentiated "wage labor" may serve the theorems defining capitalist accumulation, the concept is inadequate to the realities of personal experience and political action. When a socialist party fails to understand this fact, it will necessarily describe itself as representing an undifferentiated universal interest. In fact, socialist movements are shaped by the limited interests of socially differentiated groups. It is thus a mistake to attribute the SP's failure to an inherent American culture of individualism that made class consciousness difficult to achieve (Salvatore 1982, 267–71).[13] Members of the working class were, during this period, highly involved in a variety of collective identities. It was the collective identity of socialist that was lacking; those based in race, sex, union, nationality, and religion flourished. *The unfortunate contrast to socialism was not individualism but social differentiation.*

Similarly, appeals to the "success" of American capitalism or the party's own strategic mistakes as explanations of the SP's failure are inadequate if not joined to an understanding of the social primacy of social differentiation.[14] The success of American capitalism was precisely its capacity, during this period, to meet the needs of some segments of the working class and not others. The waves of radicalism moving through different segments of the American working class—from populist farmers to craft workers and then to nonskilled workers in the early 1900s—indicate the socially differentiated areas variously undermined and co-opted by capitalist development and the state. Criticisms of SP strategy—too left, too right, too sectarian—are also invoking social differentiation. Overly reformist and ultraleftist politics necessarily stem from taking one segment of the working class as its "universal" element. Sectarianism, in turn, is a manifestation of the social differentiation of socialists.

The first form of social primacy, the mode of production, made the emergence of the Socialist Party possible. The weakening of social authority due to the undermining of socialization processes (the realm of the second form of social primacy) allowed members of the working class to challenge authority. Within these contexts, social differentiation determined different sets of experiences and different motivations for political action. The radicalism of the SP, in turn, was a series of waves, based on the sometimes intersecting and often contradictory immediate interests and social fortunes of different groups.

16

The Communist Party and the CIO: History and Subjectivity in the 1930s

IN THE 1930S THE SELF-CONSCIOUS ACTIVITIES OF CLASSES DETERMINED HOW the structural failures of capitalist accumulation would be resolved. In this unfolding of History and Subjectivity we find the characteristic effects of the three forms of social primacy. The economic structure shaped classes as the dominant collective subjects. Other socially differentiated groups did not break through socialization processes and political oppression to embed a collective consciousness in political organization; rather, they were largely dependent on the dynamic of groups that did. In the absence of widespread and continuous self-organization by women or blacks, for instance, gender and race functioned as dependent aspects of social life.

As I have argued above, this claim does not imply that gender or race, to name two of the many forms of social differentiation, were not socially significant. Gender was essential for the reproduction of societywide political acquiescence. Both gender and race were essential elements in personal experience, deterring adequate solidarity among oppressed groups. Socialization processes, the second form of social primacy, were essential because prospects for revolution or reform were not simple products of economic conditions. Only an understanding of how unemployment, poverty, and bank failures were experienced will give us a sense of the political possibilities of the period. This experience, in turn, depended on beliefs and attitudes largely shaped by socialization processes.

The expression of group interest in the political unity or disunity of contending groups is the realm of the third form of social primacy. In the face of economic and social crisis, the ruling class, despite shared interests, was divided on its choice of strategies, at least until the decade's end. The capitalist state attempted various policies to resolve contradictions between accumulation and legitimation in the face of an at times insurgent working class. Despite its successes, the working class lacked a coherent political identity. The Communist Party (CP) received worker support only when it organized for limited reforms and supported Roosevelt. The CIO, with its unprecedented success among industrial workers, did not include the growing number of white-collar workers, offered little for women, and was divided from the craft labor of the AFL. Political unity was greatest in the New Deal coalition. However, except for certain issues such as welfare benefits, political initiatives and power in this coalition remained with the state. The CP followed the CIO, and the CIO accepted Roosevelt's efforts to preserve capitalism. Explanations of these facts are mistaken if they appeal mainly to the strategic failures of the CP and the CIO.[1] The simple truth is that the working class was bound by forms of socialization that had been weakened but not broken; it was still fragmented by social differentiation.

This chapter briefly describes the economic and social crisis of the 1930s, then attempts to show how the effects of socialization and the complementary unity and disunity of the ruling class and the working class determined how this crisis would be resolved. I focus on two central causes of the limitations of socialist politics during this period: the weaknesses of the CP, and the way a militant working class remained bound by bourgeois hegemony.

The Economic Context

From 1890 to 1930, centralization and monopolization drastically limited the unrestrained price competition that had caused the slump of 1873–96. Craft unions gained grudging acceptance, though even their few prerogatives were often under attack. Partly in response to such unions, however, employers altered the labor process to undermine the autonomy and power of craft workers. Through "technical control," manufacturing processes were redesigned so that the skills of individual workers no longer contributed significantly to the work process. Also, the pace of work was determined by the structured assembly line. This "drive system" substituted the impersonality of plantwide technology for the personal and direct commands of a foreman (Edwards 1979, 111–30; Gordon, Edwards, and Reich 1982, 100–164). Simultaneously, attempts to control the work force through industrial psychology and separate "personnel" departments increased. While more women (including married women) joined the paid labor force, they were occupationally segregated. Similarly, though a significant postwar migration of blacks increased their participation in the northern, especially industrial, work force, they continued to enter that work force in specifically "black" positions (Green 1980, 124–27; Spero

and Harris 1931; Tentler 1979, 13–57; Ware 1982, 21–26). With the breaking of the 1919 steel strike and the post–World War I repression of the left,
the power of the working class was at an extremely low ebb during the
1920s (Davis 1980). Membership in the AFL was down, and the number of
strikes in 1929 was about one-third its 1919 level.

Ruling-class profits were high. New markets had been discovered and
raw materials cheapened; production of the automobile and associated
commodities absorbed huge amounts of surplus; and monopolization lessened competition. This economic abundance supported "welfare capitalism": the self-conscious and well-publicized attempt by employers to win
the loyalty of workers through company unions and benefits (Brody 1980,
48–81).

The combination of improving working-class living standards and a
high rate of profits made for social peace during the 1920s. It could not
last: despite certain inroads into the autonomous economy brought about
by the Progressive Era and by government direction during World War I,
the basic movement of capitalist accumulation remained unrestrained; consequently, competitive capitalism's tendency to business cycles of increasing severity inevitably made itself felt. The enormous concentration of
profits led to a failure of demand. Simultaneously, U.S. capital became
increasingly underutilized. With much of American society, especially
those who had prospered during the decade, tied to a belief in the uninter-
rupted expansion of the American economy, consumer spending and stock
market speculation continued until the crash of 1929 (Baran and Sweezy
1967, 234–48; Gordon, Edwards, and Reich 1982, 167–74; McElvaine 1984,
25–50). By 1933, fifteen million people, at least 25 percent of the work
force, were unemployed, and some forty million (one-third of the nation)
were without normal income. Manufacturing had declined by 54 percent
and hovered at about 50 percent of capacity (Baran and Sweezy 1967, 232,
242; Boyer and Morais 1976, 249–53; Green 1980, 135). These cold figures
were lived out in an emotional devastation affecting much of U.S. society.
Consequently, the ideological mechanisms that had integrated the working
class into the capitalist system could not be sustained, for they were dependent on continually expanding accumulation. There followed U.S. capitalism's greatest legitimation crisis, a crisis that demanded significant
changes from the state and other social authorities.

This economic and social context set the stage for the political successes
of the CP and the CIO. However, although the authority essential to the
reproduction of capitalist society had been shaken, only a small number of
the basic prerogatives of capitalist power were challenged. And most of
those challenges were dropped after the promises of the 1920s seemed to
have been made good in the 1940s and 1950s, and after the dominant force

of the left proved to be both strangely alien and in certain ways indistinguishable from other forms of social authority.

Socialization and Authority

In the 1920s a fundamental transformation of American culture occurred. Images of personal identity and relations to authority took on a form that lasted to the 1960s. As the 1920s introduced mass consumption to the American public, personal identity became increasingly identified with such consumption, and social authority was legitimated by facilitating it. In such "civil privatism" (to use Habermas's (1975) term), people accept high living standards and privatized (that is, familial) relationships while giving up significant participation in political life. When joined to an increasingly ubiquitous mass culture, civil privatism lays the seeds of what I have defined as the "dominated self"—that self confronted by images which purport to represent it but from which it is essentially estranged.

In a context of high consumption and welfare capitalism, there is necessarily a transition in workers' attitudes toward authority. In 1931, already two years into the Depression, conservative AFL leader John Frey lamented: "So many workmen here have been lulled to sleep by the company unions, the welfare plans, the social organizations fostered by the employer. . . . that they . . . look upon the employer as their protector" (Brody 1980, 78). Simultaneously, advertising budgets rose by 150 percent in the 1920s, reaching $1.5 billion in 1928 (Carter 1970, 32). This money helped create role models that the public could identify with solely on the basis of shared consumption, not action or virtue. Studying the biographies of personalities featured in popular magazines, Leo Lowenthal (1961) found a change from "idols of achievement" to "idols of consumption." This change involved an implicit redefinition of the meaning of success. Paul Carter summarizes Lowenthal's observations that for these people success "is not something they achieve, but something that happens to them, through forces as far beyond their control as earthquake or flood" (Carter 1970, 29). Similarly, the new movie magazines portrayed stars in terms of their consumption of particular commodities (Prince 1984).

Mass society, technological development, and the bringing together of culturally heterogeneous groups weakened traditional authority. The rise of an ethic of consumption corresponded to the devaluation of work, the use of technical control, and the increased size and scope of social institutions. Similarly, the degradation of work and the increasingly sophisticated technology of the work process drastically reduced the impact of the ordinary individual. Two essential elements of early capitalist ideology—individual accomplishment in work, and the resources of one's community—

were thus undermined by structural changes in the economy. A socialist response would have been possible had not the working class and its political "leaders" retained the effects of an authoritarian form of socialization: the belief that authority is reserved for an elite, the acceptance of male domination, and a comparable attachment to hierarchy in areas of life outside the family.

The identification of personhood with consumption, and social authority with the capacity to provide or manage consumption, was supported by the actual possibilities of working-class life during the 1920s. Real weekly earnings increased by nearly 15 percent between 1922 and 1927. Even more important was the "qualitative leap in living standards" accompanying that rise: electricity, indoor plumbing, central heating, home appliances, the radio, and automobiles became available. With the advent of a consumer lifestyle, in turn, leisure became oriented more toward consumption and less to communal activities.

The working man was granted access to the goods of the productive system beyond the dreams of earlier generations. If his share in making a Chevrolet was the endless repetition of a single task, the assembly-line worker stepped into one of those machines and drove it home at the end of the day. (Brody 1980, 65)

Simultaneously, the worker was confronted with ever more pervasive images of sexuality and consumption to which he or she could only aspire. Enormously appealing images of beauty and accomplishment dazzled the workers with all that they would never attain. As consumers fervently pursued these images, an explosion of credit saw a great many American workers living beyond their weekly income. The new culture was thus "weaning workers from their traditional values and remolding them into acquisitive, amoral individualists" (McElvaine 1984, 202). What was left, then, was the endless pursuit of more material goods combined with the occasional feeling that it was never enough.[2]

The complex interplay of consumerism, a rising standard of living, and the social presence of images of attainment from which most people were excluded was essential to the subsequent political dynamic of the 1930s. Working-class militancy during the decade did not seek state power or collective control of the means of production. Rather, workers sought to alter or create institutions to ensure their participation in a consumer-oriented society. The demand was not for social power but for guaranteed consumption or, at least, for social power insofar as it would guarantee consumption.

Consciousness and the Depression

The mistakes of the Communist Party were essential to the left's inability to create a lasting political presence in the United States. Unemployment, poverty, militant strikes and actions by the unemployed did suggest the prospect of radical social change. However, even an ideal CP would have been limited by the working-class consciousness of the Depression period. Without an understanding of the limited scope of working-class response to the terrible conditions of the 1930s, the failure of the left becomes incomprehensible. Neither the general economic crisis nor the militancy of parts of the working class signaled the possibility of a large leftist movement. That either contemporaries or later critics thought such a possibility existed indicates a failure to understand the interrelation among the different forms of social primacy, especially an inability to see how a full break with traditional socialization is a necessary condition for a socialist revolution.[3]

Many workers initially responded to the Depression by blaming themselves: "The mood of the downtrodden in the Hoover years is one of defeat, resignation, and self-blame" (Boyer and Morais 1976, 254–59; Garraty 1978, 177–87; McElvaine 1984: 81; Piven and Cloward 1979, 48–49; Ware 1982, xiii). However, there were numerous examples of violent action on the part of the unemployed in the early years of the 1930s. Such militancy was essential to the creation of federal relief programs; many government, business, and even conservative union leaders believed that government action was necessary to forestall a revolution (McElvaine 1984, 90–94; Piven and Cloward 1979, 108–10). The decade also saw a variety of mass political movements claiming to support the interests of the poor against those of the rich.[4] The CP rose from a tiny and isolated political sect in 1929 to a significant political presence ten years later. At decade's end, nearly six million industrial workers had formed the CIO.

Yet what is remarkable about all these movements is how quickly they either disappeared or lost their radical politics. Francis Townsend, Father Coughlin, and Huey Long, with millions of followers in the mid-1930s, were politically irrelevant by the beginning of World War II. The CP, through which perhaps a half-million people passed during the decade and which influenced millions, was by 1941 clearly on the decline; by the late 1940s an anti-Communist crusade would eliminate virtually all of its remaining influence. The CIO, whatever the original intentions of some of its rank-and-file and lower-level organizers, was by the war years pretty much committed to bargaining for improved conditions for its members within the existing distribution of social power.

The objective condition of poverty; the subjective reactions of disappointment, despair, and self-blame; the rising tide of anger and disillusionment; militancy in the streets and in factories—all these fell far short of the necessary conditions of a socialist movement. However angry people were, the vast majority were not ready to alter the social order fundamentally: that is, to replace capitalism with socialism. Those few who supported a revolutionary social transformation retained an elitest model of authority. The majority in these movements were militant mainly in pursuit of the values that had come to shape working-class consciousness during the 1920s: participation in the American Dream of mass consumption; a reasonable amount of respect at the workplace:

> *We dont want a revolution* in this country where innocent men, women and children will be shot down without mercy. . . . With the majority of us poor people *we desire good things* as well as the higher classes of society. For instance we desire a *nice home* to live in with sanitary surroundings . . . a *nice refrigadaire, electric stove, fan, nice furniture, radio, a nice car with money to take a vacation.* (A 1936 letter to Eleanor Roosevelt, quoted in McElvaine 1983, 193; my emphasis)

> The industrial union organizing drive of the 1930s was a movement for democracy. Talk to the mass production workers who took part in it, and they will tell you that *what they wanted more than anything else was dignity.* They wanted freedom from the petty harassment of a foreman who would send a man home at will and reward those who curried his favor. . . . They wanted "unions of their own choosing" . . . to stand up to . . . corporate employers and bargain on equal terms. (Lynd and Lynd 1973, 1; my emphasis)

The radicalism of the 1930s diminished when the demands described in those quotations were satisfied. The wartime economy of the early 1940s brought back the high consumption of the 1920s, and on a "sounder" footing that would last for another three decades. Simultaneously, a sizable percentage of the working class received a certain amount of government protection of their income. Meanwhile, the development of mass production unions and a resurgence of the AFL gave the industrial working class a public presence to represent their interests.

It is significant, however, that the two demands cited above do not speak of new forms of social organization or any real transformation in social authority.[5] Not surprisingly, the CP and the CIO retained the same principles of authority and hierarchy as other political organizations. Likewise, the sexual division of labor and power within the family remained pretty much unchanged (McElvaine 1983; Ware 1982, 13–17).

The 1930s saw the rise of subjectivity on the part of the American working class. The breakdown of the social structure of accumulation frustrated workers' desire for a comfortable material life—perhaps the first time in history that such a thing had even been within the reach of a sizable portion of a nation's "lower" classes. Despite the political ferment of the time, the goal of the class was never to attain collective social power. Only a small minority of highly politicized workers could conceive of such a goal. For the most part, even the Communist minority possessed a vision of a changed society in which the forms of authority were not really so different from those of patriarchal capitalism.

The Communist Party in the 1930s

Made up mainly of the left wing of the SP and radical European immigrants, a unified American Communist Party emerged in 1923. During the 1920s the party toiled in comparative obscurity and exhausted itself in internal squabbles. Its membership failed to regain the high of 1919, never exceeding ten thousand. The CP's union strategies had begun with the attempt to radicalize the AFL by "boring from within." By 1928 it was focusing on a "dual union" strategy of forming separate, CP-led unions (Cochran 1977, 20–81; Klehr 1984, 28–40, 118–34; Weinstein 1976, 41–44). Neither strategy had much success. Its relations with liberal or left-wing groups, such as the Farmer-Labor Party in 1922–24 and the NAACP, led to little of lasting value. The party did, however, create a considerable "cadre" of totally committed, disciplined political organizers (Glazer 1974, 26–89; Klehr 1984, 4–27; Weinstein 1976, 26–43).

The CP's isolation in the later 1920s and early 1930s was partly caused by its "Third Period" political strategy. This Comintern strategy assumed that capitalism's stabilization of the 1920s would be followed by a period of crisis and wars, leading to fascism or communism (Klehr 1984, 11).[6] Motivated by past experience and internal political conflict, Soviet leaders directed Comintern to identify social democrats, liberals, and socialists as "social fascists." From 1928 to 1933 the American party publicly vilified any left-wing or liberal leader or group that did not follow it or accept its policies.

The rise of fascism in Germany and the prospect of a militarily hostile Europe led Comintern to alter its policies decisively. By 1934 priority had shifted to working with all antifascists. The CP supported Roosevelt, the Democratic Party, and liberal political organizations of all types; most significantly, it gained great influence in industrial unions by helping shape the organizing drives of the CIO. The Hitler–Stalin peace pact of 1939 led to another decisive change. The CP remained committed to the Popular Front, but its analysis of foreign affairs stopped making sharp distinctions between fascist and democratic governments and assumed an essentially antiwar position. After Hitler's invasion of the Soviet Union, the CP switched again and supported the war effort.

By 1938–39 much of the New Deal was in force, and industrial unions were coming to be accepted even by many members of the ruling class. The

CP was taking virtually no public political position that might distinguish it from the other members of the Popular Front. Then began the elimination of the CP from unions—and thus from its only effective institutional connection to American political life. The purge of the CP started in 1939, paused during the war years, and resumed soon after. By 1948 the party was no longer politically significant in the United States.

The strengths and contributions of the CP are numerous. Significantly, it never fell prey to the divisive effects of social differentiation as the Socialist Party had done. While its treatment of blacks had weaknesses, it possessed a serious commitment to racial equality (Allen 1983, 216). Unlike that of the SP, most of the CP's southern organization was made up of blacks (Klehr 1984, 273). Through its campaign for the "Scottsboro boys," support of interracial hiring of blacks in New York department stores, publicized "trials" of members for "white chauvinism," and defense of black rights in the unions (especially the CIO), the party won some support from the black community and increased its black membership (Allen 1983, 273; Klehr 1984, 324–48; Naison 1978a and 1978b; Weinstein 1975, 87–92).[7] Similarly, the CP systematically encouraged the participation of women in the party, analyzed women's oppression theoretically, included women in leadership positions, supported women in the trade unions, and formed all-women locals (Shaffer 1979). Also unlike the SP, the CP was not tied to the upper strata of the working class. During the early years of the Depression it was instrumental in organizing marches and demonstrations of the unemployed, forcibly preventing evictions, and leading groups of the destitute to demand relief (Boyer and Morais 1976, 259–66; Klehr 1984, 49–68; Piven and Cloward 1979, 41–64).

Once it was clear that industrial unionism would develop outside of the framework of the AFL, the CP devoted enormous energies and resources to the CIO. It provided dedicated and experienced organizers, formed part of the intellectual and legal staff around the CIO leadership, and cooperated with non-Communists (Cochran 1977, 82–127; Klehr 1984, 223–24; Milton 1982, 77–85). By 1938 the party had influence in or controlled between a third and a half of the CIO's unions (Klehr 1984, 230–51; Milton 1982, 121–22).

Finally, while membership in the CP never rose above a hundred thousand, its participation in other organizations gave it influence over millions. The energy and singlemindedness of its members necessarily extended its impact. At its best, the party provided a sense of comradeship and community that brought out the best in a whole generation of political radicals.

These accomplishments, as well as the prestige that necessarily accrued to an anticapitalist organization during capitalism's worst depression, could not prevent the CP from losing its role in American politics by the 1940s. Three major factors were at work. Internally, Communists manifested an extreme form of the social differentiation of radicals. Externally, party success was necessarily limited by the essentially nonrevolutionary character of the American working class during the period. Finally, that nonrevolutionary character was matched, in the late 1930s, by the return of political unity to the American ruling class. Let us examine each of these factors.

The Social Differentiation of the Communist Party

Hundreds of thousands passed through the CP. Millions belonged to organizations directed or affected by it. The party organized demonstrations of up to one hundred thousand unemployed, created international support systems for its causes, and provided a rallying point for progressive intellectuals. At times its organizers responded directly to the needs of a particular community and forged political alliances somewhat free from party control (Gornick 1979, 95–101; Naison 1978a). Yet these activities did not create a solid leftist national presence or long-lived organizational support for the CP. Little response was forthcoming when it was expelled from unions, its leaders were jailed, and its ideology became anathema to most of American society.

One explanation for this long-term failure is that for those who stayed more than a year or two, the CP became an entire social and moral universe, isolated from the rest of American society. Party directives determined political activity and judgment. Political activity became the center of personal life. And the entire experience was shaped by the faith that communism combined moral righteousness and science. Two party members recall:

I had been a devout Christian and now I was a devout Communist. I have always responded to structured authority in this way, once the idea behind the authority seemed absolutely right to me.

After a while I wasn't afraid anymore. I had the Party and I had my comrades, and they made me strong, strong on my feet. . . . In those days I had an answer for everything. . . . I knew what I was talking about. (In Gornick 1979, 108, 63)

This secular religion required a faith in the essential correctness of Marxism as interpreted and applied by the authorities of the Communist world. Party policy was accepted, not debated: "Many Communists did not mind these limitations. . . . Marxism-Leninism was a science: like any science, it had its experts" (Klehr 1984, 157). In more practical terms, the party would command members to change cities, jobs, and friends; spy on their comrades; and turn their backs on family members who held "dangerous" (for example, Trotskyite) opinions (cf. Gordon 1976; Gornick 1979; Klehr 1984).

Since Communism was a "science," whatever line was dominating the party was represented and experienced as absolute truth. The CP could tolerate working-class denials of this truth, for party teachings "guaranteed" that eventually the class would come around, but it did not tolerate political disagreements from articulate sources. This intolerance was most obvious during the Third Period, when the CP attracted but failed to hold groups of intellectuals, blacks, students, and workers. The party tried to rule any group with which it came in contact and castigated any articulate political person who expressed even minor reservations. An intellectual who criticized the Soviet treatment of Trotsky's family was expelled from a CP-dominated writers' group and "denounced for echoing the same line as Archduke Cyril, Pope Pius [and] Alexander Kerensky" (Klehr 1984, 83). This attitude, repeated in political coalitions and trade unions, inevitably branded Communists as single-minded, sectarian, and hostile.

It might seem that the party's totalitarian attitude would have ended in the Popular Front. During this period the CP did make alliances with and work under liberal trade union groups and political organizations which it would have (or had) pilloried as social fascists a few years before. But the CP's invective and sense of political certainty were not eliminated; they simply shifted. Supporting F.D.R., it condemned as traitors or "agents of Fascism" all who criticized him (Klehr 1984, 221). When A. Philip Randolph organized a March on Washington to protest racial discrimination in war industries, the CP accused him of sabotaging the war effort. Less than two years before he had been condemned for not being sufficiently critical of Roosevelt's "imperialist" foreign policy (Allen 1983, 221–22).

Not only were American Communists isolated by virtue of their socially differentiated form of life; they were accurately perceived as following directives from a foreign country. Viewing politics and revolution as expressions of objective social structures knowable on a quasi-scientific basis, American Communists could accept policies determined by the Soviet Union and changed drastically with virtually no consultation (cf. Weinstein 1976, 54). The concept of the Third Period came from the Soviet CP via the Comintern. It accompanied Stalin's consolidation of power and his policy of forced collectivization (Draper 1972, 300–11; McKenzie 1964, 113–30). Besides the obvious stupidity of trying to adapt foreign politics to the needs of the totally different U.S. society, this line isolated the CP from the rest of the American left and from American workers during the initial years of economic crisis and rank-and-file militancy (Weinstein 1975, 43–46). As part of the Third Period strategy, the dual union strategy cut the CP off from the steelworkers who in 1934 sought Communist aid in organizing industrial unions in opposition to the AFL; the CP would help only if this rank-and-file group would join the CP's small steel union. A year later the party switched from the dual union to a Popular Front policy and would aid the rank-and-file only if strikes were carried out within the AFL's steel union (Lynd 1972). Similarly, while the CP had the best record on race of any U.S. political party, its Comintern-directed support of black territorial separation and self-determination "ran contrary to the aspiration of blacks for legal equality and integration" (Weiss 1983, 297).

The Popular Front policy was also determined from abroad (Klehr 1984, 167–85; McEnzie, 140–65). While it enabled the CP to make contact with a larger part of the American population, its singleminded pursuit of "unity" led it to abandon any attempt to promote socialism as a political ideal. The problem was not that the CP stopped seeking members. Rather, as its earlier program had been alien to American working-class culture (Green 1980, 164), so its later position presented little, if anything, more radical than the progressive wing of the Democratic Party. The party's intention, stimulated by the rise of fascism and signaled by the Franco-Soviet pact of May 1935, was that the Popular Front should keep the United States and the Soviet Union from becoming military enemies. To this end independent leftist or rank-and-file movements were sacrificed. In 1939, for example, Communists in various unions were instructed by the party to support right-wing union leaders (Milton 1982, 136). Thanks to its rigid and blind adherence to a line laid down from abroad, claims Harvey Levenstein (1981), the CP abandoned the power it might have had in auto and steel, the major unions of the CIO.

Whether the CP could have retained its power and influence in the face of the anti-Communist initiative of the Cold War is uncertain. However, there seems to be little doubt that its adherence to a political strategy laid down from abroad led to a fundamental political blindness. Most important was the mistaken confidence that the New Deal coalition could lead to socialist consciousness. On the one hand, the party believed that it was the political and intellectual vanguard of the working class, even if not recognized as such (Gordon 1982, 41). Yet its theories were not based in the reality of American political life. Past crises of capitalism had led to revolutionary movements and to fascism. Accepting a mechanical application of traditional Marxist theory, the CP expected a leftward movement of the working class and the creation of socialism as long as fascism did not develop. It interpreted the American present in terms of the European past, seeing the reorientation of American politics and the formation of industrial unions as the prelude to a mass socialist consciousness (cf. Lynd 1974). The capital–labor accord, which used industrial unions to integrate the modern working class into capitalism, was simply not perceived. Therefore, the CP could willingly abandon its presence or power in trade unions or have one of its own members introduce a resolution barring Communists from union office (Cochran 1977, 145).[8] It would view the use of the army to break the North American Aviation strike of 1941 as an attempt to destroy the union—when in fact the government's goal was only to rationalize the role of unions and eliminate wildcat activity (Cochran 1977, 180–81).

The CP was comparatively obscure when it adopted the Third Period strategy and switched to the Popular Front. But its support of the Hitler–Stalin pact in 1939 could not go unnoticed. Such an abrupt change in policy demonstrated to the American working class how fundamentally alien the party was. Support dropped away in the unions and among "fellow-traveler" organizations of students and intellectuals. The tendency of blacks to see the CP as using their concerns for its own ends—ends determined by the Soviet Union—was confirmed (Allen 1983, 217–23). Even left-wing unionists now saw Communists as foreign to the interests of labor (Cochran 1977, 145–50). Political coalitions in Washington, California, Wisconsin, Minnesota, and New York were weakened or shattered (Gordon 1982, 44; Klehr 1984, 400–409). Party membership never again reached the high of 1939, and the CP's influence drastically declined.[9]

In the context of religious devotion, scientific certainty, and foreign allegiance, then, Communists necessarily became an isolated subculture. New members often felt unwelcome because they had not mastered the complex social rules of cell meetings. Until the mid-1930s the Party was dominated by European political traditions and keyed to the needs and demands of the Soviet Union. From celebrating May Day instead of Labor Day to carrying "Defend the Soviet Union" signs on marches of the unemployed, the party continually introjected strange and often incomprehensible elements into its contacts with the American working class.[10]

While the CP was socially differentiated from the American working class in the ways I have outlined, it shared certain fundamental attitudes and beliefs with the rest of American society. Its politics was essentially "bourgeois" in Reich's sense. Political strategy, based in a supposed expertise, was to be decided by the party leadership and obediently followed. This "made for a certain aura of efficiency, but it also resulted in extreme bureaucracy, mechanical rigidity, stifling of free discussion, witch-hunting, major political errors, and enhanced membership turnover" (Gordon 1982,

42). Ironically, the frequent top-down decisions, lack of respect for opponents, and attacks on members and its own public leaders when they lost favor with Comintern confirmed the impression that the CP was not, really, so different from the rest of society. Like society at large, it functioned on the basis of male forms of authority: domination, control, and destruction of the "enemy," all "objectively" justified. Like other authorities, it sought power detached from feeling, considered "difference" to be the enemy, and repressed doubt. Its treatment of dissidents exactly mirrored the anti-Communist crusades of the right (cf. Cochran 1977, 171–72). Its self-righteousness duplicated that of such competitors for influence in the American working class as the Association of Catholic Trade Unionists.

Ideological space in the United States was thus dominated by exclusive and competing doctrines, all of which were predicated on domination and hierarchy, and all of which were in that sense compatible with class society. Whatever their political differences, left and right alike expressed the same perspective on social authority: it was reserved for experts. Perhaps a sizable portion of the American working class could have been won from civil privatism to active involvement in effectively controlling social institutions. Certainly, however, no significant political group sought to promote such self-activity. Consequently, the social primacy of authoritarian socialization processes meant that a massive economic crisis would result only in a reorganization of American capitalism, not its overthrow.

The CP was accepted when it joined in political struggles, valued when it helped give public and institutional form to demands and needs actually present. But it failed to see that it had accepted a conservative form of political authority. In the choice between the CP and a more familiar authority—a John L. Lewis, an F.D.R., or even a Catholic Union movement — American workers, not surprisingly, rejected the CP. Why choose something both so alien and so familiar? Ironically, the following claim by a member of the Young Communist League was true:

Some people have the idea that a YCLer is politically minded, that nothing outside of politics means anything. Gosh no. . . . We go to shows, parties, dances and all that. In short . . . *members are no different from other people except that we believe in dialectical materialism as the solution to all problems.* (In Liebman 1979, 493; my emphasis)

The Limits of Radicalism: The Need for Leadership

The militance of the American working class during the 1930s took place within extremely circumscribed limits. There was no nascent socialist movement somehow co-opted or misled by its leaders. The CP and the

CIO were limited by the fact that the fundamental structure of social authority was not at issue. Rather, the question was whether the working class would reap the benefits of mass consumer society and achieve its own "presence" in the social order. To accomplish these goals, workers had to create new institutions (such as the CIO), politicize the economy, and increase the state's role as mediator between workers and capitalists. Workers did not "need," nor did they seek, socialist revolution. Four aspects of working-class politics during the 1930s support this analysis: (1) working-class action was often a response to government initiatives; (2) spontaneous working-class action usually required support from unions or political organizations; (3) mass insurgence was not directed toward undermining the capitalist system; (4) unions and working-class parties retained a hierarchical form of authority.

Government Initiatives

Two key initiatives mark the development of union activism in the 1930s: Section 7(a) of the National Industrial Recovery Act (NIRA) in 1933, and the Wagner Act in 1935. According to many historians, these actions convinced workers (rightly or wrongly) that the government would support their attempts to unionize. Although Section 7(a) actually offered workers much less protection than they thought it did, work stoppages in 1933 involved almost four times as many workers as in 1932. It was not the Depression alone that produced working-class militancy. Rather, "to an extraordinary extent at this time, the laboring people of the United States looked to the federal government and especially to Roosevelt for leadership and comfort" (Bernstein 1971, 170; Cochran 1977, 82–83; Green 1980, 140–44; McElvaine 1984, 160–62; Milton 1982, 29–31; Raybeck 1966, 329–34).

The "leadership and comfort" of the NIRA was partly a response to countrywide discontent that seemed, in 1932, to threaten mass radical action (McElvaine 1984, 90–94; Piven and Cloward 1979, 108–10). The act attempted to allow businesses to evade the strictures of antitrust legislation, at the same time encouraging unions and providing codes to govern wages and hours. This "something for everyone" approach was doomed by the conflicting interests of American society, especially since business interests dominated the application of the codes. Yet it did lead American workers to see their attempt at unionization as legitimate.

Union/Party Support

The bureaucrats of the AFL resisted the influx of masses of new, industrially organized, and potentially uncontrollable members. The state, though exercising remarkable restraint, was essentially siding with employers in their struggle with the new union movement. The escalation of working-class violence in 1934 then led to the Wagner Act, which provided significant federal protection for unions.

Piven and Cloward (1979, 107–15) correctly view the Wagner Act as motivated by fear of increased worker militancy and Roosevelt's desire to regain political support from workers (Green 1980, 150; Klare 1978; McElvaine 1984, 258–59; Milton 1982, 71–74). They also correctly criticize the essentially conservative AFL and the self-interested CP for following, rather than leading, the insurgency. Yet they mistakenly conclude that large organizations tend to impede political struggle rather than support it, and that political radicals should therefore support mass militance rather than build organizations. What Piven and Cloward ignore is the extent to which *the militant workers of this period yearned for institutional leadership from established organizations.* I have mentioned already the failed 1933–35 effort by rank-and-file steel locals to affiliate with either the AFL's or the CP's steel union. This movement could not succeed without the help of established groups. Lack of experience, funds, and self-confidence crippled it. A leader of the group recalls: "Most of us were capable local or district leaders, but *we had very little idea what the national picture was like. . . . We were completely unprepared for a strike. We had no funds, no central leadership, no national organization* except Amalgamated's officers, and they were opposed to strike action" (in Lynd 1972, 45; my emphasis).

Lynd (1972, 57) favors popular over organizational power and claims that such power might have been retained by the rank-and-file:

The critical weakness of the rank and file was its inability to organize on a national scale. Had the Communist Party thrown its organizers, its connections and its access to media, lawyers and money into a different direction, there might have come about an industrial unionism not only more militant . . . but more independent politically. (My emphasis)

Since the CP never supported popular power, however, but sought to channel insurgency to its own ends, Lynd's argument here supports the dependence of rank-and-file movements on established institutions.

Similarly, the 1933 walkout at Briggs Manufacturing in Detroit, cited by Piven and Cloward (1979, 136) as an example of a "spontaneous" strike, was marked by workers' need for direction from an established organization. One strike leader recalls: "We decided we weren't going to walk out as individuals. . . . Soon there were hundreds of workers milling round in the street. *They didn't know what to do. They had no organization, no one to speak for them*" (Lynd and Lynd 1973, 55, cf. 57; my emphasis). These points suggest that whatever the weaknesses of radical organizations, such organizations are necessary.

Insurgency's Limited Goals

With passage of the Wagner Act in 1935, workers took advantage of its promise of government protection for unions and of the current economic upswing to launch mass production unions. Rank-and-file workers organized locals, initiated strikes, and introduced the sit-down as a new tactic against employers. The sit-down was labor's response to the drive system: in an integrated plant, work stoppage by a small group could paralyze the entire operation. These initiatives came neither from the CP (which hesitated to join with the CIO until 1937) nor the CIO leadership. Yet the goal of the militance was to form powerful industrial unions that would follow the leadership of the CIO and function within capitalism (Brody 1980, 100–111, 150–57; Cochran 1977, 100–134).

Many writers have described the labor history of the 1930s as a process in which the working class exchanged political militancy for union recognition. There also seems to be general agreement that by the late 1930s the CIO and the CP were restraining rank-and-file militance and giving union leadership all decision-making power. Both CIO and CP leadership opposed or attempted to constrain the initial outbreak of sit-down strikes in the rubber industry, and by the late 1930s the CP was supporting the CIO leadership, even at the expense of the rank-and-file. The CIO leadership, on the other hand, appears to have been essentially conservative from the beginning. Whatever political differences divided them, the various factions at the top of the CIO all agreed that authoritarian and hierarchical organization was essential for industrial unions, and that the goal of such unions was to achieve a "fair" place for union members within the continuing framework of capitalism (Carey 1972; Green 1972: 13; Milton 1982, 122; Nelson 1982; Piven and Cloward 1979, 155–60; Weinstein 1975, 77–86).

Traditional Forms of Authority

Thus it is not surprising that writers explain the deradicalization of the working class by the failures of its leaders. Yet such an explanation ignores the fundamental question, Why were these ultimately conservatizing or restraining figures *accepted* as leaders? This question can only be answered by a response to another question: what was the political character of rank-and-file militancy during this period?

My answer is that the Depression had undermined the new forms of socialization of the consumer society. Both stimulating and responding to government action, the working class expressed, during the 1930s, its refusal to tolerate a society in which workers' economic interests were not represented. In 1934 more than 15 percent of the work force was involved in work stoppages. Violent major strikes broke out in Toledo, Minneapolis, and San Francisco, where unions were led or influenced by Communists, Socialists, and Trotskyists. Nationwide, three hundred and fifty thousand to half a million textile workers fought for union recognition in twenty states. In two years at least fifty-five workers were killed and thousands wounded; troops had been called out in sixteen states (Green 1980, 140–49; Levinson 1938, 56–57; Piven and Cloward 1979, 111–30; Raybeck 1966, 320–32).

The violence of the mass strikes of the early 1930s and the disrespect for some key prerogatives of private property in the wave of sit-downs of 1936–38 made it clear that certain key restraints of the socialization process had been broken through. Further, the high level of class consciousness and unity among the working class was unique in American history: there was a partial erosion of ethnic and racial barriers, a willingness of workers in different industries to learn from and support one another, and a refusal to be broken by employer violence or red-baiting (Boyer and Morais 1976, 317–29; Foner 1977: 214–37).

Within this context of militance and violence, however, the central goal remained union recognition. As some of the accounts cited above indicate, the working class was not capable of generating a sustained radical leadership from within itself. Its rebelliousness was expressed, for instance, in a rash of sit-down strikes in the rubber industry over fairly trivial incidents (Nelson 1982); or by the auto worker who, after the victorious Flint sit-down, was cheered by workers when he said of foremen, "I'll be goddamned if I ain't gonna smack the first one that looks the least bit cockeyed at me" (in Milton 1982, 101). Demands were focused mainly on union recognition and the reduction of the arbitrary power of foremen. There was militance in pursuit of those goals but not toward the creation of a long-standing political organization to increase working-class control of production in particular or the social order as a whole.

Piven and Cloward (1979, 153) argue that "it was the strike movement that created the CIO" but also correctly state that "the workers . . . were fighting for unionization" (cf. Millis and Montgomery 1945, 692, 701). If that is the case, it makes little sense for Piven and Cloward (e.g., 1979, 155, 157) then to suggest that the CIO had limited, co-opted, or sold out the rank-and-file by leading them to exchange worker militance for union recognition. This was precisely the exchange the workers wanted.

Similarly, David Milton (1982, 121) is mistaken when he argues that the CIO possessed enormous left-wing potential because of Communist control and influence in CIO unions. At that point the CP was not acting any more leftist than other sections of the labor coalition; indeed, its Popular Front strategy had, in effect, ended its identity as a leftist political party. Its power in the unions was a result of its organizers' dedication and experience, and their initial support for rank-and-file action. Yet that action was directed toward union recognition and limited improvements in shop-floor conditions, not a leftist movement. Furthermore, Milton (1982, 122) himself acknowledges that "the Communist Party ... shared with social-democratic rivals ... the same desire to secure positions of power by creating alliances at the top, an orientation that guaranteed the eventual purge of the Left from the CIO" (see also Green 1980, 164; Klehr 1984, 243–51; McElvaine 1984, 294).

Responding to attempts by historians such as Staughton Lynd and James Green to stress the difference between rank-and-file militancy and conservative leadership, Klare (1978, 291) summarizes the key facts that render suspect any attempt to identify rank-and-file *militance* with rank-and-file *radicalism*:

Collective bargaining was almost universally and uncritically viewed by working-class activists, both within and outside of the organized left-wing groups, as the cornerstone of all programs for social justice ... in contrast, the concept of workers' control as such, and workers' councils, public ownership, state planning or decentralized planning, and direct state regulation of the terms and conditions of employment never became dominant rallying cries.

The ultimate result of such a politics could be only what David Montgomery refers to as the "New Deal Formula": "state subsidization of economic growth ... legally regulated collective bargaining, and the marriage of ... unions ... to the Democratic Party." (1979, 161).

While the contradictions of the economic system had caused a social crisis, the power of socialization led the working class not to believe in its own capacity to rule as a collective subject. The "dominated self" of advanced capitalism was broken through to the extent of allowing for mass militance but in support of only limited ends. Rebelliousness, not revolution, was on the agenda. In this rebelliousness the working class remained tied to authority: of its conservative union leaders, of the authoritarian CP, and ultimately of Roosevelt. Within the social and psychic context of the times, no other options were available. Though economic structures created a variety of possibilities for social change, socialization processes were undermined but not transformed. The resulting political struggle was therefore limited at the outset, while the social differentiation of workers and ruling-class unity in the state determined the final outcome.

It is therefore not surprising that the CIO's antiracist policies would deteriorate during and after the war (Meier and Rudwick 1982; Foner 1977, 238–331); that the limited inclusion of women into industrial unions would be eliminated; that the massive strike waves of 1941, 1943, and 1946— often opposed by CIO leaders and the CP and also often overlapping with "hate strikes" against black workers—remained within the parameters of union recognition, decent wages, and attempts to make good on wartime patriotic ideology (Davis 1980–81, 65–69; Lichtenstein 1975). While many workers were capable of wildcat strikes, they were not interested in establishing a socialist mass movement (Keeran 1979). The ultimate conclusion was the curtailment of labor's political position after the war and the Taft-Hartley Act's restriction of labor to legal bargaining. An essentially racist, sexist, and pro-imperialist AFL-CIO took shape in the 1950s and 1960s. The industrial union movement had won essential gains for workers, often at great personal cost to militants. It had not been a movement for socialism.[11]

Authority and the State

The working class was limited by more than its own partially undermined socialization and the alienating social differentiation of the CP. These limitations were complemented by the state and other traditional forms of social authority.

That the state would become a central terrain of class struggle was made clear during the early years of the Depression. The emerging concern with electoral politics at the AFL's 1932 convention, the militant demands of unemployed workers for government relief, and the sweeping electoral victory for F.D.R. and the Democratic Party indicated that people were turning to the state to deal with economic crisis (McConnell 1966, 299). In the first years of the Depression the state apparatus was inconsistent. Influenced by the desperation of all sectors of the population, it often lacked a coherent political strategy to meet that desperation. Later, the introduction of Keynesian economic policies and the capital-labor accord became the "new common sense" of a transformed American society.

During the 1930s the state reflected a variety of interests. Its response to the rising tide of discontent included federal relief, government protection of unions, and public works projects. Also, politicians' limited, autonomous self-interest in their own jobs necessitated certain policies directed toward achieving electoral support: for example, F.D.R.'s turn to the left in the "second new deal" of 1935–37. Finally, the state was responsive to the power and interests of the ruling class. With some exceptions, the New

Deal was administered by individuals who accepted capitalism. Moreover, in the absence of a direct attack on ruling-class power, that class's control over investment gave it the trump card in relations between the state and the working class. The labor militance of the mid-1930s was restrained by the depression of 1937–38, which, in turn, reduced F.D.R.'s electoral support and made him more responsive to business interests (Zinn 1966, xviii–xxxvi).

The need to transform the social structures of accumulation was not immediately recognized by the capitalist class. They violently opposed Roosevelt's early programs and fought the "leftism" of labor, the New Deal, and such groups as the "Share the Wealth" and "production for use" movements. Yet, by the end of the decade it was becoming increasingly clear that mass industrial unions might help manage workers. In any case they did not spell the end of capitalism. Lynd (1974, 32) finds a "sophistication on the part of the Federal Government and a part of American business" that allowed, for instance, U.S. Steel to accept the CIO as a bargaining agency without either losing the open shop or enduring a potentially costly strike. The Wagner Act named as two of its goals the promotion of "industrial peace" and the overcoming of underconsumption. Klare (1978) describes how its potentially radical elements were "deradicalized" by a series of judicial interpretations.

The state's management of the economy and labor conflict was not the only element of ruling-class authority evident in the period. It is interesting that a highly important role in the conservatizing of the CIO was taken by the Association of Catholic Trade Unionists. Formed to counteract the influence of the CP in the labor movement and promote hierarchy over rank-and-file power, it had dozens of branches in the industrial states and was staffed by well-supported and well-trained organizers (Milton 1982, 146).

With the stabilization of capitalism in the late 1930s, the state started direct attacks on radical elements in the labor movement. War preparations made for a natural blend of anti-Communist and patriotic ideology, especially given the CP's obvious subservience to Moscow.[12] The first victims of the anti-Communist Smith Act were Trotskyist labor leaders in Minneapolis in 1941. Their prosecution was applauded by the CP, which was then deeply committed to the war effort, but the weapon would be turned against the party after the war (Milton 1982, 145–46).

Finally, we might observe that the personality of F.D.R. was itself an essential element in the preservation of social authority. His easygoing paternalism and manipulation of the media gave him a following not shared by any other public leader. His political inconsistency and failure to support an ongoing leftist movement seemed less important than the way he projected concern for the victims of the Depression. That projection was taken by many as more real than their own dilemmas. Many observers reported the widespread feeling that during the worst of times people tended to believe that F.D.R. would help "if only he knew or could." He was everyone's good daddy, paternal authority written larger than life. Workers loved him, even when he condemned labor and capital equally during the failed steel organizing drives of 1937. John L. Lewis, hero to millions of workers, opposed him in 1940, but it was Lewis who lost position in the CIO, not F.D.R. who lost the support of workers.

The nation reachieved a kind of political unity during the war. Class conflict and social differentiation, while still present in the racism against blacks in defense plants and the wildcat strikes of 1941 and 1943, were muted. The American working class responded to the threats posed by the working classes of Japan, Germany, and Italy. The war saved the economy, inducing a recovery from the paralyzing slump of 1937–38. It also helped save capitalist hegemony in the United States by preying on that perhaps most potent form of social differentiation: nationalism.

17

The New Left: A Political Memory

I SUGGESTED IN CHAPTER 9 THAT AUTOBIOGRAPHICAL SELF-REFLECTION should be part of political theory. Since political activity stems from the experiences of personal life; theorizing reflects the subjective political identity of the theorist. In this concluding section I offer my own experience as an illustration of this thesis. The following discussion of the New Left is a personal/political account of some aspects of my participation in a decade and a half of radical politics. Unlike the rest of *History and Subjectivity*, this chapter does not build on the work of scholars; neither is it meant to be objective history. Not surprisingly, however, an autobiographical sketch of my involvement in the New Left is consistent with my claims concerning the political significance of social differentiation and the role of the three forms of social primacy in determining social life. My own experience "confirms" the theory to which it gave rise.

Three Moments

Fall 1967

After a day of rallying and marching against the war, there are maybe five thousand of us left on the steps of the Pentagon. It is midnight. I am surrounded by the hard-core politicos and crazies of the political present: the self-described witches who tried to exorcise the military machine; the Trotskyists passing out leaflets about vanguards; the draft-card burners and dollar-bill burners ("fuck the draft, fuck money"); and . . . me.

What was I doing there? In memory I cannot be sure. Some of the leaders of the demonstration had tried to enter the Pentagon. But I stayed on the steps, periodically blinded by the television camera lights, facing the clubs and bayonets of federal marshalls and the 82nd Airborne Division. I had no plan or strategy. But I knew I should be there.

Three years earlier, in 1964, I had attended my first antiwar demonstration, where I had very little in mind except a vague rebelliousness and the conviction that the war was wrong. (Marching at the very end of a line on the Boston Common, we come to the end of the street and the line reverses itself. Suddenly I'm at the front, and six guys in black suits are snapping my picture while a hostile onlooker yells, "Go back to Russia!" "Russia?" I think. "I came from White Plains. And have I, with the turning of the line, become a major American Communist?") Four years later, in 1971, I at least had a clear purpose when I returned to block traffic as part of a mass effort to stop a government that would not stop the war.

But now, in 1967, what was I doing there? I can at least be sure that I was expressing my anger at what I thought was an unjust war, an unjust system, and the unjust men who made the wars, controlled the universities, turned what could have been a beautiful world into an ugly one—and who threatened to draft me when I graduated from Brandeis in six months' time. And I knew, without thinking about it, that I belonged among these politicos and crazies and not on the other side.

In ideology I was somewhere to the left of Timothy Leary but shared a few of his illusions about LSD; somewhere at a slant from the Leninists who thought the working class was the key; and completely ignorant of the earliest stirrings of feminism. I was a white, male, culturally Jewish student radical from a comfortable middle-class background. My politics was shaped by sit-ins for student power, revulsion at American imperialism, the Marcuse of *Eros and Civilization* and the Marx of the *1844 Manuscripts*. My rejection of capitalism went along with the belief that the Soviet Union had nothing to do with socialism and that the American Communist Party and the labor movement were irrelevant to social change. I saw no contradictions between my life and that of workers or blacks or women or the Viet Cong, or if I saw those contradictions, I did not feel them.

I smoke some dope on the steps, scared of the troops but heartened by the crowd around me. At midnight the lights go out and they charge us, clubs flailing. I move back down the steps, keeping out of range of the clubs, not running away but not standing my ground and getting beaten as the bravest do.

1976

I'm sitting in a basement room of some Harvard building, at a meeting of the Boston chapter of the New American Movement (NAM). The high tide of the mass antiwar movement has given way to little, self-conscious, theoretically sophisticated leftist groups. And I have gone from mass demonstrations and the terror of the clubs to these constant meetings. I work on NAM's newspaper, and we do our best to "reach the working class." We are, we think, the nonsectarian left. We are committed to a feminism I had discovered in 1971 after having been out of the country for two and a half years. We are committed to a mild-mannered and pleasant neo-Marxism. We are committed to sharing tasks and skills and power in the group. We are committed to an endless cultivation of sensitivity to a variety of oppressions. Somehow, all of this is supposed to overcome the real contradictions of social life.

NAM supports farmworkers and opposes racism, reports on labor news and rejects Leninism, seeks a base in unions and in white-collar workers. It has a politics I can respect. And in Boston it goes nowhere. Its sophisticated theoretical discussions (over half of the members of our chapter are college faculty or graduate students), its sincerity, the total absence of anyone with children and virtual lack of anyone over thirty-five or anyone who's not white, make it utterly foreign to those we wish to organize.

Like the rest of the chapter members, I am painfully sincere. Still, I leave most meetings irritated, bored, and frustrated with the endless debates over "principles of unity"; resentful of the militant women who seem always on the lookout for some political slight; and angry at the macho intellectual men.

I leave each meeting in a hurry to get home and sleep before getting up to drive two hours to my college teaching job in Connecticut—where I ambivalently both flaunt my radicalism and try to get a tenure-track position. I live in a commune in Boston—where we have five-hour house meetings to discuss our feelings. We try hard to be politically correct, to love people after knowing them for two weeks, to "smash couplism" while creating an alternative to the nuclear families that we're all trying both to escape and to re-create.

April 1981

A small group of us present *They Fought Back: Jewish Resistance to the Nazis.* It has taken us a year and a half to find or create the words, images, and music that tell the usually ignored story of how Jews had resisted. We sell out a medium-sized theater; advance tickets are sold at a nonpolitical Jewish crafts store, at the local women's and the local left-wing bookstore.

Somewhere in later 1970s I had discovered my Jewishness, prompted by the growing realization that the left had ignored and continued to ignore Jewish oppression. Angered by the United Nations' "Zionism is Racism" resolution, I wrote an editorial for NAM's paper supporting a two-state solution for the Arab–Israeli conflict. My comrades' response, full of hostility to any self-conscious Jewish identification and reflecting a callous amnesia with regard to the Holocaust, further awakened my Jewish consciousness.

I left NAM after four years, left the long meetings discussing political principles in university basements, and moved toward a gradually evolving Jewish radicalism: a radicalism that started with an attempt to counter the left's failures to understand Zionism, then was embodied in a Boston organization that sought to be a Jewish voice on the left and a leftist voice among Jews. This was no bland group of university intellectuals. Along with a few Marxists like me, there were lesbian separatists who were doing their first political work with men in years; temperamentally progressive but politically unformed Jews alienated from the dominant Jewish community; experienced community organizers alienated from the anti-Semitism of the left.

In this context I confronted the history of my own oppression or, at least, a tradition of oppression with which I could personally identify, whose effects I could see in the faces of my parents-in-law—Holocaust survivors who'd lost their families in Treblinka and Auschwitz—and in the consciousness of my wife, who was born in a Displaced Persons camp in Germany after the war. In this context I discovered the passion of my own social differentiation: grief and fear as I immersed myself in reading and thinking about the Holocaust; anger and self-righteousness in defense of Jews and Jewishness; pride in our survival and resistance. The rootless, politically correct universalism of NAM gave way to a sense of community in which I tried to join the theoretical insights of Marxism with a personal passion. The ethical abstractions of concern for women, the working class, or the Vietnamese joined to identification with fighters for Jewish self-defense and liberation.

Eventually, that sense of community dimmed somewhat—partly because I exhausted myself on *They Fought Back*, partly because in fall of 1981 I had a son who died, partly because after fifteen years I was simply tired of meetings and organizations and platforms and demonstrations, and partly because I decided to write this book and didn't have the time to keep up those connections *and* be a father to my daughter *and* teach philosophy . . . at a college in Worcester, Massachusetts . . .

Origins

I became a leftist, in part, out of rebellion against parental authority. I accepted feminism relatively easily (at least in theory) because I felt damaged by the traditional male authority of my father—an irrational and sometimes brutal authority that I feared and hated for much of my childhood and adolescence. My father's sentimentalism and self-righteousness made me distrust the self-justifications of all authorities. By the time I got to college, a hypnotic attraction for intellectual life was easily combined with a permanent distrust of all the irrational powers I saw around me.

I became a leftist, in part, because other people did: a cousin who explained to me in thirty minutes why the Vietnam War was wrong; a college roommate who told me about that first demonstration on the Boston Common; a speech by Mario Savio (leader of Berkeley's Free Speech Movement): "Stop the machine. Don't let the deans talk down to you. Take it over. They don't know what they're doing. We do."

I became a leftist, in part, because I was searching for a community to re-create the love I'd received from my parents in my infancy. At the London School of Economics I took part in the first student occupation at an English university and got involved in a free-wheeling group of acidheads, Trotskyists, and left Laborites who made radical politics fun.

I became a leftist, in part, because I decided to become a philosopher, and I believed that wisdom should make people happy. During that time it seemed to me that Marxism was the only wisdom being used to make people happy and not to promote someone's career or power.

Was it my personal psychology? the movement of the times? an accident of autobiography? an intellectual quirk? all of these? Whatever it was, it was a *personal* fact about me. Though personal, it was not *individual*. My adolescent rebellion and intellectual leanings would have meant little had so many others not been making a similar journey. And my rejection of my father's male power would have meant little had that power not been writ so much larger and so much more brutally in the rest of the world. But my political life was not just a social product. As others influenced me, so I influenced others. I was both product and producer, an effect of History and an active Subjectivity.

Reflection

Thinking back, it is not hard to find a personal logic in my political history: the movement from childhood rejection of male authority to student politics in a rebellious era to "rational" Marxism to feminism to a Jewish consciousness, with later stages not replacing but building on earlier ones. At each stage I was part of a group shaped by a particular history. At each stage my actions reflected that social history. And at each stage up to the present, I lived out the illusion that I had found some kind of universal answer to social misery.

Thinking back, it is too easy to see the limitations of my political history: the absence of theoretical or historical perspective in the early stages; the male presumptions of deracinated Marxist politics in the NAM period; the angry, at times hostile, passion of social differentiation during my years on the Jewish left. It is too easy because noting these past limitations from my present perspective necessarily ignores my limitations in the present.

More important, it is too easy because political life is necessarily limited, presumptuous, and passionate. It is only the world as a whole that we attempt to change as leftists. Yet what are the tools we have for that attempt? We have our personal histories, our theory, and our passion. Each of these is problematic: our personal histories and our passions unite us with some and divide us from others, others whom we need if we are to succeed in really changing the world. Our theory inevitably reflects the denial of our partiality and limitations, for theory is necessarily universalizing. Theorists, however, can only be persons—situated and partial, not universal.

At least, so my years of action and study have led me to believe. Reflection on those years led me to this book, to an attempt to integrate the abstractions of Marxist theory with the passion of political action and to formulate a theoretical vision in which Marxism and feminism, the white working class and Jews and blacks, History and Subjectivity, all find their place.

Such reflection also leads me to believe that they did not all have their proper place in my years of active politics in the New Left. While my ideal object was the whole of social life, my understanding of that life was based on a fragment of experience. Whatever universal experience was contained in that fragment—the truths of the antiwar movement, the rebirth of Marxism in America, contemporary radical feminism and socialist-feminism, the Jewish left—was always combined (I see in retrospect) with the partiality of social differentiation. There was, in our attempt to see everything, so much we did not see: how we were living a form of life possible only for people without children; how the conservative working class had a life our politics could not possibly reach; how easily our movement could be undermined by a failing U.S. economy and a shift of mood; how easily our heroes in Vietnam and Cuba, for all their courage, could turn into Communist bureaucrats.

Not surprisingly, we failed, for we faced at every turn the power of a ruling class which, if not in perfect harmony, possessed far more unity of thought and action, and far more resources, than we. Our scraggly troops, inevitably divided among themselves, always faced army clubs, a well-organized bureaucracy, a class that sought to preserve its rule. And we could offer against that force only our limitations; we were powerful in our passions, groping for a theory of the whole, but always so fragmented by the social differentiation of social groups and of the left that our resources were only a pale shadow of theirs.

I do not regret the effort. I think I have some perspective on the failures. I hope that my reflections in these pages may provide some insight, perhaps even some inspiration, as we in the United States engage in the next round of a mass struggle of human Subjectivity against the dreadful and threatening powers of History.

Notes

1. Because (as I argue in Chap. 2) Marxism is founded on critical norms, it seeks to awaken human subjectivity, not see it as the product of impersonal structures. Because Marx believed that forces of production derived much of their historical meaning from the social relations in which they were inserted, he was not a technological determinist. Developed versions of my interpretation of Marx may be found in Avineri (1970), Lefebvre (1968), and Schmidt (1983). Schmidt in particular argues against Althusserian interpretations of Marx in which the human subject is essentially absent or dependent on nonintentional structures. Feenberg (1981, 27–59) describes the relation in the early writings between Marx's political perspective and his concepts of freedom and reason. In recent years, a school of "analytical Marxism" has reformulated and defended as true the view that Marx was a "technological determinist": i.e., made a rigid distinction between productive forces and social relations of production and believed that forces were socially primary. The most important exponent of this view is G. A. Cohen (1978). I have already given my reasons for rejecting Cohen's book as either a version of Marx or a theory of history in its own right (Gottlieb 1985a). Similar criticisms from a more analytic perspective can be found in Miller (1984, 171–270).

2. Other recent criticisms of traditional historical materialism have been made by Aronowitz (1981), Balbus (1982), Giddens (1981), and Habermas (1968, 1970, 1973, 1975). They criticize Marxism for generalizing the features of capitalism to all of human history; for mistakenly reducing all types of domination to forms or effects of economic exploitation; for uncritical confidence in the revolutionary mission of the working class; and for acceptance of an instrumental attitude toward nature. In different ways they all argue for the autonomous importance of structures of human interaction. While I am in agreement with many of their criticisms, my reasons for rejecting their proposed alternatives to Marxism are spelled out in Gottlieb 1981 and 1985b.

3. See Cohen's (1978, 28) discussion of different senses of "mode of production."

4. Many surveys of Marx's economic system exist. I believe Sweezy (1942) remains the clearest.

5. There are many attempts to clarify the notion of the "economic." See those by Braudel (1973), Cohen (1978), and Godelier (1972).

6. The role of economic structure in determining historical change in feudal society is the subject of Chap. 3.

7. One classic version of this is found in Polanyi (1957).

8. These claims are developed in Part II.

9. Balibar defends his position by citing a famous passage from *Capital* (Marx 1967, 1: no. 82) Some of his critics, claims Marx, agree "that each special mode of production and the social relations corresponding to it, in short that the economic structure of society, is the real basis on which the juridical and political super-structure is raised . . . that the mode of production determines the character of the social, political and intellectual life in general, all this is very true for our own times . . . but not for the middle ages, in which Catholicism, nor Athens and Rome, where politics, reigned supreme. . . . however . . . the middle ages could not live on Catholicism, nor the ancient world on politics. On the contrary, it is the *mode in which they gained a livelihood that explains why here politics, and there Catholi-cism, played the chief part*" (my emphasis). Unfortunately for Balibar, Marx here includes in the "economic structure" the "social relations corresponding to a mode of production." While in the Middle Ages these might not include knight errantry or Catholicism, they do include the lord's power to expropriate labor rent.

CHAPTER 2

1. Bernstein (1978; 1983) surveys the terrain here. Other references include Giddens (1979), Habermas (1968, 1973), Hann and Bellah (1983), Horkheimer (1972; 1974), Lukács (1971), Radnitsky (1973), and Taylor (1983)

2. A wide variety of examples can be found, from the "speaking bitterness" meetings of the early years of the Chinese revolution to the consciousness-raising sessions of the women's liberation movement.

3. This point is developed by radical and socialist feminists.

4. This point is essential to Greenspan's (1983) account of female psychology and to writings about blacks under slavery (e.g., Genovese 1976). See my remarks about "resistance" in Gottlieb 1983.

5. See Quine (1976) and Rorty (1979) for discussions of "evolutionary episte-mology," in which frameworks of rationality are seen as themselves historically evolving. Both writers can be considered within the broad tradition of pragmatism.

6. In different ways, Althusserian Marxism and sociobiology both seek to elimi-nate the subject from the analysis of social life.

7. The literature is very large here. See Hann and Bellah (1983) for a recent collection of articles and references.

8. Schmidt (1983) shows how alien to Marx is Althusser's (1971; 1979) denial of human agency and rejection of history as an analytical category.

9. Socialist-feminist arguments criticizing the limitations of traditional Marx-ism are presented in Chap. 9.

10. I argue this point in greater detail at the end of Chap. 9. It should be remem-bered that general claims here are historically limited; i.e., the present wave of feminism may embody itself in long-lived political forms that will make gender relations co-primary with those of class.

11. See, e.g., Bowles's and Gintis's (1976) description of the role of class in-

terests in the history of American education; or David Noble's (1979) account of the rise of modern technology.

12. By implication, this question could be asked of any class society but it is particularly appropriate to contemporary capitalism for two reasons. First, as a modern society, it has created the technological and cultural preconditions of a rational and free society. Second, as opposed to most forms of the bureaucratic state, advanced capitalist societies tend to be reasonably democratic. Unlike, e.g., Poland, we cannot say of the United States that class rule is based in the frequent use of military force.

13. See Gottlieb (1975) for discussion of a noncognitive sense of ideology.

14. I use "dependent on wages" rather than "wage-earning" in order to include unpaid household laborers and thus avoid from the outset any false opposition between the (supposedly male) working class and women. I refer to the absence of "individual control" in order to allow for collective control exercised by unions or political parties. My use of the traditional term "working class" includes the great majority of oppressed groups defined by gender, race, nationality, and so on.

15. Historical developments make these categories more or less important and add new ones. Thus at times a person's age or the distinction between tenants and homeowners may be crucial.

16. This argument is developed in Chaps. 13–16.

CHAPTER 3

1. This highly condensed summary is based on Anderson (1978; 1979), Bois (1976), Brenner (1976; 1978), DeVries (1976), Dobb (1947), Duby (1973), Garraty and Gay (1972), Hilton (1951; 1978; 1979), LeGoff (1973), Miskimin (1977), Tawney (1912), Tilly (1975), and Wallerstein (1974a; 1980). Among other factors, I have ignored wide variations in the conditions of peasants (only some of whom were the classical "serfs" of feudalism), the variety of holdovers from the Roman empire (e.g., the persistence of urban culture in Italy), and tribal or communal cultures (e.g., parts of rural England, which were not enserfed until the eleventh century).

2. Sweezy (1979b, 35) claims that feudalism "is a system of production for use. . . . There is . . . none of the pressure which exists under capitalism for continual improvements in methods of production. . . . There is a very strong tendency for the whole life of society to be oriented toward custom and tradition." It is therefore not surprising that Sweezy looks for external forces to explain the dynamics of feudalism and the transition to capitalism. Like Pirenne (1937), he finds them in the disruptive effect on feudalism of the growth of trade and towns from the tenth century on. For Sweezy, trade, the growing use of money, and towns exercise a kind of dissolving effect on feudalism. They introduce motivations to end customary economic relationships and replace them with ones that lead not to, but in the direction of, capitalism. Feudalism is, in itself, stable. Factors that destabilize feudalism— such as demographic growth and competition among lords over vassals and land— "have no creative or revolutionizing influence on feudal society" (Sweezy 1979, 36)

Sweezy's position challenges Dobb's claim (1947, 42, 46) that the forces which transformed feudal society were internal to it. My arguments in the text make clear my disagreements with Sweezy. In essence, the point is that trading may often be largely unconnected with the process or relations of production. Marx's explanation of why trade does not decisively change the mode of production is accepted by many writers on this subject: "[Trade] exploits the difference between the prices of production of various countries ... [and] appropriates an overwhelming portion of the surplus-product partly as a mediator between *communities which still substantially produce for use-value* and for those whose economic organization the sale of products at their value, *is of secondary importance*" (Marx 1967 3: 330–31; my emphasis). This explanation is accepted by both Marxists (e.g., Dobb 1947, 19–22; Hilton 1979, 23, 149–52) and non-Marxists (e.g., Baechler 1976, 34–39; Pirenne 1937, 46). Note also that Sweezy's account cannot explain why social crisis followed the initial feudal expansion.

3. Anderson (1979, 404–8) shows how extremely wary Marx was of applying the term "feudalism" beyond the borders of western Europe and without a duplication of a wide variety of economic, political, legal, and even cultural conditions. Interestingly, Anderson's position accords with Marx's own writings in two ways. First, Marx often stressed that the effects of economic changes (e.g., the growth of trade) depended on the overall organization of social life (1967, 3: 331–32). As Anderson shows (1979, 404–8), Marx suggested that industrial capitalism required the prior emergence of an autonomous sphere of economic activity in the medieval towns, where private property, independent of community controls and used for expanded accumulation, could develop.

4. Following Marx's lead, the class-struggle theorists could have gone beyond rejecting the Pirenne–Sweezy thesis concerning the role of trade and their own detailed analysis of the effects of the relations of surplus extraction. As Marx tried to describe the differential effects of trade in different social settings, they should also have been concerned to show the differential effects of "extra-economic coercion" in different social settings. That they did not do so can be explained, I believe, only by their belief that it was necessary to search for a "prime mover"— and that this prime mover had to be the core economic relation of the society. This belief, again, stems from accepting Marx's theory of competitive capitalism as *the* model of a theory of *any* type of society.

5. Baechler (1976, 40, 77) makes a similar argument, claiming that the distinctive feature of European feudalism was its political structure. For him, economic activity develops most when least interfered with by the state; thus the rise of capitalism was determined by the independent city. Baechler's thesis is weakened by his dubious suggestion that the "political anarchy" of western Europe can qualify as a causal principle. Also, he ignores the role of the state in the rise of capitalism and forgets that capitalism had to leave the cities to develop.

6. Baechler (1976, 34–40) describes a variety of civilizations that possessed organized merchants, banks, pooled capital, and even (in the Abbasid Empire) a prototypical form of the putting-out system. Baechler claims the decline of these societies stemmed from too much state involvement in the economy. This fits into

Wallerstein's theory that the capitalist world-system requires multiple centers of political power rather than world empire.

7. Anderson's position (1978, 198) on the crisis is somewhat different again. He claims that class struggle—especially in the form of state action—may *resolve* a crisis. The *cause*, however, lies in the structural limitations of the use of the forces of production within a given set of social relations. This distinction does not bear up, for a crisis in production is experienced as a crisis of the social system only if it is politically appropriated as such by the major contending social actors. A crisis is such only when seen as one; otherwise, it is simply a fall in production, increased poverty, starvation, or the like.

8. Theda Skocpol (1977, 84–87) misconstrues Wallerstein's position when she accuses him of claiming a factual correspondence between strong core states and core positions in the world economy. For Wallerstein (1974a, 133–67, 113–25), the claim that "core states have strong states" is not susceptible to refutation, because he defines a "strong" state as the kind of state that can do the sorts of things it needs to do to support a dominant position in the world economy. His position is weak, but not because it is factually incorrect, as Skocpol's references to the "weak" (in the traditional sense) core state of the Netherlands and the "strong" peripheral state of Spain are designed to show. Rather, it is weak simply because it is a tautology. The "political and social features" Wallerstein identifies with strength are just those that enable the national "owner-producers" the highest possible profit on the world market. Since by definition the owner–producers of the core countries are enjoying these profits, it is not surprising that the states of these countries are "strong."

9. Skocpol (1977, 82) quotes similar evidence from Blum, Slicker, von Bath, and Malowist.

CHAPTER 4

1. See Thompson (1963) on the development of the English working class; Hobsbawm (1975) on the fruition of capitalist development; and Polanyi (1957) on the social, legal, and economic developments.

2. Marx devoted the final section of the first volume of *Capital* to this theme. He describes the separation of peasants from the land, the legal and ideological pressures that shaped them into a compliant labor force, other sources of free laborers, the role of the state, and the ways in which farmers, traders, and petty producers become capitalists (for summaries, see Marx 1967, 1: 732, 737, 748, 757, 761). While the origins of capitalism clearly require a "free" labor force, the case is less clear when developed capitalism penetrates a noncapitalist area.

3. For later periods, see arguments by Braverman (1974) and Edwards (1979).

4. This is a highly schematized account. Urban commodity production never ceased in parts of Italy.

5. These developments did not flower fully until the late eighteenth century, but they built on developments that had begun long before. Modern forms of credit and

commerce evolved from the eleventh century on (Cipolla 1976, 190–97; Pirenne 1937, 211–12). In production, Nef (1954) describes developments in the production of coal, sal, glass, ships, alum, soap, and gunpowder and the growth of mining and manufacturing generally during the period 1540–1640. Crouzet (1968, 140–44) reviews a series of challenges to Nef's claims. Though he believes that Nef overstates the case, he agrees that industrial development was considerably higher in England than in France by 1700.

6. Space restrictions do not allow details of the Dutch role as precursor to English development except for two interesting facts about the Dutch economy. First, the Dutch *fluytship*, the merchant vessel developed as part of their sixteenth-century domination of the Baltic carrying trade, was the first merchant vessel not intended to serve also (at least potentially) as a warship (DeVries 1976, 117–18; Wallerstein 1980, 212). Second, the commercialization of agriculture in Holland led to massive capital investment. For instance, by mid-seventeenth century, urban investors—utilizing new advances in windmill technology—had spent more to drain floodland in northern Holland than the combined capitalization of the Dutch East India and West India companies (DeVries 1976, 37–38).

7. Of course a simple preference for *rentes* by the French bourgeoisie does not explain the failure of capitalist development in France. Rather, I am suggesting that such a pattern of investment must be overcome if capitalism is to develop.

8. My comments about the "efficiency" of capitalism are not meant as a defense or glorification of it. Apologists for capitalism like Baechler (1976) identify capitalism as the "model" of an economically efficient society as such, especially because the producers work only for profit. The consequences of such a system—its periodic crises, need of war and imperialism, use of racism and sexism, crippling effects on the intellectual and moral development of its members—are ignored by such a conception of efficiency.

CHAPTER 5

1. It might be argued against this thesis that the behavior of the state is itself a product of capitalism, that government action is an extension of the "logic" of capital accumulation. I discuss various theories of the state in Chap. 11.

2. I omit an account of the historical evolution of politicized capitalism, adequate attention to significant differences in the content of state involvement in different countries, and the way such "dependent capitalisms" as those of India, Brazil, and Thailand were always conditioned by the economies and political actions of the dominant capitalist powers.

3. As others have noted, the falling tendency of the rate of profit may be avoided if the rate of exploitation increases faster than the organic composition of capital.

4. Overuse of credit led to inflation; high corporate taxes supporting the social wage cut into profits; government protection of industries diminished competitive productivity; socialization of the costs of constant capital and the reproduction of labor power led to a fiscal crisis of the state; see *Dollars and Sense*, Gordon, Hill,

McEwan, Seltzer, all in Economics Education Project (1978); Castells (1980, 81–103); Mandel (1978 and 1980); Wright (1979, 145–62).

5. Baran and Sweezy (1966) claim that the crucial fact is an unabsorbable surplus produced by monopoly control over prices. Mandel (1978) argues that the law of value determines capital flow even under restrained competition. Castells (1980) sees a rising organic composition leading to a falling rate of profit and inadequate consumer demand.

6. Mandel (1980, 182) suggests that the economic crises of the 1970s combined with an increase in anticapitalist worker militancy constituted "a crisis of capitalist relations of production." My criticism of this position appears in the text.

7. For an overview of Late Capitalism (Mandel 1978), see Rowthorn (1980, 95–128), where some of my points are developed in greater detail.

8. Articles by Barr (1979), Kondratieff (1979), Pomain (1979) and the Research Working Group (1979) provide detailed accounts of long-wave theory.

9. The dramatic increase in the service sector of advanced (especially U.S.) capitalist economies is sometimes thought to pose a new barrier to capitalist expansion (Castells 1980, 164–69; Dolnick 1984; Gough 1975, 163–64; Rothchild 1981; Rowthorn 1980, 124–26). Since the service sector resists the concentration of constant capital characteristic of industrial production, an economy dominated by service faces a structural obstacle to the bunching of investment that marks the expansion of a long wave. Of course, some industrialization of service (e.g., banking machines) can occur. It is hard, however, to replace labor with machines in those areas (medicine, social work, teaching) in which human contact is essential to the "commodity" consumed.

CHAPTER 6

1. Giddens (1979, 154–55) makes a similar claim in relation to Marx: "Marx gave so much of his effort to studying capitalism that he underestimated its distinctiveness, as compared to other historical forms of society . . . we may suggest that it is only with the advent of capitalism that the evolution of the forces of production characteristically occurs on the level of the forces of production."

2. Rexford Tugwell, one of Franklin Roosevelt's economic advisors, made the direct plea for a government-administered capitalism as a response to the Depression. Tugwell's ideas were not adopted, but they indicate how the capitalist state can assess the need to change the system as a whole in order to preserve its essential class character (Zinn 1966, 53–56, 84–90). More recently, French President François Mitterand proposed the recoordination of the economies of the major capitalist powers to deal with the 1982 economic crisis.

3. It might be objected that my treatment of traditional Marxism omits the way that tradition describes capitalist development as the outcome of political struggles between capital and labor; e.g., Marx (1967, 1: 231–302) has an extended discussion of the struggle to limit the length of the working day: "The creation of a normal working-day is, therefore, the product of a protracted civil war, more or less dis-

sembled, between the capitalist class and the working-class." (299) Yet my argument is not that traditional Marxism omitted accounts of political struggle; any familiarity with the historical works of Marx disproves that claim. Rather, my position is that Marx and traditional Marxism tended to believe that the long-term political behavior of economic classes was a more or less predictable product of their place in the economic system. For Marx, working-class political consciousness and action is a product of workers' economic position. The working-class movement "on both sides of the Atlantic" to limit the working day "had grown instinctively out of the conditions of production themselves." (301). The worker, Marx explains, "comes out of the process of production other than he entered." (301). This particular account is consistent with Marx's more programmatic statements (e.g., in *The Communist Manifesto*) that repeatedly speak of the dynamic of capitalist development creating the political forces that will overthrow capitalism.

4. This is in some ways a restatement of Marx's claim that "men" make history but not in conditions of their own choosing. The point, however, is that we are increasingly in a position to "choose" our conditions, at least subject to the choices of others and our own ideological limitations. Giddens (1979, 9–95) develops this view against both French structuralism and traditional sociology.

CHAPTER 7

1. Stress on the political centrality of antiimperialist movements is a direct implication of a variety of Marxist writings, writings partly inspired by anti-imperialist movements. Writers such as Wallerstein, Amin, and Frank argue that the advanced capitalist nations and underdeveloped Third World are directly related in a world-system of exploitation and unequal exchange. To the extent that capitalist development depends on unequal exchange, the ending of imperialist relations is thought to be an eventual cause of economic crisis in developed nations. It is also hoped that Third World movements will serve as examples of and catalysts for political activity in advanced nations. The political implications have been stressed regularly in the writings of the journal *Monthly Review* and in the political practice of certain segments of the New Left. On Marxist theories of imperialism, see Brewer (1980). For particular accounts of underdevelopment, see Amin (1976), Frank (1969), and Wallerstein (1974b).

2. Engels's (1977) "dialectical materialism" represented both social life and the natural world as following universal "laws" of dialectics. Kautsky's commentary on the SPD's important Erfurt Program of 1891 speaks of the "natural necessity" of an "inevitable" breakdown of capitalism. Colletti's essay on the Second International (1972, 45–110) forms the basis of much of my interpretation. See also Lichtheim (1965, 203–304) and Cole (1950–65). For a detailed account of the last years of the SPD before World War I, see Schorske (1965).

3. Luxemburg was a leader of the Second International who recognized the historical variability of democracy and criticized the Second International for failing to see the necessity of dealing with working-class consciousness and capacity

for self-organized political action (1971, 52–134; 223–72). Also, Lenin and Rudolf Hilferding were clear on the role of imperialism and the future threat of a war over imperialist profits.

4. They also failed to see how socialist organizations could themselves recapitulate relations of domination. It was out of the failure of the Second International that disappointed socialist Robert Michels would write his classic *Political Parties* (1962) which stressed the inevitable separation between the interests of leaders and the interests of the led in mass organizations.

5. He justified the vanguard party but also, during times of mass insurgency, criticized the Bolsheviks for lagging behind the masses. Although he spent much of his energy seeking to purify party doctrine to justify its vanguard role, during the last year of his life he also struggled against the bureaucratic and totalitarian behavior of the party. He sought rigid discipline in the party, but his vision of socialism in *State and Revolution* (1965) emphasized the withering away of the state and the possibility of all administrative tasks being shared by the population. See Carr 1964, 134–50; Cliff 1980; Harding 1977; Leonhard 1974, 47–94; Lichtheim 1965, 325–80; Menashe 1973; Siranni 1975.

6. My interpretation of the Russian Revolution and Soviet Marxism is based in the sources listed in n. 5 and Carr (1966), Cliff (1980), Daniels (1960; 1969), Deutscher (1959; 1963; 1965), Kingston-Mann (1983), Lichtheim (1965, 355–80), Marcuse (1958), Rowbotham (1974, 134–79), Trotsky (1970).

7. In 1921 Lenin argued against self-described "representatives of the proletariat": "What do you describe as proletariat? That class of labourers which is employed in large-scale industry. But where is [your] large-scale industry? What sort of proletariat is this? Where is your industry?" At the party congress he 1922 he claimed: "Since the war it is not at all working-class people but malingerers that have gone to the factories. And are our social and economic conditions at present such that genuine proletarians go to the factories? No. They should go, according to Marx. But Marx wrote not about Russia—he wrote about capitalism in general, capitalism as it has developed since the fifteenth century. All this has been correct for 600 years, but it is incorrect in present-day Russia." A representative of the Workers' Opposition later argued: "Vladimir Illich said yesterday that the proletariat as a class, in the Marxian sense, did not exist [in Russia]. Permit me to congratulate you on being the vanguard of a non-existing class." (These quotations are from Deutscher 1959, n. 14–15.)

8. For accounts of Comintern, see Borkenau (1962), Daniels (1960, vol. 2), Deutscher (1959), Gruber (1972), Novack (1974). The effects on the American Communist Party are described in Chap. 16.

CHAPTER 8

1. Jay (1984, 2) is right that a precise definition of "Western Marxism" is still disputed. He identifies the tradition with reactions against theories of economic determinism and political practices of Communist tyranny, and with the claim that

"true praxis was a collective expression of self-emancipation involving all of mankind" (see 1984, 1–20 for references to recent debates).

2. Bernstein (1983) and Radnitsky (1973) survey the arguments.

3. Kaptchuk (1983) is the most accessible exposition of Chinese medicine.

4. Not surprisingly, images of a different kind of science stem either from a vastly different society (Chinese medicine) or the most profound of failures of our society (ecology).

5. For Habermas the distinct interest that makes scientific processes possible, the need to master nature, is for the earlier Frankfurt School a distortion of the proper relations between human beings and nature. See Habermas 1984 (366–99) for his critique of Horkheimer's and Adorno's views of science. Therborn (1978) criticized Marcuse's (1964) description of the role of technology in domination as a "step backwards" from his earlier account (Marcuse 1958) of its "essentially neutral character." Similarly, Therborn attacks Horkheimer and Adorno for the "ultraradicalism" of their rejection of bourgeois science in *Dialectic of Enlightenment*. Therborn follows Althusser in holding that science is necessarily objective, decisively emerging at a specific point in time from prescientific ideologies. The useful technology created by science has beneficial or harmful effects depending on class relations. Colletti (1973) makes a similar attack on Horkheimer, Adorno, Marcuse, and Lukács. It is not science that is at fault, claims Colletti, but the class relations that dictate science's use.

6. Al-Hibri (1981) provides a useful summary of this position.

7. Keller (1983) describes male bias in biology. For a politicized account of contemporary scientific practice, see Arditti (1979).

8. Habermas (1984, 377–78) claims that Horkheimer and Adorno require a "conceptual apparatus that will allow them . . . to denounce the whole as untrue." Yet Habermas is mistaken when he thinks that they are totally alien to the "pretensions of the great philosophical tradition." In seeking to ground critical theory in the intentions of the theorists, Horkheimer—at least in the essays from the 1930s— shares those pretensions.

9. Foundationalism is an example of what Dewey called the "quest for certainty." Certainty has been justified in many ways; e.g., the theory's relation to an external metaphysical reality (Plato); the theory's relation to the history of the acquisition of knowledge (empiricism); the theory's connection to a self-developmental process of spiritual evolution (Hegel). Analytic philosopher Rorty (1979) and Continental philosopher Derrida (1977) provide contemporary critiques.

10. See Merchant (1983).

11. Ryan (1982) makes a similar argument by invoking an interpretation of Derrida's tactics of deconstruction. In this view any attempt to provide a theory of the totality of social life inevitably leads to a totalitarian (in theory or practice) rejection of those inescapable facts, tendencies of values that break out of the constraints of the (supposed) totality. More important, such false totalizations (e.g., Lukács's identity of the subject and object in the proletariat, or Gramsci's notion that the productivity of the working class should be the basis for a new hegemony) always contain within themselves the principle, value, or limitation they have

sought to exclude. However, like all theorists who support relativity and a plurality of viewpoints, Ryan forgets that one point of view is, or ought to be, a basis for action. One may intellectually qualify one's point of view and be willing to change it; nevertheless, one's position possesses a certain kind of "absoluteness" if one is willing to act and, in the ultimate case of political struggle, perhaps do violence on its basis. In short, beliefs become absolutized by their role in action, not just by their epistemological status.

12. Reification may be seen as a combination of Weber's concept of rationalization and Marx's concept of alienation.

13. This is the obvious conclusion of any analysis of radical politics in the post–World War II United States, as well as of antiimperialist movements in the Third World.

14. See Lukács's account (1971) of the need for the proletariat to sacrifice its immediate interests in order to industrialize; or the essay "Towards a Methodology of the Problem of Organization" (in 1975) in which he discusses the role of the revolutionary party as moral exemplar.

15. Gramsci is both respected highly and interpreted in contradictory ways. He is hailed as the inspiration of the Italian Communist Party's (PCI's) support of democracy and pluralism, and identified as a supporter of working-class self-organization, which would run directly counter to the PCI's heavily bureaucratic organization. He is described as both a Leninist and an anti-Leninist; as part of the Hegelian Marxist tradition of Lukács and the Frankfurt School and an anti-Hegelian precursor of Althusser's attacks on the Frankfurt School. See Boggs (1976), Buci-Glucksman (1975), Merrington (1978), Mouffe (1979), Salvadori (1979).

16. Gramsci (1971, 238–39) stressed that the density of civil society made a quick military victory (as in the Soviet Union) unlikely in the West. Yet he saw economic structure, political-cultural balance, and military power as codetermining the outcome of social instabilities (cf. 1971, 160–80).

17. During the struggles of 1920, Gramsci expected (to his later disappointment) that members of this "technical class" would side with the proletariat. Adler (1977) develops a criticism of Gramsci for ignoring complexities in productive life.

18. See Ferguson (1979) and Chap. 9.

19. Hartmann (1981) develops this point.

20. Thus Anderson's (1976–77) criticisms of one of Gramsci's formulations of the relation between state and civil society are questionable. Gramsci sometimes suggests, claims Anderson, that both the state and civil society contribute both force and consent to bourgeois hegemony. This mistaken position, he argues, obscures the essential asymmetry between the state and civil society. While both support the ideological supremacy of the ruling class, the state possesses a monopoly on violence. Thus "consent" is a moment of both the state and civil society but a "force" only of the former. The widespread character of rape and wife-battering refute Anderson's distinction. We might also note nonstate violence by right-wing terrorists and organized crime.

21. Brownmiller (1975) on rape and Dworkin (1979) on pornography describe two characteristic aspects of male violence.

22. Benjamin (1978, 56) criticizes Horkheimer's account of the relation between socialization and authority. She focuses on his belief that resistance to mass culture requires a socialization based in a relation to a powerful father: "Had Horkheimer ... seeking in the past an image of what the future might hold, sought his image of the anti-authoritarian mother, he would probably have found a lost utopia ... of women's kinship and friendship ... of sisterhood ... [and] perhaps he would have seen an image of revolt based upon identification with others stemming from awareness of one's own suffering and oppression." Chodorow and Dinnerstein (1977) offer accounts of the family emphasizing the role of the mother rather than that of the father.

23. For historical accounts of women's family role, see Clark (1920) and Malos (1980).

24. These relations are described by the essays in Sargent (1981).

25. Even leftists highly conscious of sexism believed women would be liberated by men. See Rowbotham (1974) and Hartmann (1981b).

26. Miller (1976) and Greenspan (1983) link female psychology to women's social position under patriarchy.

27. This assumption is not backed by argument, but it seems that no activist could reject it. During the 1950s, capitalism appeared to have created a character structure whose needs it could completely satisfy. Marcuse, e.g., 1964 denied that workers retained any radical political destiny. Yet the stasis was only temporary.

CHAPTER 9

1. Jagger (1968) gives a detailed account of different forms of feminism.

2. Marxism has to avoid describing its universal in terms of the characteristics of one particular form the universal may have taken: it should not analyze "mode of production" so that all precapitalist modes of production are described by concepts germane only to capitalism. I have noted similar difficulties in an overuniversalized concept of patriarchy, but such difficulties should not lead us to reject concepts that can embody this tension between the universal and the concrete.

3. In 1979 only 15 percent of women with children under six and 27 percent of women with school age children worked full time, compared to 48 percent of childless married women. In Europe part-time work is even more prevalent for married women (Brenner and Ramas 1984, 60 n.60)

4. Women's economic situation persists in this form: "By the 1980s women still occupied limited kinds of jobs with limited opportunities; and a disproportionate degree of poverty still characterized female-headed families" (Kessler-Harris 1982, 318).

5. Gardiner (1979) also observes that different segments of capitalism have opposing interests, and the needs of capitalism as a whole vary during different parts of the business cycle. Capitalists seeking cheap female labor or the commodification of housework will be at odds with those using housewives' unpaid labor to

cheapen the cost of male laborers. In a recession, state services will be cut, requiring that women take up the slack for government welfare programs. In a boom period, wages and consumption can rise simultaneously, and expansion into the home and replacement of unpaid labor by commodities becomes attractive.

6. In the United States, 1830–70, an ideology of domesticized femininity developed. A public image depicted an idealized wife who "would assuage all the alienation men confront in the work force . . . save her husband from any temptation to drink, gamble, or carouse . . . [and] restrain competitive excesses" (Ryan 1979, 158).

7. For another account of selfhood, see Chap. 10.

8. I am leaving out other forms of social differentiation; e.g., race or ethnicity. See Chaps. 12–13.

9. Capitalists were ambivalent participants in this process. Ruling-class agencies supported the most extreme forms of sexist ideology, but employers often welcomed women as cheap and docile laborers. (Similar ambivalence can be found in the relations between employers and blacks; see Chap. 12.) Brenner and Ramas (1984) argue that the modern family was centrally determined by the interaction of the biological limitations imposed by women's role in reproduction and child care, and by the practical and economic constraints of early capitalism. They claim that the sexual division of labor in the modern household was made necessary by working-class poverty and the need of women to nurse and care for children. Their argument challenges claims (by Hartmann (1981b) and others) that trade unions and workers' political parties enforced women's inequality. Unfortunately, the authors acknowledge but fail to take seriously the way the modern family embodies gender inequality as well as gender differentiation. If low wages, factory work separated from the home, and women's biological relation to children make the wage-earning husband and the homebound wife "rational," these facts do not explain women's systematic political and ideological inequality.

10. Young (1981, 44) seeks a theory that "can comprehend capitalist patriarchy as one system." Besides the difficulty noted in the text, Young's tough-minded essay suffers from some confusion when she tries to explain women's unequal access to labor and social power by a "gender division of labor." Surely gender division of labor *is* this differential access.

11. Kessler-Harris (1982, 300–319) shows how women's entry into the labor force predated and provided the basis for feminism.

12. Chodorow 1978; 1979. Other theorists stressing the importance of mothering include Balbus 1982), Dinnerstein (1977), and Harding (1981).

13. The mothering theorists are often inconsistent on the social primacy of mothering. For some of their clearest statements supporting its primacy, see Chodorow (in Lorber et al. 1981), Balbus (1982), Dinnerstein (1977, 28, 36–37, 102–4), and Harding (1981). My points here summarize the detailed treatment in Gottlieb 1984. Other criticisms can be found in Lorber et al. (1981) and Young (1983).

14. Recent studies of Japanese management techniques suggest that the dominant ideology of the large Japanese corporation is not individualism and competi-

tiveness; rather, a sense of mutuality and family prevail. This ideology is not simply an illusion but corresponds to the typically lifelong commitment of managers and workers to the firm and the existence of various services of the firm to its employees (Ouchi 1981; Athos and Pascale 1981). The values and emotional styles attributed by Chodorow to exclusively female mothering may be a product of a certain phase of competitive capitalism, especially as it unfolded in the political and cultural context of the United States.

15. On the family, see Aries (1965), Oakley (1976), Poster (1980, 166–205), Tilly and Scott (1978, 42–60). For a sense of the variety of sex roles and gender personalities, see the essays in Rosaldo and Lamphere (1974) by Denich, Paul, Hoffer, Wolf, Tanner, and Stark.

16. Anderson (1984, 91) makes a similar claim: "If the structures of sexual domination stretch back longer, and go deeper, culturally than those of class exploitation, they also typically generate *less collective resistance*, politically."

17. Even much of their political activity since that time has expressed an ideology in which women were viewed in sexist terms. Rothman (1980, 64–134) describes how female-led reform political activity in the late-nineteenth and early-twentieth centuries saw women possessing a special "civilizing mission," the embodiment of the virtues of motherhood, or the product of educated mothers transforming the "world of men." As the head of the Women's Christian Temperance Society put it, her organization would be "the home going forth into the world" (Rothman: 67).

18. With the development of modern forms of capitalism, men no longer have an interest in large families. It is both men and women who are "resisting" having many children; indeed, many men seem to have less interest in having families as such (B. Ehrenreich 1983). Also, the impetus for women's struggle over housework comes not simply from the conflict of interests between men and women under patriarchy. If it did, we might wonder why that struggle is such a recent phenomenon. The basis for the current struggle is the conflict between women's private and public roles in contemporary capitalism. That Hartmann (1981a) might agree with this last claim is suggested by the fact that she provides no explanation of changes in women's relation to housework that appeal to housework or the family in and of themselves.

19. Hartsock (1983, 230–39) argues that since women's paid and unpaid labor is more concerned with quality and use-values than with commodities, women's "viewpoint" is more conducive to the formation of a liberating social order than is men's. On a more psychological level, Miller (1976) claims that women possess a fundamentally different ego structure from men because of their need for and capacity to be in close affective contact with others. Greenspan (1983) relates this ego structure (condemned by male psychiatry as a product of "weak ego boundaries") to the affective work women do in both families and the public world.

20. The "intimacy" between men and women, and women's confinement in the private sphere make female oppression qualitatively different from that affecting classes, races, or ethnic groups.

CHAPTER 10

1. My argument is not intended as a complete account of the problem. On other levels of explanation, it may be quite appropriate to appeal to people's conscious beliefs, to short-term interests, or to ruling-class physical power. These approaches, however, presuppose the continued inability of the working class to achieve correct conscious beliefs, see beyond their short-term interests, or resist ruling class power. My account will help explain the validity of this presupposition. Also, my discussion of the dominated self continues the focus placed on selfhood by Reich, feminists, and other thinkers. Finally, it should be noted that the rejection of the self by certain contemporary French thinkers (Derrida 1977) is in contradiction to a critical and moral perspective on human action and to concepts of personal responsibility and self-conscious political action.

2. A similar argument is developed at length in Schmitt's *Alienation and Class* (1983). Schmitt claims that alienation emerged when capitalism combined individual freedom and personal powerlessness.

3. I am opposing Marcuse's account in *One Dimensional Man* (1964), in which he claimed that repressive desublimation, which made for what might be called a "happy consciousness" among the ruled, was responsible for the absence of radical political activity.

4. The alienation of experience was a basic theme in the "anti-psychiatry" movement of the 1960s (Laing 1960; 1967).

5. This type of analysis was first performed on changing sexual mores by Marcuse's concept of "repressive desublimation." Marcuse (1964) argued that the seeming end of sexual puritanism masked a continued repression. The impersonal sex of the sexual revolution, he maintained, did not liberate our sexuality but simply changed the form of sexual repression.

6. This may be one way to make sense of Althusser's often quoted but highly obscure claim (1971, 162) that "ideology is a 'representation' of the imaginary relationships of individuals to their real conditions of existence."

7. In Foucault's (1975) accounts of the "gaze" in medicine and the penal system, subject groups (patients or prisoners) are rendered passive before a seemingly objective source of knowledge and power.

CHAPTER 11

1. In addition to Poulantzas (1978, 190–250), see also Wolfe (1977, 322–48) and, more philosophically, Habermas (1975, 117–41).

2. For Marxist political theories, see Carnoy (1984), Jessop (1982), Offe (1984).

3. In this dismissal of the subject, Poulantzas is following the lead of Althusser (1971), whose essay "Ideology and the State" takes subjectivity to be an expression and product of ideology.

4. Consider, e.g., the following comment on the increased integration of the state

and the economy as a whole: "While the capital accumulation process now directly dictates the rhythm of state activity, it finds expression in the State only to the extent that it is *articulated to and inserted into its global policy*. Every state economic measure therefore has a political content . . . [partly] in the sense that *it is necessarily adapted to the political strategy of the hegemonic fraction*" (Poulantzas 1978, 169; my emphasis). Any appeal to a political strategy belies the attempt to explain history as the outcome of structures without subjects.

5. Anderson (1984, 44–45, 54) presents two effective arguments against structuralist, antisubjectivist theories. First, he notes that the structuralist tendency to base an analysis of social life on an analysis of language ignores three crucial distinctions between language and politics: that languages change much more slowly than other aspects of society; that while a language may change slowly, individual language users can be extremely creative in their use of it; and that while speech acts are performed almost always by individuals, "the relevant subjects in the domain of . . . [social] structures are first and foremost *collective*: nations, classes, castes, groups, generations." Second, eliminating subjectivity from social theory makes the concept of structure questionable, "for once structures [are] freed from any subject at all, delivered over totally to their own play, they . . . lose what *defines* them as structures—that is, any objective coordinates of organization at all."

6. A similar dilemma haunts O'Connor's *Accumulation Crisis* (1984), which stresses American individualism while paying little attention to collective social experience.

7. The politicization of the economy means that in advanced capitalism clear distinctions between economic and political power are often extremely difficult to make. States order the accumulation process and sometimes control economic resources. Nordlinger (1981) has argued that there exist a variety of forms of state autonomy. His argument fails, I think, because he ignores the connection between state revenues and capitalist accumulation.

8. These interests may not always be uniform. The military may be temporarily opposed to those who seek economic modernization rather than arms. Unions of government employees may want a different tax program than do members of industrial unions, since the former derive their incomes from taxes paid by the latter.

9. Here Foucault's work (1975) is central. One need not accept his metatheoretical conception of a seemingly declassed drive for power to appreciate his accounts of the evolution of prisons, social theory, medicine, and psychiatry as forms of authority.

10. Suzanne Arms (1977) provides detailed and graphic descriptions of the negative consequences of male control of childbirth, a control motivated by the interests of men and professionals. My description in the text is complicated by the commodification of health care under capitalism, in which medical procedures are produced for profit. For a Marxist analysis of the modern health care practices stressing the needs of capitalism, see Doyal (1979).

11. Althusser (1971, 140, 143) obscures this point when he claims that "the whole of the political class struggle revolves around the State" but then goes on to identify religious institutions, private schools, the family, the media, and culture as

"ideological state apparatuses." Such an analysis precludes understanding the specific characteristics of different forms of social authority as well as potential conflicts between different authorities; e.g., between the private patriarchy of individual men in their families and the public patriarchy that uses women as cheap paid labor.

12. These reforms expressed the "corporate liberalism" previously described, and included standards of universal public education, civil service reforms, limits on the length of the working day, and government standards for industrial products.

13. Domhoff (1976, 223) makes it clear that his stress on ruling-class institutions and strategy is not meant to deny the effects on state action of working-class struggle. He correctly denies any false opposition between "instrumental" and "class struggle" views of the state. The mediating and organizing state apparatus is a product of "real people who are part of classes and interest groups." Domhoff also claims that this balance is historically variable. Thus a reform (e.g., the Wagner Act) may preempt an intensification of class conflict rather than be a defensive response after that conflict has developed. Guttman and Willner (1976) describe in detail the enormous degree to which government programs are formulated and implemented by management consultants, "experts," and think tanks. Despite the inefficiencies and boondoggles of these institutions, it is also the case that they represent the most concerted effort in history by a ruling class to produce the cognitive bases of its own reproduction.

CHAPTER 12

1. Edwards (1979) and other segmentation theorists have been criticized (cf. Lever-Tracy 1984). I am not concerned here with the details of the theory (e.g., with whether or not "secondary" jobs occur in the largest corporations or whether jobs that are primary in terms of income and union representation always promise the chance for upward mobility). I do, however, accept the general claim that among the broadly conceived types of jobs, racism is used to channel blacks into the worst.

2. Schmitt (1982, 25) makes the same point for immigrant communities: "It gives employers too much credit to say they divide the workers. Workers divided themselves along ethnic lines; employers merely used lines that workers drew themselves." Gutman's (1977, 3–78) account of the role of immigrant cultures in resisting capitalist workplace discipline supports this point.

3. Black United Mine Workers leader Richard Davis was an exception. Yet Davis's position was highly unusual for a black and had little effect on the overall policies of American labor (Gutman 1977, 109–208).

4. Also, Bonacich sees blacks' political powerlessness as an independent variable helping to explain why employers can use them in opposition to white workers. Yet their lack of power is itself surely as much a product as a cause of racism (Saxton 1979).

5. Such an experience does not rule out the formation of classes within the

colonized group, since colonialism requires "an alliance between the occupying power and the indigenous forces of conservatism and tradition" (Allen 1970, 11). Under colonialism, however, these "forces of conservatism" possess power at the discretion of the dominant group. Also, the experience of the colonized is sufficiently homogeneous to allow for some solidarity among colonized peoples of different classes.

6. However, as I argue later, nation-classes themselves are fragmented by other forms of social differentiation.

7. I do not wish to deny the survival of a certain amount of African culture in the new-formed culture of American blacks (Herskovits 1924). And I am *not* claiming that blacks have a "deficient" culture. The culture of all groups facing oppression is partly a response to that oppression. The point, rather, is that forced immigration and slavery destroyed cultural resources available to other groups— such as the capacity to set up, soon after arrival, self-help organizations or religious institutions with traditional leaders.

8. The same issues can be found in Litwack's detailed account (1979, 502–56) of black political conventions immediately after the end of the Civil War. There is a mixture of anger and self-justification, criticism of slaveholders and recognition of the crippling effects of slavery, negative judgments of white society and a desire to be accepted by it, self-assertion and confusion over the nature of the self being asserted. It might be argued that ambivalence over personal identity and rootedness in oppression are limited to the black intelligentsia, an elite who necessarily experience their lives in terms of conflict between black and white culture. It is true that the attempt to escape racial oppression by denying one's blackness is a familiar theme in the lives of the black middle class (Frazier 1957). Yet the writers I have been quoting are among the most non-assimilationist black intellectuals. Analysts of black music and religion, two non-elite and widely shared aspects of black culture, find that they too are partly based in oppression (Frazier 1974; Levine 1971).

9. While the Public Works Administration fought discrimination in employment in public works, "other New Deal programs showed prevailing discrimination" (Weiss 1983, 53). In the distribution of relief "There were large inequalities" (Fox 1971; Harris 1982, 96–100; Weiss 1983, 58). The Agricultural Adjustment Administration, designed to "save" the American farmer through price supports and reduced production, gave payments to middle and large farmers, not their black tenants and sharecroppers. Its policies also reduced black farm labor. The Civilian Conservation Corps, seeking to hire the unemployed, hired fewer blacks, housed them in segregated camps, and allowed almost no black leaders. The National Recovery Administration failed to set codes for black workers, or allowed for regional (and thus racial) differences in pay scales. Sitcoff's estimation (1978, 328–29) of the effects of the New Deal are more positive than Weiss's, yet even he admits that "little had changed in the concrete aspects of life for most blacks" and that the Roosevelt administration was guilty of "timidity, half measures, and concessions."

10. The racism of the Socialist Party is discussed in Chap. 15. The Communist Party (Chap. 16) was more complicated: it opposed racism in a variety of ways;

nevertheless, its commitment to blacks depended on a theoretical framework in which blacks remained subsidiary to "workers," with the interests of that class defined by a distorted communist ideology and practice.

11. It has been argued that the south could desegregate because its economy no longer needed Jim Crow; that public violence against blacks conflicted with U.S. attempts to forge anti-Communist alliances with Third World nations; and that the black middle class is simply a neo-colonial elite (Allen 1970; Piven and Cloward 1979; Hill 1980; Wenger 1980).

12. Conversely, racism makes black family structure and social position different from that of whites. Therefore, black women's relation to sexism is different from that of white women.

CHAPTER 13

1. "The working men [sic] have no country. . . . National differences and antagonisms between peoples are daily more and more vanishing, owing to . . . uniformity in the mode of production and in the conditions of life corresponding thereto" (Marx 1964a, 50–51). For Marx's view of the progressive role of colonialism in India, see Avineri (1969, 94) and Tucker (1972, 586). For a summary of Marxist positions, see Davis (1967). For a contemporary critique of limitations in Marxist thinking about nationalism, see J. Ehrenreich (1983).

2. J. Ehrenreich (1983) shows that this position ignores class differences in both imperialist and imperialized countries.

3. "Is it not strange that after the Marxists reduced the whole Jewish situation to its economic aspects, they have never undertaken an actual examination of it? As if they were afraid of discovering something that would invalidate their original premise" (Memmi 1962, 143).

4. Let us recall Robert Allen's claim (1976, 123): "Black nationalism is in essence a defensive reaction to racial oppression; it is group solidarity in the face of a hostile environment."

5. On Jewish national identity and anti-Semitism, see Chutzpah (1977b), Dreier and Porter (1973), Leon (1970), and Memmi (1962).

6. Marx (1964a, 53) believed that "one fact common to all past ages" was the "exploitation of one part of society by another." Because of this fact, "the social consciousness of past ages . . . moves with certain common forms, or general ideas, which cannot completely vanish except with the total disappearance of class antagonism." See also Marx 1967, 1: 71–83; and 1970 (Preface) for his discussion of general features of precommunist societies.

7. Leon (1970) discusses this process; see also Wallerstein (1974a, 149): "As the indigenous bourgeoisie grew stronger in the core states [1400–1650] intolerance to Jews made substantial legal progress."

8. For the uses of anti-Semitism in late nineteenth-century Germany, see Margolis and Marx (1927, 690–91). For similar uses in Russia, see Levin (1977, 3–

64). Sartre (1965) describes the psychological structure of petty bourgeois anti-Semitism.

9. "Private property and capital *inevitably* disunite people, inflame national enmity and intensify national oppression, collective property and labour just as *inevitably* bring people closer, *undermine national dissension* and destroy national oppression" (Stalin 1935, 272; my emphasis).

10. Gottlieb (1981b) discusses some philosophical implications of the Holocaust.

11. Halbrook's (1974) "materialist" account of Zionism makes peripheral mention of anti-Semitism and none of the Holocaust.

12. This pattern can be found in the specifically Jewish radicalism of the Bund, U.S. Jewish socialist and labor groups, Jewish ex-Communists, and members of the New Left.

13. Theodor Herzl founded political Zionism, though his ideas had been anticipated, especially by Moses Hess in *Rome and Jerusalem*. Herzl—like Lenin among Russian Social Democrats in 1903—had an organizational program as well as an ideology. On political Zionism's view of anti-Semitism, see Hertzberg (1971, 120, 209).

14. Hattis (1970, 147), chronicling Zionist binationalism, quotes Ben-Gurion in 1936: "It is possible that the whole question of an agreement [between Arabs and Jews] is not within practical realization. Not only because of the bitterness and hatred which have been intensified during the disturbances, but because of *the basic political contradiction between ourselves and the Arabs, primarily on the question of immigration*" (my emphasis).

15. Arab opposition to Zionism began with the first wave of Jewish immigrants in the 1880s (Mandel 1976; Porath 1977).

16. "The radicals subscribed to proletarian internationalism, regarding the Arab worker as an ally in the class struggle. . . . [But] once their settlements were attacked, they had to defend themselves regardless of the class origins of those firing the guns" (Laqueur 1972, 335–36).

17. Consider the 1970 discussion of the meaning of "secular democratic state" by representatives of various Palestine Liberation Organization factions. No participant recommended national rights for Jews in what would be an essentially Arab state (Harkabi 1974, 90–102). Speaking of the two-state solution, Farouk Kadoumi—then head of the PLO Political Department—was quoted in *Newsweek* (March 1977): "We have to be flexible . . . to establish peace. . . . So we have to accept, in this stage, this state on only part of our territory. But this doesn't mean we are giving up the rest of our rights."

18. Initial Soviet support for Israeli independence was short-lived and tied to Soviet desire to lessen British influence in the region. See McLaurin (1975) and MERIP (1975).

19. Israel's ties to South Africa are often referred to in this context. These ties should be condemned; however, it should be remembered that France, e.g., sold over $3 billion of arms to South Africa in the 1960s and 1970s. Other nations selling arms to South Africa include Great Britain, West Germany, the U.S.S.R., and Czechoslovakia (*Chutzpah* 1977a).

CHAPTER 15

1. The American working class "was continually altered . . . by infusions . . . of peasants, farmers, skilled artisans, and casual day laborers who brought ways of work and other habits and values not associated with industrial necessities and the industrial ethos" (Gutman 1977, 15; see also 19). These infusions required, Gutman shows, self-conscious attempts to resocialize workers to industrial society.

2. Karson (1974, 198) describes the antisocialist activities of the Catholic Church; he is tentative about their precise effects but points out that "no Catholic worker in early-twentieth-century America could be unaware that his church was an adversary, not an ally, of socialism." Conversely, the church's power came not solely from religion but also from its role as protector of Irish immigrants against Protestant nativism (Davis 1980, 20–22).

3. In my perspective it is a mistake to stress, as several commentators have (see many essays in Laslett and Lipsett 1974), either "external" or "internal" factors as causes of the SP's failures. Social differentiation was both reflected in and reproduced by the SP, thus was neither simply external nor internal.

4. Brody (1980, 23) suggests that while craft unions were strongly rooted in their communities, craft organization also created "an abiding particularism that made each trade look to itself, and, emphatically, to hold apart from the unskilled and the alien." To the extent that the SP tied itself to the AFL, a comparable particularism in its own politics was inevitable. Lane (1984, 25) claims that when the AFL accepted the literacy test as part of its immigration policy in 1906, "solidarity had been eclipsed by the instinct for survival." The question remains, Why is survival defined to include a smaller rather than a larger segment of the working class?

5. Laslett (1970, 295) suggests that the SP's union work failed "not so much because they were unpragmatic, but because they were too much so." As in Wilhelm Reich's distinction between bourgeois and socialist politics, when socialist organizations focus their energy on state reforms to the neglect of helping to awaken class consciousness, the success of those reforms will signal the collapse of the movement.

6. The IWW focused on workers highly differentiated from AFL members by lack of skill, racial or national exclusion, and poverty (Dubofsky 1969, 146–70).

7. My criticisms of the SP's treatment of women and blacks should not diminish the fact that it was far in advance of other political organizations in its concern for both groups. The point, however, is that the social primacy of social differentiation severely limited the SP's advances.

8. My argument agrees with that of Davis (1980). He adds to the forms of social differentiation I have already discussed the conflict between Protestant and Catholic and describes correspondences among position in the new division of labor, type of union membership, party affiliation, and ethnic grouping.

9. Bedford (1976, 245–47) describes the resistance of the Massachusetts SP to the presence of the IWW at Lawrence as fear of alienating reformist supporters, of

associating with "Wobbly" radicalism, and of the entry of southern and eastern Europeans into unions.

10. Another example is the unity of Socialists, supporters of women's suffrage, and some unions in the successful 1917 New York campaign for women's suffrage.

11. Here another paradox of politics asserts itself. On the one hand, as Gutman and others have argued, much of the working-class capacity to resist ruling-class socialization and integration into industrial capitalism stems from the power of their traditional culture. Forms of work, community, solidarity, religion, and the rest, sustained waves of immigrants in resisting capitalist control (Gutman 1977, 65). At the same time, traditional cultures tended to be sexist and authoritarian. We therefore must balance respect for working-class culture with appreciation of the progressive role of "outside agitators" and explicitly radical ideology (Green 1982).

12. Cf. Davis's description (1980, 41) of the party's divisions: "Neither of the two major tendencies of American socialism in 1912 offered a realistic strategy for uniting the working class or coordinating trade union strategy with socialist intervention in the urban political arena. The reformists had no plan for building industrial unionism, while the revolutionaries saw no point in attempting to influence skilled workers or in contesting Gompers's domination of the AFL. Similarly, neither the 'sewer socialism' of the right . . . nor the apoliticism of the syndicalist left met the need for a socialist political solution to the urban crisis and the plight of the slum proletariat."

13. "All recent analysis of mass voting patterns in the U.S. between 1870 and 1932 have corroborated the persistent primacy of *ethno-religious* cleavages as determinant of party loyalty and voting preference" (Davis 1980, 15–16). Voting in the 1980s—often based in race, gender, age, and geography—shows this phenomenon in a different form.

14. Arguments on this theme can be found in Laslett and Lipsett (1974).

CHAPTER 16

1. See discussions by Gordon (1976), Levenstein (1981), Milton (1982), and Weinstein (1975; 1976).

2. Many workers did not enjoy the general rise in the standard of living. Davis (1981, 46) speaks of the base for the industrial unionism of the 1930s as being found in "second generation workers in the steel mills, anthracite mines, packinghouses, coke ovens, foundries, and auto assembly lines" who witnessed the nation's affluence but did not share it (see also Fells 1973, 11–12).

3. This is perhaps an overstatement. The main point, however, is that obedience to authority is so central to class power that changes in socialization are essential to any radical political program which is not to degenerate into economism or bureaucracy.

4. These include statewide movements to develop "production for use" or "share the wealth" in California, Louisiana, Minnesota, and Wisconsin; the twenty million radio listeners of Father Coughlin, who attacked capitalism, Communism, the

banking system and the Jews; and the Townsend Movement's attempt to combine a nationwide sales tax with government payments to the elderly.

5. Mike Davis's (1981) often excellent account of how the Democratic Party captured the working class in the 1930s and 1940s is limited in this area. When Davis focuses on the failures of the late thirties, he stresses a lost opportunity and concentrates on actions by AFL leaders, the CP, and state repression. While in both this and his earlier (1980) article on the historical failures of the U.S. left he emphasizes the role of social differentiation, he never addresses the basic question of the attitude of the U.S. working class toward authority in general.

6. In 1934 Eugen Varga, formerly chief economist of the Soviet Union and then director of a Moscow research institute, wrote that the current depression was "of a special kind, without any prospect of a new prosperity phase" (in Garraty 1972, 81–82).

7. Naison (1978b, 20–21; 1978a) argues that in Harlem the Communist Party introduced direct action techniques on a hitherto unknown scale, helped direct that action against government, and for a time helped the black community to see the white working class as a potential ally. Black support for the party faded in the later 1930s when the CP asked blacks to subordinate their interests to unions. It ended with the Nazi-Soviet pact.

8. John Williamson (1969, 156), one of the designers of the CP's union strategy, claims that the party erred in three basic ways: it failed to build socialist consciousness in unions, to create a mass CP presence there, and to organize a left in the AFL.

9. In a personal conversation, I asked Dorothy Healey, who had served as director of the CP in California, why she thought the radicalism of the 1930s had failed. Without hesitation she named the Nazi-Soviet pact as by far the most important cause.

10. Such tendencies remain a part of the contemporary American left. In a local ice cream shop I recently saw a large poster inviting the neighborhood to help celebrate the fortieth anniversary of the Albanian Communist Party.

11. Cochran (1977, 332) generalizes: "Industrial unionism did spell greater labor solidarity, but not for anticapitalist assaults; mass political activities, but not for Socialist or Labor party candidates; the conversion of unions into more socially purposeful, less discriminatory mechanisms, but for social service, not radical, purposes."

12. Davis (1981, 74–75) suggests that "what ultimately created the basis for a new cultural cohesion within the postwar American working class was the rise of wartime nationalism." He qualifies this claim by noting that this cultural cohesion was based in a definition of that working class as white.

References

ADLER, Franklin, 1977. "Factory Councils, Gramsci, and the Industrialists." *Telos*, no. 31 (Spring): 67–90.

ALEXANDER, David. 1984. "Feminization in Clerical Work: Gender and Labor in the Office, 1890–1930." Unpublished.

AL-HIBRI, Azizah. 1981. "Capitalism Is an Advanced Stage of Patriarchy: but Marxism Is Not Feminism." In Sargent (1981).

ALLEN, Robert. 1970. *Black Awakening in Capitalist America*. New York: Anchor Books.

———. 1976. "Racism and the Black Nation Thesis." *Socialist Revolution*, no. 27 (Jan.–March).

———. 1978. "A Reply to Harold Baron." *Socialist Review*, no. 37 (Jan.–Feb.).

———. 1983. *Reluctant Reformers*. Washington, D.C.: Howard University Press.

ALTHUSSER, Louis. 1971. *Lenin and Philosophy and Other Essays*. New York: Monthly Review Press.

ALTHUSSER, Louis, and Etienne Balibar. 1979. *Reading Capital*. London: Verso.

AMIN, Samir. 1976. *Unequal Development*. New York: Monthly Review Press.

———. 1978. *The Arab Nation*. London: Zed Press.

ANDERSON, Perry. 1976–77. "The Antinomies of Antonio Gramsci." *New Left Review*, no. 100 (Nov.–Jan.): 5–80.

———. 1978. *Passages from Antiquity to Feudalism*. London: Verso.

———. 1979. *Lineages of the Absolutist State*. London: Verso.

———. 1980. *Arguments within English Marxism*. London: Verso.

———. 1984. *In the Tracks of Historical Materialism*. Chicago: University of Chicago Press.

ANTONIUS, G. 1939. *The Arab Awakening*. Philadelphia: Lippincott.

Arab-Israel Debate. 1970. New York: Times Change Press.

ARDENT, Gabriel. 1975. "Financial Policy and Economic Infrastructure of Modern States and Nations." In Tilly (1975).

ARDITTI, Rita. 1979. *Science and Liberation*. Boston: South End Press.

ARIES, Philip. 1965. *Centuries of Childhood: A Social History of Family Life*. New York: Vintage.

ARMS, Suzanne. 1977. *Immaculate Deception*. New York: Bantam.

ARONOWITZ, Stanley. 1981. *The Crisis in Historical Materialism*. South Hadley, Mass.: Praeger.

ASHER, Robert. 1982. "Union Nativism and the Immigrant Response." *Labor History* 23, no. 3 (Summer).

ATHOS, A. G., and R. T. Pascale. 1981. *The Art of Japanese Management*. New York: Simon & Schuster.

AVINERI, S., ed. 1969. *Karl Marx on Colonialism and Modernization*. New York: Anchor.

———. 1970. *The Social and Political Thought of Karl Marx*. Cambridge: Cambridge University Press.

BAECHLER, Jean. 1976. *The Origins of Capitalism*. New York: St. Martins Press.

BAIROCH, Paul. 1973. "Agriculture and the Industrial Revolution." In Cipolla (1973).

BALBUS, Isaac D. 1982. *Marxism and Domination*. Princeton, N.J.: Princeton University Press.

BALDWIN, James. 1964. *Nobody Knows My Name*. New York: Dell.

BALIBAR, Etienne. 1979. *The Basic Concepts of Historical Materialism*. In Louis Althusser and Etienne Balibar, *Reading Capital* (London: Verso).

BARAN, Paul. 1957. *The Political Economy of Growth*. New York: Monthly Review Press.

BARAN, Paul, and Paul Sweezy. 1966. *Monopoly Capital*. New York: Monthly Review Press.

BARON, Harold M. 1971. "The Demand for Black Labor." *Radical America* 5, no. 2, pp. 1–46.

———. 1978. "The Retreat from Black Nationalism: A Response to Robert L. Allen." *Socialist Review*, no. 37 (Jan.–Feb.): 109–11.

BARR, Kenneth. 1979. "Long Waves: A Selective, Annotated Bibliography." *Review* 2, no. 4 (Spring): 675–718.

BARRETT, Michele. 1980. *Women's Oppression Today*. London: Verso.

BEAUVOIR, Simone de. 1953. *The Second Sex*. New York: Knopf.

BEDFORD, Henry F. 1976. *Socialism and the Workers in Massachusetts, 1886–1912*. Amherst: University of Massachusetts Press.

BEECHEY, Veronica. 1978. "Women and Production: A Critical Analysis of Some Sociological Theories of Women's Work." In Kuhn and Wolpe (1978).

BENJAMIN, Jessica. 1978. "Authority and the Family Revisited; Or, A World without Fathers?" *New German Critique*, no. 13 (Winter).

BERGESEN, Albert. 1980. "Cycles of Formal Colonial Rule." In Hopkins and Wallerstein (1980).

BERGIER, J. F. 1973. "The Industrial Bourgeoisie and the Rise of the Working Class, 1700–1914." In Cipolla (1973).

BERNSTEIN, Irving. 1971. *Turbulent Years: A History of the American Worker, 1933–41*. Boston: Houghton Mifflin.

BERNSTEIN, Richard J. 1978. *The Restructuring of Social and Political Theory*. Philadelphia: University of Pennsylvania Press.

———. 1983. *Beyond Objectivism and Relativism: Science, Hermeneutics, and Praxis*. Philadelphia: University of Pennsylvania Press.

"Black Sisters." 1970. In B. and T. Roszak, eds., *Black Nationalism in America* (New York: Bobbs-Merrill).

BLAUNER, Robert. 1972. *Racial Oppression in America*. New York: Harper & Row.

BLOCK, Fred L. 1977a. *The Origins of International Disorder.* Berkeley: University of California Press.

———. 1977b. "The Ruling Class Does Not Rule." *Socialist Revolution,* no. 33 (May–June).

BOGGS, Carl. 1976. *Gramsci's Marxism.* London: Pluto Press.

BOIS, Guy. 1976. *Crise du feodalisme.* Paris.

———. 1978. "Against the Neo-Malthusian Orthodoxy." *Past and Present,* no. 79, pp. 60–69.

BONACICH, Edna. 1976. "Advanced Capitalism and Black/White Relations in the United States: A Split Labor Market Interpretation." *American Sociological Review* 41 (Feb.): 34–51.

———. 1980. "Class Approaches to Ethnicity and Race." *Insurgent Sociologist* 10, no. 2 (Fall): 9–24.

BORKENAU, Franz. 1962. *World Communism.* Ann Arbor: University of Michigan Press.

BOTTOMORE, T., and P. Goode, eds. 1978. *Austro-Marxism.* Oxford: Oxford University Press.

BOUSQUET, Nicole. 1980. "From Hegemony to Competition: Cycles of the Core." In Hopkins and Wallerstein (1980).

BOWLES, Samuel, and Herbert Gintis. 1976. *Schooling in Capitalist America.* New York: Basic Books.

———. 1982. "The Crisis of Liberal Democratic Capitalism: The Case of the U.S." *Politics and Society* 2, no. 1, pp. 51–94.

BOYER, Richard O., and Herbert M. Morais. 1976. *Labor's Untold Story.* New York: United Electrical Workers Union.

BRAUDEL, Fernand. 1973. *Capitalism and Material Life, 1400–1800.* New York: Harper & Row.

BRAVERMAN, Harry. 1974. *Labor and Monopoly Capital.* New York: Monthly Review Press.

BRENNER, Johann, and Maria Ramas. 1984. "Rethinking Women's Oppression." *New Left Review,* no. 144 (March–April).

BRENNER, Robert. 1976. "Agrarian Class Structure and Economic Development in Pre-Industrial Europe." *Past and Present,* no. 70, pp. 30–74.

———. 1978. "The Origins of Capitalist Development: A Critique of Neo-Smithian Marxism." *New Left Review,* no. 104, pp. 25–92.

BREWER, Anthony. 1980. *Marxist Theories of Imperialism.* London: Routledge & Kegan Paul.

BRIDGES, Amy. 1974. "Nicos Poulantzas and the Marxist Theory of the State." *Politics and Society* 4, no. 2.

BRODERICK, Francis L. 1971. "The Gnawing Dilemma: Separatism and Integration, 1865–1925." In Huggins, Kilson, and Fox (1971).

BRODY, David. 1980. *Workers in Industrial America.* New York: Oxford University Press.

BROWN, Carol. 1981. "Mothers, Fathers and Children: From Private to Public

Patriarchy." In Sargent (1981).

BROWNMILLER, Susan. 1975. *Against Our Will: Men, Women, and Rape.* New York: Bantam.

BUCI-GLUCKSMAN, Christine. 1975. *Gramsci et l'État.* Paris: Librarie Aetheme Fojard.

BUHLE, Mari Jo. 1983. *Women and American Socialism, 1870–1920.* Urbana: University of Illinois Press.

BUHLE, Paul. 1968. "The Meaning of Debsian Socialism." *Radical America* 2 (Jan.–Feb.).

———. 1973. "Debsian Socialism and the New Immigrant Worker." In William L. O'Neill, ed., *Insights and Parallels.* Minneapolis: Burgess.

BUTTERFIELD, Stephen. 1974. *Black Autobiography in America.* Amherst: University of Massachusetts Press.

CADE, Toni, ed. 1970. *The Black Women.* New York: Signet.

CAGAN, Leslie, Margaret Cerullo, et al. 1982. "Peace at Any Price?: Feminism, Anti-Imperialism and the Peace Movement." *Radical America* 16, no. 2 (Jan.–April).

CAREY, Lorin Lee. 1972. "Institutionalized Conservatism in the Early C.I.O.: Adolph Germer, A Case Study." *Labor History* 13, no. 4 (Fall): 475–504.

CARNOY, Martin. 1984. *The State and Political Theory.* Princeton, N.J.: Princeton University Press.

CARR, E. H. 1964. *Studies in Revolution.* New York: Grosset & Dunlap.

———. 1966. *The Bolshevik Revolution,* vols. 1–3. 1966. London: Pelican.

CARROLL, Bernice A., ed. 1976a. *Liberating Women's History.* Urbana: University of Illinois Press.

———. 1976b. "Mary Beard's *Woman As Force in History*: A Critique." In Carroll (1976a).

CARSTEN, F. L. 1969a. "Introduction: The Age of Louis XIV." In Carsten (1969b).

———, ed. 1969b. *The New Cambridge Modern History.* Vol. 5, *The Ascendancy of France, 1648–88.* Cambridge: Cambridge University Press.

CARTER, Paul. 1970. *The Twenties in America.* New York: Trowell.

CARUS-WILSON, E. M., ed. 1954. *Essays in Economic History,* vol. 1. London: Edwin Arnold.

CASTELLS, Manuel. 1980. *The Economic Crisis and American Society.* Princeton, N.J.: Princeton University Press.

CAYTON, Horace M., and George S. Mitchell. 1939. *Black Workers and the New Unions.* College Park, Md.: McGrath.

CHESLER, Phyllis. 1980. *About Men.* New York: Bantam.

CHODOROW, Nancy. 1974. "Family Structure and Feminine Personality." In Rosaldo and Lamphere (1974).

———. 1978. *The Reproduction of Mothering: Psychoanalysis and the Sociology of Gender.* Berkeley: University of California Press.

———. 1979. "Feminism and Difference: Gender, Relation, and Difference in Psychoanalytic Perspective." *Socialist Review,* no. 46 (July–August).

CHOMSKY, Noam. 1969. *Peace in the Middle East?* New York: Vintage.

Chutzpah. 1977a. "Israel Arms South Africa?" Vol. 12 (Spring).

Chutzpah. 1977b. *A Jewish Liberation Anthology.* San Francisco: New Glide.

CIPOLLA, Carlo M., ed. 1973. *The Fontana Economic History of Europe: The Industrial Revolution.* London: Fontana.

———. 1976. *Before the Industrial Revolution.* New York: Norton.

CLARK, Alice. 1920. *The Working Life of Women in the Seventeenth Century.* New York: Harcourt Brace & Row.

CLARK, George. 1969. "Social Foundation of States." In Carsten (1969b).

CLEAVER, Eldridge. 1968. *Soul on Ice.* New York: Delta.

CLIFF, Tony. 1980. *Lenin,* vols. 1–2. London: Pluto Press.

COBBAN, A. 1970. "The Decline of Divine-Right Monarchy in France." In Lindsay (1970b).

COCHRAN, Bert. 1977. *Labor and Communism.* Princeton, N.J.: Princeton University Press.

COHEN, Aharon. 1970. *Israel and the Arab World.* Boston: Beacon Press.

COHEN, G. A. 1978. *Karl Marx's Theory of History: A Defence.* Princeton: Princeton University Press, 1978.

COLE, G. D. H. 1950–65. *History of Socialist Thought,* vols. 1–4. London.

COLLETTI, Lucio. 1972. *From Rousseau to Lenin.* New York: Monthly Review Press.

———. 1973. *Marxism and Hegel.* London: New Left Books.

COLLINS, Larry, and Dominique Lapierre. 1973. *O Jerusalem.* New York: Pocket Books.

COORNAERT, E. L. J. 1967. "European Economic Institutions and the New World: The Chartered Companies." In E. E. Rich and C. H. Wilson, eds., *Cambridge Economic History of Europe,* vol. 4 (Cambridge: Cambridge University Press).

COX, Oliver. 1948. *Caste, Class and Race.* New York: Monthly Review Press.

CROUZET, F. 1968. "England and France in the Eighteenth Century: A Comparative Analysis of Two Economic Growths." In R. M. Hartwell, ed., *The Causes of the Industrial Revolution* (London: Methuen).

CRUSE, Harold. 1965. *Marxism and the Negro Struggle.* New York: Merit.

———. 1967. *The Crisis of the Negro Intellectual.* New York: Morrow.

———. 1968. *Rebellion or Revolution.* New York: Morrow.

CURRIE, Elliott, Robert Dunn, and David Fogarty. 1980. "The New Immiseration: Stagflation, Inequality, and the Working Class." *Socialist Review,* no. 54 (Nov.–Dec.).

DANCIS, Bruce. 1976. "Socialism and Women in the United States, 1900–1917." *Socialist Revolution,* no. 27 (Jan.–March): 81–144.

DANIELS, Robert Vincent. 1960. *A Documentary History of Communism,* vols. 1–2. New York: Vintage.

———. 1969. *The Conscience of the Revolution.* New York: Simon & Schuster.

DAVIES, Margery. 1979. "Women's Place Is at the Typewriter: The Feminization of the Clerical Labor Force." In Eisenstein (1979).

DAVIS, Horace B. 1967. *Nationalism and Socialism.* New York: Monthly Review Press.

DAVIS, Mike. 1980. "Why the U.S. Working Class Is Different." *New Left Review,* no. 123 (Sept.–Oct.).

———. 1980–81. "The Barren Marriage of American Labour and the Democratic Party." *New Left Review,* no. 124 (Dec.–Jan.).

DAVIS, Uri. 1977. *Israel: Utopia Incorporated.* London: Zed Press.

DEANE, Phyllis. 1965. *The First Industrial Revolution.* Cambridge: Cambridge University Press.

DERRIDA, Jacques. 1977. *Of Grammatology.* Baltimore, Md.: Johns Hopkins University Press.

DEUTSCHER, Isaac. 1959. *The Prophet Unarmed.* New York: Vintage.

———. 1963. *The Prophet Outcast.* New York: Vintage.

———. 1965. *The Prophet Armed.* New York: Vintage.

DEVRIES, Jan. 1976. *The Economy of Europe in an Age of Crisis, 1600–1760.* Cambridge: Cambridge University Press.

DINNERSTEIN, Dorothy. 1977. *The Mermaid and the Minotaur.* New York: Harper & Row.

DOBB, Maurice. 1947. *Studies in the Development of Capitalism.* New York: International Publishers.

———. 1967. *Capitalism, Development, and Planning.* New York: International Publishers.

———. 1979. "A Reply" and "A Further Comment." In Hilton et al. (1979).

Dollars and Sense. 1978. "Corporate Debt: Obstacles to Recovery." In Economics Education Project (1978).

DOLNICK, Edward. 1984. "We Won't All Be in High-Tech." *Boston Globe,* Aug. 20.

DOMAR, Evsey D. 1970. "The Causes of Slavery and Serfdom: A Hypothesis." *Journal of Economic History* 30, no. 1, pp. 18–32.

DOMHOFF, William. 1976. "I Am Not an Instrumentalist: A Reply to *Kapitalistate* Critics." *Kapitalistate,* nos. 4–5.

———. 1979. *The Powers That Be: Processes of Ruling Class Domination in America.* New York: Random House.

DOYAL, Leslie. 1979. *The Political Economy of Health.* Boston: South End Press.

DRAPER, Theodore. 1972. *American Communism and Soviet Russia.* New York: Octagon.

DREIER, P. and J. N. Porter, eds. 1973. *Jewish Radicalism.* New York: Grove Press.

DUBOFSKY, Melvyn. 1969. *We Shall Be All: A History of the Industrial Workers of the World.* Chicago: Quadrangle Books.

DU BOIS, W. E. B. 1970. "Of Our Spiritual Strivings." In Storing (1970).

DUBY, Georges. 1973. "Medieval Agriculture, 900–1500." In Cipolla (1973).

DWORKIN, Andrea. 1979. *Pornography: Men Possessing Women.* New York: Perigee.

Economics Education Project. 1978. *U.S. Capitalism in Crisis.* New York: Union of Radical Political Economists.

EDWARDS, Richard. 1979. *Contested Terrain*. New York: Basic Books.

EHRENREICH, Barbara. 1983. *Hearts of Man*. New York: Random House.

EHRENREICH, Barbara, and John Ehrenreich. 1979. "The Professional-Managerial Class." In Walker (1979).

EHRENREICH, Barbara, and Deidre English. 1975. "The Manufacture of Housework." *Socialist Revolution*, no. 26 (Oct.–Dec.).

———. 1979. *For Her Own Good: 150 Years of Experts' Advice to Women*. Garden City, N.Y.: Doubleday.

EHRENREICH, John. 1983. "Socialism, Nationalism and Capitalist Development." *Review of Radical Political Economics* 15, no. 1 (Spring).

EISENSTEIN, Zillah, ed. 1979. *Capitalist Patriarchy and the Case for Socialist Feminism*. New York: Monthly Review Press.

ELLMAN, Mary. 1968. *Thinking About Women*. New York: Harcourt, Brace & World.

EMMANUEL, Arghiri. 1972. *Unequal Exchange*. New York: Monthly Review Press.

ENGELS, Frederick. 1977. *The Origin of the Family, Private Property, and the State*. New York: International Publishers.

ESPING-ANDERSON, Gosia, Roger Friedland, and Eric Olin Wright. 1976. "Modes of Class Struggle and the Capitalist State." *Kapitalistate*, nos. 4–5.

EVANS, Sara. 1980. *Personal Politics*. New York: Vintage.

FANON, Franz. 1968. *The Wretched of the Earth*. New York: Grove Press.

FEENBERG, Andrew. 1981. *Marx, Lukacs, and the Sources of Critical Theory*. Totowa, N.J.: Rowman & Littlefield.

FELDBERG, Roslyn L. 1981. "Women, Self-Management and Socialism." *Socialist Review*, no. 56 (March–April): 141–52.

FELLS, Richard H. 1973. *Radical Visions and American Dreams: Culture and Social Thought in the Depression Years*. New York: Harper & Row.

FERGUSON, Ann. 1979. "Women as a New Revolutionary Class." In Walker (1979).

FERGUSON, Ann, and Nancy Folbre. 1981. "The Unhappy Marriage of Patriarchy and Capitalism." In Sargent (1981).

FINEGOLD, Kenneth. 1982. "From Agrarianism to Adjustment: The Political Origins of New Deal Agricultural Policy." *Politics and Society* 11, no. 1.

FIRESTONE, Shulamith. 1970. *The Dialectic of Sex*. New York: Bantam.

FLAX, Jane. 1978. "The Conflict between Nurturance and Autonomy in Mother-Daughter Relationships and within Feminism." *Feminist Studies* 4:2.

FLEXNER, Elenor. 1974. *Century of Struggle*. New York: Atheneum.

FONER, Philip S. 1972. *The Voice of Black America*, vol. 2. New York: Capricorn.

———. 1977. *American Socialism and Black Americans*. Westport, Conn.: Greenwood Press.

FORCEY, Charles. 1961. *The Crossroads of Liberalism*. New York: Oxford University Press.

FOUCAULT, Michel. 1975. *The Birth of the Clinic: An Archeology of Medical Perception*. New York: Vintage.

FOX, Daniel M. 1971. "Black Americans and the Politics of Poverty, 1900–70." In

Huggins, Kilson, and Fox (1971).

FRANK, A. G. 1967. *Capitalism and Underdevelopment in Latin America.* New York: Monthly Review Press.

———. 1969. *Latin America: Underdevelopment or Revolution.* New York: Monthly Review Press.

FRAZIER, E. Franklin. 1957. *Black Bourgeoisie.* New York: Free Press.

———. 1974. *The Negro Church in America.* New York: Schocken Books.

FREIDMAN, Isaiah. 1973. *The Question of Palestine, 1914–18.* New York: Schocken Books.

FRIEDAN, Betty. 1968. *The Feminine Mystique.* New York: Dell.

FRIEDBERG, Gerald. 1974. "Comment." In Laslett and Lipsett (1974).

GARDINER, Jean. 1979. "Women's Domestic Labor." In Eisenstein (1979).

GARFINKEL, Alan. 1981. *Forms of Explanation.* New Haven, Conn.: Yale University Press.

GARRATY, John. 1972. "Radicalism in the Great Depression." In *Essays on Radicalism in Contemporary America* (Austin: University of Texas Press).

———. 1978. *Unemployment in History.* New York: Harper & Row.

GARRATY, John A., and Peter Gay, eds. 1972. *A History of the World.* Vol. 1, *The World to 1500.* New York: Harper & Row. 1972.

GARVEY, Marcus. "The Principles of the Universal Negro Improvement Association." In Foner (1972).

GENOVESE, Eugene D. 1976. *Roll Jordan, Roll: The World the Slaves Made.* New York: Random House.

GERAS, Norman. 1978. "Althusser's Marxism: An Assessment." *New Left Review*, no. 104, pp. 232–72.

GERSON, Joe. 1976. *Middle East: U.S. Deeply Involved Again.* Boston: American Friends Service Committee.

GESCHWENDER, James. 1978. *Racial Stratification in America.* Dubuque, Iowa: Wm. C. Brown.

GEUSS, Raymond. 1981. *The Idea of a Critical Theory.* Cambridge: Cambridge University Press.

GIDDENS, Anthony. 1979. *Central Problems in Social Theory.* Berkeley: University of California Press.

———. 1981. *A Contemporary Critique of Historical Materialism.* Berkeley: University of California Press.

GILLIGAN, Carol. 1983. *In a Different Voice.* Cambridge, Mass.: Harvard University Press.

GITELMAN, H. M. 1984. "Being of Two Minds: American Employers Confront the Labor Problem, 1915–19," *Labor History* 25, no. 2 (Spring).

GLAZER, Nathan. 1974. *The Social Basis of American Communism.* Westport, Conn.: Greenwood Press.

GODELIER, Maurice. 1972. *Rationality and Irrationality in Economics.* New York: Monthly Review Press.

GOLD, David, Clarence Lo, and Eric Olin Wright. 1975. "Recent Developments in Marxist Theories of the Capitalist State." *Monthly Review* 27, no. 6 (Nov.).

GORDON, David. 1978. "Up and Down the Long Roller Coaster." In Economics Education Project (1978).

———. 1980. "Stages of Accumulation and Long Economic Cycles." In Hopkins and Wallerstein (1980).

GORDON, David M., Richard Edwards, and Michael Reich. 1982. Segmented Work, Divided Workers. Cambridge: Cambridge University Press.

GORDON, Linda, and Allen Hunt. 1977–78. "Sex, Family, and the New Right." Radical America 11, no. 12 (Winter).

GORDON, Max. 1976. "The Communist Party of the Nineteen-thirties." Socialist Revolution, no. 27 (Jan.–March): 11–47.

GORNICK, Vivian. 1979. The Romance of American Communism. New York: Basic Books.

GOTTLIEB, Roger S. 1975. "A Marxian Concept of Ideology." Philosophical Forum 6, no. 4. (Summer).

———. 1981a. "The Contemporary Critical Theory of Jurgen Habermas." Ethics 91, no. 2 (Jan.).

———. 1981b. "Some Implications of the Holocaust for Ethics and Social Philosophy." Philosophy and Social Criticism 8, no. 3 (Fall).

———. 1983. "The Concept of Resistance: Jewish Resistance during the Holocaust." Social Theory and Practice 9, no. 1 (Spring).

———. 1984. "Mothering and the Reproduction of Power." Socialist Review, no. 77 (Sept.–Oct.).

———. 1985a. "Forces of Production and Social Primacy." Social Theory and Practice 11, no. 1 (Spring).

———. 1985b. "Three Contemporary Critiques of Historical Materialism." Philosophy and Social Criticism 11, no. 2 (Fall).

GOUGH, Ian. 1975. "State Expenditure in Advanced Capitalism." New Left Review, no. 92 (July–Aug.): 53–92.

GRAMSCI, Antonio. 1971. Selections from the Prison Notebooks. Ed. Quentin Hoare and G. N. Smith. New York: International Publishers.

GREEN, James R. 1972. "Working Class Militancy in the Depression." Radical America 6, no. 1 (Nov.–Dec.): 1–35.

———. 1978. Grass-Roots Socialism. Baton Rouge: Louisiana State University Press.

———. 1980. The World of the Worker. New York: Hill & Wang.

———. 1982. "Culture, Politics and Workers' Response to Industrialization in the U.S." Radical America 16, Nos. 1–2 (Jan.–Feb.).

GREENSPAN, Miriam. 1983. A New Approach to Women and Therapy. New York: McGraw-Hill.

GRUBER, Helmut, ed. 1972. International Communism in the Era of Lenin. New York: Anchor.

GUTMAN, Herbert. 1977. Work, Culture, and Society in Industrializing America. New York: Vintage.

GUTTMAN, Daniel, and Barry Willner. 1976. The Shadow Government. New York: Pantheon.

HABERMAS, Jurgen. 1968. *Knowledge and Human Interests*. Boston: Beacon Press.
———. 1970. *Towards a Rational Society*. Boston: Beacon Press.
———. 1973. *Theory and Practice*. Boston: Beacon Press.
———. 1975. *Legitimation Crisis*. Boston: Beacon Press.
———. 1979. *Communication and the Evolution of Society*. Boston: Beacon Press.
———. 1984. *The Theory of Communicative Action*. Vol. 1, *Reason and the Rationalization of Society*. Boston: Beacon Press.
HALBROOK, S. 1974. "The Philosophy of Zionism: A Materialist Interpretation." In I. Abu-Lughod and B. Abu-Laban, eds., *Settler Regimes in Africa and the Arab World* (Wilmette, Ill.: Medina University Press).
HALL, Catherine. 1980. "The History of the Housewife." In Malos (1980).
HAMILTON, Earle J. 1934. *American Treasure and the Price Revolution in Spain*. Cambridge, Mass.: Harvard University Press.
HANN, Norma, and Robert Bellah, eds. 1983. *Social Science as Moral Inquiry*. New York: Columbia University Press.
HARDING, Neil. 1977. *Lenin's Political Thought: Theory and Practice in the Democratic Revolution*. New York: Columbia University Press.
HARDING, Sandra. 1981. "What Is the Real Base of Patriarchy and Capital?" In Sargent (1981).
HARKABI, Y. 1974. *Palestinians and Israel*. Jerusalem: Keter.
HARRIS, William H. 1982. *The Harder We Run: Black Workers since the Civil War*. New York: Oxford University Press.
HARTMANN, Heidi. 1979. "Capitalism, Patriarchy, and Job Segregation by Sex." In Eisenstein (1979).
———. 1981a. "The Family as the Focus of Gender, Class, and Political Struggle: The Example of Housework." *Signs: A Journal of Women and Society* (Spring).
———. 1981b. "The Unhappy Marriage of Marxism and Feminism: Towards a More Progressive Union." In Sargent (1981).
HARTSOCK, Nancy. 1983. *Money, Sex, and Power: Toward a Feminist Historical Materialism*. New York: Longman.
HATTIS, Susan. 1970. *The Bi-National Idea in Palestine during Mandatory Times*. Tel-Aviv: Shikmona.
HEGEL, G. W. F. 1967. *The Phenomenology of Mind*. New York: Harper & Row.
HELD, David. 1980. *Introduction to Critical Theory*. Berkeley: University of California Press.
HERSKOVITS, Melville J. 1924. *The Myth of the Negro Past*. New York.
HERTZBERG, Arthur, ed. 1971. *The Zionist Idea*. New York: Atheneum.
HIBBERT, A. B. 1963. "The Economic Policies of Towns." In M. Poston, *Cambridge Economic History of Europe, vol. 3*, ed. E. E. Rich and E. Miller (Cambridge: Cambridge University Press).
HILL, Christopher. 1961. *The Century of Revolution, 1603–1714*. New York: Norton.
HILL, Jack. 1978. "Financial Instability, Debt, and the Third World." In Economics Education Project (1978).

HILL, Richard Child. 1980. "Race, Class, and the State: The Metropolitan Enclave System in the United States." *Insurgent Sociologist* 10, no. 2 (Fall): 45–59.

HILTON, R. H. 1951. "Y eut-il une crise générale de la feodalité?" *Annales E.S.C.* 6: 23–30.

———. 1978. "A Crisis of Feudalism." *Past and Present*, no. 80, pp. 3–19.

HILTON, Rodney, et al. 1979. *The Transition from Feudalism to Capitalism*. London: Verso.

HOBSBAWN, E. J. 1975. *The Age of Capital*. New York: Signet.

HOFFMAN, Stanley. 1978. "Who Can Salvage Peace?" *New York Review of Books*, Aug. 17.

HOPKINS, Terence K., and Immanual Wallerstein. 1980. *Processes of the World-System*. Beverly Hills, Calif.: Sage.

HORKHEIMER, Max. 1932. "Geschicte und Psychologie," *Zeitscrift fur Sozial-furschung* 1, nos. 1–2.

———. 1972. *Critical Theory*. New York: Seabury.

———. 1974. *Critique of Instrumental Reason*. New York: Seabury.

HORKHEIMER, Max, and Theodor Adorno. 1974. *Dialectic of Enlightenment*. New York: Seabury.

HOROWITZ, David. 1969. *Empire and Revolution*. New York: Vintage.

HOWARD, Dick, and Karl E. Klare. 1972. *The Unknown Dimension: European Marxism since Lenin*. New York: Basic Books.

HUGGINS, N. I., Martin Kilson, and Daniel M. Fox, eds. 1971. *Key Issues in the Afro-American Experience*, vol. 2. New York: Harcourt Brace Jovanovich.

HUSSEINI, H., ed. 1975. *Toward Peace in Palestine*. Washington, D.C.: Arab Information Center.

ISMAEL, T. Y. 1976. *The Arab Left*. Syracuse, N.Y.: Syracuse University Press.

JACOBSON, Julius, ed. 1968. *The Negro and the American Labor Movement*. New York: Anchor.

JAGGER, Alison. 1983. *Feminist Politics and Human Nature*. Totowa, N.J.: Anchor.

JAY, Martin. 1973. *The Dialectical Imagination*. Boston: Little, Brown.

———. 1984. *Marxism and Totality*. Cambridge, Mass.: Harvard University Press.

JESSOP, Bob. 1982. *The Capitalist State*. New York: New York University Press.

JOHNPOLL, Bernard K. 1967. *The Politics of Futility: The General Jewish Workers Bund of Poland, 1917–1943*. Ithaca, N.Y.: Cornell University Press.

JOLL, James. 1966. *The Second International, 1889–1914*. New York: Harper & Row.

KAMEN, Henry. 1972. *The Iron Century: Social Change in Europe, 1550–1660*. New York: Praeger.

KAPTCHUK, Ted. 1983. *The Web That Has No Weaver*. New York: Congdon & Weed.

KARSON, Marc. 1974. "Catholic Anti-Socialism" and "Reply." In Laslett and Lipsett (1974).

KEERAN, Roger. 1979. "Everything for Victory: Communist Influence in the Auto Industry in World War II." *Science and Society* 43, no. 1 (Spring): 1–28.

KELLER, Evelyn Fox. 1983. *A Feeling for the Organism*. New York: W. H. Freeman.

KESSLER-HARRIS, Alice. 1982. *Out to Work*. New York: Oxford University Press.

KILSON, Martin. 1971. "Political Change in the Negro Ghetto, 1900–1940's." In Huggins, Kilson, and Fox (1971).

KINGSTON-MANN, Esther. 1983. *Lenin and the Problem of Marxist Peasant Revolution*. New York: Oxford University Press.

KLARE, Karl. 1978. "Judicial Deradicalization of the Wagner Act and the Origins of Modern Legal Consciousness, 1937–1941." *Minnesota Law Review* 62 (March): 265–339.

KLEHR, Harvey. 1984. *The Heyday of American Communism*. New York: Basic Books.

KODSY, Ahmed El, and Eli Lobel. 1970. *The Arab World and Israel*. New York: Monthly Review Press.

KOENIGSBERGER, H. G. 1958. "The Empire of Charles V in Europe." In G. R. Elton, ed., *New Cambridge Modern History*. Vol. 2, *The Reformation*. London: Cambridge University Press.

KOLKO, Gabriel. 1967. *The Triumph of Conservatism*. Chicago: Quadrangle.

KONDRATIEFF, N. D. 1979. "The Long Waves in Economic Life." *Review* 2, no. 4 (Spring): 519–62.

KORSCH, Karl. 1971. *Marxism and Philosophy*. New York: Monthly Review Press.

KOVEL, Joel. 1970. *White Racism: A Psychohistory*. New York: Random House.

KRADITOR, Aileen S. 1981. *The Radical Persuasion, 1890–1917*. Baton Rouge: Louisiana State University Press.

KUHN, Annette, and AnnMarie Wolpe, eds. 1978. *Feminism and Materialism*. London: Routledge & Kegan Paul.

KULA, Witold. 1976. *An Economic Theory of the Feudal System*. London: New Left Books.

LAING, Ronald D. 1960. *The Divided Self*. New York: Penguin.

———. 1967. *The Politics of Experience*. New York: Ballantine.

LANE, A. T. 1984. "American Trade Unions, Mass Immigration, and the Literacy Test." *Labor History* 25, no. 1 (Winter).

LAQUEUR, Walter, ed. 1970. *The Israel-Arab Reader*. New York: Bantam.

———. 1972. *A History of Zionism*. New York: Schocken.

LASLETT, John M. 1970. *Labor and the Left*. New York: Basic Books.

LASLETT, John M., and Seymour Martin Lipsett. 1974. *Failure of a Dream? Essays in the History of American Socialism*. New York: Doubleday.

LAZONICK, William. 1974. "Karl Marx and Enclosures in England." *Review of Radical Political Economics* 6, no. 2 pp. 1–59.

LEFEBVRE, Henri. 1968. *The Sociology of Marx*. New York: Random House.

LEGOFF, Jacques. 1973. "The Town as an Agent of Civilization." In Cipolla (1973).

LEINENWEBER, Charles M. 1968. "The American Socialist Party and the "New" Immigrants." *Science and Society* 30, no. 1 (Winter): 1–25.

———. 1977. "Socialists in the Streets." *Science and Society* 51, no. 2 (Summer): 152–69.

LENIN, V. I. 1943. *What Is to Be Done?* New York: International Publishers.
———. 1960. *Lenin on Proletarian Revolution and Proletarian Dictatorship.* Peking: Foreign Languages Press.
———. 1963. *Collected Works,* vol. 21. Moscow: Progress Publishers.
———. 1965. *The State and Revolution.* Peking: Foreign Languages Press.
———. 1970. *Two Tactics of Social-Democracy in the Democratic Revolution.* Peking: Foreign Languages Press.
LEON, Abram. 1970. *The Jewish Question.* New York: Pathfinder.
LEONHARD, Wolfgang. 1974. *Three Faces of Marxism.* New York: Putnam.
LERNER, Gerda, ed. 1972. *Black Women in White America.* New York: Random House.
LESTER, Julius. 1970. "Look Out, Whitey! Black Power's Gon' Get Your Mama." In Storing (1970).
LEVENSTEIN, Harvey. 1981. "Leninists Undone by Leninism: Communism and Unionism in the United States and Mexico, 1935–39." *Labor History* 22, no. 2 (Spring): 37–62.
LEVER-TRACY, Constance. 1984. "The Paradigm Crisis of Dualism: Decay or Regeneration?" *Politics and Society* 13, no. 1 (Spring).
LEVIN, Nora. 1977. *While Messiah Tarried.* New York: Harper & Row.
LEVINE, Lawrence W. 1971. "The Concept of the New Negro and the Realities of Black Culture." In Huggins, Kilson, and Fox (1971).
LEVINSON, Edward. 1938. *Labor on the March.* New York: Harper.
LICHTENSTEIN, Nelson. 1975. "Defending the No-Strike Pledge: CIO Politics during World War II." *Radical America* 9, no. 2 (July–Oct.): 49–76.
LICHTHEIM, George. 1965. *Marxism.* New York: Praeger.
LIEBMAN, Arthur. 1979. *Jews and the Left.* New York: Wiley.
LILLEY, Samuel. 1973. "Technological Progress and the Industrial Revolution, 1700–1914." In Cipolla (1973).
LINDSAY, J. O. 1970a. "Introductory Summary." In Lindsay (1970b).
———., ed. 1970b. *New Cambridge Modern History.* Vol. 7, *The Old Regime.* Cambridge: Cambridge University Press.
LIPPMANN, Walter. 1975. "On Municipal Socialism, 1913: An Analysis of Problems and Strategies." In Stave (1975).
LITWACK, Leon F. 1979. *Been in the Storm So Long.* New York: Knopf.
LONG, Norton E. 1969. "Politics and Ghetto Perpetuation." In R. L. Warren, ed., *Politics and the Ghettos* (New York: Atherton).
LORBER, Judith, Rose Coser, Alice S. Rossi, and Nancy Chodorow. 1981. "On The Reproduction of Mothering: A Methodological Debate." *Signs: A Journal of Women and Society* 6, no. 3 (Spring).
LOUGH, J. 1969. "France Under Louis XIV." In Carsten (1969b).
LOWENTHAL, Leo. 1961. "The Triumph of Mass Idols." In *Literature, Popular Culture and Society,* ed. Henry May (Englewood Cliffs, N.J.: Prentice-Hall).
LUKÁCS, Georg. 1971. *History and Class Consciousness.* Cambridge, Mass.: MIT Press.

————. 1975. *Tactics and Ethics.* New York: Harper & Row.

LUXEMBURG, Rosa. 1971. *Selected Political Writings.* New York: Monthly Review Press.

LYND, Alice, and Staughton Lynd. 1973. *Rank and File.* Boston: Beacon Press.

LYND, Staughton. 1972. "The Possibility of Radicalism in the Early 1930's: The Case of Steel." *Radical America* 6, no. 4 (Nov.–Dec.): 37–65.

————. 1974. "The United Front in America: A Note." *Radical America* 7, no. 2 (July–Aug.): 29–37.

MCCONNELL, Grant. 1966. *Private Power and American Democracy.* New York: Vintage.

MCDONOUGH, Rosin, and Rachel Harrison. 1978. "Patriarchy and the Relations of Production." In Kuhn and Wolpe (1978).

MCELVAINE, Robert S., ed. 1983. *Down and Out in the Great Depression.* Chapel Hill, N.C.: University of North Carolina Press.

————. 1984. *The Great Depression: America, 1929–41.* New York: Times Books.

MCEWAN, Arthur. 1978. "The Development of the Crisis in the World Economy." In Economics Education Project (1978).

MCINTOSH, Mary. 1978. "The State and the Oppression of Women." In Kuhn and Wolpe (1978).

MACINTYRE, Alasdair. 1973. *Against the Self-Images of the Age.* New York: Schocken.

————. 1981. *After Virtue.* Notre Dame, Ind.: Notre Dame University Press.

MCKENDRICK, Neil. 1966. "Josiah Wedgwood and Factory Discipline." In *The Rise of Capitalism,* ed. David S. Landes (New York: Macmillan).

MCKENZIE, Kermit. 1964. *Comintern and World Revolution 1928–1943.* New York: Columbia University Press.

MCLAURIN, R. D. 1975. *The Middle East in Soviet Policy.* Lexington, Mass.: D. C. Heath.

MCLENNAN, Gregor. 1981. *Marxism and the Methodologies of History.* London: Verso.

MAGDOFF, Harry. 1969. *The Age of Imperialism.* New York: Monthly Review Press.

MALAND, David. 1970. *Culture and Society in 17th-Century France.* New York: Scribner.

MALOS, Ellen, ed. 1980. *The Politics of Housework.* London: Allison & Busby.

MANDEL, Ernest. 1962. *Marxist Economic Theory.* New York: Monthly Review Press.

————. 1978. *Late Capitalism.* London: Verso.

————. 1980. *The Second Slump.* London: Verso.

MANDEL, N. J. 1976. *The Arabs and Zionism before World War I.* Berkeley: University of California Press.

MANDELBAUM, Maurice. 1977. *The Anatomy of Historical Knowledge.* Baltimore, Md.: Johns Hopkins University Press.

MANDLE, Jay R. 1978. *The Roots of Black Poverty.* Durham, N.C.: Duke University Press.

MARABLE, Manning. 1980. *From the Grassroots*. Boston: South End Press.
———. 1983. *How Capitalism Underdeveloped Black America*. Boston: South End Press.
MARCUSE, Herbert. 1941. "Some Social Implications of Modern Technology." *Studies in Philosophy and Social Sciences*, 9.
———. 1958. *Soviet Marxism*. New York: Vintage.
———. 1962. *Eros and Civilization*. New York: Vintage.
———. 1964. *One Dimensional Man*. Boston: Beacon Press.
———. 1969. *An Essay on Liberation*. Boston: Beacon Press.
———. 1972. *Counterrevolution and Revolt*. Boston: Beacon Press.
MARGLIN, Stephan. 1974. "What Do Bosses Do? The Origins and Functions of Hierarchy in Capitalist Production." *Review of Radical Political Economy*, no. 2 (Summer).
MARGOLIS, M., and A. Marx. 1927. *A History of the Jewish People*. New York: Meridian.
MARX, Karl. 1964a. *The Communist Manifesto*. Chicago: Gateway.
———. 1964b. *The Economic and Philosophical Manuscripts of 1844*. New York: International Publishers.
———. 1967. *Capital*, vols. 1–3. New York: International Publishers.
———. 1970. *A Contribution to the Critique of Political Economy*. New York: International Publishers.
MEDVEDEV, Roy A. 1973. *Let History Judge*. New York: Vintage.
MEIER, August, and Elliott Rudwick. 1979. *Black Detroit and the Rise of the UAW*. New York: Oxford University Press.
———. 1982. "Communist Unions and the Black Community: The Case of the Transport Workers Union 1934–44." *Labor History* 23, no. 2 (Spring).
MEMMI, Albert. 1962. *Portrait of a Jew*. New York: Viking.
MENASHE, Louis. 1973. "An Essay on Lenin." *Socialist Revolution*, no. 18 (Nov.–Dec.).
MERCHANT, Carolyn. 1983. *The Death of Nature: Women, Ecology and the Industrial Revolution*. New York: Harper & Row.
MERIP 1975. *Middle East Research and Information Project*. Report No. 39.
MERRINGTON, John. 1978. "Theory and Practice in Gramsci's Marxism." *New Left Review* pp. 140–75.
———. 1979. "Town and Country in the Transition to Capitalism." In Hilton et al. (1979).
MICHELS, Robert. 1962. *Political Parties*. New York: Collier.
MILLER, Jean Baker. 1976. *Toward a New Psychology of Women*. Boston: Beacon Press.
MILLER, Richard. 1983. "Fact and Method in the Social Sciences." In *Changing Social Science*, ed. D. R. Sabia and J. Walliu. Albany: SUNY Press.
———. 1984. *Analyzing Marx*. Princeton, N.J.: Princeton University Press.
MILLER, Sally M. 1971. "The Socialist Party and the Negro." *Journal of Negro History* 56, no. 3 (July).
———. 1973. *Victor Berger and the Promise of Constructive Socialism, 1910–20*.

Westport, Conn.: Greenwood Press.

———. 1975. "Milwaukee: Of Ethnicity and Labor." In Stave (1975).

———. 1983. "Other Socialists: Native Born and Immigrant Women in the Socialist Party of America." *Labor History* 24, no. 1 (Winter): 83–105.

MILLETT, Kate. 1971. *Sexual Politics*. New York: Avon.

MILLIS, Harry A., and Royal E. Montgomery. 1945. *Organized Labor*. New York: McGraw-Hill.

MILTON, David. 1982. *The Politics of U.S. Labor*. New York: Monthly Review Press.

MISKIMIN, Harry A. 1977. *The Economy of Later Renaissance Europe*. Cambridge: Cambridge University Press.

MITCHELL, Juliet. 1972. *Women's Estate*. New York: Vintage.

MONTGOMERY, David. 1979. *Workers' Control in America*. Cambridge: Cambridge University Press.

Monthly Review. 1976. "The New Reformism." Vol. 28, no. 2 (June).

MOORE, Barrington Jr. 1966. *Social Origins of Dictatorship and Democracy*. Boston: Beacon Press.

MORGAN, Glenn. 1981. "Class Theory and the Structural Location of Black Workers." *Insurgent Sociologist* 10, no. 3 (Winter).

MORGAN, Robin, ed. 1970. *Sisterhood Is Powerful*. New York: Vintage.

MOUFFE, Chantal, ed. 1979a. *Gramsci and Marxist Theory*. London: Routledge & Kegan Paul.

———. 1979b. "Hegemony and Ideology in Gramsci." In Mouffe (1979a).

MOUSNIER, Roland. 1970. *Peasant Uprisings in Seventeenth Century France, Russia, and China*. New York: Harper & Row.

MURPHY, M. Brian, and Alan Wolfe. 1980. "Democracy in Disarray." *Kapitalistate*, no. 8.

MURRAY, Martin. 1977. "Recent Views on the Transition from Feudalism to Capitalism." *Socialist Revolution*, no. 34 (July/Aug.): 64–91.

———. 1979. "Inflation, Unemployment, and the Contemporary Business Cycle." *Socialist Revolution*, no. 44 (March–April): 75–98.

MURRAY, Pauli. 1970. "The Liberation of Black Women." In *Voices of the New Feminism*, ed. M. L. Thompson. Boston: Beacon Press.

NAISON, Mark. 1978a. "Harlem Communists and the Politics of Black Protest." *Marxist Perspectives* 1, no. 3 (Fall).

———. 1978b. "Historical Notes on Blacks and American Communism: The Harlem Experience." *Science and Society* 24, no. 3 (Fall): 324–43.

NEF, J. U. 1954. "The Progress of Technology and the Growth of Large-Scale Industry in Great Britain, 1540–1640." In Carus-Wilson (1954).

NELSON, Daniel. 1982. "Origins of the Sit-Down Era: Worker Militancy and Innovation in the Rubber Industry, 1934–38." *Labor History* 23, no. 2 (Spring): 198–225.

New Left Review. 1978. *Western Marxism*. London: Verso.

NEWMAN, Dorothy K. 1965. "The Negro's Journey to the City: Part II." *Monthly Labor Review*, June.

NICHOLSON, Linda. 1977. "Rationality and Gender." Unpublished.

NOBLE, David. 1979. *America by Design: Science, Technology and the Rise of Corporate Capitalism.* New York: Oxford University Press.

NORDLINGER, Eric. 1981. *On the Autonomy of the Democratic State.* Cambridge, Mass.: Harvard University Press.

NOVACK, George, Dave Frankel, and Fred Feldman. 1974. *The First Three Internationals.* New York: Pathfinder Press.

OAKLEY, Ann. 1976. *Women's Work.* New York: Vintage.

O'CONNOR, James. 1973. *The Fiscal Crisis of the State.* New York: St. Martin's Press.

———. 1984. *Accumulation Crisis.* New York: Basil Blackwell.

OFFE, Clause. 1972a. "Advanced Capitalism and the Welfare State." *Politics and Society* 2, no. 4.

———. 1972b. *Sturkhurproblem Das Kapitalistichen Stautes.* Frankfurt: Suhrkamp.

———. 1984. *Contradictions of the Welfare State.* Cambridge, Mass.: MIT Press.

OLLMAN, Bertell. 1972. "The Marxism of Wilhelm Reich: The Social Function of Sexual Repression." In Howard and Klare (1972).

OMI, Michael, and Howard Winant. 1983a. "By the Rivers of Babylon: Race in the United States." *Socialist Review,* no. 71 (Sept.–Oct.): 31–66.

———. 1983b. "By the Rivers of Babylon: Race in the United States, Part Two." *Socialist Review* no. 72 (Nov.–Dec.): 35–70.

OPPENHEIMER, Martin. 1974. "The Sub-Proletariat: Dark Skins and Dirty Work." *Insurgent Sociologist* 4 (Winter): 6–20.

ORTNER, Sherry. 1974. "Is Female to Male as Nature Is to Culture?" In Rosaldo and Lamphere (1974).

OSOFSKY, Gilbert. 1963. *Harlem: The Making of a Ghetto.* New York: Harper & Row.

OUCHI, Z. 1981. *Theory Z.* Reading, Mass.: Addison-Wesley.

PIERCY, Marge. 1970. "The Grand Coolie Damn." In Morgan (1970).

PINDAR, John. 1976. "Europe in the World Economy, 1920–70." In *The Fontana Economic History of Europe.* Vol. 6, *Contemporary Economies, Part 1.* London: Collins.

PIRENNE, Henri. 1937. *Economic and Social History of Medieval Europe.* New York: Harcourt, Brace & World.

PIVEN, Frances Fox, and Richard A. Cloward. 1979. *Poor People's Movements.* New York: Vintage.

PLOTKE, David. 1980. "The United States in Transition: Towards a New Order?" *Socialist Review,* no. 54 (Nov.–Dec.).

POLANYI, Karl. 1957. *The Great Transformation.* Boston: Beacon Press.

POMAIN, Krzystof. 1979. "The Secular Evolution of the Concept of Cycles." *Review* 2, no. 4 (Spring): 563–647.

PORATH, Y. 1977. *The Palestinian Arab National Movement.* London: Frank Cass.

POSTAN, M. M. 1954. "The Rise of a Money Economy." In Carus-Wilson (1954).

POSTER, Mark. 1980. *Critical Theory of the Family.* New York: Seabury.

POULANTZAS, Nicos. 1975. *Political Power and Social Classes.* New York: New Left Books.

———. 1978. *State, Power, Socialism.* New York: New Left Books.

PRINCE, Stephan. 1984. "Cinema, Personality, and the Production of Culture." Lecture, Popular Culture Association, Toronto, March.

PROCACCI, Guilano. 1979. "A Survey of the Debate." In Hilton et al. (1979).

QUANDT, W. 1973. *The Politics of Palestinian Nationalism.* Berkeley: University of California Press.

QUINE, W. V. O. 1973. "Posits and Reality." In *Theories and Observation in Science,* ed. Richard E. Grandy (Englewood Cliffs, N.J.: Prentice-Hall).

———. 1976. *Ontological Relativism and Other Essays.* Cambridge, Mass.: Harvard University Press.

RADNITSKY, Gerard. 1973. *Contemporary Schools of Metascience.* Chicago: Henry Regnery.

RAYBECK, Joseph. 1966. *A History of the American Worker.* New York: Free Press.

REDKEY, Edwin S. 1971. "The Flowering of Black Nationalism: Henry McNeal Turner and Marcus Garvey." In Huggins, Kilson, and Fox (1971).

REICH, Michael. 1980. *Racial Inequality: A Political-Economic Analysis.* Princeton, N.J.: Princeton University Press.

REICH, Wilhelm. 1946. *The Mass Psychology of Fascism.* New York: Orgone Institute Press.

———. 1976. *Character Analysis.* New York: Simon & Schuster.

———. 1972. *Sex-Pol.* New York: Vintage.

REITER, R. R., ed. 1975. *Towards an Anthropology of Women.* New York: Monthly Review Press.

Research Working Group. 1979. "Cyclical Rhythms and Secular Trends of the Capitalist World Economy: Some Premises, Hypotheses, and Questions." *Review* 2, no. 4 (Spring): 483–500.

RODINSON, Maxime. 1968. *Israel and Arabs.* New York: Pantheon.

———. 1973. *Israel: A Colonial-Settler State?* New York: Pathfinder.

RORTY, Richard. 1979. *Philosophy and the Mirror of Nature.* Princeton, N.J.: Princeton University Press.

ROSALDO, Michelle. 1974. "Women, Culture and Society: A Theoretical Overview." In Rosaldo and Lamphere (1974).

ROSALDO, Michelle Zimbalist, and Louise Lamphere, eds. 1974. *Women, Culture, and Society.* Stanford, Calif.: Stanford University Press.

ROSEN, Sumner. 1968. "The CIO Era, 1935–55." In Jacobson (1968).

ROTHCHILD, Emma. 1981. "Reagan and the Real America." *New York Review of Books,* Feb. 5.

ROTHMAN, Sheila M. 1980. *Women's Proper Place: A History of Changing Ideals and Practices, 1870 to the Present.* New York: Basic Books.

ROWBOTHAM, Sheila. 1973. *Women's Consciousness, Man's World.* New York: Penguin.

———. 1974. *Women, Resistance and Revolution.* New York: Vintage.

ROWBOTHAM, Sheila, Lynne Segal, and Hilary Wainwright. 1979. *Beyond the*

Fragments: Feminism and the Making of Socialism. London: Merlin Press.

ROWTHORN, Bob. 1980. *Capitalism, Conflict and Inflation.* London: Lawrence & Wishart.

RUBIN, Gayle. 1975. "The Traffic in Women: Notes on the 'Political Economy' of Sex." In Reiter (1975).

RUBIN, Lillian. 1976. *Worlds of Pain.* New York: Basic Books.

RYAN, Mary. 1979. "Femininity and Capitalism in Antebellum America." In Eisenstein (1979).

RYAN, Michael. 1982. *Marxism and Deconstruction.* Baltimore, Md.: Johns Hopkins University Press.

SACKS, Karen. 1974. "Engels Revisited: Women, the Organization of Production, and Private Property." In Rosaldo and Lamphere (1974).

SALVADORI, Massimo. 1979. "Gramsci and the PCI: Two Conceptions of Hegemony." In Mouffe (1979a).

SALVATORE, Nick. 1982. *Eugene V. Debs: Citizen and Socialist.* Urbana: University of Illinois Press.

SARGENT, Lydia, ed. 1981. *Women and Revolution.* Boston: South End Press.

SARTRE, Jean-Paul. 1965. *Anti-Semite and Jew.* New York: Schocken.

———. 1976. *Critique of Dialectical Reason.* London: New Left Books.

SAXTON, Alexander. 1979. "Historical Explanations of Racial Inequality." *Marxist Perspectives* vol. 2, no. 2 (Summer).

SCHMIDT, Alfred. 1983. *History and Structure.* Cambridge, Mass.: MIT Press.

SCHMITT, Richard. 1982. "Class, Culture, and Ethnicity." Unpublished.

———. 1983. *Alienation and Class.* Cambridge: Schenkman.

SCHORSKE, Carl E. 1965. *German Social Democracy, 1905–1917.* New York: Wiley.

SELTZER, Rich. 1978. "The Development of the Crisis in the United States." In Economics Education Project (1978).

SENNETT, Richard. 1981. *Authority.* New York: Random House.

SENNETT, Richard, and Jonathan Cobb. 1973. *The Hidden Injuries of Class.* New York: Random House.

SHAFFER, Robert. 1979. "Women and the Communist Party, USA 1930–40." *Socialist Review,* no. 45 (May–June): 73–118.

SHANNON, David. 1967. *The Socialist Party of America.* Chicago: Quadrangle.

SHULMAN, Stephen. 1981. "Race, Class, and Occupational Stratification: A Critique of William J. Wilson's *The Declining Significance of Race.*" *Review of Radical Political Economics* 13, no. 3 (Fall): 21–31.

SID-AHMED, Mohamad. 1976. *After the Guns Fall Silent.* New York: St. Martin's Press.

SIDEL, Ruth. 1978. *Urban Survival.* Boston: Beacon Press.

SIRANNI, Carman. 1975. "Rereading Lenin." *Socialist Revolution,* no. 23 (April).

SITCOFF, Harvard. 1978. *A New Deal for Blacks.* New York: Oxford University Press.

SKLAR, Holly, ed. 1980. *Trilateralism.* Boston: South End Press.

SKOCPOL, Theda. 1977. "Wallerstein's World Capitalist System: A Theoretical and Historical Critique." *American Journal of Sociology* 82, no. 5, pp. 1075–80.

————. 1980. "Political Responses to Capitalist Crisis: Neo-Marxist Theories of the State and the Case of the New Deal." *Politics and Society* 10, no. 2.

SLATER, Phil. 1977. *Origin and Significance of the Frankfurt School: A Marxist Perspective.* London: Routledge & Kegan Paul.

SPEAR, Allen. 1971. "The Origins of the Urban Ghetto, 1870–1915." In Huggins, Kilson, and Fox (1971).

SPERO, Sterling D., and Abram L. Harris. 1931. *The Black Worker.* New York: Columbia University Press.

STALIN, Joseph. 1935. *Marxism and the National and the Colonial Question.* Moscow: International Publishers.

STARR, Paul. 1982. *The Social History of American Medicine.* New York: Basic Books.

STAVE, Bruce, ed. 1975. *Socialism and the Cities.* Port Washington, N.Y.: Kennikat Press.

STONE, Lawrence. 1977. *The Family, Sex, and Marriage.* New York: Harper & Row.

STORING, Herbert, J., ed. 1970. *What Country Have I? Political Writings by Black Americans.* New York: St. Martin's Press.

STORK, Joe. 1975. *Middle East Oil and the Energy Crisis.* New York: Monthly Review Press.

STRONG, Bryan. 1971. "Historians and American Socialism, 1900–1920." *Science and Society* 34, no. 3 (Winter): 387–97.

SWEEZY, Paul. 1942. *The Theory of Capitalist Development.* New York: Monthly Review Press.

————. 1979a. "A Crisis in Marxist Theory." *Monthly Review,* June.

————. 1979b. "A Critique" and "A Rejoinder." In Hilton et al. (1979).

SWEEZY, Paul, and Harry Magdoff. 1981. "Reagan and the Nemesis of Inflation." *Monthly Review* 32, no. 8 (January): 1–10.

SYZMANSKI, Albert. 1979. "Racial Discrimination and White Gain." *American Sociological Review* 41 (June): 403–14.

TAWNEY, R. H. 1912. *The Agrarian Problem in the Sixteenth Century.* London: Longman's.

TAX, Meredith. 1970. *Women and Her Mind: The Story of Daily Life.* London: Bread and Roses.

————. 1980. *The Rising of the Women.* New York: Monthly Review Press.

TAYLOR, Charles. 1983. "Political Theory and Practice." In *Social Theory and Political Practice,* ed. C. Lloyd (Oxford: Oxford University Press).

TENTLER, J. W. 1979. *Wage-Earning Women.* New York: Oxford University Press.

TERKEL, Studs. 1970. *Hard Times.* New York: Pocket Books.

THERBORN, Goran. 1978. "The Frankfurt School," in *New Left Review,* 83–139.

————. 1980. *What Does the Ruling Class Do When It Rules?* New York: Schocken.

THOMPSON, E. P. 1963. *The Making of the English Working Class.* New York: Vintage.

THRUPP, Sylvia. 1973. "Medieval Industry, 1000–1500." In Cipolla (1973).

TILLY, Charles, ed. 1975. *The Formation of National States in Western Europe.*

Princeton, N.J.: Princeton University Press.

TILLY, Louise, and Joan W. Scott. 1978. *Women, Work, and Family.* New York: Holt, Rinehart & Winston.

TOBIAS, H. T. 1972. *The Jewish Bund in Russia.* Stanford, Calif.: Stanford University Press.

TREBLICOT, Joyce, ed. 1983. *Mothering.* Totowa, N.J.: Rowman & Allenheld.

TROTSKY, Leon. 1970. *The Revolution Betrayed.* New York: Pathfinder.

TUCKER, Robert V. 1972. *The Marx-Engels Reader.* New York: Norton.

VILAR, Pierre. 1956. "Problems of the Formation of Capitalism." *Past and Present,* no. 10, pp. 15–38.

WALKER, Pat, ed. 1979. *Between Labor and Capital.* Boston: South End Press.

WALLERSTEIN, Immanuel. 1974a. *The Modern World-System,* vol. 1. New York: Academic Press.

———. 1974b. "The Rise and Future Demise of the World Capitalist System." *Comparative Studies in Society and History* 16, no. 4.

———. 1980. *The Modern World-System.* Vol. 2, *Mercantilism and the Consolidating of the European World-Economy, 1600–1750.* New York: Academic Press.

WARE, Susan. 1982. *Holding Our Own: American Women in the 1930s.* Boston: Twayne.

WARREN, Bill. 1980. *Imperialism: Pioneer of Capitalism.* London: Verso.

WEINBAUM, Batya, and Amy Bridges. 1979. "The Other Side of the Paycheck: Monopoly, Capital, and the Structure of Consumption." In Eisenstein (1979).

WEINRYB, B. D. 1970. "Anti-Semitism in Soviet Russia." In *The Jews in Soviet Russia,* ed. L. Kochan (London: Oxford University Press).

WEINSTEIN, James. 1967. *The Decline of Socialism in America, 1912–25.* New York: Monthly Review Press.

———. 1968. *The Corporate Ideal in the Liberal State.* Boston: Beacon Press.

———. 1975. *Ambiguous Legacy: The Left in American Politics.* New York: New Viewpoints.

———. 1976. "Response." *Socialist Revolution,* no. 27 (Jan.–March): 48–58.

WEISS, Nancy. 1983. *Farewell to the Party of Lincoln.* Princeton, N.J.: Princeton University Press.

WELLMER, Albrecht. 1974. *Critical Theory of Society.* New York: Seabury.

WENGER, Morton G. 1980. "State Responses to Afro-American Rebellion: Internal Neo-Colonialism and the Rise of a New Black Petite Bourgeoisie." *Insurgent Sociologist* 10, no. 2 (Fall): 61–72.

WEST, Jackie. 1978. "Women, Sex and Class." In Kuhn and Wolpe (1978).

WHITE, Ronald C., and C. Howard Hopkins. 1977. *The Social Gospel.* Philadelphia: Temple University Press.

WIEBE, Robert H. 1967. *The Search for Order, 1877–1920.* New York: Hill & Wang.

WILLIAMS, Robert G. 1981. "The Political Economy of Hub Currency Defense: Sterling and the Dollar." *Review of Radical Political Economy* 3, no. 3 (Fall): 1–20.

WILLIAMSON, John. 1969. *Dangerous Scot.* New York.

WILSON, C. H. 1970. "The Growth of Overseas Commerce and European Manufacture." In Lindsay (1970b).

WILSON, William J. 1978. *The Declining Significance of Race.* Chicago: University of Chicago Press.

WOLFE, Alan. 1977. *The Limits of Legitimacy: Political Contradictions of Contemporary Capitalism.* New York: Free Press.

WORTHMAN, Paul B., and James R. Green. 1971. "Black Workers in the New South." In *Key Issues in the Black African Experience*, vol. 2, ed. N. I. Huggins et al. (New York: Harcourt Brace Jovanovich).

WRIGHT, Erik Olin. 1979. *Class, Crisis, and the State.* New York: Schocken.

YOUNG, Iris. 1981. "Beyond the Unhappy Marriage: A Critique of Dual Systems Theory." In Sargent (1981).

———. 1983. "Is Male Gender Identity the Cause of Male Domination?" In Treblicot (1983).

ZARETSKY, Eli. 1976. *Capitalism, the Family, and Personal Life.* New York: Harper & Row.

ZINN, Howard, ed. 1966. *New Deal Thought.* New York: Bobbs-Merrill.

Index